SEND A GUNBOAT

SEND A GUNBOAT

THE VICTORIAN NAVY AND SUPREMACY AT SEA, 1854–1904

ANTONY PRESTON
and
JOHN MAJOR

Foreword by
ANDREW LAMBERT

Afterword by
ERIC GROVE

CONWAY

Half title: Gunboats at Aden, on the route to India.
(Stephen Dent)

Frontispiece: The composite sloop *Icarus* (1885)
off Royal William Yard, Devonport.
(Conway Maritime Press)

TO OUR PARENTS

… to extend the protection and shield of England to her wandering sons, who are carried by commerce, or by pleasure, or by necessity, to the various regions of the world – to extend over them, as much as the rules of civilized nations will permit, the great aegis of England's protection, that it may follow them wherever they may go, into the despotism of Russia, or into the bleak countries of America – whether they be within the limits of ocean, or within the confines of any Power, great, insignificant, or almost helpless.
John Roebuck, 1850

I often think … that it is a good job no one called our bluff very often.
Ernest Bevin, 1945

A Conway Maritime Book

© Antony Preston and John Major 1967
Revised edition © Antony Preston and John Major 2007

Originally published in 1967 by Longmans, Green and Co. Ltd.

This edition first published in Great Britain in 2007 by Conway,
an imprint of Anova Books Ltd, 151 Freston Road, London W10 6TH
www.anovabooks.com

British Library Cataloguing in Publication Data:
A catalogue record for this book is available from the British Library

Library of Congress Cataloguing in Publication Data Available

ISBN 10: 0 85177 923 9
ISBN 13: 9 780851 779232

Printed by WKT Co. Ltd, China

CONTENTS

Preface to the Original Edition

This book could not have been written without a great deal of help and encouragement. We would like to thank Dr D. M. Schurman and Miss M. J. Rooney for allowing us to use their unpublished works on imperial defence, and Mr G. Osbon of the National Maritime Museum, Greenwich, and Mr J. Colledge for letting us draw on their incomparable knowledge of the Victorian Navy. We must also express our gratitude to Miss E. Drus, Mr G. E. Metcalfe and Dr D. K. Bassett, of the History Department of the University of Hull, not only for their advice, but for their generosity in allowing us to use some of their own original material. We acknowledge a special debt to the Parker Gallery, the Imperial War Museum, the Radio Times Hulton Picture Library and the National Maritime Museum for providing illustrations and plans, and to Mr J. Day for preparing the drawings. We are also indebted to the British Museum, the Public Record Office and the London Library for the use of their facilities. We are very grateful to Mrs Joan Kirwan for her work on typing this book. Finally, we wish to thank Lieutenant Berridge of *Navy News*, and those who provided us with first-hand recollections of their experience in sloops and gunboats sixty years ago.

Antony Preston and John Major

Preface

I first met Antony Preston at a drinks party in Bayswater one summer evening in the early 1960s. Against the surrounding bibulous chatter he outlined his project for an account of the small ships of the Royal Navy in the Victorian era. I gladly came on board the venture and, better still, embarked on a friendship that lasted forty years. *Send a Gunboat* was very much Antony's idea, and as his co-author it gives me the greatest pleasure to see his plan for a re-launch glide down the slipway. It is a tribute to one of the foremost naval historians of his generation, and all those who knew Antony will only wish he could have lived to see it.

John Major, August 2006

Publisher's Note to the New Edition

The central part of this volume consists of a faithful presentation of Antony Preston's and John Major's original work of 1967. However, a few changes have had to be made – in particular one or two of the captions and headings have been changed – to take into account both the passage of time and the different way that this edition has been put together. Nevertheless, readers should keep in mind that there are occasions when terms such as 'the present day' in fact refer to the late 1960s. One major structural change from the original book is that the notes and references are now gathered together in one section, on pages 137-141, rather than as footnotes on individual pages.

As well as the numerous new illustrations and photographs (almost all the original illustrations have been retained), this edition features a new foreword by Andrew Lambert, Laughton Professor of Naval History at Kings College, London; a postscript by Dr Eric Grove, Director of the Centre for International Security and War Studies at the University of Salford; and an appendix on the restoration of HMS *Gannet* by Lindsay Doulton, Curator of Maritime Technology at The Historic Dockyard, Chatham.

Particular thanks are due to Stuart Robertson, Stephen Dent and David K Brown. In addition many other people have helped in various ways, including John Brooks; Andrew Connor and Helen Taylor at Heriot Watt University; Debbie Corner at the Royal Navy Submarine Museum; Geoffrey Dennison; Andy Field; Mark Frost at Dover Museum; Katy Goodwin of Portsmouth Museums and Records Service; Sara Grove at the National Maritime Museum; Jean Hood; Vic Jeffrey, Regional Manager, Public Affairs, Royal Australian Navy; John Jordan, editor of *Warship*; Mr Pound and Pound's Yard, Portsmouth; Gerry Rendle of Plymouth Naval Base Museum; and Dr Duncan Veasey of the Naval Photographic Club.

SEND A GUNBOAT

FORTY YEARS ON

Andrew Lambert
Laughton Professor of Naval History
Kings College, London

*S*end a Gunboat was a pioneering book. Not only did it draw together in compact, accessible form the naval highlights of many Victorian colonial campaigns, but it did so in combination with a development history of the ships that conducted these missions, and an examination of the underlying political and economic issues that impelled Britain to use force across the globe. While these strands of thought reflected the interests of the two authors, the result was a seamless work that has remained the standard text to this day. Despite the emergence of much new work since 1967, addressing almost every aspect of the subject, from the aims and strategies of the British Empire to technology of the Victorian warship, the book remains the baseline for any study of naval force in British Imperial diplomacy between the Crimean War of 1854-56 and the Entente Cordiale of 1904.

Rather than revisit the original text, and trifle with the details, it seems more appropriate and more useful to address broader themes that will enlarge the story.

The term 'gunboat diplomacy' was developed and given strong twentieth-century flavour by retired diplomat Sir James Cable in his classic book *Gunboat Diplomacy* of 1971.[1] Daniel Headrick placed the gunboat among the 'tools of imperialism' that enabled the west to subdue and dominate the non-European world.[2] The key to any serious appreciation of what this term means in the nineteenth century is sophisticated understanding of what actually constituted the British Empire. Here Headrick's work benefited from the pioneering work of scholars like Gerald Graham, Donald Schurman, Ronald Robinson and Jack Gallagher, Nicholas Tarling and others.[3] Without this political framework the events recorded might easily be dismissed as a random collection of stories, but the in-depth analysis of the context of the engagements ensures they make sense to a modern audience, and strike a chord with contemporary naval officers. This is an example for all naval historians: what

happened is merely the starting point for an examination of why and to what purpose.

The British Empire was not a classic imperial model, seizing land to control people and markets by military power. Instead it relied on capital and commerce to develop a system of informal empire, in which the cost of local administration was borne by nation states which were beneficially owned by British institutions. The literature on this subject is large, and interlocks with that on foreign policy and regional activity.[4] Gunboats were used to support British policy in three distinct categories.

1. Wars with major powers, either actual or planned. While the Crimean War was the only serious conflict of the period there were significant crises with the United States, Russia and France between 1861 and 1898. Gunboats were assigned critical roles in projected operations in every case.

2. In defence of British commerce, either against piracy which caused a rise in insurance rates, or defaulting regimes that threatened the security of the capital market.

3. To persuade powers to alter their tariff regime to open hitherto closed markets to British trade, be they Imperial China or minor West African kingdoms.

Design

The gunboat was one of the first purpose-built warship designs to exploit the potential of the screw steam machinery. The new propeller allowed designers to create a small, shallow-draft warship that could operate effectively close inshore. From the start the gunboat was designed for offensive operations. The first Admiralty design was prepared in 1845, the basis for the iron-hulled screw propeller Royal Yacht HMS *Fairy* as a mobilisation prototype and test bed.[5] A small, steam-powered warship could attack a naval base at any state of wind or tide, exploiting the limited arcs of fire provided for batteries that were only intended to engage large sailing ships in the main navigable channel. While there were many foreign naval bases and port cities which might be targets for such operations, the focus of British concern in the mid-1840s was the expanding French base at Cherbourg, only 200 miles from the south coast of England. If warships could take up position off such bases they could bombard the dockyard facilities, the fleets that they harboured and anything else in range. If they were small, and could fire at very long range, the chance of being hit by return fire was minimal. All the gunboat needed to be effective in this role was a long-range, heavy calibre gun.

During his nine-year term (1845-1854) as Captain of the Gunnery Training and Experimental ship HMS *Excellent*, Henry Chads considered that 'the real question of the day was how to destroy ships and arsenals with shells, and render such forts as Cherbourg useless to their possessors'. His solution was to focus development on increased range, through rifled weapons and larger charges.[6] In 1850 a group of British officers visited Cherbourg. Chads reported that the base would be at the mercy of long-range guns, and that an early attack on it was essential, because a substantial French fleet based at Cherbourg would paralyse British naval operations.[7] In consequence of his observations at Cherbourg, Chads devoted his efforts to increasing the extreme range of British guns. He saw in the latest gun designs, and the use of eccentrically cast shot for longer ranges:

> that Cherbourg was not secure against a bombardment, that most assuredly a large fleet could not lie securely in the roadstead within the breakwater, and that even the Arsenal might be assailed by a enterprising enemy, having command of the sea.

The results exceeded his hopes. In 1851 eccentrically cast 10-inch shells ranged out to 5,700 yards, 34 degrees elevation, although the gun burst at the 54th round. Chads reduced the range to 5,000 yards, so that ships lying 2,500 yards beyond the breakwater could bombard at night. Even at 28 degrees elevation the projected results were impressive. The arsenal would be badly damaged, and the anchorage rendered untenable.

> I have also reason to believe not only Cherbourg, but most of the other French Ports on the Channel inside Ushant, St Malo, Havre, Boulogne, Calais etc. might be

assailed in a similar manner, the necessary preparations for which would be neither extensive nor expensive, if the experiments now in project should realise my expectations.[8]

The experiments with the heavy 68-pounder gun of 95 cwt soon had shells reaching out to 6,500 yards. This gun was mounted on all naval steamers.[9] In addition the promising eccentric-bore Lancaster-rifled 68-pounder offered greater range and precision, at a price.[10] Improved rockets would complement the guns.[11] A year later Chads concluded:

> That this port may be successfully assailed by a naval force having the superiority in the Channel, I trust will be considered satisfactorily established from these recent experiments.

At such long ranges the chances of the bombarding craft being hit were 'extremely remote'. He recommended that this information be kept strictly confidential, to ensure the French did not throw out advanced works beyond the breakwater.[12]

The Crimean War, 1854-1856

The combination of improved guns and experimental screw gunboats meant that when the Crimean War broke out in 1854 the Royal Navy was ready to begin series production of well designed and highly effective gun vessels and gunboats. The whole package had been built to bombard Cherbourg, but the shift of foe required little more than redirecting the focus towards Kronstadt and Sevastopol. This would be a maritime war, projecting power from the sea against the vast, but inflexible and antiquated land mass of Imperial Russia.[13]

Gun vessels and gunboats took part in most of the significant naval operations after they reached service in mid-1854. The astonishing rise in orders reflected the success of the gunboat design, and failure of the Russians to contest command of the sea. The only targets for the allied fleets were ashore, and in the rocky waters of the Baltic, and the shallows of the Sea of Azov, only gunboats could get close enough to project power ashore. The failure of an attack on Kokkola in the Gulf of Finland in June 1854 was caused by the lack of shallow-draft warships with heavy guns.[14] Once the Admiralty had accepted that it would have to build steam gunboats to fight Russia effectively, which it did in October 1854, the Royal Navy quickly applied 'Cherbourg Strategy' and commenced the mass production of flotilla craft, after

Gunboat prototypes ordered 1844–1845

	Launched	Hull	Length	Breadth	Depth	Tonnage	Armament
Fairy	1846	iron	144' 8"	21' 1½"	9' 10"	317	unarmed
Rifleman	1848	wood	150'	26' 6"	15' 6"	624	2 x 10" & 4 x 32 pdrs
Teazer	1848	wood	130'	22'	9' 2"	192	1 x 10"[15]

the initial half dozen *Arrow* class gun vessels proved too large, the first twenty classic Crimean gunboats were ordered in October 1854.

The initial flotilla of six gun vessels and twenty gunboats were employed to remarkable effect in the Black Sea and Baltic in 1855. In the Black Sea they opened the Sea of Azov and crippled the logistics of the Russian army in the Crimea, and bombarded the fortress of Kinburn. In the Baltic they opened up the coastal waters of the Russian Empire before incinerating the dockyard and gunboat sheds at Sveaborg. The gunboats and mortar bombardment of Sveaborg was so similar to the planned attack on Cherbourg as to make the presence of French forces alongside the British bizarre. In a little under three days the whole dockyard complex was destroyed by long-range fire from mortars, heavy guns and rockets to which the Russian forts could make no effective reply. The allies did not lose a single man.[16] Following these successes gunboats were mass-produced, so that there were almost three hundred gunboats built or building when the war ended in March 1856. Along with over one hundred mortar vessels and rafts, eleven armoured batteries, mortar frigates and a host of factory, store and depot ships, the gunboats were central to the 'Great Armament', designed for a full-scale assault on Kronstadt, using an advanced base selected in 1855, and relying on sustained firepower at long range, protected by armoured batteries, to demolish the most powerful collection of sea forts in the world. The viability of this operation remains unknown, but the threat was too much for the Russians, who were quick to make peace.

The 'Great Armament' was the first mass-mobilisation of national shipbuilding resources of the industrial age. It demonstrated the depth of Britain's resources, should the war be prolonged, resources that would hardly be touched for the rest of the century. Quite simply Britain could out-build the world in warship tonnage, in quantity and quality. To power the gunboat armada the Admiralty turned to their two preferred marine engine suppliers, Maudslay, Sons & Field, and John Penn & Sons. The two great Thameside firms divided the contracts, and called in their smaller competitors to produce many of the cast and forged parts, assembling the engines in-house. So successful were these engines that several sets were re-used in new hulls a decade later.[17] Although the gunboats were built in private yards, along with their machinery, they were fitted out and commissioned at the Royal Dockyards. This led to a serious shortage of skilled engineers, and increased costs.[18] At the same time battleship and large frigate programmes went on unabated, keeping the Royal dockyards fully engaged constructing huge ocean-going types, which would be needed for war with France, not Russia.

To ensure the rest of the world understood the nature of British power, and thereby to deter future aggression, the Baltic Fleet planned for the 1856 campaign was assembled at Spithead on St George's Day, 23 April 1856 for a Grand Review to celebrate Britain's victory. No one was left in any doubt of the purpose: the flotilla craft staged a mock attack on Southsea Castle, which bravely stood in for Kronstadt, Cherbourg, or New York. As *The Times* observed:

> A new system of naval warfare had been created... We have now the means of waging really offensive war, not only against fleets, but harbours, fortresses and rivers, not merely of blockading, but of invading, and carrying the warfare of the sea to the very heart of the land.[19]

It was the humble gunboat that allowed machine-age seapower to move into coastal waters with confidence, using long-range artillery to attack the most powerful sea forts. The object of the Review was, in large measure, to demonstrate this new power to the assembled diplomatic corps. The 'Crimean' War demonstrated that the 'Cherbourg Strategy' developed by British planners in the 1840s could be applied equally well elsewhere.[20] By the late 1850s it was widely believed that naval blockades were no longer required; a superior fleet could always call up enough firepower to destroy a naval base. Operations at Sveaborg and Kinburn had shown that maritime sieges were now possible.[21]

The Gunboat and Grand Strategy

In 1859 General Sir Howard Douglas, the godfather of modern naval gunnery, stressed that this new possibility would change the strategic needs of the British Empire:

> Amongst the changes which steam propulsion for ships of war will introduce in naval operations, may be included the abandonment of the blockade system. For a steam fleet superior in strength to the fleet blockaded – if well supplied with Armstrong's incomparable gun… will be able to destroy from afar the fleet, or the arsenal in which the ships are crowded, and probably both at the same time. Thus it will not be necessary to keep a steam fleet before an enemy's port during long intervals of time, as was the case formerly with our blockading fleets.[22]

If Cherbourg and any French fleet within could be destroyed by bombardment, there was no prospect of France making war on Britain. Small and simple they may have been, but the screw steam gunboats of the 1850s effected a profound change in the balance of strategic power between the land and the sea, by enabling a dominant navy to destroy any hostile forces, even if they remained in port. The response of the other major powers demonstrated that this threat was very real, and very difficult to counter. France, Russia and the United States all added millions to their coast defence budgets, and developed coast defence warships to counter the offensive threat posed by the Royal Navy's new flotillas. Because the

British had a superior battlefleet they would always be the attacking force, and would like nothing better than for an inferior enemy fleet to come to sea and give battle in defence of their base. States that went to war with Britain would lose their fleets, either at sea, or in harbour.

After the war many of the gunboats were taken ashore and laid up under cover at Haslar using a marine railway and shed complex designed and engineered by Isambard Kingdom Brunel.[23] They could easily be mobilised. Little wonder the decision to fit out the support craft for the flotilla was enough to deter the United States in December 1861.[24] When a Federal cruiser stopped a British mail steamer on the high seas and seized two Southern agents, Britain demanded an apology. New York, Boston and the approaches to Washington DC were all vulnerable to flotilla attack, and with the support of armoured warships British planners were confident that they could break into New York harbour. Already waging war on the Southern Confederacy, the Federal Government was quick to apologise and retreat.

Other gunboats and gun vessels were sent out to China, to force open the trade of the Celestial Empire. As Preston and Major demonstrated, these campaigns were the longest running gunboat operations of the period, but the gunboats made it possible to coerce the largest, and most inward-looking empire on Earth, with relatively little loss. Thirty years before, this would have been impossible.

When the Crimean gunboats wore out, the Admiralty built two divergent, specialist types. The first, which features strongly in *Send a Gunboat*, was an improved colonial police vessel, a sea-worthy craft, equipped with a full rig and armed with small quick-firing guns. (One of these sloops, the *Gannet*, survives and is being restored at Chatham dockyard.) In the process the gunboat had grown rather large, and moved away from the initial

impulse, merging into the sloop class. It has been argued that after the 'Crimean' war the British armed services 'remained chiefly specialists in colonial warfare'.[25] While this argument may gain some credence from a list of what the Royal Navy did between 1856 and 1900 it fails when confronted with a dimension missing from *Send a Gunboat*.

While the colonial gunboats and sloops saw much active service on the imperial margins, the defence of empire and the maintenance of British influence in Europe required a very different type of vessel. The Crimean coast-assault function was taken to new levels with the 'Flatiron' gunboat of the 1870s. Based on a small craft used by the Armstrong factory to test heavy guns, George Rendel's design, developed with the assistance of Admiral Sir Astley Cooper-Key, a leading gunnery expert, was an ideal weapons system for a power largely focussed on coastal offensive operations as the basis of deterrence and war-fighting. Armed with a single very heavy gun, initially a 12-ton 9-inch muzzle-loading rifle, entirely worked by Armstrong hydraulic machinery, the 'Flatirons' would have operated on the flanks of a British assault on Cherbourg, Kronstadt or New York, supporting the larger ironclad turret ships. The order dates for the *Ant* class tie in with concern for the security of Belgium during the Franco-Prussian war, the *Gadfly* group to the Russian war scare of 1878. This design would have been turned out in large numbers, had a major war broken out. The hull was deliberately designed to facilitate towing at a far higher speed than their engines could attain. These gunboats would, like the Crimean War gun and mortar boats, have operated from coastal shallows, where they could find good opportunities to bombard hostile forts, suppress defensive fire and facilitate a direct assault by heavy turret ironclads. Twenty 'Flatirons' were built between 1870 and 1880. In *Send a*

HMS *Staunch*, one of the two prototypes of the 'flatiron' gunboats. This photograph was probably taken on trials – note the clothing being worn by the men on deck, their headgear in particular. *(Private collection)*

Gunboat they are simply described as 'Coast Defence' types, and condemned as failures.[26] In truth the 'Flatirons' were more accurately described on the confidential Pink List of the Royal Navy as 'Gunboats for the Attack and Defence of Coasts'. They formed an integral part of the naval capability to assault forts, and could be mass-produced in wartime. So durable were these little craft that more than one survived to fight, as originally intended, on the Belgian coast in the First World War.[27]

Far from being a gunboat force, the Royal Navy between 1860 and 1900 was dominated by European concerns and spent the bulk of the construction budget on first class warships for operations against major powers. It employed obsolete and economical types for colonial police work and imperial suasion, but only because such minor vessels were backed up by the armed might of the ironclad battlefleet. In 1882 the Mediterranean Fleet was used to coerce Egypt, with gunboats supporting the ironclads. In fact between 1860 and 1890 the Royal Navy was incomparably superior to any rival fleet in the number of warships and the efficiency of the men. Consequently, therefore, it could afford the luxury of preparing for offensive operations, with 'Flatirons' as part of a sophisticated, layered approach to the tactical problems of defeating large-scale coastal defence systems.[28] This capability was well understood in Paris and St Petersburg.[29] By adopting an offensive strategy Britain could take the initiative in war, attacking hostile naval assets and bases, to deny them any offensive options at sea. The 'Flatiron' was a key asset to this strategy, which underpinned the British reliance on deterrence to secure their interests without the economically dislocating business of waging war.

Deterrence continued to work, as part of the process whereby Britain constrained the dynamic elements that threatened her vital interests. In 1878 Britain met Russian advances into Turkey by assembling a coast service fleet at Portland. Russian pressure on Afghanistan repeated that response. In both cases Russia backed down. Her naval exercises between 1879 and 1884 revealed that Kronstadt was still vulnerable to superior naval forces, while her fleet was incapable of meeting the British at sea. The Russian economy remained as vulnerable as it had been in 1854. While Britain could not overthrow Russia she was quite invulnerable to any Russian action, and could wage a long war of limited commitment, relying on economic damage to undermine the very fabric of the Tsarist state.[30] In 1898 the Royal Navy responded to the Fashoda crisis by preparing to bombard Cherbourg. The French hurriedly moved their fleet to Brest and backed down, convinced the arrogant British would be only too pleased to finish what they had begun at Trafalgar.[31] Two years later the Germans were convinced that the British fleet had the power to steam past all their fortifications, enter the River Elbe and sink their fleet.[32] In the diplomacy of the

'free hand' the Royal Navy provided the power to deter France and Russia, and by protecting Italy, to hold together the Triple Alliance. It alone gave Britain the status of a first-class power.[33]

The gunboat era came to an end because other powers finally decided to challenge Britain's naval mastery. The combined naval building programmes of France, Russia, the United States and finally Germany forced Britain to temporarily re-deploy naval manpower from gunboats at the colonial margins to a battlefleet at the Imperial centre. This was neither unprecedented, nor a retreat signalling the end of British power. It was merely a strategic adjustment to meet prevailing circumstances. After 1918 the navy shifted back to the Empire, until Hitler and Mussolini once again shifted the focus.

Ultimately the function of navies is to exert influence ashore, where men live and work, a point succinctly and skilfully made by the brilliant maritime strategist Sir Julian Corbett in 1911:

> Since men live upon the land and not upon the sea, great issues between nations at war have always been decided – except in the rarest cases – either by what your army can do against your enemy's territory and national life, or else by what the fear of what the fleet makes it possible for your army to do. Men do not live at sea, and therefore it is what your navy can enable your army to do that is important.[34]

Context

Send a Gunboat was written at a time when the Royal Navy was in decline, the Empire was disappearing, and the ability of the British state to act alone outside the NATO area, or even within it, was in serious doubt. The Cold War had seen the very term gunboat take on a perjorative, dismissive meaning. Little wonder the original conclusions were downbeat, although defiant. For those who like their history symmetrical, with rise followed by fall, the last forty years have been most annoying. Britain was not finished in 1967, and while the flag was hauled down around the globe, the underlying British Empire, world trade and invisible exports, was largely undamaged. In 1982 the failure to keep a gunboat on station laid the Falklands open, but that failure was swiftly redeemed by a highly successful demonstration of naval capability. At the end of the 1980s the Soviet Union collapsed, allowing naval forces to recover their interventionist role. The function of modern navies is to deliver power from the sea, just as it was 150 years ago. There is a very striking parallel between those Victorian marvels of technology – a weapons system that opened up the non-European world, in concert with quinine and the quick-firing gun – and the latest American concept, the Littoral Combat Ship, a small, heavily armed platform with the ability to enter and leave coastal battle spaces at speed, and outrange existing defences.[35] The contemporary relevance of *Send a Gunboat* has never been greater.

On a fine morning in 1896, the 1st Class gunboat H.M.S. *Bramble* (1886), moored off Devonport. *(Conway Maritime Press)*

PART 1

SEND A GUNBOAT

Chapter 1

INTRODUCTION

Send a gunboat! What other phrase can evoke the spirit of nineteenth-century imperialism in such a powerful way? What phrase could rouse such deep conflicting emotions, the nostalgic longing for vanished glory or a passionate rejection of Victorian arrogance? Yet 'gunboat diplomacy' is a phenomenon largely misunderstood by its supporters and its detractors.

This book seeks to examine the story of the gunboat's part in British imperial history, and to show how fact often differs from myth. It does not attempt a detailed history of gunboat operations or an analysis of gunboat diplomacy's origins. It is a description of the gunboat as an instrument of British foreign policy in the fifty years between the Crimean War and the advent of Admiral Fisher as First Sea Lord in 1904.

Gunboat diplomacy might be broadly defined as the use of warships in peacetime to further a nation's diplomatic and political aims. As such it is neither new nor old. Since the days of Danegeld the physical threat of a warship in a peaceful anchorage has often been more effective than a regiment of soldiers. By this definition the whole of the nineteenth century was an age of gunboat diplomacy, for the Royal Navy remained throughout the major instrument of British national policy.

The gunboat itself is harder to define, for the term has been loosely used for as long as guns have been mounted in ships. During the seventeenth and eighteenth centuries oared craft with one or two guns served in most navies, but these gunboats disappeared from the Royal Navy early in the nineteenth century. Some of the early screw-steamships were rated as gunboats to distinguish them from their sisters which carried no offensive armament. H.M.S. *Teazer* (1846) came into this category, being rated at various times as gunboat, gunvessel and mortar-vessel. But this vessel and others like her constituted only a small fraction of the Royal Navy's strength,

and until 1854 the word 'gunboat' was a generic term for a few minor vessels. Not until the steam gunboat came into service in the Crimean War did the gunboat-type become associated with the Navy's 'diplomatic' role, and we have therefore limited our study to its brief fifty-year life-span.

Great Britain's victory in 1815 gave her an unassailable position in the world, one unlikely to be equalled by any other nation. Although much of her new empire was poor, it held great promise for the future. On the credit side were Canada and Australia, which, it was thought, needed only capital and immigrants to make them flourish; on the other hand there were expensive commitments, colonies unlikely to prosper but nonetheless essential to the Empire's defence. The once-valued sugar islands in the West Indies were in decline, and India was still regarded as an economic liability. Yet many of these unprofitable areas could not be allowed to go by default to Great Britain's rivals, since this would jeopardise communications between the mother country and her rich foreign markets The best example is India, the linchpin of Britain's trading interests in the Far East, but later to become an enormous commercial prize in its own right.

The pattern of British expansion between the Napoleonic and Crimean Wars shows that colonies came second to trade, and that bases to protect trade-routes were more highly prized than new dominions. Although Captain Mahan wrote later that the three 'interlinking rings' of world power were colonies, commerce and sea power, by 1820 colonial trade was only a small part of Britain's overseas commerce. Trade with the once rebellious United States expanded enormously, as did trade with Asia, and continued to outpace trade with the colonies.[1] For this reason the steady process of annexation which went on during the first half of the nineteenth century concentrated on acquiring only what would facilitate world-wide trade. Coaling stations and naval bases on the route to the Far East frequently developed as entrepôts and trading centres of their own accord, but their primary role was strategic. Labuan, the Falkland Islands and Aden were all in this category, for they served as springboards for trade, not for conquest.

Geography favoured British expansion in a way which was unique, and even now plays a not inconsiderable part.[2] Being to the west of Europe gave British sailors the advantage of the prevailing westerly winds in wartime for the very winds which carried them to the enemy shore kept the enemy penned in his harbours. In peacetime London commanded her natural share of seaborne traffic through the Channel and the North Sea at a time when few merchantmen dared to brave the wintry seas north of Scotland. The large deposits of coal in the British Isles also played their part, for the export of coal was a form of invisible subsidy to British merchants. A British ship on her way to Chile to load a cargo of nitrates could make the outward voyage with a cargo of coal as ballast; by making the ship earn revenue on both legs of the trip British owners were able to quote lower freight rates than their foreign rivals,[3] an advantage which continued to accrue as British factories turned out an ever larger supply of cheap manufactured articles for export. Without the benefit of this two-way earning capacity British shipping might not have won such a monopoly of world trade, and the great maritime empire might not have attained the limits which it did.

The long peace which followed Waterloo had the rare quality of being a genuine peace, in that there was no concerted attempt to break the British monopoly of world power. It is fashionable to think of the *Pax Britannica* as something which was enforced by armed might, but this was hardly the case. An exhausted Europe offered no serious competition to the English Industrial Revolution after twenty-two years of intermittent warfare, and it was another fifty years before Europe began to reap the first benefits of industrialisation. The pace of British expansion could therefore afford to be leisurely, and there was no need to maintain strong naval and military forces.

The navy which had smashed Napoleon's dreams was allowed to dwindle away, from ninety-nine sail of the line in 1814 to twenty-three in 1838.[4] Each year the Naval Estimates were cut in any way possible, either by Parliament or by the Board of Admiralty. Even that great administrator Sir James Graham, who did so much to effect reforms from within the Navy, was adept at paring costs ever further.[5] Efficiency is not easily bred by such means, for the retention of obsolescent ships and weapons for the sake of economy discourages new tactics and inhibits realistic training. One glaring example was the standing Admiralty instruction to captains of steam vessels to economise in the use of coal at all times; on several occasions valuable men-o'-war were wrecked while trying to ride out a storm under canvas, when their engines could have saved them.[6]

Representative of an era – the composite gunboat H.M.S. *Rattler*. (© National Maritime Museum, London)

H.M.S. *Osprey* and H.M.S. *Opossum* destroying Chinese junks in Sama Bay. *(Radio Times Hulton Picture Library)*

Despite this grinding parsimony the Royal Navy kept an overwhelming preponderance over its nearest rivals for many years. In the first half of the nineteenth century individual foreign ships of the line might be handier or faster, but no competitor tried to outbuild the Royal Navy in sheer numbers. Even the advent of steam power had only a slow impact on naval rivalry, for it was first applied to small auxiliaries, such as tugs and dispatch vessels, and only fitted in bigger ships as an adjunct to sail

power after much vacillation. The greater part of the battle fleet was laid up 'in Ordinary' (Reserve) to save money and manpower, while the majority of peacetime tasks were left to minor warships, frigates, sloops and brigs. The strength of the battle fleet was maintained by desultory building progammes, excepting the spurts of activity occasioned by the 'panics' of 1844-45 and 1847, when war with France seemed imminent.

In a world untroubled by conflict between the Great

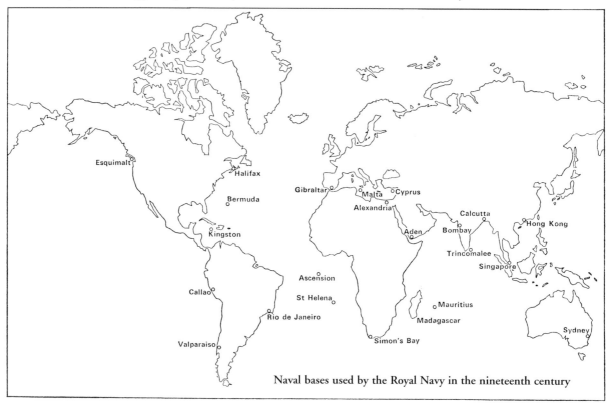

Naval bases used by the Royal Navy in the nineteenth century

Powers the minor warships of the Royal Navy were force enough to oversee British interests abroad. There was no conscious design about this, for it was 'a fact of life resulting from the French wars'.[7] When the steam gunboat came on the scene the Navy was already accustomed to acting as a world police-force. Outside Europe and the eastern seaboard of North America there were few countries with settled populations of European descent. To the Victorians this meant that the rest of the world was inhabited by savage races, 'half devil and half child', who would be protected if they remained well-behaved or chastised if they became unruly. 'Good behaviour' was equated with co-operation in helping European traders to establish themselves in their midst, and correspondingly, opposition from Asians or Africans was interpreted as resistance to progress.

To understand how the machinery of gunboat diplomacy was administered we must try to understand the paternalism and authoritarianism which was part of the Victorian outlook. When assessing their motives and intentions it must be remembered that Victorians *believed* in the virtues of Christian Progress and the 'civilising influence of Law and Order'. The missionary zeal, the passionate desire to enlighten the heathen may be explained away as a subconscious desire to atone for the greed and cruelty of preceding generations of Englishmen, but it was nonetheless one of the most powerful forces in nineteenth-century England. The success of the Anti-Slavery Lobby was proof of the influence wielded by English humanitarians, for they defeated powerful vested interests to get Government support for their campaign.

An Englishman abroad was a British Subject, and therefore the responsibility of the Crown. No matter how barbarous his conduct it was inconceivable that a 'savage' nation should be allowed to pass judgement on one of its benefactors. Palmerston expounded this doctrine in the famous Don Pacifico Debate in 1850:

> I am convinced these principles are calculated… to conduce to the maintenance of peace, to the advancement of civilization, to the welfare and happiness of mankind… as the Roman, in days of old, held himself free from indignity, when he could say *Civis Romanus sum*, so also a British subject, in whatever land he may be, shall feel confident that the watchful eye and the strong arm of England will protect him against injustice and wrong.[8]

The Palmerstonian view did not lack critics, needless to say. Victorians could be high-minded as well as high-handed, and conflict between the 'will to rule' and humanitarian concern for those on the receiving end of colonial government continued throughout the nineteenth century. In the early 1880s, for example, one naval officer sent on a punitive expedition in the Pacific Islands later wrote:

> These wretched people… have been hunted and worried till it will be long before they settle again… I regret that my whole voyage in these islands has been one of apparently ruthless destruction, but no other course has been possible.[9]

More often than not, however, the doubts were suppressed and the bringers of the *Pax Britannica* went unswervingly ahead. When the first gunboats arrived on the scene the policy they were to serve had been taken for granted by the bulk of British opinion, and the confidence that upheld it was to last for most of their active life.

In making our assessment of gunboat diplomacy, therefore, we make only one reservation. The moral attitudes implicit in certain examples of gunboat actions are neither condoned nor condemned, and the actions should be judged by the prevailing standards of the age.

Chapter 2

CRIMEAN DEBUT

The Baltic 1854

The first of the Royal Navy's long gunboat line was launched in the Crimean War, that aimless conflict which wrought so many changes in naval warfare. The destruction of the Turkish fleet at Sinope in 1853 hastened the extinction of the wooden line-of-battle ship, but also led to the introduction of the steam gunboat, an entirely new type of warship.

To understand how this new category came into being we must look at the course of the Crimean War. After Russia's invasion of Turkey in 1853 the British and French Governments decided to assist the Turks by aggressive action in the Black Sea. Russia's naval power

was to be restrained by the capture and destruction of Sevastopol, her main naval base. To capture this magnificent arsenal and dockyard the British and French soldiers endured the long agony of the Crimea. The Allies had no intention of occupying the Crimea permanently, so the campaign was aimless and futile; it was also foolhardy as the Russians needed only to wait for the British and French armies to be weakened by frostbite and disease before overwhelming them with superior forces.

The plan for military operations in the Crimea had been favoured principally by Napoleon III, because the French Army was felt to be large enough for the task. His

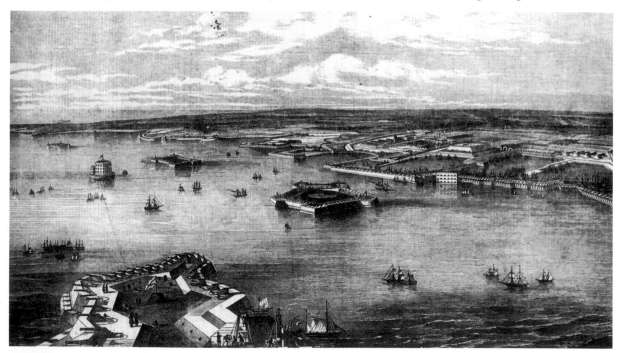

Kronstadt: a contemporary illustration showing the fortifications and naval base. *(Conway Maritime Press)*

British partners, although dubious about the wisdom of his scheme, had every reason to want Russia's naval power reduced. But British thoughts turned instinctively to a naval plan for inflicting more lasting damage on Russia. While the Mediterranean Fleet was ordered to transport and support the British Army in the Crimea, the main British offensive effort was directed to the Baltic, still the main source of the Royal Navy's timber, pitch and cordage.

In December 1853 *The Times* had published a telegram from Paris announcing that France and Britain would send an expedition to the Baltic in the early spring of 1854. The source was unofficial, but remarkably well-informed, for it also forecast that Vice-Admiral Sir Charles Napier would be Commander-in-Chief. Napier had earned a reputation for pugnacity in the past and everyone had high hopes of his leadership. But Napier, by now sixty-eight years old, had little inclination to be a dashing hero. While the Press acclaimed the strength of the Baltic Fleet Napier gloomily told one of his captains that he was going out 'with a raw squadron to attack an efficient fleet in their own waters'.[1]

Raw the Baltic Fleet certainly was. Even after years of patient reform from within, the Royal Navy had been caught napping, still largely a fleet of sail and smooth-bore guns, and worse, a fleet of senile admirals. The stately three-deckers, differing little in essentials from H.M.S. *Victory*, took months to make up full crews and prepare for foreign service. The Admiralty's belated introduction of retirement for admirals had not yet had much effect, and the Flag List still featured gouty old dodderers who had last seen service in the reign of George IV. The few steamships in service were allowed to play only a minor role; only the conditions of real warfare could bring them into the limelight.

Sir Charles Napier was well aware that England expected him to achieve glorious results however great his difficulties might be. After rejecting the passive concept of blockading the Gulf of Finland and the militarily impossible one of attacking the main Russian base at Kronstadt he decided to attack the Aland Islands, then belonging to Russia. These isands command the Gulf of Bothnia between Sweden and Finland, and inevitably they were defended by a large fortress, Bomarsund (see map). But even this modest effort took months to get under way, and Napier did not succeed in taking Bomarsund until mid-August 1854. This was the only major operation of the campaign for that year, although the humdrum work of blockade went on throughout 1854. There were many difficulties, for the British and French fleets had very poor charts of the Baltic and had to employ their ships cautiously. As the Baltic is a relatively shallow sea long stretches of the coastline were inaccessible to Napier's deep-draught sloops and frigates.

There was clearly a need for a new type of vessel more suited to the job. As *The Times* ruefully admitted, 'We

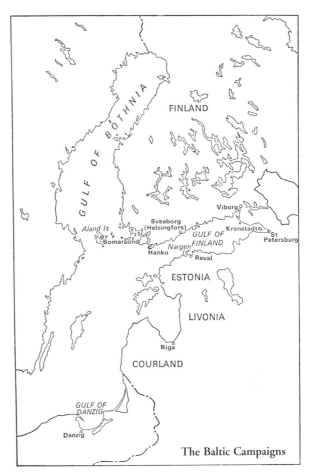

The Baltic Campaigns

have to deal with shallow waters and granite walls, and find ourselves too gigantic for the petty warfare, and giants though we are, we are so far baffled.'[2] With Sveaborg, the great naval arsenal at Helsingfors (now Helsinki), in mind Napier wrote: 'The only successful manner of attacking Sveaborg that I can see … is by fitting out a great number of gunboats carrying one gun with a long range, and placing them west of Sveaborg and south of Helsingfors…'[3] The dispatches went to and from the Secretary of the Admiralty, showing how much the idea of attacking the Russians' bases appealed to the Board and the Cabinet, and how hopeless it seemed to Napier. His towering three-deckers lumbered about imposingly in deep water but did little to enforce the blockade of Russian ports beyond sending their boats in to burn stores of timber and pitch. In one raid in the Gulf of Bothnia the boats of H.M.S. *Leopard* destroyed shipping and supplies valued at £380,000, and all within ten days. But this only served to show how much more could have been achieved with ships designed for this sort of work.

Changes were already in sight, however. Another *Times* leader, attacking Napier for his rumoured intention of withdrawing from the Baltic, contained a reference to a startling new development:

What, too, we may ask, if operations are to be thus prematurely closed, was the object of proceeding lately with such urgency in the equipment and dispatch of gunboats for special service in the Baltic waters? Everybody observed that the chief risk encountered in the recent proceedings was that of grounding in the shallows while the chief advantage experienced by our forces was in the superior range of our artillery. By a judicious application of these lessons we have constructed vessels with offensive powers of a most formidable character, vessels drawing only very little water, and yet armed with guns of an enormous calibre and prodigious range. One piece of ordnance capable of throwing a shot nearly four miles has already reached the fleet, and though this may seem of no great moment, it should be remembered that a single ten inch gun, well placed and worked had no inconsiderable share in the destruction of Bomarsund. But there is time enough, we presume, before the end of this month, to reinforce the fleet with some of the gunboat Flotilla and there would then still remain another month available for putting their powers in requisition. Why stop short at the fall of Bomarsund, with such fair opportunities left for successful progress?[4]

This flotilla of gunboats was the Admiralty's answer to the problem of Baltic operations, just as the peculiar problems of World War II produced the Tank Landing Ship. A year before, in 1853, the Royal Navy had no gunboats – the term had all but lapsed since Georgian times. During the previous century the term 'gunboat' had been widely used to describe any small craft with one or two guns and relying usually on oars. Napoleon's vaunted Boulogne Flotilla had a number of these oared gunboats to support his invasion of England; and the term was also applied to the singularly useless craft ordered by President Madison in 1812 to oppose the British landings in the United States. In 1854 the Russians still had a number of gunboats of this type, but they were never used offensively and so achieved nothing. The Royal Navy, more accustomed to fighting on the high seas, had developed the 250-ton brig-sloop as the most useful type of small armed vessel, and only in the last years of the 1840s was a screw-propelled, steam-powered replacement designed.

There were only six warships which could have answered Napier's requirements for inshore work in the Baltic. These were the *Arrow* class, originally dispatch vessels, but later upgraded to sloops; this new rating was rather too flattering as they carried far fewer guns than any existing sloop, so the Admiralty compromised by coining the new term 'gun-vessel' for them. Carrying two Lancaster guns, a new type of rifled muzzle-loader firing a 68-pounder shell, they had a fair turn of speed and shallow draught. This was the perfect combination of qualities for watching an enemy's harbours or bombarding his fortifications, but unfortunately only one, H.M.S. *Wrangler*, joined Napier's command, while her five sisters went to the Black Sea, where they proved

H.M.S. *Arrow*, a gunvessel designed before the war, in action off Sevastopol. *(Private collection)*

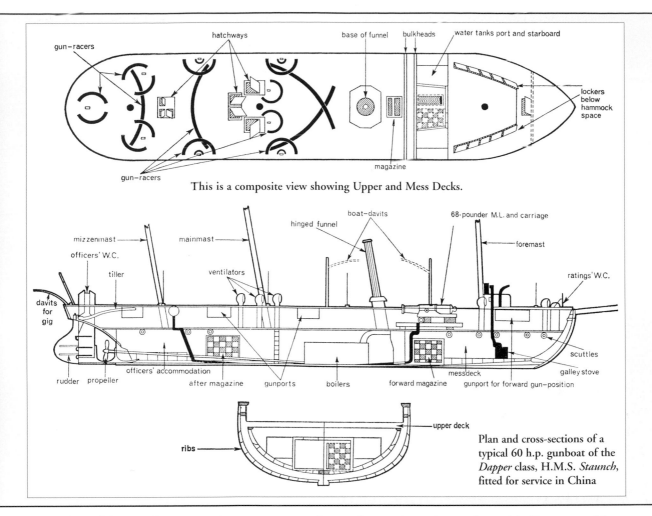

This is a composite view showing Upper and Mess Decks.

Plan and cross-sections of a typical 60 h.p. gunboat of the *Dapper* class, H.M.S. *Staunch*, fitted for service in China

extremely useful. *Wrangler* seems to have spent most of her time carrying mails from Danzig to the main fleet base at Nargen, but by herself she would have been of little use. As *The Times* hinted, Napier was resigned to lifting the blockade and withdrawing from the Baltic. *The Times* had been misled, however, in assuming that the Admiralty's new gunboats could be finished before the winter of 1854. As the French were already leaving the Baltic it would have been foolish to send a fresh force out to Napier to serve for only a few weeks before the ice closed in.

The first new gunboats were ordered in midsummer, when the Admiralty gave out contracts for six *Gleaner* class vessels. The main requirements were that the gunboats should be able to float in six-and-a-half feet of water and mount two 68-pounder guns. To accomplish this, the Admiralty's naval architects produced a strange and novel type of vessel. The hull was timber-built and there was only ten feet between deck and keel, resulting in dreadfully cramped accommodation. The bows were bluff, almost square when compared with those of modern ships, and the tubby hull was less than five times as long as it was broad. Below deck half the space was taken

up by a reciprocating engine and boilers crowned by a hinged funnel on the deck above. The first plans show such a light rig that it is clear that they were meant to rely on their engines rather than their sails – in itself a new departure for warships. In time they emerged with more canvas, due mainly to the fact that they could not carry enough coal for a long voyage. Although sixty feet shorter than the *Arrow* the little *Gleaner* also carried her guns in the same manner. Instead of the old truck mountings one can still see in H.M.S. *Victory* the big guns of 1854 were on wooden slides and could be slewed round with tackles and handspikes to fire through gunports on either broadside. To prevent the decks from being continually swamped with water they were enclosed by solid wooden bulwarks standing four feet high, and the guns fired through hinged double ports rather like swinging gates. When not needed the guns were lashed securely in a fore-and-aft position, where they had the minimum effect on the ship's stability. Stability was a vital factor as these little ships had three tall masts, a hull only twenty-two feet in the beam, and a completely flat bottom.

In October 1854, while the six *Gleaners* were still being built, the Admiralty took the plunge with an order for twenty more. These differed only slightly and became known as the *Dapper* class. Experience was to show that the weight of the second 68-pounder gun (ninety-five cwt) was too much for these gunboats, and they finally received a 32-pounder weighing nearly forty cwt less. Even then they were far too lively in any sort of rough weather, and heeled disconcertingly when both big guns were trained on the same broadside.[5] To keep up the ammunition supply when in action, every officer and rating except the lieutenant in command was either at the guns or down below passing ammunition. Even though each gunboat carried two 24-pounder howitzers amidships, no one could be spared to fire them if the other guns were manned!

To give one an idea of the relative firepower of these first steam gunboats it must be remembered that the 68-pounder was the second largest gun then used in the Royal Navy and fired a shell eight inches in diameter. The 32-pounder's solid round shot was over six inches in diameter and the gun weighed fifty-six cwt. Both guns were usually mounted in sloops and frigates, as well as ships of the line, and putting them in a gunboat could be compared with mounting 6-inch guns in a modern minesweeper. Such tremendous fire-power in a small hull made previous standards of comparison useless, for the two-gun *Gleaner* with her speed of seven knots and greater manoeuvrability under steam was more than a match for any twelve-gun sailing brig. In common with larger vessels gunboats abandoned the ancient system of rates, whereby the fighting value of a ship was rated by the number of guns carried. Soon the sailors were calling the gunboats the 'sixties' because their machinery developed a nominal sixty horsepower, although this was a figure much like the Treasury rating of motor-cars' horsepower, an arbitrary figure calculated on cylinder capacity and quite unrelated to the power developed.

The Black Sea

As a result of Napoleon III's infatuation with the idea of confining and weakening Russian power in the Black Sea the Anglo-French fleet found itself convoying troopships first to Varna in July 1854 and then to the Crimea itself in September. At the same time the Allies faced the problem of how to deploy their naval strength against the Russians. Since the Black Sea is not as shallow as the Baltic and does not have the myriad creeks and islands which frustrated the Baltic Fleet's efforts, the big ships were put to better use. Vice-Admiral Dundas was a mediocre Commander-in-Chief, but his second-in-command, Rear-Admiral Sir Edmund Lyons, was an energetic and unorthodox seaman. Lyons saw active service in the war of Greek Independence and had also been British Minister at Athens, in Switzerland and at Stockholm. His diplomatic experience made him well suited for the delicate task of administering a blockade against an enemy with whom friendly nations were still trading.

The British flag officers were unwilling to enforce a close blockade of the Russian ports, which would employ too many vessels and make other operations impossible. Dundas even put forward the idea of 'dis-

H.M.S. *Magnet*, typical of the *Albacore* class gunboats, seen here on the Thames. *(NPC, Antony Preston Collection)*

The iron paddle gunboat *Recruit* was being built by Scott Russell for Prussia but was taken over by the Royal Navy. She served in the Sea of Azov. Though well liked, the design was inferior to Admiralty types with screws. *(Private collection)*

tant' blockade, much the same as that enforced against Germany in both world wars. This meant that all neutral vessels should be examined for contraband when they tried to pass through the Bosphorus. But all such schemes were rendered futile when the Allied armies went to the Crimea, for the Navy's first duty was to supply and protect the troops besieging Sevastopol. By the autumn of 1854 the scope of the Crimean operations became so wide that very few ships could be spared from blockading Sevastopol, while hundreds of seamen and marines were ashore fighting in the Naval Brigade. In this way the Fleet's offensive role was severely limited, as Dundas had foreseen.

Perhaps the greatest potential exceptions to this state of affairs were the gunvessels. There were five *Arrow* class gunvessels under Dundas's command, and they soon began to feature in dispatches. *Lynx*, for instance, helped to rescue the three-decker *Rodney* when she ran aground within range of the Sevastopol forts; and later *Beagle* and *Arrow* landed their Lancaster guns for use ashore. Lyons was pressing for a bolder use for such handy craft, and his fertile brain already envisaged them operating against the Russian supply routes in the Sea of Azov. This landlocked sea lay behind the Crimea and through it passed all the

stores and victuals of the Russian armies. For the siege of Sevastopol was not what it suggests; the Allied trenches lay south of the defences while the northern side of the city was open to supply convoys and reinforcements. The result was that the Allied armies froze to death in their first ghastly Russian winter, while the Russians continued to receive unlimited supplies of food and ammunition.

The Admiralty also took exception to the wasteful employment of the five *Arrows* off Sevastopol. When Dundas wrote to say that he had landed the guns of *Arrow* and *Beagle* as the ships were quite useless in the heavy swell, the Secretary of the Admiralty's reply was:

My Lords can well understand that the motion of small vessels in a seaway must be unsteady; but considering that much care has been bestowed on the construction of these vessels, and that others of the same class are still in progress, it is important to know that your observation is not intended to apply to the use of these vessels in shoal water upon a weather shore, or under other circumstances in which they are not likely to be exposed to the effects of a heavy sea.

The operations reported by Captain Goldsmith of the *Sidon*, of his endeavours to check the march of the

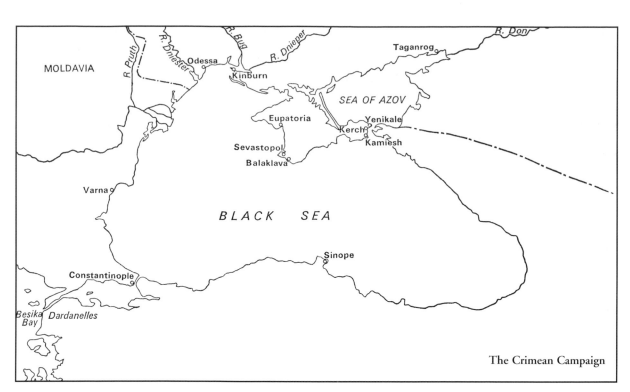

The Crimean Campaign

Russian forces proceeding along the shore in the neighbourhood of the Bay of Kherson, affords one, among other instances, in which the proper use of such vessels as the *Beagle* and the *Arrow* might be of great service,...[6]

Dundas was under pressure to do more than he was able, and wrote to the Admiralty in October:

I have always been fully aware of the value of the Sea of Azoff to the enemy and that it could only be attained by the possession of Kerch. Some weeks ago I urged that 2,000 men should be embarked for that place, but their Lordships are aware that from disease and the action at Alma our troops have suffered great loss, and the French Admiral, when he applied to his general for assistance to attack Kerch, was told of the impossibility of sending a man. The last report, by a neutral, that we have is, that the navigation through the straits at Kerch is entirely prevented by the enemy sinking ships and stones; and under existing circumstances all I can do is, when I have steamers to spare from the duty here, to send them off the port to damage the enemy as much as possible.[7]

Dundas also reported that the *Arrow* and her sisters *Beagle*, *Lynx* and *Viper* were fully occupied off Sevastopol and that all his steamers were suffering much wear and tear. To add to the Navy's endless responsibilities fifteen Allied warships and transports were driven ashore during a great gale on the night of 14 November 1854.

Nevertheless *Lynx* was detached with the frigates *Tribune* and *Highflyer* to 'proceed along the coast of the Crimea from Balaklava to Kerch... for the purpose of

preventing any supplies being conveyed coastways for the Russian Army at Sebastopol'.[8] The three vessels had orders to destroy every vessel seen, and any public property wherever it could be reached safely. As the weather was bad this raid accomplished little, but a good omen for the future was the destruction of a martello tower near Kerch. After the ships had shelled the fort and driven the defenders out, seamen and marines landed and blew the place sky high.

With the approach of winter all naval activity was reduced and so the opportunity was taken to recall most of the sail-powered battleships. The long, frustrating campaign had produced new ideas at last, and the admirals hoped to see better results in the spring of 1855. Little could be done to alleviate the Army's sufferings beyond improving the harbour at Balaklava, so the Navy very wisely prepared for a much greater contribution to the war when its new screw-battleships and gunboats arrived.

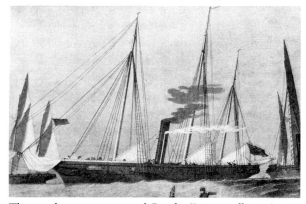

The wooden screw gunvessel *Beagle*. *(Private collection)*

In 1855 the Mediterranean Fleet was ready for a new campaign. In command at last was Sir Edmund Lyons, who was known to favour an intensified policy of amphibious warfare, and this reshuffle in the naval command was followed by political changes at home. Lord Aberdeen's government fell in January 1855, on the grounds of mishandling the war, and the new government under Palmerston immediately set up a Select Committee to enquire into the conduct of military operations.

It was clear that the Allies were still undecided about their grand strategy. The British and French naval commanders favoured a combined naval and military attack on Kerch, with the aim of weakening the Russian strength in the Crimea. Napoleon III also wished to divert the Allied efforts away from the siege of Sevastopol, but he hoped to use the troops to encircle and destroy the large Russian armies still at large in the central Crimea. This plan was approved in principle at a Council of War at Windsor on 18 April 1855.

The Allied forces were strengthened by the arrival of 40,000 Turks, whose victory over the Russians at Eupatoria is said to have broken the Tsar's heart (he died on 2 March 1855). With these troops and 15,000 Sardinians now available Lyons and Bruat, the French naval commander, were encouraged to press for an expedition to Kerch. They had good reason to hurry, for a reconnaissance by *Viper* showed that the defences were being strengthened, but they were unaware that Napoleon was secretly opposing their plans; his A.D.C. in the Crimea, General Niel, had instructions to hinder the naval expedition as much as possible.

The gunboats building in England were not yet available for service in the Black Sea, for in a letter on 19 February the Secretary of the Admiralty gave Lyons instructions about the proposed operations in the Sea of Azov:

The land-batteries once silenced, a narrow passage through the barrier is known to be open; and this passage may, if necessary, be widened by submarine explosion, the means of which, together with divers, have been long ago provided from England, and are now ready at Balaclava… The shallowness of the water, both at the entrance and within the sea itself, presents the most serious obstruction. Even in the mid-channel the depth is less than 3 fathoms [eighteen feet] in many places; and no ships of war would seem fit for this service if they draw more than 14 feet of water. The *Swallow* and the *Curlew*, and the six ships of the *Wrangler [Arrow]* class under your command, are probably available for this particular object… But it would be prudent immediately to prepare at Constantinople some sailing-vessels of light draught to be fitted as gun-boats…

An extract of this despatch has been transmitted to Captain the Honourable George Grey, at Gibraltar, in order that he may ascertain whether any gunboats or other vessels, suitable for the above service, can be procured in that neighbourhood.[9]

Lyons was writing to the Admiralty at the same time to say that he believed that the Kerch channel was no longer blocked by sunken ships after the winter gales; he also gave instructions that the Russians were to see no sign of unusual activity in the area. When the expedition was ready to leave at the end of April 1855 Lyons had only been able to collect a few pontoons for carrying 32-pounders, but the force sailed on 3 May full of enthusiasm, 11,000 men and over thirty ships.

Now Napoleon's deviousness showed itself. By telegram from Paris (the link had been completed at the end of April) he ordered his Commander-in-Chief, General Canrobert, to land men from Constantinople in the southern Crimea. To do this was simple enough, and need not have interfered with the Kerch expedition, but a second telegram ordered Canrobert to concentrate *all* his forces at once. The dispatch vessel carrying the fatal order reached the Allied force at the very entrance to the Straits of Kerch, and the French contingent was recalled. Fortunately the British force was withdrawn as well, for it would have been hopeless to attack alone. British and French, officers and men alike, were disgusted at this turn of events, and Lyons wrote a furious dispatch to London as soon as he returned to Balaklava. His attacks on Canrobert should be forgiven, for he was unaware of the part the French Emperor had played in ruining his plans.

The luckless Canrobert, never renowned for firmness, resigned in a welter of criticism and was replaced by General Pélissier, a 'rude, resolute and energetic' commander, whose first action was to deal with Niel. The Emperor's A.D.C. now found himself treated like a subaltern, told to speak only when spoken to, and forbidden to communicate privily with Paris on pain of being put on the first ship homeward bound. Niel clearly feared

General Pélessier.
(US Library of Congress)

Pélissier, and since Napoleon's master plan had already been rejected at a meeting of the Allied commanders on 12 May there was no audible complaint when the second Kerch expedition sailed on 22 May. This time Lyons and Bruat had 15,000 men, ample artillery and fifty-six ships, among them all six *Arrows*.

In spite of the warning the Russians must have had three weeks earlier, they were stunned when this overwhelming force landed at Kamiesh under covering fire from ships' guns. They blew up all their stores and magazines, spiked their guns and withdrew without a fight. Their immediate material losses were 4,000,000 lb. of corn and 500,000 lb. of flour, and within four days the Allied squadron destroyed 250 ships and more grain depots. All this represented about four months' rations for an army of 100,000 men.

With the Russians cleared from both sides of the Kerch channel the Allied 'inshore' squadron moved into the long-forbidden Sea of Azov. Besides the *Arrow* and her sister gunvessels *Beagle, Snake, Lynx, Viper,* and *Wrangler,* eight larger sloops and five French steamers began to scour the Sea of Azov systematically. By great good fortune the Russians left 17,000 tons of coal at Kerch and Yenikale, thus providing the flotilla with more than it needed.

Having destroyed the Russians' fleet of coastal shipping without difficulty the Azov Flotilla began to attack the enemy on shore as well. Since the Russian hinterland was devoid of railways and lacked any usable system of roads, their supply system relied very heavily on that very

coastal shipping so lately destroyed. With so few good roads the overland supply route to the Crimean armies was kept as short as possible and even that was threatened, for the Flotilla had orders to destroy all the important bridges near the shore.

As the sailors worked their way along the coast they were astonished at the growing evidence of Russia's vast resources. Close to the shoreline, ready for shipment to the Crimea, they found stocks of corn, salt, coal and flour. The countryside was infested with Cossack patrols, so the sailors adopted tactics remarkably like the Commando raids of World War II, destroying granaries and supply depots and retreating to the ships before the redoubtable Cossack lancers could cut them off.

Admiral Lyons was told by the Admiralty to relax his efforts to procure makeshift gunboats locally as six of the new *Dapper* class were on their way out to him. A month after the forcing of the Straits of Kerch all six – *Boxer, Clinker, Cracker, Fancy, Grinder* and *Jasper* – were at work in the Sea of Azov. They were particularly active in the shallow, desolate waters around the mouth of the Don, landing men wherever possible to destroy forage, wheat, boats, fisheries, windmills and grain-stores. The gunboats were also kept on the move to pin down large numbers of enemy troops who might otherwise have been at Sevastopol.

Under close surveillance was the port of Taganrog at the north-eastern corner of the Sea of Azov, a vital link in the traffic route between central Russia and the Crimea. Taganrog was one of the first targets of the Azov Flotilla,

The gunvessel *Snake* engaging Russian steamers near Kerch, 24 May 1855. (*Parker Gallery*) The inset shows a Lancaster 68-pounder RML on board *Snake* in 1854. This was the first rifled gun in the Royal Navy, and the weight was such that it was only suitable for operations in sheltered waters, being shipped on board larger vessels during sea passages. (*NPC, Antony Preston Collection*)

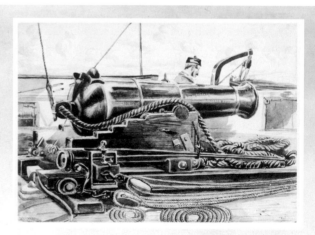

The gunvessel *Grinder* chasing Russian boats in the Sea of Azov, 31 August 1855. *(NPC, Antony Preston Collection)*

and suffered bombardment early in June. Soon feelings were running high in the town, and on 20 July an Englishman living there, Mr John Martin, wrote to the British Consul to complain that gunboats had recently fired wantonly on women and children. Martin claimed that he had seen the officers of one gunboat 'dining under an awning … and drinking toasts with brutal hilarity'.[10] The letter was said to have been written at the instance of Count Tolstoy, Governor of Taganrog.

Commander Sherard Osborn, the senior British naval officer, indignantly refuted the charges.[11] He had himself reconnoitred Taganrog in *Jasper* on 19 July, when only a few shots were fired. *Jasper* was subsequently detached with orders to harass the area, and on 23 July succeeded in capturing seven Russian field-guns 'within a stone's throw of the fortifications', giving covering fire to the gig which carried out the operation. 'Count Tolstoi', remarked Osborn tartly, 'asserts that he gave orders for our people not to be fired on; all I can say is, his orders were not obeyed, and even if they had been Lieutenant Hudson [commanding officer of *Jasper*] could not be expected to be prepared for the humane eccentricities of the Governor of Taganrog.'[12]

Mr Martin may have derived some consolation from the fate which overtook

Commander Sherard Osborn.
(US Library of Congress)

the *Jasper* only a few hours after her exploit at Taganrog. On the night of 23 July the little gunboat was making for Crooked Spit, the appointed rendezvous with Osborn in the paddle-sloop *Vesuvius*, where one of the Flotilla reported every forty-eight hours. Gunboats carried only one commissioned officer, the lieutenant in command; being constantly on patrol in enemy waters meant that Hudson had been able to take only snatches of rest during the previous six days. Exhausted beyond endurance, he lay down that night on the deck next to the man at the tiller after giving the order: 'Wake me at midnight or as soon as you see the lights.' But he had forgotten to tell the helmsman that the course he was steering would run the ship aground if no alteration were made, and the next thing Hudson felt was a mighty lurch as *Jasper* ran hard aground on Crooked Spit at about four-and-a-half knots.

It was just after midnight when Hudson was woken by the crash as his ship struck. Frantically he and the ship's company worked through the rest of the night to try to lighten the ship and repair the damage. When the sun came up they realised how desperate their situation was. They were so close inshore that some of the ubiquitous Cossacks were firing at them from the cover of ruined buildings on shore. Hudson's reaction was spirited. While not slackening his efforts to salvage his ship he ordered all the hammocks to be stowed around the bulwarks at the bow to give protection against Russian musket balls. To keep the Cossacks at a respectful distance one small brass howitzer was manhandled from amidships up to the bows where it could bear on the enemy riflemen, while the five Royal Marines replied with their Minié rifles. The big 68-pounder shell-gun would have dispersed the Russians very quickly, but Hudson knew that its weight was helping to keep *Jasper* firmly aground. Sweating and cursing, the seamen managed to heave the gun clear of its carriage with rope tackles, and dropped it over the side with a mighty splash, followed by its heavy wooden carriage and the newly-taken field-guns. *Jasper* was lighter by some four tons.

Luckily, their squadron-mate *Swallow* had been alerted by the sound of firing and came to their rescue later that morning. But the combined efforts of both ships' companies could not help *Jasper*, and *Swallow*'s captain, Commander Craufurd, ordered Hudson to abandon ship. Bad weather was in the offing, and *Swallow* dared not dally so close inshore. Hudson and his gunner stayed on board to fire the magazine, but while loose powder and other combustibles flared up and set the whole fore part ablaze, the magazine obstinately refused to detonate. Hudson volunteered to go back, but Craufurd refused to allow it, and *Swallow* stood out for the open sea, leaving the Russians nothing more than a smouldering wreck.

Four days later, when the storm had blown itself out, Commander Osborn himself sailed for Crooked Spit. He found that the Russians had stripped *Jasper* of everything movable, including her howitzers and her signal books (a singularly careless omission by Hudson). With the forward half of the ship completely burned to the waterline and the after part badly damaged by shellfire, it was clear that the Russians could never raise her. However, Osborn hoped that the Russians had not found the jettisoned gun, and after clearing Crooked Spit of riflemen with a few rounds of shellfire, *Vesuvius* and her consorts started dredging. They soon found the 68-pounder, and fished up three of the seven field-guns before Osborn decided to give up.

The loss of the *Jasper* had little effect on the Azov Flotilla's depredations. Right up until the Azov began to freeze the Flotilla worked hard and the dispatches from Osborn show just what benefits were reaped from energetic leadership. No records seem to exist of the Russian view of their losses, but they must have been severe, and the knowledge that the spring of 1856 would bring more gunboats and sloops into the Sea of Azov must have disheartened the local peasantry and townspeople. When Osborn, now a Captain, wrote to Sir Edmund Lyons on 24 November 1855 to report the end of the Azov operations,[13] he brought to a close not only the most envied of the Royal Navy's war exploits but also its most significant contribution to the war effort.

The last major action of the war in the Black Sea was the reduction of the fortress of Kinburn which guarded the mouth of the Dnieper and the Bug and which, in the Allies' hands, would have been a grave threat to Odessa. This fortress is said to owe its existence to John Paul Jones having advised Suvorov to fortify the position to protect Odessa from attack.[14] Both the French and British navies were anxious to test their new armoured warships against Russian fortresses, and since Sevastopol had fallen on 12 September Kinburn offered the only opportunity for such an assault.

The decision to go ahead with a combined operation was taken at a conference on 29 September and a force of 10,000 men sailed a week later under the supreme command of General Bazaine, later branded as the archtraitor of the Franco-Prussian War. The *Arrows* and *Dappers* had all been withdrawn from the Sea of Azov for the expedition, and *Boxer*, *Clinker*, *Cracker* and *Fancy* in company with four French gunboats forced an entrance on the first day. All six *Arrows* took part in the saturating barrage which led to the garrison's surrender, and four of the gunboat contingent remained behind when the main body returned to Sevastopol at the end of the month. As at Kerch and Sveaborg, the Navy's specialised warships demonstrated the power of armour and shellfire over a hitherto impregnable defence.

After Kinburn operations in the Black Sea virtually ceased for the winter, but not before a final destructive sortie in the Sea of Azov. A highly publicised Council of War was held in Paris in January 1856, at which numerous plans of campaign were said to have been discussed,

General Bazaine.
(*US Library of Congress*)

but by this time military strategy was being overtaken by the peace negotiations. On 29 February an armistice was declared and the formal peace treaty was signed in Paris on 30 March, bringing to an end a war which had cost the lives of close on half a million men.

Return to the Baltic, 1855

There had never been any doubt that the Navy would return to the Baltic in 1855 but this did nothing to stop speculation about the identity of the new Commander-in-Chief and the composition of his command. By the end of February 1855 everything was settled: Rear-Admiral the Hon. Richard Dundas (no relation of the former C.-in-C. in the Mediterranean) was to command a fleet comprising steamships only.

The new fleet sailed in two divisions, the first of which left Spithead with great ceremony, under the gaze of the Queen and the First Sea Lord in their respective yachts. By June the fleet was reunited at Nargen and had been reinforced by a French squadron, making a total of over fifty ships, including eighteen gunboats.

The dispatches were soon bristling with details of captures of Russian vessels running the Allied blockade, and the names of several new 60 h.p. gunboats crop up continually. For example, on 12 June the little gunboat *Badger* under the watchful eye of H.M.S. *Hogue* was sent into Hanko, where she used her 68-pounder to destroy a Russian telegraph station. This sort of random raiding may seem wasteful and petty to the modern reader, but

when carried out on a large scale it tied down thousands of Russian soldiers on garrison duty. Exactly sixty years later a handful of British submarines had much the same effect in the Sea of Marmora, when by shelling trains and landing demolition parties they drew off thousands of Turkish troops from the trenches at Gallipoli.

The monotonous work of blockade went on right through the summer, and although the Navy felt left out of the war, its silent pressure on the Russians was slowly taking effect. By October 1855 the Tsar had more men guarding danger points along the coasts of Bothnia and Finland than the entire strength of the British Army, and prowling sloops and gunboats had snapped up 80,000 tons of shipping. As the little wooden gunboats carried so little coal they invariably cruised in company with a larger warship, from whom they drew not only coal but ammunition and victuals. Living conditions were so primitive that this was the only way of keeping the ship's company efficient and healthy. The parent ship had no cause to begrudge this service to her satellite, for she shared in the prize-money awarded for the gunboat's capture, and if the gunboat ever took on an opponent too strong for her she could always fall back on the parent ship for support.

The gunboat *Ruby* had the rare experience of seeing a Russian man-o'-war at sea while operating in the Gulf of Finland in July. She was sent into Kounda Bay near Viborg (now Viipuri) and was towing the boats of *Magicienne* and *Arrogant* when she sighted a large

Practicing 68-pdr gun drill on board H.M.S. *Starling. (NPC, Antony Preston Collection)*

Operations in the Baltic, carried out in a very similar manner to those of the Azov campaign. *(NPC, Antony Preston Collection)*

Russian warship towing two oared gunboats. *Ruby* opened fire and the Russians retired smartly with the whole cavalcade in pursuit. When *Ruby* tried to enter the sound leading to Viborg she was held up by a barrier of stakes. Suddenly, while she was helping the boats to cross the obstruction the Russians sprang their trap; the little gunboat was at the mercy of a battery of guns concealed on shore only 350 yards away.

For a few minutes there was utter chaos as enemy riflemen joined in, firing volleys at the huddle of boats, but *Ruby*'s guns spoke out and drove the riflemen from their position. The confusion was doubled when a rocket burst in one of the boats, but the seamen and marines rallied under the gunboat's protection. The force withdrew, for by this time three Russian gunboats and a steamer were coming up the sound, attracted by the sound of firing. In spite of the galling fire at such close range the British force lost only a midshipman from one of the cutters, and got away from a very tight corner with the aid of *Ruby*'s covering fire.[15]

The gunboat *Ruby* and rocket boats in action in Kounda Bay, 13 July 1855. *(© **National Maritime Museum, London**)*

In August permission was given for the cherished attack on Sveaborg, and a careful reconnaissance was made of the island-dotted approaches to the sprawling anchorage. For the first time in its history the Royal Navy had to sweep for mines, for the Russians had recently introduced moored 'explosive machines', the beginning of their pre-eminence in this branch of undersea warfare. Mooring positions for the bombarding vessels were carefully surveyed and buoyed, clear of reefs and yet as far as possible from the heavy batteries to the east and west of the town.

Dundas had assembled sixteen gunboats and sixteen mortar-vessels for the main bombarding force, and it was these vessels, with ten French craft, which bore the brunt of the action. Although some thirty larger vessels were present they remained passive onlookers as they drew too much water. However, they gave up a number of heavy guns to strengthen the gunboats' armament; as the gunboats were in sheltered waters, they could take the risk of the extra weight. *Stork* and *Snapper* each carried three of the new Lancaster guns, despite this weapon's increasingly familiar habit of bursting. The mortar-vessels were little more than barges, but each one had squatting amidships a mortar to lob 13-inch bombs over parapets to destroy fortified buildings. Once these ungainly craft had the range they methodically dropped their deadly missiles through roofs and into gun-positions, dismounting guns and detonating magazines.

Just after seven o'clock on the morning of 9 August 1855 the inshore squadrons of Allied ships opened fire on the Russian batteries, and although the Russians replied vigorously the gunboats' constant movement prevented them from being hit. An eye-witness described them as 'pirouetting in a witches' dance'. Even the mor-

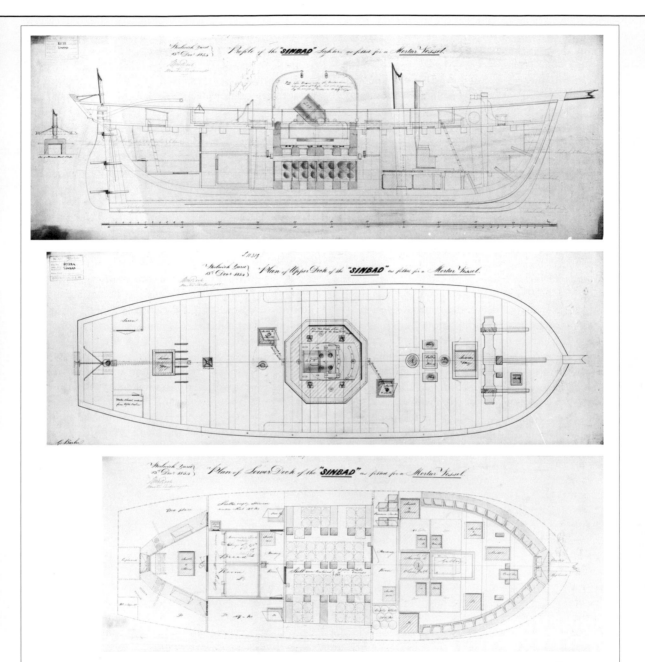

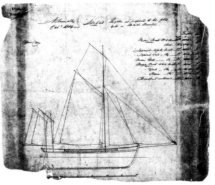

Profile, plans and sail plan of the mortar vessel *Sinbad*, converted from a dockyard lighter in 1854-55. Of 105 tons, she and her sister *Drake* measured 60 ft 1 in long by 20 ft 9 in beam, with a depth in the hold of 9 ft, and were armed with a single 13-inch mortar. They took the numbers *Mortar Vessel No.2* and *Mortar Vessel No.1* respectively; twenty similar purpose-built vessels taking numbers 3–22. Seventeen, including *Sinbad*, were dispatched to the Baltic, where all but one were involved in the bombardment of Sveaborg.
(NPC, Antony Preston Collection)

tar-vessels were able to confuse the aim of the enemy gunners by warping themselves to and fro. After three hours of cannonading fires could be seen ashore and three enormous explosions were heard. The bombardment went on through the afternoon, but when night fell the gunboats withdrew to avoid running aground in the dark. To maintain the Russians' discomfiture rocket-boats were sent in during the night, while the mortar-vessels kept up an intermittent fire.

Next day the gunboats returned, this time closing to within 2,200 yards of the forts. Although firing went on into the night of 10 August, it became less severe as defects began to develop in the mortars. Eventually the ships were withdrawn on this account, after expending over 100 tons of powder and 1,000 tons of shells and mortar bombs; the Allies lost only one man killed and fifteen wounded, mainly by bursting rockets. Although the London dailies made extravagant claims, a conservative estimate later put the Russian losses at 2,000 men, twenty-three ships and a number of detonated magazines.

The immediate results of the bombardment were nil, but the Allies gained much in the long run. Nothing further was achieved that year as the Anglo-French fleet confined itself to maintaining the blockade, but the new Tsar and his advisers knew that the Allies had only flexed their muscles. There can be little doubt that fear of an all-out attack on Kronstadt and St Petersburg, coupled with the adherence of Sweden to the Allied cause in

November 1855, helped to persuade the Russians to accept the peace terms proposed by Austria and bring the war to a close early in 1856.

In the spring of 1856 the Royal Navy would have had over a hundred gunboats ready. At least half this armada would have been available for Baltic operations and it is interesting to speculate on what might have been achieved. *The Times* of 8 December 1855 forecast that 'a formidable fleet… will re-enter the Baltic in 1856 … and blockade all coasts, while the army commanded by General Canrobert will simultaneously operate in Finland, and the three Russian provinces of Courland, Esthonia and Livonia…'[16] This again reflected Napoleon III's new strategy of withdrawal from the profitless Crimea in favour of large-scale military operations in the Baltic, a change of heart due principally to the achievements of the men and ships of both navies.

An unsigned memorandum was drawn up at the end of 1855, setting out three plans for the naval contribution to the projected 1856 campaign.[17] The first was a close blockade of the Russian coast, attacking their coastal trade, particularly in the Gulf of Finland. Significantly, the second plan, calling for a purely naval attack on Sveaborg and Kronstadt, received little sympathy. The third plan obviously seemed promising and was set out in great detail. A large-scale attack on Sveaborg based on the 1855 bombardment was planned, but with more ships and gunboats, as well as

The mortar vessel H.M.S. *Pickle* (*MV22*) at Sveaborg, August 1855. (*NPC, Antony Preston Collection*)

The attack on Sveaborg. *(Private collection)*

some of the new armoured batteries. This time a landing force of up to 50,000 men would be provided to capture the base after it had been pounded to rubble. An attack on this scale could hardly have failed and would probably have been followed by a similar onslaught on Kronstadt.

Impressed at last with the need for gunboats by the Baltic and Azov operations, the Admiralty ordered more and more gunboats of the *Dapper* type from May 1855 onwards. In all ninety-eight were built, all practically identical to the original twenty, and the Admiralty might have gone on ordering them until the end of the war had a change not been indicated. By midsummer 1855 the Baltic dispatches contained many references to the *Gleaners* and *Dappers*, and mentioned several instances of gunboats grounding in five or six feet of water.

To overcome this problem two new classes of shallow-draught gunboats were ordered. The first twenty *Cheerfuls* were not a success; weight-saving was carried to extremes, so that they suffered from very frail hulls. Their faults were rectified in the next class, known as the *Clown* type, by installing a bigger engine and making the scantlings stronger. Instead of the puny 20 h.p. engine of the *Cheerful*, these tiny gunboats boasted a one-cylinder

40 h.p. engine. Out of the original dozen boats seven saw a good deal of service, whereas all but two of the other class never left Home waters.

This vast programme of gunboat-building, calling for the completion of more than 120 boats by 1856, resulted in unprecedented exertions by English shipbuilders. Only two firms, Penn & Co. and Maudslay, Son & Field, were awarded the contracts for engining all these gunboats. As neither of these firms, in spite of being the finest marine engineers in the world, could hope to have produced half the machinery required, it is believed[18] that they resorted to some form of sub-contracting, and only completed the final assembly and installation themselves.

The assembly-line was unheard of in 1855, and so was precision engineering. Nevertheless engineering firms all over England turned out batches of components such as cranks and connecting-rods, which were sent in turn to the two parent firms for assembly. It must be remembered that even a small batch of pistons turned out by one firm might vary considerably, while there was no guarantee that they would match the cylinders turned out by another company. Yet the gunboats' machinery worked, and some of these engines were still working thirty years later.

The gunboats *Thistle* and *Weazel* engaged in cutting out trading craft off Kronstadt, 1855. *(Conway Maritime Press)*

These large orders for gunboats came right on top of a spate of warship-building which was straining the Royal Dockyards' resources to their limits. By 1855 the Royal Navy's precious store of seasoned oak was almost exhausted, so the Chief Constructor gave the builders of minor warships permission to use a variety of woods. But this was still not enough, and eventually the use of 'green' unseasoned timber was used, on the grounds that gunboats and gunvessels were expendable, and unlikely to be retained in the postwar fleet.

A wartime stopgap often becomes a workhorse in peacetime, when it is cheaper to use an unsuitable ship than it is to build a new vessel to do the job properly. So it was with the little gunboats, which carried out a variety of tasks long after the Crimean War. As tenders to bigger ships, as survey vessels and sail training ships they served quite successfully for years, and as we shall see, a few saw active service abroad. But false economy always reveals itself; as the inevitable result of being built of green timber nearly forty gunboats and gunvessels developed dry rot before they were ten years old. This resulted in a great outcry when the news reached Parliament,[19] for the taxpayer was not normally asked to foot a bill for warships which rotted on the slipway. In the mid-1860s the Crimean gunboats achieved a certain notoriety on account of this, and their replacement was the cause of some extraordinary measures (see Chapter 7).

At the time the Allied and Russian delegates gathered in Paris for the Peace Conference the Royal Dockyards were frantically preparing gunboats for the Baltic.

Gunboat after gunboat was commissioned at her builder's yard and towed round to Deptford, Woolwich and other southern dockyards to receive her guns and engines, for each one was launched without fittings of any sort. But suddenly the feverish haste vanished, for the declaration of peace meant no Baltic campaign. Many gunboats went straight into the Reserve, and over fifty spent their entire lives hauled up on slipways in Haslar Creek, roofed over against the weather, and waiting for the next war.

To celebrate the Peace the Queen inspected her Navy off Spithead in April 1856. Among the vast throng were sixty-four gunboats, with the bigger gunvessels acting as divisional leaders, but for most of them it was their last commission. By the end of that year only a handful were still in full commission.

The Admiralty was not satisfied with the design of the existing gunboats, and in 1856 an improved class was put in hand. The new *Algerine* class followed the general lines of the *Dapper*, but reflected the influence of the bigger *Philomel* class of gunvessels. By the simple expedient of increasing length by nearly twenty feet, and depth of hold by a foot and a quarter the *Algerine*'s designers produced a gunboat which could make an ocean passage in relative safety. Her greater size enabled her to carry a more substantial rig, more powerful engines and with it all a good armament. Indeed, she made such an impression when compared with the earlier gunboats that she and her sisters were referred to for a few years as gunvessels. H.M.S. *Algerine* was in many ways an epoch-mak-

The gunboats *Lapwing* and *Ringdove* under construction at White's shipbuilders, Cowes, Isle of Wight, in 1855. This view shows work being carried out by gaslight, which was introduced by the company to enable them to bring in a night shift in order to cope with the volume of work that the Admiralty required. Nevertheless they were eventually forced to turn down some Admiralty contracts rather than compromise on standards or delivery times. *(Private collection)*

ing vessel, for she was more than a link between the gunboat and the gunvessel. She was the link between the wooden gunboats of the Crimean War and the sturdy composite-built ships which served right through the rest of the century.

There was a spurt in gunvessel-construction at this time, but it never approached the scale of the various gunboat programmes. After the *Arrows* there was an increase in size with the *Vigilants* and *Intrepids*, almost big enough to be rated as sloops. Just as the *Algerines* were sometimes called gunvessels, so the *Arrows* were called gunboats at various times. The gunvessel *Victor* when taken into the Confederate Navy in 1863 was re-rated as the frigate *Rappahannock*.[20] This confusion was just another symptom of the uncertainty in naval design in this revolutionary period. To add to the confusion Victorian writers on naval affairs had the habit of calling anything below the rank of frigate a 'gunboat', and any vessel on detached duty such as slavery patrols or pirate-hunting was technically 'cruizing'; hence the term 'cruizer' was applied to many of the sloops and gunboats which were to be the backbone of the small-ship Navy in years to come.

Chapter 3

THE GUNBOAT HEYDAY

The flotillas of small craft produced for the Crimean War were not to lack employment. Several of them, as we shall see, were soon in action against the Chinese. Their success in helping to browbeat the Manchus meant that for a generation thereafter the gunboat and gunvessel were to form an indispensable element of the Victorian Navy. The arrival of the gunboat did not, of course, mark a new departure, for it fitted conveniently into the context of a policy which had been developing since Waterloo. The gunboat simply carried out this policy more efficiently than its predecessors of the days of sail.

For over forty years the Royal Navy had added the duties of world policeman to its traditional role as the chief agent of British interests abroad, and the outcome had been grandiloquently christened *Pax Britannica*. Chastising pirates, slavers, and savages the Navy waged a relentless war on everyone who resisted the sacred Liberal virtues of parliamentary government, scientific progress and free trade. By the 1850s the ships of Her Britannic Majesty had already done much to pave the way for the Liberal millennium, but the fire-power and shallow draught of the gunboat made her the perfect weapon for pushing the Western advance to unprecedented limits. Enemies who had hitherto relied on coastal forts, inshore reefs and unnavigable rivers as barriers against British penetration were now practically defenceless.

It should be remembered, however, that once they secured their entry the British rarely moved forward to annexation and direct rule of any newly penetrated territory. In the years between the close of the Napoleonic Wars and the Scramble for Africa in the 1880s the British Empire was predominantly an 'informal' empire, an empire of influence rather than government. The returns accruing from foreign trade and investment and the profits from British banking, shipping and insurance were

infinitely more important than the possession of colonies. Whenever the gunboat was used it exerted pressure at some point to prod the local inhabitants into an appreciation of the benefits of Western civilisation, not to force an opening for an occupying army. This was the time when the white constituents of the Empire were moving steadily towards independence. Even India, the largest non-white colony, was ruled after 1857 in no spirit of imperial fulfilment, but rather as a painful and distasteful duty. Almost everywhere the merits of indirect imperialism seemed to outweigh the burdensome and expensive chore of governing alien races.

This is not to say that there were not British consuls and traders in Africa, China and the Pacific who had other ideas. The consuls in particular, forgotten in their remote outposts, often dreamed megalomaniac dreams of planting the Union Jack on every possible acre of foreign soil, and occasionally enlisted the support of a sympathetic naval officer. But these petty empire-builders were invariably overruled by the Foreign Office, anxious above all to avoid the risk of direct involvement and international dispute. Throughout its career the gunboat remained the tool of a strictly limited Imperial policy. Naval commanders on foreign stations were kept as far as possible under surveillance, and the Admiralty was constantly on guard against committing its ships and men any more than it could help.

The gunboat was sustained by other basic elements of mid-Victorian political philosophy. For one thing, she was the ideal craft for a government and a nation dedicated to defence on the cheap; comparatively low costs of production and maintenance made her the perfect weapon for a country with rigid public thrift as one of its articles of faith. These mid-century years were the noontide of *laisser faire*, when income tax was held at a negligible rate and government expenditure was cut to the

bone. For years the arch-exponents *of laisser faire* eco-nomics, the Liberal Gladstone and the Radicals Cobden and Bright, fought to keep government spending to a minimum. As a profound distrust of militarism was another part of the Radical and Liberal creeds the naval and military estimates were inevitably the first to go under the axe. This regardless of the fact that it was the Navy which constantly underwrote the international peace extolled by Radicals, and the Navy which alone guaranteed the undisturbed international trade demand-ed by Liberals.

The high point of this tight-fisted doctrine came dur-ing Gladstone's first administration from 1868 to 1874, when Imperial commitments were drastically cut by the withdrawal of nearly half the British troops serving on garrison duty in the colonies. This 'return of the legions' had been demanded for at least a decade, partly for rea-sons of economy, partly as a step in the movement towards colonial self-government, but also, as we shall see, for strategic reasons. In 1861, a Select Committee of the House of Commons had recommended that the cost of defending the 'white' colonies such as Canada, South Africa, Australia and New Zealand 'ought mainly to

The heyday of the gunboat navy. Above: cutlass and gun drill on deck. Below: one of the later wooden gunboats (left) with the battleships *Sans Pareil* and *Donegal*, off the Hamoaze. Both battleships had steam and sail propulsion, with funnels that could be lowered when not in use, as in this photograph. *(NPC, Antony Preston Collection)* devolve upon themselves', while Great Britain continued to shoulder the responsibility for such small Imperial outposts as Malta, Gibraltar, Aden, Hong Kong, parts of the West Indies, the Falkland Islands and the West African settlements. Three years later reductions began with the removal of 10,000 men from New Zealand, and this at the height of the Maori Wars! Further withdrawals took place under the direction of Gladstone's Secretary for War, Cardwell. In 1869 Cardwell proposed a reduction in British troops overseas (excluding India) from 50,000 to 26,000, in an attempt to slash the Imperial defence budget by a third. Despite bad relations with the United States garrisons in Canada dropped from 16,000 to 6,000 men, and after the *Alabama* dispute had been settled by arbitration in 1871 the only British troops left were the garrisons of the naval bases at Halifax and Esquimalt. By 1870 *all* British troops had left Australia and New Zealand.

From this time the chief responsibility for defending the colonies rested not on the Army but on the Navy (indeed, after the withdrawal of the garrisons it is hard to see how the Army could have defended the Empire at all). The 1861 Committee recognised this in stating that the country should 'trust mainly on naval supremacy for securing against foreign aggression the distant dependencies of the Empire'. The type of vessel best fitted for this job was, in the Committee's view, the gunboat. Backed by floating batteries the gunboat would provide an economical form of coastal defence which, it was hoped, would be more than a match for anything a potential rival could set against it. The small-ship navy, scattered across the world, was to be the mainstay of British and colonial interests.

The greatest threat to this point of view came, paradoxically enough, not from the advocates of the ironclad, but from the leadership of the Liberal party. As we have pointed out, the Navy was the only possible means of colonial defence once the Army had been withdrawn, but the Liberals were still determined to cut defence expenditure on all fronts. So when Gladstone's First Lord of the Admiralty, Hugh Childers, presented his first Naval Estimates in March 1869 he announced that the number of men serving on foreign stations would be reduced in the coming year from 17,000 to 11,000 – in other words, he was proposing to parallel Cardwell, regardless of the consequences. With this reduction in manpower came cuts in the available shipping; gunboats on foreign stations were reduced in number while five of the new *Plover* class gun-vessels were held in reserve for two or three years before their first commissions. Despite the protests of the First Sea Lord, Sir Alexander Milne, Childers had his way and manpower abroad was slashed to 11,500.

It is interesting to see how Gladstone himself justified his policy. Speaking in the Commons in the early stages of the Franco-Prussian War, he rested his case on arguments curiously similar to those later deployed by such 'Big Navy' fanatics as Fisher.

> What is the use [asked Gladstone] of a system of naval defence which dots your vessels over the whole globe, multiplying occasions of difference, of quarrel, of danger and of conflict, into which Parliament finds itself hurried by the act of some subordinate agent abroad, but which would never have been accepted on recommendation of a Cabinet? What is the use for the purpose of defending these shores, and of enabling you to assert the dignity of the United Kingdom, at a great European crisis, of that sporadic system which enables you, if you think fit, to vaunt your strength in those parts of the world where the flags of the Queen's ships may be flying but which, instead of adding anything, actually deducts from the real strength and energy of the country?[1]

But the additional estimates voted for the Navy were not spent on a battle-fleet to guard against a European threat; that was to wait another nineteen years. Gladstone, as one commentator has put it, 'shared Cobden's distaste for the possibility that two drunken naval captains of frigates in the Antipodes might cause a war between European powers'.[2] His reflexes were defensive, not aggressive like Fisher's, and they were reinforced by the endless quest for economy that he was to pursue to the very last day of his political career.

> That for which I have been disposed to contend [he wrote to Childers's successor, Goschen, in 1871] is that we are to have a powerful fleet in and near our own waters, and that outside of this nothing is to be maintained except for well-defined and approved purposes of actual service, and in quantities of force properly adjusted; and not under the notion that there are to be fleets in the various quarters of the world ready when a difficulty arises with a foreign country, or an offence to our own ships, *then and there* [Gladstone's italics] to deal with it with a strong hand.[3]

Faced with these stern admonitions, Goschen was no doubt expected to go even further than Childers in the direction of parsimony but it was not to be. The view took hold that the total of 11,500 men was an irreducible minimum, and the waning of the fancied European danger ended the call for concentration on the Channel. At the same time an alarming increase in the slave trade off East Africa, with the growth of 'blackbirding' in the South Pacific (the illegal transportation of native labour from the islands to the Australian colonies), meant still heavier calls on the Navy's resources. The gunboat fleet had survived its first attack.

A second important factor pushing gunboats and other small ships to the fore in the mid-Victorian era was the emergence of the strategic concept of 'Fortress

England'. The Army had turned its back on the colonies partly in order to be free to concentrate on the defence of the British Isles. With the advent of steam propulsion at sea in the 1840s the idea had gained ground that the Navy was no longer capable of acting as Britain's first line of defence. Thanks to steam power the French Fleet could, in the opinion of the Navy's critics, escort an invasion force across the Channel overnight and establish a beach-head before the Admiralty could react. In spite of their Lordships' contemptuous dismissal of this sacrilegious charge, the feeling that the Regular Army and the Militia must be relied on to stem a French invasion gradually took hold.

Public outcry on the score of invasion came to a head on three occasions – the so-called 'Three Panics' of 1846-47, 1851-52 and 1858-59. After the first the Army's partisans let it be known that the venerable figure of the Duke of Wellington was on their side (or so it seemed). 'As we stand now and if it be true that the exertions of the fleet alone are not sufficient to provide for our defence,' wrote the Duke, the French were in a position to set troops on the English coast 'at any time of tide, with any wind, and in any weather'. The fact that he had also written, 'We have no defence, or hope of chance of defence, excepting in our Fleet', was discreetly overlooked. But the damage was done, and the apparent ambitions of Napoleon III, culminating in the laying-down of the revolutionary French ironclad *La Gloire* in 1858, only added fuel to the fire. By the close of the 1850s the majority of informed opinion was convinced that the Royal Navy could play only a supporting part in the defence of the British Isles.

Hereafter the main reliance for home defence was placed on the Army and an elaborate system of coastal fortifications. For a time, indeed, nothing less than fortress mania swept the country – there was even a request for the fortification of the entire north-western coastline of Scotland! The Navy's task was seen as the provision of coastal defence vessels – gunboats – to supplement the shore batteries, and while the Admiralty was not unnaturally apoplectic at this assessment of its importance, it was a long time before it could make any headway against its critics. Gunboats stationed in Home waters were earmarked for coastal defence duties in the vicinity of all main ports and dockyards. A proposal was even made by Laird, the Birkenhead shipbuilder, in the 'invasion summer' of 1859 for the conversion of Mersey ferry-boats into a gunboat flotilla carrying a 68-pounder or two 32-pounder guns each (to repel the French in the unlikely event of their steaming into Liverpool).[4] Characteristically, Laird's scheme was turned down on the grounds of expense.

The speed of the technological revolution in naval architecture after the Crimean War also tended to favour the development of the small warship. 1860 saw the commissioning of the British answer to *La Gloire*, the ironclad H.M.S. *Warrior*, and the next twenty-five years saw more changes in the design and construction of warships than the previous four centuries. By 1865 the wooden ship of the line was obsolete; a decade later steel was introduced, and opened another round in the contest between armour and the gun. By 1885 the Fleet boasted such monsters as the *Benbow*, with 16.25-inch breech-loaders, and the *Inflexible* with twenty-four inches of armour. But these freak battleships were doomed to remain sisterless, for as Gladstone acidly pointed out, the fashion in ships of war was as fickle as that of ladies' hats. No government in the period from the Sixties to the Eighties would sanction more than a 'fleet of samples', when the newest vessel could be obsolete almost before her launch. It is not surprising, therefore, that small warships came to enjoy the esteem that stemmed from cheapness and long life.

Fortunately for the Navy this was a time when Great Britain had little to fear from the European Powers, or from any other part of the world. Her Majesty's ships had nothing to contend with but pirate junks, slaving dhows or native war canoes. Only the occasional blockade-runner with a superior turn of speed presented them with any serious problems; for most operational requirements small ships were all that was needed. The Navy's chief rival in Europe was France, which took a brief lead with *La Gloire*. But French shipbuilding resources did not match the technical skill of her naval architects, and the British ironclad building programme swiftly overtook the French. Her discomfiture was completed by the decline in the French Navy after the Army's catastrophic defeat at the hands of Prussia in 1870. This reverse did nothing to threaten British naval supremacy, for the Prussian Navy, like those of Russia, Austria, Italy and the United States, was no serious rival. Nothing in the North Sea, the Atlantic or the Mediterranean called for a declaration of war by Great Britain.

So there was little incentive to alter the structure of a service that had stood the country in good stead since the downfall of Napoleon, no reason to substitute a war machine for a world police-force quite adequate for its tasks. Some Liberals like the Financial Secretary to the Admiralty, G. O. Trevelyan, might grouse that:

> The call for gun-boats is incessant from the Foreign Office, from the British residents in ports abroad, who like the sense of security they feel at the sight of the British flag, and from other quarters where, without being bound by the ties of Treaty, or even nationality, we are urged to yield assistance by the claims of humanity.'[5]

But to the great majority of the British public this was only right and proper, the plain duty of the greatest maritime power in the world. In this atmosphere of nonchalant primacy, and fortified by a sublime confidence in the future, the gunboats went about their business.

Chapter 4

THE SECOND CHINA WAR

In one sense there never was a Second China War. Between 1856 and 1860 British and French forces clashed with local Chinese forces in a series of 'incidents' which never escalated into all-out war between the three nations. Fighting began ostensibly because the conditions of a treaty signed in 1842 were not honoured by the Chinese; it was ended in 1858 by a further treaty honoured in the breach, and was only stopped finally in 1860. In that time Anglo-French naval and military detachments went into action against the inhabitants of Canton, then against rebels seeking to overthrow the Emperor of China, and ultimately, on only two occasions against Imperial forces. It could hardly be called a war against China, either defensive or aggressive.

The Second China War was, in fact, a trade offensive like the earlier Opium War of 1839-42. British merchants traded peacefully with the Chinese Empire from 1715 to 1834 under the East India Company's monopoly, but they were kept at arm's length by the Chinese without difficulty. Only the city of Canton was open to Western trade, for the Chinese were well aware that small trading posts could blossom into annexation and alien rule, as had happened to India. Even at Canton, the ships had to anchor downriver, and Europeans were confined to their small concessions on shore.

The end of the East India Company's monopoly in 1834 brought a huge increase in trade to China, for British merchants saw the sprawling Celestial Empire as an untapped source of wealth. But they soon found that conditions good enough for 'John Company' were too restrictive in a competitive market. Not until 1842 were the five 'treaty ports', Canton, Amoy, Foochow, Ningpo and Shanghai, fully open to Western traders and their protecting warships. To add to the friction British merchants found that opium (grown in India exclusively by the Honourable East India Company) could fetch an exorbitant price in China. It had to be smuggled in, for the Chinese Government inflicted severe penalties for trafficking in the drug.

The treaty ports had been opened by the terms of the Treaty of Nanking in 1842, which also ceded the naval base at Hong Kong to Great Britain. But it was soon apparent that the Cantonese had no intention of honouring the treaty; they refused to allow any Europeans to enter their city, despite the terms agreed by the Emperor. The Cantonese – or, as they were once called, the 'Irish of China' – were truculent and the Imperial Government chose to ignore their recalcitrance. But there were more and more incidents between Cantonese and British traders. A proclamation was issued stating their intention of killing any of the 'vile race' of English who entered the city; evidently the English 'deceitfulness of heart, untameable as the wild horse, and voracious as the vulture' so provoked the burghers of Canton that they could not answer for their actions.

The greatest source of dispute was the Chinese refusal to allow British diplomats to approach Peking. The Chinese would not allow the Son of Heaven to have any truck with Outer Barbarians – an attitude contradicted by the Nanking Treaty but still tacitly maintained. The British negotiators for their part were woefully ignorant of the awe and veneration in which the Chinese held their Emperor; the concept of an enthroned godhead meant little to the loyal subjects of Napoleon III and Victoria. But to the Chinese it was unthinkable that foreign traders should come to the capital, for the Emperor could not even be seen by the Chinese people. In the Chinese hierarchy soldiers and merchants vied for bottom place; for foreign merchants, therefore, to approach the Imperial court was almost sacrilegious. Lest this be thought merely quaint protocol, it should be remembered that China was prepared to go to war to uphold this principle. Only when it seemed that worse indignities were to be inflicted on the Emperor and his court did his advisers admit the Western envoys.

The first gunboats to arrive at Hong Kong in 1857 found a good deal of work waiting for them. After more than six months of desultory warfare in the Canton River the British and French naval forces had achieved very little. After occupying Canton they abandoned it through lack of troops to defend the position. They could not hold the river either, for the Chinese attacked the Allied warships constantly with fire-rafts and drifting boats packed with powder-barrels. Although these 'incendiary appliances' caused no casualties they did undermine the sailors' morale, for warships in confined waters are particularly vulnerable to attack from weapons of stealth.

The senior naval officer was Rear-Admiral Seymour.[1] At the age of fifty-three he had a reputation for patient planning and attention to detail. He had distinguished himself in action in the Baltic in 1855 and lost the sight of his right eye when examining a Russian mine. The problem for the British and French in the Canton River was much the same as the one they faced in the Baltic in 1854: how to get to grips with an enemy who refused to fight, and chose to shelter behind shoals and islands.

Seymour chose much the same solution as Napier had; he retreated downriver to Macao until gunboats arrived from England. In a letter to the Secretary of the

Rear-Admiral Sir Michael Seymour. (© *National Maritime Museum, London*)

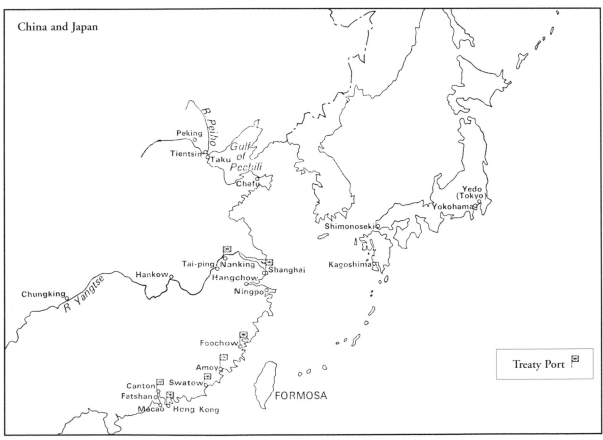

China and Japan

Treaty Port

Admiralty he reiterated his request for a 'further number of light-draughted steamers to those already on their way'.[2] With seven 60 h.p. gunboats at his disposal and two or three gunvessels, the Commander-in-Chief could at last retaliate against his tormentors and bring some pressure to bear on the Chinese Government.

After the frustrations of the previous six months, the arrival of the gunboats in the spring of 1857 put new heart into the sailors, for up to this point they had conducted all their cutting-out operations in open boats, and had been roughly handled by the Chinese on one or two occasions. As soon as the gunboats had received their guns from the bigger ships and carried out any repairs needed they were sent to attack a force of mandarin junks hiding in Escape Creek. This was not the main Chinese force, which lay in Fatshan Creek, but it was necessary to prevent the Escape Creek junks from coming to the rescue at a crucial moment if an attack was made on Fatshan Creek.

On 28 May 1857, *Bustard*, *Starling* and *Staunch* moved off with a force of paddle-steamers and ships' boats. They encountered nearly forty junks in Escape Creek, and chased them for over ten miles up the winding channel. The action became like a steeplechase as the gunboats and paddlers grounded one by one, leaving the pulling boats to capture or burn every junk. These junks could have been formidable opponents for the gunboats, as they had a 32-pounder gun in the bows and several smaller weapons; drawing only three feet, they were ideal for river warfare if well handled.

The gunboats were unharmed by grounding, and

were soon mustered for an attack on the Fatshan Creek junks. Sir Michael Seymour was commanding in person, flying his flag in the paddler *Coromandel*. Four gunboats, *Bustard*, *Haughty*, *Plover* and *Starling*,[3] and two hired steamers helped to tow all the boats that the squadron could spare. Everyone was buoyant at the prospect of action, and the sunny First of June was a good omen – the anniversary of two of the Navy's proudest actions.

The Chinese chose their position well, for the British had to make their way upstream for three miles; at any point the larger vessels might run aground, leaving the men in open boats exposed to the fire of eighty junks moored across the creek. To make quite certain of finishing off the boat attack the Chinese moored another twenty junks four miles higher, where they commanded a narrow channel. These mandarin junks were the pride of the Imperial Fleet, and they too had every hope of success.

While Seymour in the little *Coromandel* took charge of a storming party of Royal Marines to silence a fort which could have interfered with the boats' progress, Commodore Keppel took the rest of the force towards the junks. This time the Chinese were determined to stand their ground, and there was a brisk exchange of fire between the junks and the gunboats. But again the gunboats grounded on the mudbanks, until only the *Haughty* was under way, so the boats were ordered forward. Imagine a headlong dash over a few hundred yards of water lashed by a terrific fire of cannonballs and assorted iron scraps. At the masthead of each junk were the sinister 'stink-pots' which showered burning sulphur

The gunboat H.M.S. *Bustard*. The sails are typical of the gunboat era, and are often referred to as 'gunboat rig'. *(NPC, Antony Preston Collection)*

The attack on Fatshan Creek.
(NPC, Antony Preston Collection)

on boarders. To add to the hellish uproar of gunfire the Chinese beat gongs furiously to instil fear into the enemy hearts.

In spite of a number of casualties the boats were alongside the junks before the Chinese could reload, at which the defenders jumped overboard and made for the shore. Keppel ordered the junks to be burnt, and hastened upstream to finish off the remaining twenty. To Midshipman Kennedy[4] it seemed as if it was going to be a walk-over, for the boats swept towards the second line of junks without a shot being fired.

Suddenly the British realised that they were in a trap; only 400 yards from the junks Keppel's boat grounded, followed immediately by the others. At this moment the Chinese opened fire on the huddle of boats and men. With no gunboats near to silence the junks' fire, Keppel saw that he had to retreat. However, the fire was so fierce that his galley was shot to pieces before he could withdraw. Luckily he and the survivors of his boat's crew were able to leap into the *Calcutta*'s barge as the shattered galley sank under their feet.

Keppel ordered his boats to regroup under the lee of the gunboats, which had come up closer as the tide rose. It should not be forgotten that these sailors had rowed seven miles, and had faced a fresh enemy without respite. Some boats had been left behind in the first attack, so Keppel was able to put them in the van when he returned to finish the junks.

This time there was no pause; with the gunboats

supporting them the boats rushed at the line of junks, and the Chinese did not stand to their guns. While cheering British sailors swarmed over the junks the Chinese fled across the paddy-fields. After visiting Fatshan and noting that it was unfortified, dirty and not worth molesting, the exhausted men returned to the gunboats. They had lost thirteen killed and forty-four wounded, a very low casualty list in view of the way the men had been exposed without supporting fire. In his dispatch to the Admiralty Seymour claimed that the action opened a new era in Chinese naval warfare. 'Great judgement was shown in selecting the position for the fleet,' he wrote, 'and the Chinese, particularly the last division attacked by Commodore Keppel, defended their ships with skill, courage and effect … it is to me a matter of surprise that under the circumstances of the case the loss was not greater.'[5]

Unfortunately this brilliant feat of arms was never followed up and it took a long time for the gunboats to make their presence felt in Chinese waters. The reason for this was the Indian Mutiny; the promised drafts of troops had to be diverted to Calcutta, and many of the bigger warships were withdrawn from Seymour's control. However, the Admiralty did leave the gunboats on the station, where they were of great use in keeping the Canton River open. To help the depleted China forces (by this time relying largely on the French squadron) the Admiralty dispatched another fifteen gunboats and gunvessels in the spring of 1857.

The reinforcements were sent out under Captain Sherard Osborn, C.B., R.N., who had taken over the Azov Flotilla from Captain Lyons, and was now at thirty-five a very young captain. Throughout his short life (he died in 1875), he showed qualities of leadership and initiative, and was an obvious choice for a difficult assignment. So little was thought of gunboats' behaviour in rough weather that this voyage was viewed as an extremely dangerous undertaking, and the fact that they all arrived safely cannot diminish the achievement. The little gunboats were never meant to undertake long voyages, and their shallow draught gave them little stability.

Sherard Osborn's command, the new paddle-frigate *Furious*, took under her wing four of the new *Algerine* class,[6] two more 60 h.p. gunboats[7] and six of the smaller 40 h.p. type.[8] The experiences of the Escape Creek and Fatshan actions confirmed the need for gunboats of shallower draught, but this could not have influenced the Admiralty in choosing the smaller gunboats as they all hoisted the pendant in March 1857, a month before their sisters first saw action. Completing the force were three gun-vessels, *Cormorant*, *Surprise* and *Nimrod*, which helped to take the gunboats in tow from time to time.

The squadron called at Funchal, Madeira, before striking out into the South Atlantic with the north-west trade wind behind them. After a brief rest at Simon's Bay they made a long run to Java Head; the poor little *Firm* had to burn coal bags to eke out her fuel supply until she reached the anchorage at Anger Point. In Singapore Roads they saw for the first time the great ungainly Chinese junks. With their huge square rig, these trading junks could only run south with the north-east monsoon, and had to wait for the south-west monsoon later in the year before they saw Chinese waters once more.

With the outcome of the Indian Mutiny still in doubt, and all large-scale military and naval operations consequently ruled out, it would seem there was little point in sending out extra gunboats to the Far East. But this was not the case, for there was a great need for gunboats to carry out anti-piracy patrols around Hong Kong. It was humdrum work, but no other type of warship was so eminently suited to the pursuit of junks in shallow water, or had sufficient fire-power to silence the junks when caught.

Gunboats made their name in the China Seas, and it is not hard to find the reason; their arrival coincided with the period in which the Royal Navy first energetically tackled the problem of piracy.[9] After years of vacillation and downright corruption the period 1848-60 saw British sea power exert a slow stranglehold on the sea-robbers that infested the South China coast. One may gauge the difficulties facing the Commander-in-Chief of the East Indies and China Station when it is recalled that the Crown Colony of Hong Kong was the port through which arms and ammunition reached the pirates.

Furthermore the vastly expanded opium trade offered greater temptations than the pirates had ever known. Not until the British took a stronger line with their own unruly subjects could these expensive naval operations show much result.

By the time the first gunboats were cruising off the pirates' haunts many reforms had been instituted from above, among them being specific provision for co-operation with the Chinese authorities. Both sides realised that the partial paralysis of coastal trade had to be cured, but without punishing innocent traders. By 1855 the Viceroy of Canton had arranged for a high mandarin to act as 'liaison officer' at Hong Kong; one of the paradoxes of Anglo-Chinese relations was that this arrangement remained in force at the height of the war.

If anyone should question the impact of the gunboats' arrival on the scene, the following figures are conclusive. Between June 1851 and June 1857 there were ten awards of bounties totalling £26,763. All bounties were paid to officers and men in accordance with Acts 13 and 14, Vict. C. 26.[10] However from this time until the end of 1860 the following bounties were paid.[11]

	DATE OF CAPTURE	BOUNTY PAID
		£
Magicienne (sloop) and g.b. *Algerine*	28-29 September 1858	800
Magicienne and *Fury* (sloop)	16 October 1858	1,500
Algerine and boats of *Calcutta* (frigate)	25 February 1858	180
g.b. *Clown*	13 May 1859	50
g.b. *Staunch*	4 August 1858	750
g.v. *Racehorse*	26 June and 4 July 1858	1,000
Fury, g.b.s *Firm* and *Bustard*	7-8 December 1858	1,500
g.b. *Slaney*	8 May 1859	100
Magicienne, *Algerine* and boats from *Acorn* (sloop)	17 and 19 September 1858	1,000
Magicienne, *Inflexible* (paddle-sloop) and g.b.s *Plover* and *Algerine*	26 August to 3 September 1858	3,000
Niger (sloop) and g.b.s *Clown* and *Janus*	13-15 March 1859	1,600
g.v. *Nimrod*	14-16 December 1860	1,000
Surprise g.v. and boats of *Cambrian*	23 August 1858	1,200
		13,680

The danger of awarding bounties of such magnitude was that young naval officers might in turn become worse than the pirates they hunted. Lord Elgin once said of the gunboats' forays:

It may be all right, but I fear we do some horrible injustices in this pirate hunting. The system of giving our

The attack on Wantung, 1857, showing H.M.S. *Coromandel* to the far right. *(Conway Maritime Press)*

sailors a direct interest in captures is certainly a barbarous one, and the parent of much evil; though perhaps it may be difficult to devise a remedy. The result, however, is that not only are seizures made which ought not to be made at all, but duties are neglected which do not bring grist to the mill.[12]

There was no lack of zeal among the junior commanders, and many attacks on pirates were made without Chinese advice, resulting in hardship and injustice to Chinese traders and fishermen.

The men commanding the gunboats were all young, and action against pirates offered them an easy way to distinction and promotion. At times boredom became intolerable, and in spite of the dangers officers persisted in going ashore, usually to shoot wildfowl. In December 1857 Lieutenant Pim, commanding the gunboat *Banterer*, decided to reconnoitre a creek near Sai-Lau for 'information and recreation'. With fourteen men he took a boat up the creek without seeing any Chinese, and in a rash moment decided to land. When his party returned, presumably disappointed in the recreation offered in the neighbourhood, they were alarmed to hear shouting from the direction of the river. As they raced back they saw to their horror a crowd yelling and pelting the two boat-guards with stones and refuse.

Although outnumbered, Pim's party took the Chinese by surprise with a fierce charge. The sight of a dozen men with drawn cutlasses was enough to disperse them, and the seamen were able to push the boat off the mud and scramble aboard. Now they faced greater danger, for the Chinese returned to the water's edge and fired into the press of bodies. It was impossible to miss – five sailors were killed by the first fusillade, and nearly all the others were wounded. But Pim's courage matched his reckless-ness, for he stood in the bows and held the Chinese off with his revolver; even though hit six times he kept firing and enabled the boat to escape.

Sir William Kennedy has left us a most interesting description of pirate-hunting at this time.[13] Kennedy was

not serving in gunboats at the time, but served as a mid-shipman in H.M.S. *Calcutta*, an 84-gun ship-of-the-line which supplied boats for a number of raids, including the Fatshan Creek action. In February 1858, Midshipman Kennedy was given two boats and ordered to accompany the little 60 h.p. *Forester* on an investi-gation into some acts of piracy reported in the vicinity of Hong Kong.

H.M.S. *Forester* shaped a course for Lintin Island, a well-known pirate haunt, and while still some distance away came upon a junk. This junk ran herself on shore and her crew abandoned her, which aroused the sailors' suspicions. Leaving a small party on board the junk, the gunboat pressed on to Lintin with both boats in tow. Seeing nothing, the lieutenant in command was about to return to his prize when a look-out reported something suspicious. In Kennedy's words: '...We spied a white pole rising as it were out of the ground. A closer inspec-tion proved it to be the masthead of a large junk or lor-cha, moored in a snug little harbour, the entrance of which we could not at once perceive.'

At once orders rang out, boat crews scrambled down the side of the gunboat, fumbling for oars and checking weapons. The boats cast off and made for the entrance to the pirates' lair, while the gunboat fussed about outside. The entrance was so narrow that the sailors had to 'toss' their oars (i.e. hold them upright) so as to squeeze their way in. Once inside they found a perfect harbour, in which lay a big lorcha. The cheering sailors felt some-what foolish when they boarded the lorcha in style and found it deserted. Once discovered the pirates had made off overland, and the settlement ashore was also aban-doned. Kennedy and his boarding party towed the lorcha out to where *Forester* was waiting; she turned out to be a captured English vessel with her cargo intact, which caused an amusing sequel.

That night *Forester* anchored in a safe place, but her captain took no chances and set a guard of two marines over the lorcha's cargo. He feared not so much an attack from pirates as pilfering by his own men, for part of the cargo included liquor. In the middle of the night, the sleepers wrapped in their blankets on the gunboat's deck were woken by cries for help from the lorcha, which was secured astern. Buckling on sword-belts and holsters, and rubbing the sleep from their eyes, they all tumbled into a cutter and hurried over to recapture the lorcha. They found the corporal and sentry sprawled on the deck, hopelessly drunk and roaring for assistance. While stumbling about in a stupor they had both been walloped several times by the main boom shifting from side to side as the vessel rolled in the swell.

A few days later Midshipman Kennedy was ordered to put his boats under the command of Lieutenant Forbes of another gunboat, the *Algerine*. Although one of the larger 80 h.p. gunboats, even *Algerine* was so badly knocked about in heavy seas in the Lyemun passage that her big 68-pounder gun broke loose from its lashings. The gunboat was heading for Mirs Bay, on the strength of information given by two fishermen. But for nearly a whole day *Algerine* cruised in vain among the islands in the bay, seeing only flocks of birds. The informers were questioned again, but seemed so certain that Lieutenant Forbes decided to anchor for the night.

Next day *Algerine* threaded her way among the islands, steadily moving northwards and deeper into Mirs Bay. It was at a place called Grass Island that she sighted a junk, and intercepted her. The pirates had hoped to sacrifice the junk in order to facilitate the escape of a bigger lorcha, but they were outwitted by Forbes, who took *Algerine* round the north side of the island and left the *Calcutta*'s boats on the south side. It was these boats which spotted the lorcha standing out to sea, and were able to head her off. On seeing themselves trapped by only two open boats the pirates fired a broadside of grapeshot, to which the British replied with their puny 12-pounder howitzer.

The pinnace and the cutter bore down on the pirate lorcha without flinching, and the pirates promptly turned and headed for the shore. They did not run the vessel on the rocks, but let go two anchors just a short distance from the breakers, so that the lorcha swung round with her stern touching the rocks. To the chagrin of the British sailors the pirates escaped almost dryshod, leaving the lorcha intact but almost beyond reach. The British could not leave her to become a pirate ship once more, but with half a gale blowing they would find it very hard to get near her without being driven ashore themselves. Nevertheless Kennedy decided to try and board her from the cutter.

Kennedy adopted much the same tactics as the pirates; he anchored and let the cutter veer in until she was close enough for him to jump aboard with three men. The cutter had been almost swamped by the waves and now withdrew to a safe distance to that she could bale out. Kennedy and his men found one pirate still aboard, and took him prisoner. In the hold they found an old man

heavily manacled; he had been tortured several times, and was pitifully weak. There was nothing left to do but set fire to the lorcha and be taken off by the boats. Once again the cutter approached the lorcha, and again she was nearly swamped by a heavy sea and had to retire. Now the wind was rising, fanning the flames and making it even harder for the cutter to get close.

The position was desperate, for the party aboard the lorcha were in danger of being burnt alive or blown to pieces, while the crews of the pinnace and the cutter were in equally grave danger of being wrecked or swamped. Two Chinese fishing boats which tried to help were smashed against the bows of the lorcha and their occupants drowned in the surf. In desperation Kennedy ordered the two seamen to swim to the cutter, which they did with difficulty. Then as the cutter drifted closer, he threw the old man into the boat. The remaining sailor, a coxswain, the Chinese prisoner and Kennedy jumped into the sea and were rescued by the cutter's crew, just in time to get clear of the explosion of the lorcha's magazine.

The indefatigable Kennedy never paused after his hairbreadth escape, but pressed on to link up with *Algerine* once more. He found the little gunboat engaging two big junks. Lieutenant Forbes had his hat and coat off, helping to work the 68-pounder, and had the satisfaction of seeing one of his shells hit a junk plumb in her magazine. The other junk fought on after her consort blew up, until another well-placed shell from the gunboat caused an explosion in her bow. Having had enough the pirates jumped overboard and made for the shore, followed by the boats. After burning the village everyone returned to the *Algerine* and left the pirates in peace while they had dinner. As they smoked their cigars, Forbes and his officers reflected sadly on the fact that the cash value of the day's exploits was practically nil, since they had not saved the lorcha or the two big junks. Eventually the magnificent sum of £180 was voted by a grateful Parliament, to be divided among the officers and men of *Algerine* and *Calcutta*! [14]

Meanwhile a heated diplomatic wrangle was going on between the British and French plenipotentiaries and the Imperial Government in Peking. We must retrace our steps to the point where we left Sir Michael Seymour writing hopefully to the Admiralty about a new era in Chinese naval warfare. What followed was, as we know, a period of inaction due to the Indian Mutiny. But it was not a quiet period for British diplomats. Although Palmerston's government fell early in 1857 victory in the subsequent election persuaded him to pursue his aggressive policy in China. The new Plenipotentiary, Lord Elgin, was told to obtain reparation for loss of life, full execution of the terms of the Treaty of Nanking and compensation for damage to British property. He was also to press for diplomatic representation at Peking and wider commercial facilities.

As was to be expected the Cantonese remained obdurate, and the Imperial Commissioner Yeh rejected all Elgin's demands. Finally, since Sherard Osborn's squadron had reinforced Seymour's command, Elgin was able to back his demands with force. At daybreak on 28 December 1857 some thirty ships opened fire on the walls of Canton, and demonstrated the benefits of Western civilisation by dropping shells on Yeh's residence. Seymour's force was a motley collection of sloops and frigates, with the gunvessels *Nimrod* and *Surprise* and seven gunboats, which provided men for the landing on the third day.

The landing parties encountered little resistance, and came back with three important prisoners; the general commanding the much-feared Tartar cavalry, Pih-Kwei, Governor of Canton, and Yeh himself. Having thus removed the heads of local government the Allies began to doubt their ability to control the civil population without more men. There was only one solution: the general went back to his Tartars and Pih-Kwei was reinstated as Governor. Only Yeh was kept a prisoner, and one cannot help feeling pity for him when reading of his fate. Westerners ignorant enough to dismiss the head of the most ancient civilisation in the world as a 'presumptuous savage' had no scruples about kidnapping his lawful representative and shipping him off to die in India.

Once Canton had been captured Elgin could press on with plans to go to Peking to settle his demands.[15] Accordingly he sailed for Shanghai after sending letters to the Senior Secretary of State at Peking to warn him that four Western plenipotentiaries wished to meet senior Chinese officials for a 'summit conference'. Hitherto active measures had been undertaken solely by Great Britain and France, but this time Lord Elgin included the Russian and American Ministers to underline the fact that he was bargaining for trade, not territory. In fact, only Britain and the United States had any great share of Chinese trade; apart from seeking compensation for attacks on missionaries, France was merely determined not to allow Britain to gain any unfair advantage.

At Shanghai Elgin still fenced with Chinese officials trying to prevent Western diplomats from meeting anyone of high rank from Peking. It was essential to act before the heat of midsummer affected the European troops, so Elgin wasted no time and moved to the Gulf of Pechili. Here he was at the mouth of the Peiho River, and within easy reach of Peking, provided he had naval support.

Unfortunately Elgin arrived before the gunboats, and only two gun-vessels could cross the Peiho bar – a force obviously too weak to impress the Chinese. Elgin wrote angrily to the Foreign Secretary, Lord Clarendon: '… At the moment I am writing this despatch, the French flag is represented by two gunboats within the bar of the Peiho, the English by two despatch-boats aground on top of it.'[16]

Having hoped to enter the Peiho in one of a little armada of gunboats, Elgin's disappointment and frustration can be understood. He penned a waspish attack on Sir Michael Seymour in which he gave a highly inexpert opinion on the conduct of naval affairs. Seymour was stung into making a lengthy answer to Elgin's charges, countering them one by one in what must have been the bulkiest dispatch of the campaign. However this bickering was a thing of the future, and Elgin had first to solve the problem of forcing the entrance to the Peiho.

Lord Elgin's planned stately ascent of the Peiho was out of the question anyway, for the Chinese were openly strengthening the forts around the mouth of the river. The navigable channel was only 200 yards wide, and the nearest forts 400 yards away. Over eighty guns could be seen poking their snouts over the earthworks, and thousands of Tartar cavalry lay encamped under their gay banners. To discourage the Allies further, every open stretch of river-bank had been planted with stakes to impale any assault forces.

On the face of it, the Chinese had good cause to expect the Allies to withdraw, but they reckoned without the gunboats, whose guns easily demolished the mud forts. Not even their surprise weapon, fireships filled with flaming straw, had any effect. These junks were guided from shore by ropes, so H.M.S. *Bustard* dispersed the rope-handling parties with a few rounds. After silencing the forts, the gunboats and gunvessels moved upstream and dealt with other outposts. By the night of 21 May 1858 landing parties had occupied the forts, and the warships were moored in the shelter of a barrier of junks strung across the river at Taku. All that remained was to break up this obstruction and push on upstream to Tientsin.

The gunboats had made a tremendous show, lobbing their shells over the parapets of the Chinese forts with great accuracy, even though the Chinese shot struck

The Peiho Forts from the outside – the bamboo stakes faced the storming parties.
(Imperial War Museum)

Chinese dead in one of the Peiho Forts, taken shortly after their capture in 1860. *(Imperial War Museum)*

them repeatedly. However, once the gunboats managed to pass the batteries in single file, the Chinese found themselves outflanked. Heroine of the day was the gun-vessel *Cormorant*; she led the column of ships and charged the boom of spars and chains, snapping it like thread. By a quirk of fate this little vessel had her moment of triumph at the very place where she was to sink amid a scene of disaster, almost a year later.

On 23 May the British gunboats *Firm*, *Bustard*, *Opossum*, *Slaney*, *Kestrel*, *Staunch* and *Woodcock*, with the French *Avalanche* and *Fusée*, moved off upriver, feeling their way carefully in the tortuous channel. With them were the paddle-steamer *Coromandel* (flying Seymour's flag) and a number of ships' boats. The countryside was monotonously flat, an alluvial plain only a few feet higher than the river. The intensely cultivated fields looked like an enormous market garden, with occasional clusters of mud villages.

Slowly the strange flotilla neared Tientsin, dodging from time to time the obstructions placed hurriedly by local mandarins. Unlike the fiery Cantonese the local populace were noticeably friendly. When the *Coromandel* finally gave the signal to anchor in the shadow of the walls of Tientsin there was no sign of hostility. Instead, thousands of curious Chinese came to stare at the gunboats, the first Western vessels ever seen so high upriver. Merchants sent boatloads of provisions and fresh meat, and only the Imperial officials held themselves aloof.

While the gunboat *Slaney* went downriver to tell Lord Elgin that all was ready for him, the Allied commanders tooks steps to keep their men in check. No leave was granted to sailors or marines, although officers and consular officials could go into the town. Peace was pre-served by strict discipline aided by the civility of the people of Tientsin; only one or two minor incidents occurred, when officers were pelted with mud bricks.

Tientsin had great strategic importance, being situated at the northern end of the Grand Canal, Peking's main artery of trade with central and southern China. By taking up his position there Seymour knew he was showing the Chinese that he could command the capital's commercial outlet; the authorities were not slow to see why he had moored the little *Coromandel* opposite the entrance to the canal. Within eight days Chinese plenipotentiaries met Elgin and his colleagues in a temple outside the city, and on 26 June 1858 the Treaty of Tientsin was signed, conceding all the points squabbled over for two years.

In spite of the coolness between Seymour and himself, Elgin generously acknowledged his debt to the naval forces. Announcing the treaty to Seymour he said: 'It will not, therefore, be necessary to continue any longer at this point the pressure which has been applied by your Excellency with so much effect, and at so small a cost of human life or suffering.'[17]

To the British and French it seemed their war was over. By the terms of the Treaty of Tientsin they remained in occupation at Canton until the agreed indemnity of four million taels (about £200,000) was paid by the authorities of the Kwangtung province. This was only compensation to the Allies for their trouble and inconvenience, and in practice solved none of the problems in Canton.

Although Lord Elgin intended to go to Japan to conclude a similar trade treaty with the Japanese, there was disquieting news from Canton, where fresh disturbances had broken out. Although he had misgivings about splitting his force, the Japanese proved far more amenable, and his escort of three vessels was adequate. The Mikado was particularly flattered to receive a steam yacht, a gift from Queen Victoria, and the British were established on a par with the United States and other European nations.[18]

The C.-in-C. accompanied Elgin on his mission to Japan and detached the remaining ships to Canton. It was at this time that the little *Staunch* fell in with three large pirate junks. The gunboat was proceeding on passage from Shanghai to Hong Kong, and like all of her class was disarmed for the open-sea passage to make her more seaworthy. With only her brace of 24-pounder popguns on board it was an act of foolhardiness to board a well-armed junk, but *Staunch's* commander ran her alongside the largest pirate craft and tried to grapple and board. One heroic seaman actually leapt on to the junk's deck and fixed the heavy grappling iron, but the pirates cut him down and hacked the cable through. The two ships fell away from one another, and the gunboat commander reluctantly gave the order to chase the two smaller junks, which were duly taken.

With the Tientsin Treaty in his hands as it were, Elgin was able to press the Peking Government for action against its subordinates in Canton. After ceaseless negotiation the Viceroy of the Two Kwang provinces was eventually suspended by the Emperor. Although the Allied forces continued to be plagued by incidents during the remainder of 1858, by September of that year trade tariffs were actually under discussion. It was none too soon, for two years of war had paralysed the once flourishing Anglo-Chinese trade. By November 1858 a working arrangement was achieved, and tea shipments passed down the Canton River once more.

Elgin also found time to traverse the Yangtse River, using two sloops and the gunboats *Lee* and *Dove* to show the flag. He travelled 600 miles inland to the great trading city of Hankow to establish relations with merchants. Thus another great artery of trade was opened, another 'dagger pointed at the heart of China' as the great rivers were termed seventy years later by an embittered Chinese politician.

On their way to Hankow the British ships encountered for the first time a powerful third force, the Taeping Rebellion, which was to complicate Anglo-Chinese diplomacy for many years. These Taeping rebels were a locust-swarm of ex-soldiers, rebellious hill-people and malcontents who had overrun whole provinces of northern China in less than ten years. What distinguished them was the fact that their leader, Hung-Seu-Tsien, professed a pseudo-Christianity which he had picked up from an American Baptist missionary. This Heavenly King's claim to be the younger brother of Jesus Christ may have helped to ease the consciences of those virtuous Victorians who sold guns to his disciples.

The Taeping established their capital at Nanking in 1853, and pursued a policy of goodwill towards all for-

eigners, those obliging people who provided the sinews of war while rocking the Peking Government on its heels. However, some subordinate blundered, and under the very eyes of Lord Elgin the little gunboat *Lee* was fired on by the forts of Nanking. *Lee* was flying a flag of truce, for Elgin was equally anxious to avoid a clash with the rebels. The current British view was that the internal troubles of the Peking regime were to be ignored; any taking of sides was to be avoided, but Elgin did give his approval when the ships returned the fire in self-defence. The same day, 20 November 1858, other forts at Tai-ping fired at *Lee* and *Dove*, but next day the local rebel commander assured Elgin that it was all a mistake, and the British ships proceeded without further trouble.

One of the more important stipulations of the Treaty of Tientsin was that within one year ratifications were to be exchanged *at Peking*. Although for the moment Elgin did not press the Allies' claim for a full embassy in Peking he was adamant that he must go to Peking for the ceremonial ratification, if only to establish his country's status on an equal footing with the Celestial Empire. Slowly the Westerners were being initiated into the subtle mysteries of 'saving face'.

As the Chinese repeated their delaying tactics of the year before, another naval demonstration was called for, and this time Elgin had no cause for complaint about lack of naval co-operation. The new Commander-in-Chief, Rear-Admiral Sir James Hope, succeeded Seymour in April 1859, and showed great promise of redeeming his undistinguished record in the Crimean War. With eleven gunboats and gunvessels[19] in charge of

Sir James Hope, Senior Naval Officer at the Peiho River disaster in 1859. (© *National Maritime Museum, London*)

a fire-eating admiral, the stage was set for a showdown with the Chinese.

Rear-Admiral Hope was confident that he could force the Peiho entrance as easily as Seymour's force had the year before, notwithstanding the fact that the Chinese had diligently strengthened the forts and closed the river with three barriers of stakes. The year before it had only taken the gunboats two hours to silence the Chinese guns; the ships had had little difficulty clearing obstructions, and there was no reason to expect any trouble this time.

One of the frigate captains had a young midshipman as his A.D.C. His name was John Fisher, and a photograph taken at the time shows that lowering, penetrating gaze that was still characteristic forty years later. The future First Sea Lord had his baptism of fire at the Peiho in 1859, and it impressed him deeply. 'We are just going to take the forts',[20] he wrote gaily, a short while before a series of awful sights disillusioned him for ever of the glamour of war. For this second attempt on the Peiho defences was doomed, and Fisher was to see it from the deck of H.M.S. *Plover*, Hope's flagship.

The gunboats and gunvessels found themselves trapped in a narrow channel, unable to manoeuvre or dodge the Chinese fire. Only the lowest of the three barriers could be dismantled, so the gunboats had to moor below the middle barrier. Many grounded on the mud, sitting ducks for the endless line of mud ramparts belching fire from either bank. Gun crews were mown down, and gradually the British fire slackened. The little *Plover* suffered twenty-six casualties, while *Kestrel* had only three men unwounded.

After hours of firing, both *Kestrel* and *Plover* had sunk at their moorings, and as *Plover* had been Hope's flagship he was forced to shift his flag to the gunvessel *Cormorant*. In spite of the heavy losses all around him, he lived up to his name and ordered the landing-parties away. But gallantry was not enough, and marines and sailors were smothered in the mud where they fell. Even the unwounded found themselves sinking in the evil-smelling slime, weighed down as they were with rifles and accoutrements.

To add to the horrors of the assault the Chinese were firing gingalls (a type of blunderbuss), and Fisher saw a man with his eye and part of his face burnt away by one of their dreadful fireballs. The attack withered away and the survivors withdrew, throwing away their arms to avoid sinking in the mud. Eighty-nine men had been killed and 345 wounded, including 118 casualties in the gunboats.

Sir James Hope's rashness was redeemed only by his great personal bravery. Even though he received a ghastly wound from a splinter which tore away part of his thigh he refused to leave the battle; he remained aboard *Cormorant* under heavy fire until the action was over. Fisher remembered him rallying the survivors, a great

man, very stern and stately, like the names of his three commands, *Terrible*, *Firebrand* and *Majestic*.[21]

In spite of his mishandling of the affair Hope was not superseded, for the public took a sentimentalised view of his failure. One incident was seized upon by the press to give the bloody debacle an air of chivalry. During the action U.S.S. *Toeywhan*, flagship of Flag Officer Josiah Tattnall, U.S.N., came alongside the gunboat *Plover* and offered to remove the wounded, including Sir James Hope. The story goes that Tattnall turned around to find some of his boat's crew helping to work *Plover*'s forward gun. He reprimanded them, for the United States policy was one of strict neutrality. 'Blood must be thicker than water,' he remarked to Hope; the phrase has since been handed down as part of the folklore of the Anglo-American special relationship.[22]

The losses in ships were no less heavy. The gunboats *Lee* and *Kestrel* had been sunk at their moorings under heavy fire, while the badly damaged *Plover* grounded within gun-range of the forts while going downriver after the action had been broken off. In trying to help her get off, the gunvessel *Cormorant* ran aground herself. Next day salvage parties worked to lighten the ships but only succeeded in recovering *Kestrel;* she had been torn from her moorings by the rising tide and swept downriver bottom upwards. The luckless *Cormorant* got afloat again under cover of darkness, but when the Chinese spotted her next morning they riddled her with shot until she sank. As *Lee* and *Plover* proved to be total losses the Navy lost in all three warships, its worst defeat in a century of 'peaceful' actions.

Although there was a storm of indignation in England over the rebuff to the plenipotentiaries there was also considerable criticism of their handling of the affair. It was pointed out that the United States representative had avoided a clash with the Chinese merely by using the overland route. On the other hand Elgin was aware that the American envoy had been treated with great discourtesy to point the lesson that foreigners were of inferior status.

Whatever the rights and wrongs of Hope's or Elgin's actions might have been, the British Cabinet realised that there was no acceptable alternative to demanding an apology and an unconditional ratification of the Treaty of Tientsin. Equally bellicose by this stage, the Chinese rejected the British ultimatum presented in March 1860. If the French ultimatum were also ignored both commanders had orders to occupy a convenient island off the Peiho River for use as a base, and to intercept all grain junks bound for Peking. Nothing further was to be done until the arrival of General Sir Hope Grant's Expeditionary Force and another seven gunboats.

Sir James Hope had his second chance on 21 August 1860 when his force of ten gunboats and several larger vessels (with a French squadron under Vice-Admiral Charner) attacked the Peiho forts for the third time.

This time he was successful, partly because the operation was planned more carefully and partly because Allied troops simultaneously assaulted the potentially dangerous north and south forts (the ones which had foiled him the previous year).

Once again the gunboats pushed on to Tientsin, to be greeted with the same friendliness. Keeping pace with them on land was the Anglo-French force of some 17,000 men. After yet another round of abortive negotiations the two armies moved northwards to Peking, leaving the gunboats to guard their lines of communication.

Both armies were heading for the Emperor's Summer Palace, Yuen-Ming-Yuen, hoping by this provocative gesture to bring the Chinese to battle or to terms. Yuen-Ming-Yuen, the Round Bright Garden, was a fabulous series of gardens and palaces begun in 1709 and constantly improved by succeeding emperors; it had earned the enthusiastic praise of European travellers as far back as 1743, but this did not prevent the Allied troops from looting every palace. The British and French soldiers had no idea of the value of the treasures they smashed; nothing like it had been seen except the sacking of the Lucknow palaces during the Indian Mutiny, when ignorant soldiers filled their pockets with priceless jewels.

Still the Chinese hesitated, trying to bargain with the lives of some European prisoners. Sir Hope Grant acted decisively and the city of Peking surrendered without a fight, but he was too late to save the prisoners. All had been tortured, and few survived, broken in body by savage maltreatment. As an act of revenge the British ordered the Round Bright Garden to be burned to the ground. The French demurred, but only on the grounds that they feared such drastic action might mean the end of the Manchu dynasty. In fact the intervention of the Western Powers had already all but overthrown the Manchus, and they were to need a great deal of British help to survive.

One of the Sappers entrusted with wrecking the Round Bright Garden was Captain Charles Gordon, R.E., soon to emerge from obscurity as 'Chinese' Gordon. In spite of his fury, for the Chinese had tortured one of his closest friends to death, Gordon had no stomach for such callous vandalism. 'You would scarcely conceive the beauty and magnificence of the palaces we burnt,' he wrote. 'It made one's heart sore to burn them.'[23] Forty years later the Dowager Empress of China still bewailed the fact that Yuen-Ming-Yuen could never be replaced.

By decisiveness and destructiveness the Allies obtained full satisfaction and achieved their objects. Only the question of China's survival as a nation was left unanswered, for the British had no intention of being saddled with a Chinese empire. For the moment China was left to drift on like a rudderless ship, torn by internal strife and open to plunder by any foreign invader who chose to intervene.

Chapter 5

PIRATES AND REBELS

Gunboats first went to China to fight a war, but they stayed on to keep the peace successfully for eighty more years. For years after the end of the Second China War the Admiralty maintained a large force of gunboats and gunvessels in Chinese waters, where the shallow bays and estuaries always made bigger ships useless. The force dwindled in the 1870s but the China Station always had a large proportion of shallow-draught vessels. The Treaty of Tientsin, in addition to clearing up all the points of friction that arose out of Western trading ambitions, dealt for the first time with piracy. The relevant clauses said:

> If any British merchant vessel, while within Chinese waters, be plundered by robbers or Pirates it shall be the duty of the Chinese authorities, to use every endeavour to capture and punish the said robbers or Pirates and to recover the stolen property, that it may be handed over to the Consul for restoration to the owner [Article XIX].

> British ships of war coming for no hostile purpose or being engaged in the pursuit of Pirates, shall be at liberty to visit all ports within the dominions of the Emperor of China, and shall receive every facility for the purchase of provisions, procuring water, and, if occasion require, for the making of repairs [Article LII].[1]

This was a big step forward, and a timely one, for the extension of British trading interests to the Yangtse and five new cities gave the pirates more choice of victims. The most promising development was the provision for a joint Anglo-Chinese effort against piracy, instead of the previous thirty years' haphazard measures. Moreover, at Tientsin the Chinese signed treaties with France and the United States which allowed for a degree of international co-operation. Within a decade the other European

nations concluded agreements with Peking which touched on the problem, although the burden of police work still fell mainly on the Royal Navy.

The impoverished Chinese Government was hardly in a position to honour all its obligations, pay the indemnity exacted in 1860, and fight the Taeping rebels. The Celestial Empire was crumbling and the only thing which saved China was the unwillingness of Great Britain to carve herself a Chinese empire, aided by the incredible resilience of the Chinese character. Fully aware of the danger of a European 'Scramble for China', the British had only one choice left. The feeble, bankrupt Manchu government had to be propped up and revived, but until stability returned some form of foreign intervention was essential.

The dazzling career of 'Chinese' Gordon is outside the scope of this book, but it had a naval counterpart. The Foreign Enlistment Act was suspended[2] in order to allow Regular Army and Navy officers to serve the Chinese Emperor. On land these mercenaries were meant to lead Chinese forces such as Gordon's 'Ever Victorious Army' against the Taepings, but the sailors were to fight pirates. The British Government's efforts to provide China with ships for police duties led to the creation of the notorious 'Vampire' Fleet.

Diplomatic relations with Peking improved greatly after 1860, particularly when Prince Kung became Regent. Kung's government, in spite of intrigues and plots by the anti-Western party in Peking, pursued successfully a policy of friendship with the European nations. On the advice of Sir Frederick Bruce, the first British Minister at Peking, the Imperial Government was allowed to buy seven warships in England. The fleet consisted of the specially-built sloops *Keangsu*, *Kwangtung* and *Tientsin*, the former R.N. sloop *Africa* (renamed *China*), the gunvessel *Mohawk* and the gunboat *Jasper* (renamed *Pekin* and *Amoy* respectively). To complete the force, the steamer *Ballarat* was bought for use as a store-ship, and all seven ships arrived at Hong Kong in 1863.

The new Chinese mercenary navy was not well received, in spite of being commanded by Captain Sherard Osborn, now a Chinese admiral. Some of his subordinates acted so injudiciously that there was talk of trying them as pirates in Hong Kong. But the greatest objection to the 'Vampires' came from Peking, since the new Emperor's advisers refused to agree to Prince Kung's arrangements. When they suggested that the flotilla be put under the control of local provincial mandarins Osborn refused, and Bruce supported him, for the British did not intend to subsidise the mandarins' petty wars among themselves.

The 'Vampire' ships were ordered to be sold outside Chinese waters in order to avoid their falling into the hands of either the Taepings or the pirates,[3] a confession that the Hong Kong authorities had so little control over their citizens that they could not prevent a black market in men-o'-war. In passing, it is interesting to find that one of the 'Vampires' was Captain Hugh Talbot Burgoyne, V.C., R.N., another veteran of the Azov Flotilla. After a spell of blockade-running for the Confederacy in the Civil War, Burgoyne rejoined the Royal Navy, only to drown when his ship H.M.S. *Captain* turned turtle in the Bay of Biscay in 1870.

Although the Royal Navy was deprived of any material Chinese reinforcements it kept a sizeable force of gunboats on the East Indies and China Station after 1860. The losses inflicted at the Peiho River were made good, and there were twenty-eight gunboats and two gunvessels available to hunt pirates. The Foreign Office's anxiety about China was reflected in the Admiralty's Standing Orders and Instructions of February 1859.[4] Naval officers were to use 'caution and consideration' in their dealings with the Chinese, and China was to take precedence over the East Indies. To ease the Station Commander's task his jurisdiction was reduced by making Australian waters a separate command.[5] In practice this did nothing to lighten the burden of Sir James Hope or his successor, for the Taeping Rebellion and the Japanese anti-foreign agitation threatened to destroy Great Britain's oriental trade completely.

It was the Taepings' drive on Shanghai in 1860 which alarmed Sir Frederick Bruce, for this was a 'treaty port', the largest opium market and an outlet for tea and silk. It is not surprising that the British adopted a different attitude to the rebels; before they had been treated as co-belligerents, and the Western Powers kept aloof, but from this time British naval policy showed a clear bias in favour of the Peking Government.

Gunboats were soon in action against the Taepings. In August 1860 *Kestrel* and *Pioneer* helped the European garrison to fight off a rebel attack on the town after the Imperial Tartar troops had been pushed back. With such

a thrusting man at their head as Rear-Admiral Hope the naval commanders were not slow to take the offensive. Bruce hoped to save the city of Ningpo from destruction by negotiating with the Taepings, but Hope gave orders to the man on the spot, Captain Roderick Dew of the *Encounter*, to encourage the Imperial defenders of Ningpo and 'place every obstruction in the way of the capture of the town'.[6] This was a blatant case of an over-zealous officer helping to mould official policy, for Lord Russell had to approve Hope's actions while reiterating his desire to avoid a clash unless British lives and property were threatened.[7]

Captain Dew took passage in the 60 h.p. gunboat *Flamer* to carry out Hope's orders. Hope's idea of a nego-tiated withdrawal from Ningpo took the form of an ulti-matum to the rebel leaders: if they came within two days' march of the town they would be treated as hostile by British forces. The Taepings did in fact approach Ningpo, but the gunboats *Flamer* and *Kestrel* did not open fire on them as the British and American consuls asked for a week's truce, and the town fell a week later almost without a fight. The Taepings had carefully avoid-ed harming any British or American property, a point which Hope admitted in their favour.[8]

The next obstacle placed in the way of the rebels was a request by Hope that they promise not to attack Shanghai during the following year, 1862. This was not unnatural-ly refused, whereupon Hope presented a number of impossible demands. By early 1862 Hope was actively supporting Imperial forces against the Taepings by land-ing troops and giving fire support wherever possible.

Now the Taepings felt the full weight of British naval intervention. Hitherto supreme on land, they found themselves confronted by British gunboats and gunves-sels whose withering shell-fire demoralised their soldiery. Despite protests from British merchants who saw profit in the alleged law and order of Taeping rule, Hope's sub-ordinates kept the rebels on the run. The gunboat *Flamer* destroyed 300 boatloads of food in March 1862, and soon a strong force of ships concentrated at Ningpo under Captain Dew in the sloop *Encounter*.

On 10 May the Imperial Chinese forces opened fire on Ningpo and advanced to recapture the city. Since Imperial junks manoeuvred close to Dew's ships it is not surprising that some Taeping shots whistled over British heads, and Dew lost no time in retaliating. Supported by the gun-vessel *Ringdove* and four gunboats[9] *Encounter* opened fire on the walls of Ningpo. With this encour-agement the timorous Imperial forces stormed the city without any difficulty.

Dew was the classic type of Royal Navy freebooter, doing his utmost to carry out the spirit of his instructions with little regard for the reactions of consuls or politi-cians. Having handed Ningpo over to the Imperial forces he pushed further up the Yangtse to follow up a report of a Taeping victory. A mixed force of Imperial troops and

French and British mercenaries had been defeated at Shousing, so Dew took the gunboats *Hardy* and *Confucius* (French) upriver and joined in a second unsuccessful attempt to take the town. But the Foreign Secretary was now taking a stronger line on British neutrality. It was the time of the *Alabama* dispute, and Great Britain had learned that abuse of neutrality was a double-edged weapon.

The semi-piratical Dew was recalled early in 1863, but not before his ships had landed a naval brigade to help capture Kahding. The half-disciplined Chinese force which captured the place on 24 October 1862 was promptly dubbed 'Ever Victorious' by Peking; shortly afterwards it was commanded for the first time by Major Charles Gordon.

The British attempt to influence the outcome of the Taeping Rebellion by indirect methods virtually ceased when Rear-Admiral Hope was recalled, and his successor promoted little friction. Rear-Admiral Augustus Kuper[10] was bound by the same standing instructions, but as a result of Lord Elgin's journey to Japan in 1858 the ships of the East Indies and China Squadron had to be available to show the flag in Japanese waters. By way of extra responsibility the Admiral had to report on the 'extent of the naval establishments and resources of the Russians on the River Amur, in the North Pacific, the Sea of Achotsk etc.'[11]

British Intervention in Japan

As we have seen, Japan had concluded various treaties with Western Powers after the American, Commodore Perry, had first demanded recognition in 1853. As a result of dissension among the Japanese nobles there had sprung up two parties, the pro-Western supporters of the Shogun and the anti-foreign party of Prince Mito and the Daimios. These two groups jockeyed for power and feudal Japan grew troubled by the frightening changes all around, while all the time the foreigners set up their 'concessions' as calmly as they had in China. The overwhelming self-confidence of the Victorians prevented them from feeling anything but curiosity as they moved among the Japanese people. British prestige was high as a result of her victory in China, and they were the only foreigners to have a Legation headed by a Minister. Sir Rutherford Alcock, the first man to hold the position, lived in a sumptuous Buddhist temple near Yedo (now Tokyo). Foreigners were allowed to walk or ride up to five miles from the concessions, but in view of the unsettled conditions they were warned to avoid main roads if processions of noblemen and their samurai were passing. Trading vessels could only anchor at Yokohama, while warships were allowed to anchor off Yedo if an accredited representative was in residence. Yedo was a fascinating city to European eyes in 1860. The few who passed through its streets were conscious of the curious stares of the crowds, the strange costumes and the exotic atmos-

phere. Those who went to Japan a hundred years ago remarked on the friendliness of the Japanese, and many 'went native' and settled down for life, including the artist of the *Illustrated London News*. But there was hostility towards Europeans from the Daimios, and a daring attempt on Sir Rutherford Alcock's life was defeated by sheer good luck; the long swords of a gang of samurai kept catching in the woodwork of a narrow passage, so that two of Alcock's secretaries could drive them off with their revolvers.

Although the Shogun's council encouraged foreign trade it soon showed itself powerless to protect its protégés. In September 1862 the notorious Namamugi Incident occurred, when samurai of the Prince of Satsuma attacked a small party of English tourists for a fancied insult to their lord, and hacked a young merchant to death. Palmerston's government reacted swiftly, and the Shogun was asked for a formal apology and an indemnity of £100,000 since he professed to be unable to arrest the assassin. In fact, Prince Shimazu Hisamitsu had no intention of surrendering so loyal a follower, especially as he knew that the Shogun had no way of forcing him to do so.

The British representative hoped that a show of force might suffice, and as a result he tolerated delays while the Shogun tried to find an honourable course of retreat. Eventually, in June 1863, the money was paid in silver, and taken on board the *Euryalus*, Kuper's flagship. But Kuper had orders to press a further demand on the Prince of Satsuma for £25,000 and the execution of the murderers. From his anchorage in Kagoshima Bay Kuper negotiated by a series of notes until the morning of 15 August 1863, when his small ships went in and seized three Satsuma steamers (still bearing their former English names). This action provoked the Japanese to reply at about noon. Although a heavy sea was running Kuper's squadron weighed anchor and squared up to the shore batteries. His biggest ships were the frigate *Euryalus* and the corvettes *Perseus* and *Pearl*, all screw steamers; in support were the paddle-sloop *Argus*, the gunvessels *Coquette* and *Racehorse* and the gunboat *Havock*. The little gunboat was at a disadvantage in the rough weather but worked hard enough to get a 'mention' in Kuper's dispatch.

The ensuing bombardment of Kagoshima is remembered as the baptism of fire for the famous Armstrong breech-loading guns, the first of the type to be adopted by the Royal Navy. Kagoshima also ensured that Armstrong breech-loaders were discarded, at any rate as main armament, for so many Armstrong guns burst (an aggregate of twenty-eight accidents to twenty-one guns in 365 rounds)[12] that the Navy went back to muzzle-loaders for fifteen years. At the height of the action the *Euryalus*'s forward 7-inch gun blew out its breech-block and concussed the whole crew.

The action lasted about two hours, and demonstrated that warships had still not achieved mastery over shore defences. The flagship avoided serious damage until she came up to a marker buoy, whose range was known to the Japanese. Suddenly thirty-seven guns concentrated on the big frigate as she wallowed amid the waves. As Captain Josling and Commander Wilmot were talking to Kuper they were decapitated by a round shot, and within minutes the ship had been struck by heavy shells. Meanwhile the gunvessel *Racehorse* drifted ashore when her engines seized, and had to be towed off under heavy fire by *Coquette* and *Argus*. While helping her squadron-mate *Argus* lost her mainmast, but escaped without casualties.

Admiral Kuper had no intention of landing men to occupy and destroy the Japanese positions, so when he saw that his shells had set fire to the factories in Kagoshima he led the squadron out of action to a nearby anchorage. Overnight the sailors repaired the damage to their ships and buried the dead, so that they were ready for action the next day. But Kuper contented himself with shelling the forts on either side of the straits as he set sail for Yokohama, which encouraged the Japanese in their belief that they had beaten off his attack.

At Yokohama Kuper found more warships, which had arrived from China. They included the corvette *Barrosa*, the *Encounter* and four more gunboats and gunvessels, all ready for the attack on the English settlement which was expected at any moment. But the troop detachments paraded each week impressed the Japanese suitably, and allowed tempers to cool.

Sir Rutherford Alcock, a man of great tact and decisiveness, was convinced by the events leading up to Kagoshima that the Shogun's party could be of little use to British interests, in spite of its outward friendliness. Thereafter as the Shogun's prestige declined Alcock made discreet overtures to the Imperial party. As the Prince of Satsuma wanted to restore the Mikado to his full ruling power a gentle rapprochement with the Western Powers seemed the best way to weaken the Shogun's influence. Satsuma, furthermore, was anxious to set up factories and industrialise Japan (this had already started at Kagoshima, where British shells had destroyed an iron foundry, a glass factory and a textile mill).

The Western Powers were to have one last flirtation with the Shogun's council before they switched their allegiance and before the Shogun finally fell from grace. In April 1864 Sir Rutherford Alcock learned that the Shogun was secretly supporting the Emperor's plans for expelling all foreigners. Taxed with this evidence of double-dealing, the Shogun was forced to admit that the sure way to forestall any move was to keep sufficient foreign soldiers and ships handy. The Shogun was treading a slippery path, and he was quick to turn the discussion to the misdeeds of Chosiu, Prince of Nagato. Chosiu, one of the chief anti-foreigners, had at last gone into open rebellion against the Shogun. To punish this truculent vassal the Shogun allowed British forces to assist him, or rather to do what he lacked the power to do. The Europeans in

turn wanted to teach a lesson to Chosiu since their trade had been almost completely cut off for over a year due to the disturbances.

Vice-Admiral Kuper, now a Knight Commander of the Bath, was still in command, but had seven French, Dutch and American vessels under his orders. His aim was to force the Straits of Shimonoseki in the Inland Sea in order to bring his guns to bear on Chosiu's stronghold. On 5 September 1864 the combined squadron opened fire on the batteries at Shimonoseki. From the early afternoon until darkness fell the stately columns of frigates and corvettes cannonaded while the Japanese guns replied from the heights. The massive ship-of-the-line *Conqueror* proved a distinct liability with her deep draught and managed to run aground twice. Only one gunvessel, H.M.S. *Coquette*, was there, with the gunboat *Bouncer*; as there was sufficient deep water for the squadron to manoeuvre adequate fire-power could be provided by big ships.

The following morning began well for the Japanese when they scored hits on two ships. But Kuper was not to be hurried, and preparations for landing a thousand seamen and marines began. By 4 p.m. the landing was over; more than forty guns had been disabled and three V.C.s earned. For her support of the landing *Bouncer's* lieutenant earned a step in rank.

On 8 September more guns were taken, and for the next two days parties were busy blowing up the forts and gun emplacements. It was plain that the mistake at Kagoshima had been to withdraw, for on 7 September Chosiu sent envoys to ask for a cease-fire for forty-eight hours as his troops were 'tired and hungry'. The request was repeated next day, and this time was granted, for the terms included an unhindered passage through the straits.

This battle helped the Shogun little, but improved the Europeans' position remarkably. Within two months the original indemnity which Kuper had been refused at Kagoshima was paid; unannounced, two envoys from the Prince of Satsuma arrived at Yedo with £25,000 in silver. The British Minister was so delighted that he waived the original claim for the arrest and execution of the samurai who had murdered that inoffensive merchant two years before.

Yokohama quickly degenerated under Western influence from a quaint little fishing village to a straggling series of wooden shanty brothels and saloons. Here the sailors brawled and drank themselves into a stupor until herded back to their ships. An *Illustrated London News* cartoon by Wirgman shows a missionary pointing at a grog-shop filled with fighting sailors and saying: 'In this way, and in this manner the Spirit is manifesting its wondrous work.'

Although the British officers amused themselves by founding a club and building Japan's first race-course there were rumours of a Japanese attack, and plans were made accordingly. If a signal rocket was fired H.M.S. *Kestrel*, always either under banked fires or with steam up, was to stand by to destroy the causeway at Kanagawa. This was the only line of attack open to the Japanese, so it was hoped that *Kestrel* could destroy the bridge and hold off any Japanese troops while other ships embarked the civilians. Nothing happened for some weeks, and the British continued to race their wiry ponies before enormous crowds of curious Japanese.

Suddenly one night rockets soared into the sky over Yokohama. Immediately pandemonium broke out as the darkness echoed with drum-rolls, bosun's pipes and frantic bugle-calls. But the flagship signalled imperturbably: 'From what quarter were those rockets sent up?' It turned out to be a Jardine, Matheson steamer giving a farewell party for a V.I.P. on board, but the Admiral was not amused. The whole party, by now full of alcoholic goodwill, was summarily arrested and kept under guard on the quarter-deck of H.M.S. *Euryalus* while Kuper vented his wrath on them before letting them go.

Within four years Japan changed permanently. By the time the last Shogun surrendered his power to the Mikado in 1868 Japanese students were studying in England. The Emperor Mutsuhito turned his back on feudalism and launched Japan on her spectacular career of power which culminated in Pearl Harbor and then Hiroshima.

In Chinese waters the gunboats carried on their patrols around Hong Kong and up the rivers. By the mid-sixties the routine had become an institution. The flagship was a frigate at first, then later a corvette; she originally wore the flag of a rear-admiral, but Kuper's great diplomatic responsibilities resulted in his promotion to vice-admiral just for the duration of his command. This was an unusual step, and meant that Kuper had no authority over any vice-admiral or a rear-admiral senior to him. It was no more than a symbol of prestige to assist Kuper in his dealings with Chinese and Japanese dignitaries and was abolished when Kuper was succeeded.[13] There were always three or four sloops, but the backbone of the China Squadron was the score of gunboats and gun-vessels based on Hong Kong and the treaty ports.

The large number of shallow-draught vessels on a foreign station created a problem of maintenance. How could the Admiralty keep the gunboats up to strength and at the same time replace their crews with fresh men? Running repairs could be carried out at Hong Kong, but not even the Admiralty dared keep men separated from their families indefinitely. As it was commissions lasted three or four years, and any lengthening of the time spent abroad would affect morale. Clearly the Admiralty could not repeat Sherard Osborn's convoy of 1857 every four years, so they adopted the system of commissioning ships abroad. Entire crews were sent out in troopships or transports, and the ships were recommissioned on the China

Station. Introduced in 1865, the system of relief crews saved a considerable amount of money, and kept the China Squadron at its maximum strength. Even the larger ships were recommissioned this way, and later the system spread to other stations.[14]

Life in China gunboats was not onerous, according to people who served in them. Sir Henry Woods, who later became an A.D.C. to the Sultan of Turkey, remembered with pride how he was appointed Second Master of the 40 h.p. gunboat *Kestrel* in 1863. This was the same *Kestrel* which had miraculously escaped destruction at the Peiho in 1859, and in 1863 she was stationed at Yokohama because of the anti-foreign disturbances. Woods was barely twenty, yet found himself the only commissioned officer apart from his Captain, Lieutenant 'Jock' Dunlop. He was not only navigator and paymaster but Ship's Doctor, whose duties consisted of reading the booklet supplied with a little medicine-chest. One of his brother gunboat officers is on record as having mixed all the medicines together to form a potion for the treatment of an A.B.'s obscure stomach pain!

Lieutenant Dunlop, Woods and the gunner shared the tiny wardroom table with the three engineers in more senses than one; under their feet lay a lifting board to permit oiling the bearings. The six officers shared a single wash-basin on a stand and a tiny cabinet lavatory in the stern. Even the stocky little Woods could put his head through the skylight above his cabin for fresh air, like the tall gunboat captain who used to shave in his cabin with the mirror propped up on deck.

A feature of life in gunboats was the good shooting. The monotonous lower reaches of the Canton River are given over to paddy-fields, and the young naval officers were always out shooting snipe and woodcock. The only danger was from a stray Chinese who might try to win favour with a local mandarin by bringing him a foreign devil's head. Practically every volume of naval memoirs contains chapters on shooting wildfowl, with occasional references to warning shots fired over the heads of 'menacing natives'.

Although gunboats were originally the most numerous warship type in China early in the 1860s, from then until the end of the 1870s their numbers dwindled as they were replaced by gunvessels. With more guns and more seaworthy hulls gunvessels soon ousted the little 'forties' and 'sixties' from their position of eminence. In 1860 there were twenty-four gunboats to six gunvessels, but by 1873 the proportion had changed to three gunboats and eleven gunvessels. Another factor which influenced this trend was the superior status of the gunvessel. Since the Navy was the main instrument of policy, and as we saw, even an instrument capable of wielding itself when it felt the need, many decisions had to be left to the man on the spot. Both the Senior Naval Officer and the Admiralty were therefore inclined to entrust such freedom of action to commanders rather than lieutenants.

The wooden gunboat *Grasshopper*, like *Cockchafer* a member of the numerous *Albacore* class. She is shown with the increased 'gunboat rig' fitted for service overseas. *(Private collection)*

Surveying was an important part of the duties of the Navy in Chinese waters, especially after the first Opium War. In earlier days the East India Company had a monopoly of surveying in this area, but the first comprehensive surveys began in 1840 under Sir Edward Belcher of H.M.S. *Sulphur*. Over one hundred and fifty surveys were done by 1861,[15] and an interesting point about them is that many of the earlier ones were carried out in areas officially closed to British warships. There seems to be no record of any friction caused by the survey ships calling at non-treaty ports, although similar activity in Japan was suspended because of anti-foreign feeling.

Naval hydrographers were not merely seeking to provide good charts for merchantmen. Coal was discovered in China and Formosa, as well as in Japan and the Pescadores Islands. Survey ships also had to lend a hand in any naval operations, even though they carried only a token armament. The small gunboat *Dove*, which had been disarmed to serve as a tender to H.M. Surveying Vessel *Actaeon*, was very promptly rearmed in time to see action in the Yangtse and at Taku. After the war ended she went back to survey work, but got into the headlines again when one of her boats was fired on in a bay in south Formosa; *Dove* returned the fire, and later the name Attack Bay found its way into the Admiralty charts.

During the years 1861-69 gunboats and gunvessels dealt a final smashing blow to piracy in the China Sea. In that time twelve gunboats[16] and two gunvessels[17] made no fewer than forty-six captures, for which they received £15,000 in various awards.[18] Right at the end of this period came an incident which disturbed the increasingly peaceful pattern of Anglo-Chinese relations. On hearing that some Chinese had fired on H.M.S. *Cockchafer*'s boats near Swatow the Commodore at Hong Kong ordered six ships to weigh anchor and proceed to the spot. Ignoring an order from Sir Henry Keppel to wait until the Chinese authorities could take action, the impetuous Commodore Jones landed a large force at Outingpoi on 28 January 1869. Before Keppel could arrive to take command from his reckless subordinate the landing force burnt three villages and inflicted over eighty casualties on the inhabitants.

By 1865 the responsibilities of the China Station had been delegated to four divisional commanders: the Straits of Malacca (Senior Officer, Singapore), South China under a commodore, Japan (Senior Officer, Yokohama) and North China (Senior Officer, Shanghai). Gunboats were well scattered, usually one at each consular port, where they were to protect 'life and property immediately exposed'.[19] This should not be construed as a thinly disguised mandate for naval forces to commit random acts of aggression, despite the occurrence of the '*Cockchafer*' Incident'. Rather was it the expression of Lord Clarendon's friendlier policy towards Peking, which was at last recognised to have a right to govern its subjects without interference. Clarendon's famous memorandum to Sir Rutherford Alcock contained no ambiguities. On 19 April 1869 he wrote: '... the board of Admiralty will take care that the policy of H.M. government shall not be thwarted or overborne by excessive zeal on the part of H.M. Navy... .' In retrospect all the frustration and haphazard effort of the Navy's operations in China was worthwhile. By trial and error a workable scheme of international co-operation was arrived at, while the worst malpractices of British and other Westerners were exposed and suppressed. The sanguine state of affairs evident in 1869 was to follow a fairly even pattern until the birth pangs of modern China after 1920.

Chapter 6

AMERICAN CRISES

Caribbean waters have been troubled since the days of Columbus. Long after the buccaneers had been exterminated on the Spanish Main British and French squadrons fought for possession of the West Indies, and even on the eve of Trafalgar Nelson had no hesitation in leaving the Channel unguarded to chase Villeneuve right across the Atlantic to the precious sugar islands.

After Waterloo the naval base at Kingston declined in importance, until the North American and West Indies Squadron of the Royal Navy was given the prime task of stamping out the international slave trade. The slavers were making for ports in South America to land their highly perishable cargoes, and had to make a landfall off the West Indies on account of the prevailing winds from West Africa. Unfortunately the fast slave-ships of the day could show a clean pair of heels to most warships, and not until the introduction of steamers in the 1840s could the Royal Navy score many successes.

The British squadron avoided all possible friction with the United States over abuse of territorial waters, for memories of the War of 1812 were still very bitter, but certain points of view were not reconcilable. Washington's refusal to outlaw the carrying of slaves on the high seas made it almost impossible at times to enforce the blockade. Again and again slaves were carried flagrantly under the Stars and Stripes until the legal loopholes were stopped.

Sir Henry Woods told an amusing story[1] about the difficulties encountered by Royal Navy captains in their dealings with American slavers. A common practice at this time (1859-60) was to carry two crews, one Spanish and one American. The ship was American-manned until the slaves were shipped, after which the Spanish captain and crew took over for the 'Middle Passage' to Cuba or Brazil, since United States citizens were barred from slave-trafficking.

After years of negotiations the Americans had agreed to co-operate with the British in stopping the slave trade on the high seas, but still they refused to allow the 'Right of Search', which had been wheedled or bullied out of every other nation by Great Britain. It was this same right which had led to the War of 1812 between the United States and Great Britain, and American pride prevented any compromise on this principle of neutrality. But when at last U.S. warships were sent out to the coast of West Africa to co-operate with the Royal Navy American slavers were forced to resort to endless guile. With two crews on board the slaver 'became American' if chased by a British ship; she could only be searched by an American warship. As the entire United States Anti-Slavery Squadron comprised one frigate and a store-ship in 1859 (it was later increased), this was a remote possibility.

One day the screw gunvessel *Viper*, under Commander William Hewett (who won the V.C. while serving in her sister-ship *Beagle*), fell in with a typical American slaver, who audaciously hove to, and welcomed a young British midshipman aboard. After inspecting the ship's papers the midshipman was rowed back to the *Viper*, only to return with Hewett himself.

Once aboard Hewett shook hands with the captain, gazed about him and said disarmingly: 'Why, Captain, you've got a very taut-rigged ship. You spread a lot of canvas, and it seems to me you haven't got too many men on board to handle those sails. I'll tell you what I'll do ... I've got a lot of lazy, fat-sterned fellows on board my ship. I'll lend you a few whilst we're together.'

'But,' said the American, 'I guess I don't want any of your men, and then I'm going another way.'

'Oh, that's all right! My way is yours. You don't know these waters, Captain.'

While the American captain fumed in silence and tried to think of a way to outsmart Hewett, twelve brawny British sailors were transferred from *Viper*, and lounged about on the slaver's deck with broad grins on their faces. The comedy played itself out, for nothing materialised to draw *Viper* away, and eventually the wretched Spaniards could no longer stand the heat and crowding below. They had been battened down ever since the *Viper* had drawn close (although their sufferings were slight compared to what their next cargo would endure), and when the skipper heard their shouting below he knew the game was up.

In disgust he fetched his box of genuine registration papers from his cabin, threw it overboard, and hailed the *Viper*. Once more Hewett stepped jauntily aboard and asked the skipper: 'What can I do for you, Captain?'

'Oh, I'm not the captain,' said the American. 'I'm a passenger for Luanda. Will you take me there?'

The Royal Navy had by this time broken the back of the slave trade on the west coast of Africa, and as warships knew they need not expect armed resistance there was a tacit understanding that crews of prizes were allowed to escape if possible. It saved complications and international lawsuits, and did nothing to deprive the sailors of their hard-earned 'head money' or the bounty based on the tonnage of the ship captured. Men like Hewett's American captain invariably destroyed the vital evidence which would have earned them penal servitude, and took passage to the nearest friendly port, where they had a fair chance of picking up another ship before long.

A much bigger headache for senior British officers was the activity of the filibusters in the West Indies. In the decade before the American Civil War these soldiers of fortune, nearly all Americans, waged an incredible partisan war against the tiny republics of Central America. Taking their name from the French *flibustier*, meaning a freebooter, they attempted to liberate several countries by force of arms. The most persistent of the filibusters was the notorious William Walker, whose continual abuse of United States territorial waters embarrassed Washington to such an extent that a joint Anglo-American declaration was made in 1860 to the effect that any further invasion of Nicaragua would be resisted by force.

The United States was not unduly perturbed by the filibusters' incursions into British possessions. Public opinion demanded an aggressive policy in the Caribbean, the first awakening of 'neo-colonialism'.[2] Any unrest in the area might ultimately benefit American interests, but a serious outbreak of violence could only be an invitation to Great Britain to step in and restore law and order, and incidentally provide her with an excuse for strengthening her position. At this time the Monroe Doctrine was almost a dead letter inasmuch as it did not deter Great Britain from pursuing her imperial interests in Central and South America. Although the Monroe Doctrine claimed to warn off all European colonisers, it was underwritten by the Royal Navy throughout the nineteenth century, and only kept out the French and Russians.

William Walker sailed from Mobile in 1860 with a shipload of armed followers bound for Honduras. His aim was to seize the island of Roatan (where Captain Morgan's treasure was found in 1935) for use as a base for the invasion of Nicaragua, but fate played a cruel trick on

Notorious filibuster, William Walker. *(US Library of Congress)*

him. The time seemed ripe, for Roatan had just been ceded to Honduras by Britain under the Clayton-Bulwer Treaty of 1850, and Walker hoped that the local authorities would not yet be firmly in the saddle. But when the filibusters arrived off Roatan they saw to their dismay that the Union Jack was still flying; because the government of Honduras had not paid certain debts, Great Britain had refused to complete the cession of Roatan.

With dramatic timing the British sloop *Icarus* hove in sight, carrying the officials who were to complete the cession of Roatan and the remaining Bay Islands. Baffled, Walker could only withdraw, but Commander Nowell Salmon, V.C., of H.M.S. *Icarus* was aware of his intentions. Confident that his arrival had prevented the capture of Roatan for the moment he sailed to Jamaica for further orders. When he returned he found that Walker, having given up the idea of using the Bay Islands, had landed on the mainland and captured Trujillo. This sleepy little town had been declared a 'free port', and on the face of it, a single sloop could hope to do little against a force of well-armed Americans.

Taking good care to assure himself of the legality of his actions, Salmon gave Walker twenty-four hours to evacuate Trujillo, and be repatriated to New Orleans with his men. After agreeing to these terms Walker suddenly vanished into the forest with a small band of men. When Salmon learned how he had been tricked he was determined to catch up with Walker, who could not be far from the coast. The Honduran Government asked for Salmon's help and provided 200 soldiers, so *Icarus* set off down the coast, with the soldiers crowded into a vessel towed astern.

The filibusters were finally caught at the Rio Negro, where the boats of H.M.S. *Icarus* took them by surprise. Walker told his men to surrender to avoid bloodshed, but this time there was no parleying. After being disarmed the filibusters were taken back to Trujillo, where they were put on a boat bound for New Orleans. Walker, however, was tried by court-martial in Trujillo; although he refused to claim American nationality Commander Salmon asked the nearest U.S. consul to watch the case on behalf of his government. He was found guilty on 11 September 1860 and shot next day, scarcely two months after his abortive attempt to capture Roatan. This sad, unromantic ending to Walker's life had no effect on the legends about his exploits, and many Americans have portrayed Walker and his men as liberators and patriots.

After the American Civil War filibustering continued for a while, and the North American and West Indies Squadron had to retain a number of gunvessels and gunboats to cope with fresh problems. The slave trade had been killed off at last by the Northern victory, but the following year ships had to be drafted to Canadian waters to deal with the Fenian raiders. Then came the outbreak of the Cuban Insurrection. While Cubans struggled for six years to overthrow the Spaniards it was tempting for Americans to offer money and arms to the rebels. British policy was basically favourable to the rebels, but was equally against the substitution of American rule for Spanish, and warships were disposed to intercept gunrunners running the blockade from Florida. Unfortunately the sloops and gunvessels used were rarely able to overtake the Americans unless they were caught in a flat calm. The only notable success took place towards the end of 1869, when H.M.S. *Lapwing* caught *five* blockade-runners, including one which had just landed 300 men on a British island.

The troubles of South American governments were not confined to invasions by bands of filibusters, for their endemic revolutions frequently provoked foreign powers to intervene to restore order. Such intervention was usually short and relatively painless to both sides, since the arrival of an American or British warship easily overawed the unruly mobs of soldiers and peasants who were contending for power. But one incident, typical of so many, resulted in a setback for the Royal Navy.

H.M. paddle-sloop *Bulldog* received orders to visit Haiti as soon as it was learned that an attempted *coup* had taken place, and that the rival factions were still fighting. When *Bulldog* appeared off Acul on 22 October 1865 she found that an armed rebel steamer had fired on the British Jamaica mail packet. The sloop immediately ordered the rebel captain to cease fire, which he did promptly, allowing the mail packet to escape.

The incident might have ended there, but when the rebel steamer docked at Cape Haitien the rebels' leader decided on a flamboyant but foolish gesture of defiance. In a manner familiar to modern readers the British Consulate was wrecked, and several fugitives sheltering there were captured and executed. This was ample provocation for any naval officer, and Commander Wake immediately presented a demand for satisfaction.

Wake's ultimatum expired early on the morning of 23 October 1865 so he gave the order to open fire on one of

The paddle-sloop *Bulldog* engaging rebel forts at Cape Haitien, 23 October 1865. *(Radio Times Hulton Picture Library)*

the rebel-held forts. *Bulldog* crept into the harbour exchanging shots with the batteries until she came within range of her opponent of the previous day, the steamer *Valorogue*. In very dashing manner the sloop tried to close the range, but she was heading for disaster. Commander Wake's tactics were in the best Nelsonian tradition, but they were not suited for a strange harbour in badly charted waters, and *Bulldog* ran hard aground on an uncharted reef. It was a nasty moment for the British sailors, for they were within rifle-shot of the enemy, to say nothing of the guns on shore. The sloop was doomed, but she died gamely for her guns sank the *Valorogue* and another vessel, and then hit the rebels' magazine. Rounds of grape- and canister-shot cleared the shore of riflemen, but this only gave the *Bulldog* a brief respite.

The only hope was the American warship *De Soto*, which had earlier offered to take off wounded, and Wake signalled her to try and tow his ship off the reef. After a valiant effort to get the *Bulldog* off under fire, the *De Soto* withdrew out of range while the British sloop carried on her onesided fight. That night, with no ammunition left and his position hopeless, Commander Wake set fire to the ship after transferring all survivors to a friendly steamer belonging to the Haitian Government.

Wake and his navigator returned to England to face a court-martial; contrary to popular expectation the court reprimanded them both for the navigational error which put the ship aground, and for abandoning her prematurely. However, neither officer's career seems to have suffered unduly, and they must have been gratified to learn that two squadron-mates evened the score a fortnight after their defeat. On 9 November 1865 the frigate *Galatea* and the gunvessel *Lily* bombarded the defences of Cape Haitien and supported a landing by government forces, a more usual ending to so many minor incidents in the Caribbean.

The Jamaica Rebellion

A statement made by the Governor of Jamaica in 1865 dismissed in a few sentences one of the most disquieting episodes in British colonial history:

> To the senior naval officer, Captain de Horsey, of H.M.S. *Wolverine*, we owe it that we were enabled to carry out with promptitude and efficiency the arrangements necessary to control and suppress the rebellion. Lieutenant Brand, of H.M.S. *Onyx*, is entitled to the highest praise for the unceasing and valuable services rendered by the little gunboat under his command…[3]

The summer of 1865 was hot and dry, and the poverty-stricken negro population of Jamaica was in dire straits because of widespread drought. By August Governor Eyre was receiving reports of grave distress and disaffection among the negro freedmen. The staple sugar crop, which had once made the island a shuttlecock during the Napoleonic Wars, was being priced out of foreign markets, and yielded uncertain profits. Many of the freed slaves preferred to become small landowners in the hills, and although they were more prosperous than their fellow-blacks on the sugar estates the succeeding years of drought hit them hard as well.

It took only a minor incident to turn this discontent into a rebellion. The town of Morant Bay was crowded, for Saturday was market day, when a sudden uproar in the courthouse over a fine of four shillings excited the bystanders. A man about to be arrested for shouting in the courtroom was rescued by the crowd, led by a man named Bogle. So far, nothing seemed dangerous, and it was only on the following Tuesday, 10 October 1865, that an attempt was made to arrest Bogle and his friends.

A small party of police was overpowered by an armed band of men at least 300 strong, who attacked the courthouse later that day. But the local official, Custos von Ketelhodt, had warned the Governor in time. Even as von Ketelhodt, a few civilians and a dozen or so Volunteers sold their lives dearly in the burning courthouse, soldiers were on their way, some by sea in H.M.S. *Wolverine* and others overland from Kingston.

Stories of ghastly atrocities were flying around when the Governor arrived at Morant Bay, and although many tales were proved to be exaggerations Eyre and his officers must have been in a vengeful mood as they listened to the refugees. Only eight years before Englishmen had inflicted bloodthirsty retribution on Indian sepoys, and the example of the Mutiny must have haunted Eyre in all his decisions. The immediate aim of the soldiers was to inflict such severe punishments as would overawe the negroes, leaving the Governor to get his hands on the man he considered to be the instigator of the rebellion.

George Gordon was a mulatto member of the Jamaican House of Assembly, and had been a staunch opponent of Governor Eyre for some years. His persistent petitioning for better conditions for the black population made him extremely unpopular with the white planters, and there were many who agreed with Eyre when he arrested Gordon for sedition. But Eyre knew that he had not sufficient evidence to convince a Kingston Court, so he hit on the solution of taking Gordon to Morant Bay, where he could be tried under martial law. There were only two things wrong with the Governor's scheme: first, it was blatantly unjust to arrest a man under one court's jurisdiction and then try him elsewhere, and furthermore, under English law a civilian cannot be tried by a court-martial.

Leaving aside doubts about the legality of Gordon's arrest, even Eyre's plans for the court-martial were questionable. Shortly after the outbreak of violence at Morant Bay the little 20 h.p. gunboats *Nettle* and *Onyx* had arrived from Bermuda. These two were the only specimens of their class to be employed overseas, and this was to be their only action. *Onyx* fired a couple of shells at a mob of negroes burning an estate, and was in time to rescue the planter and his family. After ferrying troops from Port Royal the two gunboats then landed most of their men for service ashore.[4]

Onyx's commander, Lieutenant Herbert Brand, R.N., was appointed to preside over the court-martial proceedings by the officer in charge at Morant Bay. Brand was still in his twenties, had no experience of court-martial procedure, and had no legal adviser; yet his own account[5] shows that his ignorance was matched by his zeal:

> On the 20th day of October last I was shown an order of Brigadier General Nelson's ordering a Court Martial to assemble that day for the trial of prisoners … after I had read it, he [Nelson's A.D.C.] took it away to show the other members, Lt. Errington of H.M.S. 'Wolverine' and Mr. P. Kelly Ensign 4th West India Regiment.
>
> In accordance with the order I assembled the Court at Mr. Marshall's Store and swore them in according to the custom of the army and the Queen's Regulations… The prisoners were arraigned on a certain charge, which was preferred by the Provost Marshall…
>
> When the case for the prosecution was over I called on the prisoner for his defence and I allowed him to say what he could or wished in his defence and also to call any witness to prove an alibi or general good behaviour. When his defence was quite finished the court was cleared and deliberated on the sentence…
>
> Two good witnesses such as owners or overseers of Estates, Justices of the Peace, Ministers and other respectable Europeans were considered sufficient evidence. When Negroes gave evidence I obtained as many as I could get.
>
> The women hung were the very worst class only such as Judy Edwards who was Captain of a Company and marched in at the head of her Men with a drawn cutlass

and cheered them on or Letitia Geoghegan who with her four sons was executed. The women sat on the still living bodies of Mr. Price and others and with their own cutlasses battered their brains out as they lay on the ground imploring mercy. No woman was hung who had not actually wielded a cutlass or assisted in some murder.

The defence as a rule was a pure and simple denial, few only attempting to prove an alibi. In case a person wished to call a witness in his defence I remanded the case until he could be procured… .

A list was then made of those to be hung or flogged and sent by the General to the Provost Marshall. The executions usually took place at 5 p.m.; at 4.30 p.m. the whole of the untried prisoners numbering, at one time about 300, were paraded in the square in front of the Court House and gallows. The Naval Brigade Troops and police under arms, such of the inhabitants as pleased also witnessed the executions…

…The Provost Marshall when all was ready opened the letter ordering the execution and called the names one by one and they walked up to the plank when they were pinioned by the party told off for that purpose and the rope was then adjusted. When all were on the plank and everything was quite ready the Provost Marshall gave the order 'Sentenced to be hung for murder and rebellion' and waving his hand the party told off tripped the plank and they were left suspended until the next morning at 6 a.m. when they were taken down carted away and buried by the other prisoners plenty of lime being used for sanitary purposes.

When all were quite dead the Corporal punishment commenced…

All prisoners were hung on the common gallows in front of the Court House, except Geo W. Gordon the Brothers Bogle and the Captain General Bonie, who were hanged in the centre arch of the building.

No duplicates or records of any court were kept. The names are from the private journal of Lieut. Errington of H.M.S. 'Wolverine'. All originals were sent to the confirming officer and I was informed that according to the Custom of Martial Law it was not even necessary to keep the proceedings. The first day of assembling was the 20th of October. 13 men were tried 11 were hung and 2 acquitted – Their names have unfortunately been mislaid.

Here follows a list of 123 men and women, with sentences ranging from hanging to fifty, sixty or even one hundred lashes; these were carried out between 21 and 30 October, after which Colonel Lewis of the Militia and Lieutenant Oxley, R.N., took over from Brand. Brand's account finishes with an abstract.

This bald narrative conceals some unpleasant truths, and Brand and Oxley were later censured by the Admiralty for their free interpretation of the rules of evidence. Several sets of cat-o'-nine tails were made on board *Onyx*, and Brand later denied a charge that they had been interlaced with wire. A Royal Commission heard some appalling stories of summary punishments for trifling offences such as answering back after a flogging – which merited another twenty-five lashes! Gordon was tried and sentenced without ceremony, although Brand is said to have improved the occasion by snatching the unfortunate man's spectacles from his face on the scaffold.[7] He nevertheless faced his executioners with dignity, and asked only one favour, that the facts of the uprising be communicated to his friends in London.

Brigadier-General Nelson was also active and under his direction parties of soldiers scoured the countryside around Morant Bay, burning houses and flogging anyone suspected of rebel sympathies. The evidence was largely hearsay, the testimony of men at gunpoint. Identifying rebels was easy; if a man fled when he saw the soldiers he was automatically a rebel. If not shot immediately he was liable to be flogged on the spot. If he was pointed out as a ringleader and survived long enough he was taken back to face Lieutenant Brand and his court. After the floggings were finished some of the prisoners were forced to run the gauntlet and were pelted with stones before they could go free. But these were only the small number brought to trial, and there is ample testimony to suggest that between summary 'justice' and martial law nearly 400 negroes were shot or hanged, and many more flogged, while over a thousand homes were burnt on the flimsy excuse that they had sheltered rebels.

England was shaken by the news of the Jamaica Rebellion, and the Governor's conduct became the subject of a fierce controversy. A hundred years later the issue has been almost completely forgotten, but for

Sentences carried out, 21-30 October 1865

COURT PRESIDED OVER BY	HUNG			FLOGGED	ACQUITTED	REMANDED	TOTAL
	MEN	WOMEN	TOTAL				
LT. BRAND 'NETTLE' GUNBOAT[6]	122	4	126	33	5	7	171
COL. LEWIS MILITIA	50	–	50	–	–	–	50
LIEUT. OXLEY 'WOLVERINE'	1	–	1	2	2	3	8
TOTAL	173	4	177	35	7	10	229

Note: Of 99 men and 40 women liberated [a gaol delivery on 4 November], most of the men were flogged.

three years it caused furious lobbying, mass protests and a remarkably acid war of words. Two parties emerged, those who saw Eyre as the judicial murderer of black subjects of the Crown, and those who saw him as the saviour of the colony. At the Old Bailey on 10 April 1867 a Grand Jury considered a possible indictment against Nelson and Brand for the murder of Gordon, a vital step before any move could be made against Eyre himself.

The main force behind the agitation was the Jamaica Committee, which had the backing of John Stuart Mill, Charles Darwin and Thomas Huxley. Ranged against them were the members of the Eyre Defence Fund, among them Carlyle, Ruskin, Tennyson, Dickens and Kingsley. This marshalling of writers and scientists gives an indication of the degree of indignation aroused, and was accompanied by enormous protest-meetings in Trafalgar Square and Hyde Park.

When the agitation died down it left hardly a trace. Despite an adverse summing-up by the Lord Chief Justice, Lord Cockburn, the Grand Jury failed to indict Nelson and Brand, making it practically certain that a similar indictment would not be obtained against Eyre. The Committee accordingly changed its line of attack, and secured an indictment for high crimes and misdemeanours under the Colonial Governors Act. The case was heard before the Grand Jury of Queen's Bench on 2 June 1868, and Eyre was acquitted the following day. But, as *The Times* pointed out, he had by no means escaped scot-free:

> He is not to be envied even for his present and, we sincerely hope, final escape from his legal persecutors. Two years in a healthy prison, or the payment of a thousand pounds, are a trifle compared with a position by the side of *Nero*, Colonel *Kirk*, Judge *Jeffreys*, *Claverhouse*, the Duke of *Cumberland*, and similar notorieties, in books for the young and religious periodicals.[8]

The significance of the Jamaica Committee's assiduous persecution of Eyre, Nelson and Brand should not be overlooked, however unsuccessful it may have been in securing retribution. In the bitter years between 1865 and 1868 the dangerously authoritarian tendencies of European rule were curbed to a marked degree. A public already incensed by reports of atrocities against the Maoris showed its opinion clearly by well-organised mass agitation. Colonial governors and the naval and military subordinates who administered the complex machinery of gunboat diplomacy were warned that public opinion could, and would, reject ruthless expediency. After the Indian Mutiny and the Jamaica Rebellion the British Empire seemed to be heading towards totalitarian oppression of its colonial subjects, while preaching democracy at home. Thanks to the work of the Jamaica Committee and its supporters the rule of law was

reasserted and Victorian humanitarianism won a much-needed victory.[9]

Another result was more rigid control by the Admiralty over junior officers. Although the Secretary of the Admiralty refused to allow the Royal Commission to see Lieutenant Brand's court-martial papers[10] on the grounds that they were confidential, there was an enquiry into the conduct of the naval officers concerned. In a letter to the C.-in-C. of the North America and West Indies Station the Secretary told him that the Board had censured Lieutenants Brand and Oxley, not because they disapproved of the military measures, but because of the irregular court-martial proceedings. It was held that Brand and other junior officers had been called on to enforce martial law without the assistance of persons acquainted with forms and proceedings of Courts of Justice. There was a reference to evidence 'which would not have been admitted before any ordinary tribunal', and the letter goes on to outline new regulations to ensure that young officers knew their duties and responsibilities in any similar situation.[11]

Canada and the Fenians

The American Civil War brought Great Britain and the United States close to war several times. The ambiguous attitude of the British Government towards the status of the Confederacy continually annoyed Washington, and in November 1861 a full-scale crisis blew up when a Federal warship held up the British steamer *Trent* and arrested two Confederate emissaries bound for Europe, James Mason and John Slidell (formerly a prominent filibuster). But Lincoln's sage observation, 'One war at a time', helped to keep the hotheads from declaring war. Ultimately the British Government took a firmer stand on prohibiting the sale of arms to the Confederacy, while Federal captains were more careful in their dealings with neutral shipping.

The end of the Civil War, however, did little to reduce tension between the two countries, for the Foreign Office was aware that the enormous increase in the strength of the Northern Army put Canada in great danger. Since the War of 1812 the defence of Canada's vast American frontier had been a major problem but the end of the Civil War suddenly released a large battle-tested army for possible use against Canada. No natural barrier exists between the two countries, and ships using the Great Lakes can be interfered with at will. The canals were at the mercy of a few batteries of field-guns, while any attempt at closing the frontier by a chain of forts would have cost millions to maintain.

The problem of defending Canada worried the Colonial Office and the Foreign Office throughout the first half of the nineteenth century. Until the Crimean War the number of troops normally stationed throughout the Empire varied from 40,000 to 47,000 (not including the entirely separate establishment of the

The 60 h.p. gunboat *Cherub* at Goderich, Lake Ontario, at the time of the Fenian Raid, 1866.
(© National Maritime Museum, London)

Indian Army). Nearly a third of these were stationed in Canada, while some thought was given to the Royal Navy's need for secure bases on the Atlantic and Pacific coasts with garrisons at Halifax and Esquimalt.

In February 1859 an Admiralty memorandum proposed that the headquarters of the Pacific Squadron be transferred from Valparaiso in Chile to Vancouver Island, to provide a base for operations against Russia or the United States. 'If these powers have dockyards and resources in the North Pacific, and we have not, for every shilling spent by either of them ... we shall spend a guinea.'[12] It was obvious that the Royal Navy could never hope to control the western coast of Canada by operating from its base at Valparaiso, which had sufficed only as long as warships were not required further north. Nothing stood in the way of this proposed change in dispositions, for it was more favourable to British interests. Great Britain had no territorial interests in South America, apart from British Guiana; her commerce could be easily protected by random visits to various ports. Vancouver Island had other great advantages, for it

shortened the time taken to reach China from three-and-a-half months to two. The Commander-in-Chief of the Pacific Squadron[13] was wholeheartedly in favour of the move, and pointed out that communication with England would be made easier by using the Pony Express from St Louis.[14] Messages from London took five weeks by this route, but the completion of the telegraph from New York to California would cut this time drastically. When the telegraphic link was extended to British Columbia the time dropped to three days. Nevertheless, owing to the snail's pace of Admiralty decisions the move did not take place until 1870.

The threat to Canada was a real one, but when it materialised it came from another direction and from an unforeseen source. The Fenian Brotherhood had been founded in the United States in 1858 to free Ireland from English rule by armed revolution. Eight years of subversion and plotting achieved very little among the disgruntled Irish of Boston. In their filthy ghettoes they could only see England as the cause of their misfortunes, and the violent secrecy of the Fenians lured them easily.

With the end of the Civil War the Fenians found recruiting easier; thousands of idle ex-soldiers looked for jobs, and arms were easy to find. Arms depots were slackly guarded, pilfering went on unchecked and vast amounts of equipment were sold to civilian contractors at knock-down prices. Nor did the Fenians suffer much interference from the U.S. Government in their efforts to embarrass the British, for every red-blooded American patriot naturally thought of America's 'Manifest Destiny' as dominion over the whole North American continent. Although Washington had no desire for a war provoked solely by its turbulent new citizens, there was no means of policing that vast frontier adequately; the Canadians could not keep the Fenians out, and the Americans could not keep them in.

By early 1866 the Fenians were strong enough to provide horses and rifles for raids across the border into Canada. These raids achieved nothing of military importance, but nevertheless called for prompt counter-measures. The Colonial Office asked the Admiralty to alert the C.-in-C. of the North America and West Indies Squadron,[15] who took his flagship to New Brunswick to checkmate a raid across the St Croix River and land the 17th Regiment for garrison duties. The sloop *Fawn* was stationed in the Bay of Fundy, but as a concession to the severity of the winter gales she was given permission to winter at St John's.

The final answer to the Fenians was to use warships to patrol the Lake Frontier of eastern Canada, leaving the garrison troops free to defend important points and round up the raiders. As the area of operations was 300 miles from Quebec only shallow-draught vessels were suitable, and so the choice fell on gunboats. Even gun-vessels drew too much water to be of much use,[16] so three of the latest 60 h.p. gunboats were sent out from England. While the Senior Naval Officer's ship *Aurora* stayed at Quebec the sloops *Pylades* and *Rosario* went upriver to Montreal, and the little gunboats *Britomart*, *Cherub* and *Heron* reached the Great Lakes through the canals which existed before the building of the St Lawrence Seaway. These canals had been built in Georgian times to handle barge traffic, and were restricted to vessels drawing not more than eight feet of water; for this reason the 80 h.p. *Algerine* class gunboats had been rejected.[17]

With *Britomart* on Lake Erie, *Cherub* on Lake Huron and *Heron* on Lake Ontario the Navy had the nucleus of a strong force to police the Lakes. Within a short time local paddle-steamers were commandeered, armed and fitted with bullet-proof plating, but nothing could equal the moral effect of the gunboats' 68-pounders. When the winter set in the Governor-General asked specifically for the three gunboats to remain on the Lakes,[18] even though this meant they would be frozen in. Accordingly *Heron* was berthed at Toronto, *Britomart* at Dunville and *Cherub* at Goderich, with temporary wooden structures

over their decks to provide extra shelter during the long dark months.

The sailors had reason to bless the Fenians for apart from a few false alarms there was no action. Instead they enjoyed Canadian hospitality, fished the trout streams and paraded occasionally to reassure the populace that the Navy was on the alert. Only one big raid took place, and that was easily frustrated by the land forces. When eventually local volunteer regiments and militia replaced the Imperial troops, the naval units were withdrawn.

With the Fenian crisis over the British Government reduced its forces in Canada as much as possible. Canada was on the verge of self-government, and was felt to be quite capable of assuming the responsibility of providing her own land forces.

Differences with the United States were smoothed over by the *Alabama* Claims settlement in 1871, by which time the number of British troops in Canada had dropped from 16,000 to 6,000 – a saving which more than offset the cost of paying for the *Alabama*'s depredations.

The Admiralty's proposal to shift the headquarters of the Pacific Squadron to Vancouver Island was followed up, and the existing anchorage at Esquimalt was provided with better facilities for refitting and repairing ships. Fixed defences and a garrison were provided for the new base, and even after 1871 when all other Imperial troops had been withdrawn from Canada the defence of Esquimalt and Halifax was considered important enough to call for garrisons composed of British regulars. Only one disadvantage plagued successive S.N.O.s and ships' captains, the possibility that seamen might desert to America, which promised high wages and adventure. Seattle was scarcely a hundred miles from Vancouver, and many A.B.s found the lure of easy money too much for them; the only cure was to restrict shore leave to petty officers and 'reliable' ratings.

In 1870 the Navy was still using Valparaiso, but on Admiralty instructions the Senior Naval Officer at Esquimalt was to be of post-rank (i.e. a captain, commanding a frigate or corvette) with two gunvessels attached. The S.N.O.'s ship was to be relieved by the C.-in-C.'s flagship every six months, and was ordered to return via the coast of Mexico and Panama, and thence to the Sandwich Islands. British investments in Mexico called for at least one ship of the squadron to be stationed off the coast during the winter months (during the rest of the year bad weather and disease made this inadvisable). Similarly the requirement for a ship to remain at Callao to watch over British interests in Peru could not always be met as yellow fever epidemics were common.

An interesting sidelight on the naval view of British financial interests occurs in a letter from Rear-Admiral Kingcome[19] to the Senior Officer of the Southern Division of the Pacific Station. Speaking of the possibility of war between Peru and Ecuador, he wrote that the

British Government was not disposed to intervene on behalf of various British investors. The instructions attached were explicit:

> As British subjects, those creditors are entitled to the good offices of H.M.G., but those who prefer the hazards of South American loans to the moderate interest of the English Funds, cannot and must not expect to derive from British Squadrons and British Influence, the security of the 3 Per Cents in addition to the high interests of the South American Republics.[20]

The Fenian troubles came too late to test a quaint trio of gunboats designed to do what the three *Britomarts* had done. The Admiralty had ordered three 'super-gunboats' in 1864, a futile attempt to match a big ship's defensive qualities with the gunboat's unique offensive strength. H.M. armoured gunboats *Viper*, *Vixen* and *Waterwitch* were like enormous black crocodiles, with long low silhouettes and blunt snout-bows. Their hulls were encased in 4½-inch armour, the same thickness as the famous battleship *Warrior*, and they each mounted two 7-inch muzzle-loading guns on centre-line pivots. In addition *Waterwitch* was driven by the revolutionary Ruthven turbine, a device which propelled the ship by emitting jets of steam underwater. Their length was restricted to 162 feet to allow them to pass through the locks on the Canadian canals.

The three new gunboats aroused great interest when they were built, for the idea of a small armoured ship had been put forward frequently in the past. But they ended their days in disgrace as absurd failures. The Board of Admiralty in its usual enthusiasm for 'sticks and string' insisted that *Viper* and her sisters carry masts and yards. The enormous weight of this top-hamper made them so unseaworthy that men refused to take them to sea, while *Waterwitch* on one occasion in the Channel was unable to get her head to wind.[21] Their miserable speed was scarcely nine knots, even on paper, and if their engines had been able to get them across the Atlantic their shocking steering and handling would have made it a highly hazardous venture.

Viper and *Vixen* did ultimately cross the Atlantic, but under tow, and ended their inglorious careers at Bermuda. *Waterwitch* gave the Ruthven turbine a bad start, and her mediocre performance gave the new machinery an undeserved bad name. The idea of armoured gunboats was quietly dropped, although it continued to crop up from time to time in technical journals. The lessons of the Crimean War seemed to be forgotten until the destroyer showed once more that small craft can only rely on a good turn of speed to keep them out of trouble.

Chapter 7

THE SECOND GENERATION

In the years following the Crimean War gunboats and gunvessels were sent to foreign stations where there was a special need for shallow-draught vessels. As we saw, the combination of piracy and friction with the Chinese caused a large number of gunboats and gunvessels to be kept on the China Station for some years. To a lesser degree this applied on other stations, and gunboats appeared wherever they could be employed.

In Home waters and the sheltered Mediterranean the little wooden Crimean gunboats were used mainly as tenders to larger warships, much as they had been in the Baltic in 1855. Many spent the rest of their lives in the Coastguard, attached to the obsolete battleships stationed around the British Isles as Port Guardships. In the days before moored mines and torpedoes made harbour defence relatively easy the Admiralty visualised Great Britain's enemies (invariably the French) descending on her ports and occupying them before embarking on a full-scale invasion. To counter this many of the Navy's older ships were stationed at important commercial ports; their reduced crews meant that they rarely left port, but they provided adequate training in gunnery, while their gunboat tenders gave the men training in seamanship.

By 1867 the Crimean gunboats were near the end of their life-span. Only twenty[1] of the original twenty-seven sent out to China remained, with three newer gunvessels. The four *Britomarts* were still stationed on the Great Lakes waiting for the Fenians to attack, but the only other gunboats on the North America and West Indies Station were the tiny *Nettle* and *Onyx* at Bermuda, by now totally ineffective and due for replacement by *Albacore* and *Delight*. At Montevideo the Navy maintained its only active base on foreign soil (Valparaiso was also used, but solely as a victualling port), and as British traders had established themselves up the great South

American rivers, this South East Coast of America Squadron always had three gunboats attached. The Senior Naval Officer commanded a frigate, normally the only warship of importance in these waters. Later the frigate was replaced by a corvette, and the gunboats by three gunvessels, but the numerical strength of the squadron remained the same until the end of the 1880s. In 1867 another gunboat was present, the 60 h.p. *Gleaner*, the first Crimean gunboat to be commissioned. Her foreign service was, however, very short, for she was put up for sale the following year and was not replaced.

Apart from five gunboats in the Mediterranean and two in the Pacific the remaining twenty-eight gunboats still in commission in 1867 were Coastguard tenders or attached to warships in Home waters. Another twenty-seven were laid up or in use as hulks in the Royal Dockyards. It was these gunboats which provoked such violent criticism in Parliament when dry-rot caused them to fall apart after only ten years' service. Indeed, service is hardly an apt description, for many had gone straight into the Reserve after leaving their builders. The Admiralty had been forced to spend a good deal of money to preserve them, and they had been hauled up on slipways under wooden sheds at Haslar in an attempt to save them for a future war.

The fault lay, as the Admiralty tried to explain to its critics, in the extraordinary haste in construction, and the inescapable need to use green timber at the height of the Crimean War. This is borne out by a memorandum from the Surveyor of the Navy, Baldwin Walker, in January 1856.[2] The building yards were given a free hand in their choice of timber, so long as the contracts were completed urgently, and in many cases work went on after dark in the winter months of 1854-55. Even the gunvessels built after the war seem to have been badly constructed in some cases, for a report from the C.-in-C.

in the Mediterranean complained of dry-rot in the two-year-old *Coquette;* by 1867 twenty-two of the forty-five gunvessels launched between 1854 and 1861 had been broken up.[3]

These early gunvessels were some of the first steam warships built in large numbers, and it is fair to assume that rapid deterioration of their engines probably helped to make the ships obsolete in the short space of six years. One reason was the excessive wear in small reciprocating steam engines revolving at speeds up to 250 r.p.m. without adequate lubrication. Later, when lower boiler pressures became more fashionable, these same engines functioned with much less trouble, but in 1856 a gunboat's boilers were expected to withstand pressures approaching 42 lb. per square inch,[4] while the inertia of a huge two-bladed screw opposed the frantic efforts of a tiny two-cylinder engine. Reports on a ship's machinery frequently described the boilers as 'expected to last for two years' even when the ship was new.

The first gunvessels, the six *Arrows*,[5] all had brief careers. *Beagle* and *Snake* were sent to China, where the latter distinguished herself by capturing fourteen pirate junks. *Viper* and *Lynx* were employed in the suppression of slavery during 1859 and 1860, *Viper* being on the west coast of Africa and *Lynx* on the east coast. Under Commander William Hewett *Viper* made a number of captures, and Hewett is said to have left West Africa a rich man.

By the middle of the 1860s the Admiralty was faced with an important problem, the outcome of which had a strong influence on the development of the gunboat. Not only were these useful little craft wearing out, but they were also in danger of being outmoded by rapid advances in warship design. The Admiralty had found so many uses for gunboats and gunvessels that some form of replacement had to be built urgently. But the naval architects of 1865 could not meet this requirement simply by designing a sturdier and more reliable copy of the gunboat of 1855, for the armament-manufacturers had produced formidable new guns which were far too heavy for the old wooden hulls.

When the Crimean War ended the standard guns were still the old 32-pounder and 68-pounder smooth-bores. The 32-pounder was basically the same weapon which had decided all the great naval battles of the eighteenth century, with certain improvements added, such as a flintlock firing-device, a rudimentary sight and a slide-carriage. All branches of military science benefited from the lessons of the Crimean War, but the revolution which followed is most easily traced in naval gunnery. The notorious Lancaster gun mounted in the *Arrows* was just one of the attempts to give a projectile greater range and accuracy. Whitworth, Blakeney, Haddan, Scott and others all put forward new ideas for rifling and gun-construction, none of which could be ignored. Even the

venerable smooth-bore gun grew bigger, and by 1857 the *Algerine* class were armed with a 10-inch muzzle-loader capable of firing an 84-pound shell.

'When in doubt, form a committee' is a time-honoured saying of government departments, and in due course a Committee on Rifled Cannon was formed to consider the rival claims. As a result of its findings 1860 saw the introduction of the Armstrong breech-loader to the Fleet. But the new gun's performance was disappointing. Not only did the breech-block tend to blow out, but tests showed that the shells were unable to pierce armour at any reasonable range. In fact, to the mortification of all the advocates of Armstrong guns the smooth-bore 68-pounder could fire steel shot through plates which defeated the 110-pounder Armstrong![6]

While the Admiralty hesitantly spent £2,500,000 on Armstrong breech-loading guns proof-testing continued to demonstrate the new guns' uselessness, but a far more decisive test was soon to settle the fate of the new weapon. Vice-Admiral Kuper's report after Kagoshima (see Ch. 5) revealed so many dangerous accidents that the bigger Armstrongs were withdrawn from service immediately. At the height of a revolution in naval architecture the Royal Navy found its latest guns defective. The truth was unpalatable to all the advocates of the new gun; the Armstrong system was dangerous and the weapon was badly constructed. By this time Woolwich Arsenal had earned the unenviable reputation of being a 'reliquary of the rifled wrecks and derelicts of the past years, with hundreds of guns awaiting repair'.[7] Even the guns passed for issue to ships had flaws, and it had become the practice to issue a gun with a list of the flaws in the bore. Not enough was known about metallurgy at this stage to blend strength with lightness in gun-construction, although Armstrong's system of *building* guns from tubes of iron shrunk on one another, as opposed to casting them, was a great advance, and remained the basis of British gun-construction until 1930.

In 1865 the superintendent of the Royal Gun Factories took the only way out. A new type of muzzle-loader was issued for testing, and the Armstrong guns were withdrawn from service. This step is often derided by naval historians as the triumph of the reactionaries at the Admiralty over the forces of progress, but this is hardly fair comment, for the Royal Navy's ordnance experts were faced with the appalling prospect of a navy without guns if they persevered with their experiments. In a word, the Navy needed guns which worked properly, and needed them quickly.

The new muzzle-loading gun promised to be a good compromise. It was built up in the same way as the Armstrong gun had been, and was rifled. But in place of the treacherous breech mechanism of the earlier guns the rifled muzzle-loader had shallow rifling which fitted soft studs around the base of the shell. The new gun was bound to find favour with the Admiralty for it was cheaper to manufacture and simpler to operate. In only one respect did it prove unreliable; the rifling often made the shell 'wobble' in flight, making accurate shooting almost impossible. But the Navy did not expect to engage its enemies at distances beyond 3,000 yards, and the M.L.R. (Muzzle-Loading, Rifled) gun remained in frontline service for fifteen years. The smaller Armstrong guns were retained for boat work, for saluting and as secondary armament in small ships.

The need for special warships to navigate Chinese rivers led the Chief Constructor of the Navy to design a new generation of gunvessels to replace the ageing Crimean gunboats. The disaster at the Peiho in 1859 showed that a heavier armament was essential, but the maximum draught had to be restricted to ten-and-a-half feet. Machinery requirements complicated the design, for the normal arrangements were not suitable. Hitherto a single-shaft installation driving a single large-bladed screw had sufficed for all warships, but if this had been used in the new gunvessels part of the screw would always be clear of the water.[8] The conflicting requirements were met in a series of unusual warships built between 1867 and 1872.

The first problem to be overcome was the weight of the armament. Wooden ships tend to lack longitudinal strength, so the new ships were built with unusually thick main keels and futtock timbers. Like all wooden ships of the period the *Plover* class incorporated a certain amount of iron for structural strength, the cross-beams being made of girder-iron. As completed they were all armed with a single 7-inch, 6½-ton gun amidships and two 64-cwt 64-pounders forward and aft. These guns were all rifled muzzle-loaders carried on the centre-line,

and gave these gunvessels an armament on a par with sloops of the Crimean period.

For the reasons already mentioned the designers were forced to discard the normal single-screw machinery because of the abnormally shallow draught called for. With many misgivings it was decided to give the *Plovers* two smaller sets of engines and twin screws. Twin-screw propulsion is so commonplace in warships today that it is hard to understand why it was so badly received in 1867. Nobody regarded it as a bold innovation but rather as a retrograde step justified only by the peculiarities of the ships' design. Unfortunately the designers committed the same mistake as they had with the Crimean gunboats in not giving them non-hoisting screws,[9] thus condemning them to sluggish steering under sail.[10]

At the same time as the *Plovers* were under construction the Admiralty placed orders for eighteen more gunvessels with heavier armament and even lighter draught. When the design was drawn up the Armstrong gun crisis was in full swing, so it was decided to give them two of the well-tried and popular 68-pounder smooth-bore guns. But when a satisfactory muzzle-loader appeared they were given a 7-inch gun, a 64-pounder and two small 20-pounder Armstrong guns. On a designed draught of less than eight feet it was felt that a wooden hull could not provide sufficient strength, so the designers compromised with a frame of iron and a teak skin, known as composite construction. Iron construction would have been ideal, but in 1868 the Admiralty would never have sanctioned the construction of an unarmoured iron fighting ship.

The gunboat *Boxer*, a member of the *Beacon* class. *(R Perkins)*

One remarkable feature of these new ships was their machinery. Like the *Plover* class they were forced to adopt twin-screw machinery in the face of widespread criticism. But what made them unique was the fact that their machinery had been installed in a different type of ship thirteen years before. When the little Crimean gunboats began to fall apart in the early 1860s their machinery had in many cases hardly seen service. When the new gunvessels were under discussion the Chief Constructor was also pondering on the disposal of nearly fifty sets of single-screw machinery from the large number of 60 h.p. gunboats which had recently been broken up. The solution was to install two sets of 60 h.p. machinery in each gunvessel, giving a total horsepower of 120 (nominal). Considering the haste with which those engines had been built it is surprising to note that they were still in service in the 1880s. The secret was the provision of more efficient boilers, but it is nonetheless a classic example of naval thrift.

The new composite-built gunvessels were launched as the *Beacon* class, destined to become some of the best-known ships of the Gunboat Navy. Every British sailor on foreign service in the 1870s and 1880s could pick them out by their familiar rig, a single thin funnel and three rakish masts with three yards on the fore and main (common to all gunvessels of the period). They served on every foreign station, in some cases for nearly twenty years, before reducing to harbour service or going to the breakers, and stand out as one of the most successful classes of small ships of the period. The *Plovers* proved almost as successful, but were the last wooden gunvessels

The gunboat *Goshawk*, pictured here at Dover, was a member of the *Ariel* class, which followed the *Beacons*. *(Conway Maritime Press)*

H.M.S. *Dwarf*, a member of the *Beacon* class, at Portsmouth. She is fitted for service in the Persian Gulf, with a topgallant foresail, square mainsail and spanker boom. H.M.S. *Victory*, flagship Commander-in-Chief, Portsmouth, to left. *(Conway Maritime Press)*

The composite gunboat *Forester*, name ship of a further class of near sisters, shown here at Plymouth. *(Private collection)*

The composite gunboat *Foxhound*,
a member of the *Forester* class.
(Conway Maritime Press)

H.M.S. FOXHOUND

to be built; for twenty years after the building of the *Beacons* most of the small warships of the Royal Navy were composite-built, from corvettes down to gunboats. Composite construction has proved extremely durable due to its combination of strength and flexibility, and today (1966) there are at least four examples of composite-built warships still in existence.[11]

Composite construction spread to larger warships, and soon both sloops and corvettes were built on the new principle.[12] The sloop also suffered a loss of status about this time; formerly a warship type inferior only to the frigate, she retained her importance for a while when the Steam Era caught up with her. For some time steam sloops continued to be built, but when gunvessels and gunboats appeared in increasing numbers the sloop lost ground. She became a lightly armed warship, more closely related to the gunvessel. When a new generation of sloops, the *Fantome* class, appeared in 1869, they were built more on gunvessel lines than sloop lines; that is to say, they carried a smaller number of guns on centreline pivot mountings instead of the more usual broadside mountings. They soon joined the smaller ships on detached duties on foreign stations where they were unlikely to encounter any vessel more powerful than themselves. Their place was usurped by the steam corvette, a cruising ship somewhat less heavily armed than the frigate,[13] but likewise designed to support the line of battle.

A glance at the disposition of minor warships at the end of 1873[14] will show how quickly the composite-built ships had displaced the older wooden ships in commission:

CHINA			TOTALS
Gunvessels	*Avon*	(comp.)	11 composite
	Curlew	(wood)	3 wooden
	Dwarf	(comp.)	
	Elk	(comp.)	
	Growler	(comp.)	
	Hornet	(comp.)	
	Kestrel	(comp.)	
	Midge	(comp.)	
	Ringdove	(wood)	
	Teazer	(comp.)	
	Thistle	(comp.)	
Gunboats	*Mosquito*	(comp.)	
	Opossum	(wood)	
	Swinger	(comp.)	

CAPE OF GOOD HOPE AND W. AFRICA			
Gunvessel	*Bittern*	(wood)	3 composite
Gunboats	*Coquette*	(comp.)	1 wooden
	Decoy	(comp.)	
	Merlin	(comp.)	

NORTH AMERICA AND W. INDIES			
Gunvessels	*Swallow*	(wood)	1 composite
	Woodlark	(wood)	5 wooden
Gunboats	*Zephyr*	(comp.)	2 armoured
	Minstrel	(wood)	
	Albacore	(wood)	
	Cherub	(wood)	
	Viper	(armoured)	
	Vixen	(armoured)	

S.E. COAST OF AMERICA			
Gunvessels	*Cracker*	(comp.)	2 composite
	Dart	(wood)	1 wooden
	Ready	(comp.)	

ZANZIBAR			
Gunvessel	*Nassau*	(wood)	1 wooden
(survey ship)			

PACIFIC			
Gunvessels	*Boxer*	(comp.)	1 composite
	Myrmidon	(wood)	1 wooden

MEDITERRANEAN			
Gunvessel	*Hart*	(comp.)	2 composite
Gunboats	*Cockatrice*	(wood)	4 wooden
	Pigeon	(wood)	
	Wizard	(wood)	
	Pheasant	(wood)	
	Ariel	(comp.)	

EAST INDIES			
Gunvessels	*Magpie*	(wood)	1 composite
	Nimble	(wood)	4 wooden
	Philomel	(wood)	
	Rifleman	(comp.)	
	Vulture	(wood)	

After five years composite-built gunboats and gunvessels made up nearly half the vessels on foreign stations. Furthermore, half the remaining wooden craft belonged to the new *Plover* class, so the Admiralty could claim that the ships on foreign stations were relatively modern, despite the fact that Childers, the First Lord, had ordered some of the *Beacons* and *Plovers* to be kept in reserve to keep expenses down.

The gunboat also had its place in this evolution from wood to wood and iron, although the attention paid to the sloop and the gunvessel put their small sister somewhat in the shade. A year after the completion of the last *Beacons* the first of nine new composite gunboats was laid down. The *Ariel* class were different in conception from the gunvessels, and quite unlike any of the old wooden gunboats. The emphasis was on seakeeping qualities rather than on river navigation, for on slightly reduced length and beam *Ariel* drew over ten feet. Her

Above: The *Forester* class gunboat H.M.S. *Firefly*. *(Private collection)*
Below: H.M.S. *Watchful* of the *Albacore* class. *(Private collection)*

H.M.S. *Raven*, a unit of the *Banterer* class. *(Craig Leaske)*

H.M.S. *Redwing*, another of the *Banterer* class. *(Private collection)*

The 'flat-iron' gunboat *Staunch*, built at Elswick, Newcastle-upon-Tyne. *(Private collection)*

A model of H.M.S. *Arrow*, showing the arrangement of the armament on jacks in a well forward. The bow was shaped thus to enable the vessels to be towed at twice their own speed – an early success for William Froude's ship model testing. *(Private collection)*

H.M.S. *Weazel*, one of the *Ant* class 'flat-iron' gunboats. *(Private collection)* rig was similar to the old *Britomart's*, but she was armed with two 64-pounders (M.L.R.) on the centreline and 20-pounder Armstrongs as bow- and stern-chasers. Being composite-built the new gunboats were the first to have watertight doors, a luxury unknown to wooden ships.

The *Ariels* proved so successful in service that within three years they were followed by another dozen near-sisters of the *Forester* class. Ten years later, when the time came to order replacements for obsolete gun-vessels, the *Banterer* class were almost carbon-copies of the *Foresters*. The importance of these new ships in the development of the Gunboat Navy lies in their superior seakeeping qualities. The very fact that gunboats were being built to sail the oceans marked the Navy's deeply-rooted faith in the 'Blue Water' philosophy, as opposed to the 'Fortress England' concept. After the Crimean War the uncertainty of future developments gave the 'Fortress Englanders' a better hearing than they had enjoyed in the 1840s, but their influence waxed and waned. In the 1870s their voices commanded respect, and some thirty small iron gunboats were built, purely for coastal defence.

The coastal defence gunboat had its supporters, as the following description shows:

... of the new gunboats we have thirty-five, grouped in two classes. One sea-going, rigged, tiny model men-of-war, the *Ariel* or *Goshawk* class, with twin-screws [they were in fact single-screw] and composite hulls, number-ing nine in all, but likely, if we mistake not, to be multiplied. The other, the well-known coast defence gunboats of the *Staunch* or *Plucky* class, with small size, fair speed, iron hulls, no masts, carrying one heavy 12-ton, or 18-ton gun, and forming a locomotive floating gun carriage. There is but one opinion as to the usefulness of this last class, which we owe to the ingenuity of Mr. Rendel of the Elswick Works (Sir W. Armstrong and Co.) and there is little fear of their going out of fashion, so that the gradual increase in their numbers in time of peace, or the provision of the means of rapidly producing them in time of war seems to be a wise policy...[15]

Short, tubby, and ludicrously slow, these 'flat-iron' gunboats were the antithesis of an Imperial navy. None of them served a full commission abroad, and even under ideal conditions their fighting value was small.

The 'flat-iron' gunboat *Mastiff*. (*Private collection*)

Bouncer (below) appears to be identical to *Weazel*, but was in fact built some eight years later to a modified, slightly longer design. (*Craig Leaske*)

Drudge (above) was a slightly larger 'flat-iron' gunboat completed in 1887 and built specifically for testing guns and mountings. She served in this capacity attached to H.M.S. *Excellent*, the gunnery school at Portsmouth, and later as a floating workshop for H.M.S. *Dryad*, until sold in 1920. *(Private collection)*

Kite (below), one of the orginal 'flat-irons', was one of a number to go on to serve as a gunnery tender (as shown). She too was sold in 1920. *(Private collection)*

The *Medina* class were larger 'flat-iron' gunboats which carried a barquentine rig as well as a heavier armament. Clearly intended for overseas service, the design nevertheless still included the requirement for them to be towed into action. *Medina* herself and a sister ship are shown above, while below is *Medway*, off Fort Blockhouse, Portsmouth, in 1897. *(Private collection)*

The composite gunvessel *Arab*.
(Private collection)

However, as they were stoutly built they lasted an amazing length of time (one, H.M.S. *Cuckoo*, was still at Devonport in the 1950s), and ended their days as gunnery tenders. But fortunately their non-existent virtues condemned them to a subsidiary role from the start, and they were never repeated. To have produced them in large numbers would have turned the clock back twenty years to the Crimean era, and not even the hoariest traditionalists at the Admiralty were prepared to do that. The future lay clearly with the second generation of gunboats, and in many ways that generation formed the backbone of the mid-Victorian Fleet.

H.M.S. *Dragon*, a composite
sloop of the *Osprey* class,
pictured in Plymouth Sound.
(Conway Maritime Press)

H.M.S. *Redwing*, a *Banterer* class composite gunboat. *(Private collection)*

Between 1873 and 1883 twenty-three armoured ships were completed for the Royal Navy, of which only four formed a class by themselves. In the same period the Navy was strengthened by twenty sloops, including six *Fantomes* and fourteen *Ospreys;* thirty-three gunvessels, including twenty-two *Beacons* and *Frolics*, two *Arabs*, four *Condors*, two *Linnets* and three *Algerines;* thirty-two gunboats, including nine *Ariels*, twelve *Foresters* and eleven *Banterers*.[16] Given a corresponding continuity in corvette-building the distant squadrons were amply catered for, and the Gunboat Navy stood at its short-lived apogee.

Another *Osprey* class composite sloop, H.M.S. *Gannet*, pictured in 1888. *(Craig Leaske)*

Chapter 8

MALAYSIAN CONFRONTATIONS

Nearly two hundred years after the Sultan of Kedah ceded Penang to the Crown Great Britain remains active in South-East Asia. Even after so much of her colonial empire has vanished she finds herself drawn into Malaya's affairs, and the age of gunboat diplomacy seems very close when one reads of R.N. ships intercepting Indonesian guerrillas.

The Napoleonic Wars gave the British their foothold in the Straits of Malacca, when they occupied all the Dutch possessions. These possessions were handed back under the London Convention of 1814, but Singapore was acquired in 1819 to safeguard the route to China. Although the new possession had great strategic value, it was developed to facilitate trade in the Malay Archipelago, and to bypass discriminatory tariffs charged by the Dutch in Java.

Singapore soon achieved great prosperity as an entre-pôt and staging post for the China trade, since the fast opium clippers called there to refit and provision after the long voyage out from England. Disputes with the Dutch were settled in 1824, when both parties agreed to refrain from establishing settlements in one another's 'spheres of influence', which had the effect of reducing Dutch competition in the Malay Peninsula. After the end of the East India Company's monopoly, control of the Straits Settlements passed to the India Office, and finally to the Colonial Office in 1867. During this time the policy towards Malaya remained unaltered; the Administration was not to become embroiled in the quarrels of Malaya's petty princes.

The appointment of Sir Harry Ord[1] as the first Colonial Governor of the Straits Settlements in 1867 marked a new stage in Britain's attitude to Malayan affairs. In place of the detailed and consistent policy of the India Office, an informal paternalism, the Colonial Office substituted a complete lack of policy.[2] Ord's attempts to define a new policy were therefore made on his own initiative, but his decisions were made without reference to people able to give information and advice. The new Governor was not popular, but he shared with most of the colony's officials the view that he should use all his authority to increase trade and exert a moderating influence on Malayan politics. Turbulence and anarchy hindered trade in most of the native states, and was to prove too great a temptation to Sir Harry. Within a year he ordered the Lieutenant-Governor of Penang to open negotiations with the chiefs of Perak, ostensibly to revise a forty-year-old treaty whereby the island of Pangkor had been ceded to the East India Company. Ord's apparent intention was to reaffirm the British claim, for the island had never been occupied, nor had the treaty been ratified. But the Perak chiefs saw this as a prelude to annexation of their territory and refused to continue the negotiations.[3] Significantly, this and other moves were not reported by Ord to the Colonial Office, and did not come to light until 1869.[4]

Malaya in 1867 was a collection of states without common allegiance of any kind. In the north some states were still nominal vassals of the King of Siam, whereas most of the southern states were under a vague sort of British protection arising out of various treaties between the sultans and the East India Company binding them not to enter into pacts with foreign Powers. The growth of tin-mining on the western coast helped to build up trade, but the internal feuds of the Chinese tin-miners contributed to political instability and made the country unattractive to investors. Outside Kedah and Johore there was perpetual strife between the traders and miners using the rivers (the only usable routes in the country) and local chiefs who exacted irksome tolls. The Sultan or Raja who was fortunate enough to be established at the mouth of a river levied dues on all who used the river, and occasionally fought with a neighbour for possession. Every contending chief and minor brigand had his stockade on the river to enable him to control his section. After 1845 the British Government's dealings with many states were confined to having the stockades dismantled to clear the rivers for trade.[5] These moves had no effect, and strongly defended stockades became part of the unending warfare among the Malays.

The two large states of Perak and Selangor were to prove particularly troublesome to the British, for here all the problems of Malaya were accentuated. Disputes over the succession led to quarrels between the factions supporting the claimants to the throne of Perak, while an unusually large number of Chinese entered the country to work the tin-mines. A characteristic of the Chinese was their habit of organising themselves into secret societies, which had tremendous influence among the immigrant miners (most immigrants were forced to join one society or another). Feuds between the societies were common, and ultimately the Chinese became involved with the native Malays. In 1867, shortly before Sir Harry Ord arrived in Singapore, a feud between two powerful societies and their Malayan allies erupted into a ten-day riot in Penang, during which the island lapsed into anarchy.

Faced with this unpromising state of affairs Ord wrote to the Secretary of State for the Colonies to suggest that 'it would be greatly to the advantage of the Settlements if our influence could ... be extended over the Peninsula', adding that he would not fail to use any opening which presented itself.[6] Without waiting for a reply to this forthright declaration Ord went ahead with negotiations with Siam to divide Malaya into British and Siamese 'spheres of influence', a realistic assessment of the problem, but too premature for Whitehall. Ord could see that more would be achieved by admitting that Siam had a real responsibility for Kelantan, Trengganu and Kedah, instead of the nominal suzerainty which the Foreign Office desired.[7] The Siamese had shown their willingness to look after British interests, which was an advantage in view of the continuing difficulties in the northern states.

The Colonial Office cracked down on Sir Harry's empire-building in a dispatch which epitomised the spirit of liberal imperialism:

> ...H.M.G. are not disposed to adopt the duty directly or indirectly, of taking steps for the security of life and property in countries where that security cannot be given by the lawful Rulers, and cannot give countenance to the trend of policy which you appear by the last sentence of your dispatch to contemplate. It is clearly of opinion that the true policy of the British Government of the Straits Settlements is not to attempt to control but to keep clear of native disorder.[8]

Unfortunately the time was ripe, if ever it was justified, for a more aggressive policy in Malaya. The Colonial

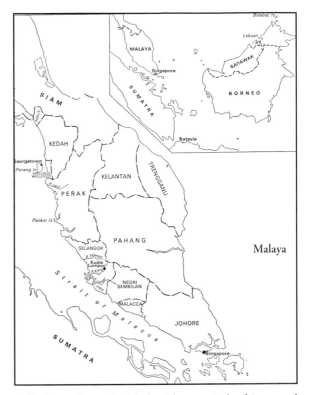

Malaya

Office's caution coincided with a period of increased lawlessness in Malaya, and the men on the spot, by now thoroughly subdued, could take no effective steps to deal with it. By 1871 a civil war was raging in Selangor, Perak had three claimants to the throne of the dead Sultan, and two societies of Chinese miners were fighting for possession of the tin-mines in Larut. The steady deterioration of the situation on the mainland was bitterly resented by officials at Singapore, who felt helpless to act, but soon a headstrong subordinate precipitated the 'Selangor Incident'.

Sir Harry Ord took his rebuke from the Colonial Office seriously, and between 1868 and 1871 there was no further attempt to extend British influence. But when he left Singapore on sick leave in March 1871 his place was taken by Colonel Anson, a man of ambition who cherished a hearty dislike for his superior. Within three months Anson was presented with a chance to act independently, when a British-registered junk was attacked by pirates between Penang and Singapore. The government steamer *Pluto* found the vessel later, lying in the Selangor estuary with her crew and cargo missing.

The police detachment embarked in *Pluto* found much of the plundered cargo in Chinese shops on shore, but when they tried to round up suspects they were attacked by followers of Raja Mahdi, a contender for the throne of Selangor. The police were lucky to escape without loss, and returned to Penang with the junk in tow. Anson immediately called on the Navy for help, and the sloop *Rinaldo* was sent to Selangor with *Pluto* in an attempt to overawe Raja Mahdi and persuade him to

H.M.S. *Leven. (Private collection)*

hand over the pirates. Early on the morning of 3 July 1871 *Pluto* began to feel her way into the estuary and made her way upriver to a point where she could land boat-parties.[9]

The men left on board became anxious when they heard firing from the shore and saw their comrades retreating to the boats. Some men were wounded, but as soon as the boats returned to *Pluto* she was able to steam out of range. The senior naval officer, Commander Robinson, decided that the situation warranted firmer action and returned to his ship *Rinaldo*, which was still anchored off the mouth of the river. Robinson sent the little steamer back to Penang to land the wounded and fetch reinforcements, confident that his sloop's guns could inflict the first reprisals in what promised to be a typical punitive expedition.

Next morning she crept into find that Raja Madhi's supporters had not lost their self-confidence. Soon *Rinaldo* was being straddled by splashes as guns on shore found her range. Five minutes of this galling fire from about 400 yards caused remarkably few casualties; three men were wounded and her hull and rigging were hit several times. But she steamed on so as to take the batteries from the rear, making it an easy matter to drive the Malay gunners from their positions. After a brisk bombardment the town began to blaze, although the inhabitants had long since taken to the jungle.

Colonel Anson followed up this hollow triumph by putting pressure on the Sultan of Selangor to appoint a Viceroy approved by the British Government. The Lieutenant-Governor's deputy made good use of one of

the new composite gunvessels, H.M.S. *Teazer*, which had replaced *Rinaldo*. For work in shallow rivers *Teazer* was far better than the clumsy sloop, and she had no difficulty in ascending first the Selangor River and then the Klang to 'show the flag' and reinforce Anson's demands. Finally *Teazer* and *Pluto* dropped anchor off the mouth of the Jugra River within sight of the Sultan's palace. The haste with which the Sultan met all the British demands can be explained by the fact that he could see *Teazer* lying only 600 yards away with her guns trained on his palace.

Teazer was left to watch the Selangor coast after the government forces were withdrawn, and soon reaped the first rewards of Anson's gunboat diplomacy. The Sultan's Viceroy, Tunku dia U'd-din, had been the man Anson wished to see confirmed in authority in Selangor, for he seemed to favour more responsible government, and co-operated with the British. Since the 'Rinaldo' Affair' had increased British prestige Commander Bloomfield of the *Teazer* decided to trade on it. He borrowed fifty of the Tunku's sepoys and attacked a stockade belonging to Raja Mahdi. Bloomfield seems to have taken the bit between his teeth by making proclamations to the effect that the British Government was supporting Tunku dia U'd-din, as he felt that this would lead to less trouble in the future.[10]

As we have seen, the Admiralty was never willing to allow junior officers to indulge in statecraft, and Bloomfield was forbidden by Sir Henry Kellett[11] to engage in any further operations, in accordance with his Standing Instructions. But as trade between the native states and Penang and Malacca increased, so were British warships called on to intervene in more cases over the years. However much the Admiralty might set its face against the use of its warships to further unofficial policies, it had a perennial commitment to suppress piracy in the Straits of Malacca. Inevitably the measures taken to suppress piracy helped to promote commercial interests to some extent.

The nature of the Malay Archipelago favoured piracy in the middle of the nineteenth century, with so much trade centred on the rivers and no strong central government to police the coast. Like the fishermen around Hong Kong, the inhabitants of the west coast of the Malay Peninsula had been accustomed to living by plunder for centuries; such piracy as existed was more an alternative form of subsistence than organised banditry.[12] In short, it was the product of a disordered social system rather than any innate wickedness in the Malay character. Nevertheless, such endemic lawlessness was never condoned by European traders, and naval officers had orders to exterminate piracy wherever it showed itself. Pirate-hunting in Malayan waters had been a favourite occupation of such redoubtable warriors as Henry Keppel, who later distinguished himself at Canton.

It is no coincidence that the naval contribution towards British intervention in Malaya relied so heavily on the gunvessel. Gunvessels found particular favour as they had enough speed to catch the big native prahus. As early as 1862 *Renard* was ordered to cruise off north-west Borneo when native marauders grew bold enough to attack an English brig.[13] In the same year Commander

Reilly of H.M.S. *Pioneer* was sent to Batavia to consult with the Dutch on a joint plan to police the area. Finally in March 1863 a formidable force gathered off Sarawak, including the sloops *Scout* and *Barrosa*, the gunboats *Bustard*, *Haughty*, *Leven* and *Janus*, and two Straits Settlement steamers. The squadron achieved little for it was, in the words of Raja Brooke, a herd of elephants searching for mosquitoes,[14] and the mosquitoes wisely chose to stay away. Once the squadron was disbanded it was almost certain that piracy would occur again. For a while Labuan was free of it, but only because the gunboat *Banterer* was stationed there. In time she returned to refit at Singapore, and *Leven* was ordered to replace her; then *Leven* developed engine-trouble, followed by an outbreak of cholera on board, and with the tiny coaling station unprotected pirates were able to swoop down on boats only thirty miles away.[15]

To counter this upsurge in piracy the C.-in-C. could only spare a sloop, a gunvessel, a gunboat and one or two auxiliaries, whereas the consul at Sarawak thought that at least three or four gunboats were needed.[16] The wretched performance of *Banterer* and *Leven* made them unsuitable for this job, so some more efficient type of vessel was needed if the area was to be properly patrolled.

Gunboats were in demand during the next three years, for H.M.S. *Forester* arrived in Brunei to investigate reports of an American filibuster, but withdrew as soon as the crisis was past. Despite appeals from local consuls the Admiralty was unwilling to allow gunboats to remain in the area, and was always suspicious of calls for naval assistance. When Governor Pope Hennessy of Labuan

H.M.S. *Gnat*, a member of the *Beacon* class, the best known of all gunvessels; a rare photograph taken in 1868 before her loss off Borneo. *(Imperial War Museum)*

heard from H.M.S. *Weazel* that a pirate fleet was heading down the Borneo coast he went to sea in *Slaney* to look for it, but confided to the Colonial Office that he felt it was just an excuse to get a man-o'-war to visit Sarawak.[17] Individual consuls might complain that the Navy was neglecting them, but in fact a number of new gunvessels were made available. Unfortunately one of the first to reach the station was wrecked on Balabac Island, north of Borneo, in November 1868. She was H.M.S. *Gnat*, one of the latest composite-built *Beacons*, and on her first commission, but others followed, and the *Beacons* soon became a familiar sight on the East Indies Station. Their size made them well suited for the open-sea voyages entailed in patrolling the Archipelago, whereas the little wooden gunboats were poor sea-boats and had a small coal-supply.

The lighter-armed *Plover* class gunvessels were also sent to the East Indies, where they proved as versatile as the *Beacons*. One improvement suggested itself after the first vessels had served their first commissions: six of the class were altered by the addition of a poop, topgallant forecastle[18] and flying deck.[19] The effect of these alterations was to give better-ventilated cabins for officers and upper-deck hammock-space for the ratings. As wooden vessels were ventilated by small plug scuttles which had to be closed most of the time the ships were at sea, conditions below soon became unbearable in hot climates. In the stifling heat of the tropics ratings were allowed to sleep on deck whenever possible to get away from the crowded messdecks below, but people sleeping on deck were liable to sudden drenching from rainstorms. The addition of a poop and topgallant forecastle provided space for airy cabins, while an awning rigged from the flying deck gave the ratings a cool and dry place to sling their hammocks. Seven *Beacons* were also taken in hand, but as they were smaller the designers could only add a poop.

After *Teazer* was withdrawn from the coast of Selangor in 1871 Tunku dia U'd-din's influence waned perceptibly. His enemies were sure that the British had tired of supporting him, and although the Viceroy could still persuade the Sultan to follow his advice he knew that his enemies were growing impatient. On the other hand the 'Rinaldo' Affair' persuaded many Chinese miners that Selangor was now peaceful, and trade expanded rapidly. Investors in Singapore, and in their wake the shareholders in London, felt that law and order would make Selangor a profitable field for investment.[20]

Sir Harry Ord returned to Singapore in 1872 to find the colonists pressing for British naval and military intervention in Selangor. The virtue of such a course was that the Singapore merchants would make a profit while the British taxpayer footed the bill for the Crown forces engaged on the expedition. Plans like this were often put forward by colonial officials but were invariably unpopular with the Colonial Office and the Treasury. Ord had

heard from Lord Kimberley, Secretary of State for the Colonies, that the Government would not support any takeover in Selangor, and he acted on this as soon as he returned to duty. But once again events conspired to make it hard for Ord to keep out of Malayan politics, for the balance of power in Selangor was suddenly upset.

Tunku dia U'd-din's 'foreign legion' of European officers and Asian sepoys tried to fight its way out of Kuala Lumpur, but was totally annihilated by the Tunku's enemies. The loss of over a hundred men was a crippling blow, but the capture of all their arms in addition dismayed those who supported the Tunku. His mercenaries had been clothed and armed by merchants in Singapore, who now saw their debtor on the verge of bankruptcy. But the Tunku was not finished, for his allies in Pahang came to his aid. By March 1873 the Viceroy regained virtual control of all Selangor, and was able to grant a concession to the Selangor Tin Mining Company, a group representing the interests of English investors.

While Selangor progressed towards stable if undemocratic rule the neighbouring state of Perak continued to enjoy sporadic violence. The dispute over the successor to the dead Sultan had thrown up one strong man, the Mantri of Perak, who ruled the rich tin-mining district of Larut. The Mantri thus controlled the revenues of the richest part of the state, and hoped, not to succeed the weak Raja Ismail, but to ensure that the new Sultan would continue to permit the Mantri to retain his independence. With money and the support of some of the Chinese secret societies the Mantri had every hope of securing the succession for his candidate, although his Chinese allies fought among themselves and changed sides frequently.

In August 1872 the Lieutenant-Governor of Penang was warned that a Chinese expedition was being equipped under his nose for an invasion of Larut. The authorities in Penang were quite accustomed to exporting firearms to Larut, but the prospect of civil war spreading to Penang was alarming. Nevertheless the expedition sailed before the police could discover any grounds for arresting the merchants responsible for supplying the arms. Then came the news that fighting had broken out in Larut, which made action imperative.

Fortunately the survey ship *Nassau*[21] was in port, and her commander was asked to delay his departure in case his ship was needed.[22] On 17 October *Nassau* accompanied the steamer *Fair Penang* with a party of police for Larut. In the Larut River they found three junks and inspected them. In each case the answer was the same; the junks were armed for self-protection, and were on peaceful trading missions. The police had to withdraw, although they did obtain the release of two Chinese prisoners. Their failure to stop the departure of the armed expedition from Penang now looked worse than ever, for the reports made it clear that fighting was widespread.

The government in Singapore was not inclined to

intervene until it received a sharp reminder that the prospect of the war spreading beyond Perak was real. First came a relatively innocuous riot in Singapore, which posed the question: what would happen if the secret societies began fighting in Singapore itself? The answer came quickly when two rival Chinese factions clashed in December 1872. The Singapore police dealt with the trouble with difficulty, only to face a dockland brawl between Macao shipwrights and coal-heavers from Fukien. But Sir Harry Ord used no excuse to stop the war in Larut until he learned of an attack on a British ship in the Larut River. The captain of the S.S. *Fair Malacca* reported at Penang that he had been fired on by eleven junks on 12 December 1872. The Acting Harbour Master verified his story and counted over thirty shot-holes in the steamer's sides.

At first sight this seemed a straightforward case of piracy, but the authorities at Penang hesitated before they called for naval intervention for the ship had been trading with the Chinese in Larut, and had merely fallen foul of the opposing faction. As traders in a foreign country the ship's owners had no claim to the protection of the British flag. The matter was referred by the commander of the sloop *Zebra* to the Solicitor-General, who declared that no piracy had occurred. Still, Sir Harry Ord felt that there ought to be some enquiry into the incident, and ordered *Zebra* to detain the junks concerned.

Zebra was too big to enter the river, so her commander asked for the gunvessel *Hornet* to be sent up to him. With boats from his own ship in tow *Hornet* went five miles upriver until eleven junks were sighted. Two were identified and towed out without difficulty, but once again the government showed it was unwilling to risk a reprimand from Whitehall by taking any decisive action. The only result was that the export of arms from Penang was prohibited, H.M.S. *Hornet* remaining in the area to enforce the ban.

Naval officers were not subject to the Colonial Office and the Senior Naval Officer, Malacca Straits, never had any doubt that the situation in Perak was serious, and sent the corvette *Thalia* and another gunvessel, *Midge*, to patrol the coastline. During the first six months of 1873 the two ships swept the area clear of suspicious junks and prahus. Few were captured but the big junks were forced to leave, while most of the war-boats and prahus were hidden up small creeks. Ashore all seemed quiet as the Mantri was at last installed as the independent ruler of Larut with the blessing of Sir Harry Ord. The ban on arms had been modified; they could now be sold, but only to the Mantri. The presence of Captain Speedy and his Sikhs from Penang, and the warships seemed to have eliminated all opposition to the Mantri, but it would not be long before the Sikhs were attacked or the White Ensign was fired on. The same dubious neutrality had drawn British ships into open conflict with the Taeping rebels in China.

On 16 September 1873 Commander Grant of the *Midge* took his gig up the Larut River, accompanied by a small schooner manned by the Mantri's men. Grant meant to seize all boats carrying supplies without the Mantri's permission, but it could hardly fail to provoke some opposition; perhaps the Navy hoped for a *casus belli*, or it may have been a move ordered by Colonel Anson in Penang.

As the tiny boat and the schooner approached a stockade the sailors saw two large twenty-oared boats pulling swiftly out of a creek. Grant ordered his gig to move upriver so as to drive the Malays out to sea, but his plan was frustrated when the schooner's helmsman dashed below in fright, allowing the ship to drift on to a mudbank. Grant's sailors and marines (only fourteen in all) kept the Malays at a distance with rifle-fire and a rocket or two while he tried to get the schooner off the mudbank. The guns in the stockade kept up a dangerous fire on the boats but only two men were hit. The tiny force got away without further loss and had to withdraw to *Midge* to plot the next move.

As soon as the tides allowed the gunvessel to cross the bar she returned to destroy the stockade. Grant had arranged to join his senior officer in *Thalia* on 19 September, and the next day her boats joined *Midge*'s for the attack. The sailors had spent weeks rowing under scorching sun or drenching rain, and the prospect of action excited them. As *Midge* took up her firing position as close in as she dared the stockade opened fire. *Midge*'s 7-inch and 64-pounder thundered back, and as the first clouds of gunsmoke billowed across the water the boats rushed forward. Suffering only two casualties the sailors took the stockade by storm, but found that the defenders had retreated into the forest. Later a second stockade was found and destroyed, but the landing-party seems to have been content to spike the guns and burn three war junks found, for the nearby town of Matang was spared.

The Larut action was a Navy affair, undertaken to work off the frustration which all officers and men felt at the boring and fruitless operations they had been engaged on. But the latest outbreak of violence did mean that more warships were sent to cruise in Malayan waters, and within three months another gunvessel, *Avon*, was in action with pirates. She sighted three native craft just as they were attacked by six prahus and was in time to drive them off with a few rounds of gunfire.

Once again the arrival of a new Governor in Singapore seemed the signal for trouble. Ord's successor was Sir Andrew Clarke, another ex-Engineer but a colonial governor of much greater promise. Before Clarke left London he had been instructed by Lord Kimberley to report on the best course of action to 'put an end to the state of anarchy and disorder'.[23] A major point about these instructions was that Clarke was to report *before* taking action, but he nonetheless interpreted them as permission to act decisively. He assumed the governorship

H.M.S. *Avon. (NPC)*

on 4 November 1873 and found himself faced with the crisis in Larut. By January 1874 he had a workable solution; the most promising of the former contenders for the Sultan's throne was to be 'encouraged to invite British intervention' in Perak in return for various promises.

Sir Andrew Clarke's choice for the new Sultan was Abdullah, but as Ismail, the man who had succeeded in 1871, was still alive he had to be pensioned off. The Treaty of Pangkor settled the disputes among the Perak chiefs and appointed a British Resident, while redefining a number of vague borders. At the same time the Mantri was reduced to the position of a lesser chief ruling part of Perak. The warring factions of Chinese were referred to an arbitration commission, which took up its duties immediately to ensure that the miners went back to work promptly. All in all, it was an example of the benevolent imperialism that made Victorians proud of their civilising mission, and the merchants of Singapore and Penang were overjoyed.

The new Governor also dealt with the other trouble-spot, Selangor. He had provocation, for on 1 January 1874 pirates attacked a lighthouse. He also had ample strength, since an unusually large number of warships was concentrated at Singapore. Vice-Admiral Shadwell's squadron[24] had arrived from Bangkok so Clarke decided to call on the Navy for help, knowing that any action against piracy on the high seas was permitted by Admiralty Standing Orders. A month later six warships were blockading the Selangor coast, the corvette *Thalia*, *Rinaldo* and *Avon* off the Jugra River, and the battleship *Iron Duke* (flagship) and *Salamis*, *Midge* and *Frolic* off the Klang River.

Sir Andrew Clarke accompanied the warships and met the Sultan, 'a jolly, good-natured opium-eater',[25] who blamed his sons for the acts of piracy and dismissed it all as a prank. This attitude could hardly commend itself to any Victorian sailor or administrator, and although by now Clarke had gone a long way beyond his instructions from the Colonial Office he felt quite justified in threatening the Sultan with reprisals. If the Sultan did not aid Tunku dia U'd-din against the pirates, said Clarke, the Admiral would sweep him and the pirates off the face of the earth.[26] The unfortunate man had little choice, and agreed to destroy all his stockades and try all suspected pirates in the presence of British commissioners.

One may ask why, if the Colonial Office was so opposed to expansion, was Clarke allowed to pursue a policy which brought some of the richest provinces of Malaya under direct British influence. The proceedings of 1874 would seem to be contrary to the prevailing pattern of informal imperialism, but there were hidden factors compelling Lord Kimberley to acquiesce in Clarke's policy. Other European Powers were staking their claims in South-East Asia by 1874; a year before the Dutch made a strong bid to control northern Sumatra, followed by French expansion in Indo-China in 1874. Vague fears about these developments coupled with a desire to develop the country's resources were probably behind the Colonial Office's relatively mild acceptance of the empire-building which went on in 1874. Indeed, when the time came to appoint Clarke's successor the choice fell on a man of similar outlook and temperament.

Sir William Jervois was yet another Royal Engineer who sought higher honours in the colonial service. When he arrived in May 1875 he inherited problems which Clarke had only just begun to solve, although all was outwardly peaceful. Residents had been appointed in Perak, Selangor and Sungai Ujong (in this case only after a punitive expedition), and trade was uninterrupted. But trouble was brewing on a greater scale than ever before; the Sultan of Perak was squandering the taxes and quarrelling with the Resident, James Birch. Clarke's puppet Sultan proved so lamentable in office that Jervois was reluctantly forced to admit that British officials would have to rule Perak instead of merely advising the ruler. The present ruler would stay, but in his name British officers would control the revenue, the police and local government.

The Governor could see no other answer to his problem; no other ruler was suitable,[27] and outright annexation would not be permitted by London. In taking these steps Jervois was risking his position, and clearly exceeding his powers, but he was confident that he would have London's backing. But before his plan could be put into effect the inhabitants of Perak took matters into their own hands by murdering the unpopular Resident, Birch. This tragedy was due as much to Birch's lack of subtlety as to the chiefs' fear that he would deprive them of their income. Debt-slavery was an ancient Malayan institution which Birch had sworn to eradicate against the advice of Sir Andrew Clarke; his failure to heed this advice led the chiefs to hire an assassin, and gave the authorities in Singapore their chance to intervene. When it was learned

in Singapore that a detachment of police and sepoys had been defeated in a rash attack on Birch's former headquarters, armed intervention was insisted upon.

Two gunvessels, *Thistle* and *Fly*, were on hand to avenge the 'insult to the flag', so Jervois sent them up the Perak River with a handful of troops on 9 November 1875. They did no more than demonstrate that one minor reverse was not the eclipse of British power. Everyone knew that the defeat would be exaggerated unless strong action were taken, but demonstrations would suffice until reinforcements arrived from the China Station. Following an urgent request to Hong Kong the corvette *Modeste*, gunvessel *Ringdove* and sloop *Egeria* sailed for Singapore. This ability to concentrate naval forces at short notice was characteristic of the gunboat era, and by 18 November the reinforcements were in position blockading the Perak coast.

The coast was soon in a ferment as British forces moved into Perak in pursuit of the chiefs who had instigated Birch's murder. A joint military and naval force defeated the Malays in the area where Birch had been murdered, and burned a number of stockades. But the wanted chiefs withdrew to the upper reaches of the Perak River, where they seemed safe until the tireless sailors sought them out in ships' boats. The remainder of the so-called 'Perak War' subsided into guerrilla warfare until March 1876, when the fugitives surrendered on board H.M.S. *Ringdove*. A brief invasion of Sungai Ujong had been defeated by a force of Gurkhas and sailors from *Thistle* three months earlier, and unrest in Selangor had come to nothing. By the end of 1876 British influence extended along the western coast of Malaya from Perak to Malacca.

Beacon class composite gunvessel H.M.S. *Fly*. *(Private collection)*

Three years later the gunvessel *Kestrel* was called in by the Governor of Labuan to bombard a stronghold on the north-east coast of Borneo. Again the excuse was piracy, whereas the underlying reason was commerce; a British chartered company had acquired rights in the area, and *Kestrel*'s action made the company's tenure more certain. Nevertheless by destroying a nest of fifteen pirate-vessels she helped to rid the area of people who had been destroying the livelihood of scores of peaceful fishermen and traders. By the 1880s Malayan piracy was almost stamped out, and although occasional outbreaks continued, both in the East Indies and in Chinese waters, it was never the problem it had been ten years before.

The only other serious incident to merit the attention of gunboats in the East Indies was the Burma War of 1885. As we have seen the Foreign Office and Colonial Office had sanctioned the virtual annexation of part of Malaya ten years before to forestall foreign expansion. In 1885 the danger of the French intervening in the internal affairs of Burma became acute. The old techniques of informal influence had sufficed for thirty years,[28] but in 1885 the British Resident reported to the Indian Government that the King of Burma was 'forming alliances with European states which have no interests in Burmah'.[29]

French influence would not be tolerated in so important an area, and in October 1885 the Indian Government issued an ultimatum to the King: complete submission or war. As it was not considered that the Burmese would submit,[30] preparations began immediately. The Navy was asked to help the Army to reach Mandalay, over 200 miles from the sea. This was done by manning the Irrawaddy Flotilla Company's steamers and using them as troop-transports, whose monotonous 'chunking' was immortalised by Kipling. The campaign presented no great tactical problems, but without the Navy's help the difficulties of supply would have been acute.

When the war broke out the only vessel at Rangoon was the gunvessel *Woodlark*, whose commander began to arm three small river-craft with light weapons from his own ship. When an officer of senior rank arrived from Trincomalee he ordered Commander Clutterbuck of *Woodlark* to take his tiny flotilla upriver. Two more improvised gunboats were armed with 64-pounder muzzle-loaders from H.M.S. *Turquoise* and sent to join the others two weeks later, in time for the first advance.

The Burma War was as good as over within a month, for the king surrendered on 29 November 1885, but owing to the absence of cavalry the Army found it difficult to pacify the country. To add to the problem cholera broke out among the Indian troops, and the naval flotilla had to be dispersed to deal with dacoits on the Chindwin River. In December a small party from *Woodlark* and *Turquoise* ascended the Irrawaddy almost as far as the Chinese border, rounding up the ex-king's soldiers and sending them back to Mandalay. This sort of police work went on until 1887, but long before then the Navy contingents had been replaced by additional drafts of troops from India.

The old wooden gunvessels remained frequent visitors to the East Indies Station, although their composite sisters were still the most popular. A few gunboats were detached from Chinese waters for special service off Labuan and Borneo, but generally gunboats were not popular in the East Indies; gunvessels could do their job better. When the *Beacons* were paid off in the late 1880s their place was taken by composite sloops, and later by 3rd class cruisers built under the Naval Defence Act. By the time the gunboat came back into favour the focus of gunboat activities had shifted from the East Indies to Africa, reducing naval commitments in Malaya to showing the flag. In 1896 there were only three sloops left in the area, and by 1901, on the eve of the Fisher reforms, only two. Replacing the once numerous *Beacons* and *Plovers* were four or five steel cruisers, all vastly more expensive to build and to run but having the great virtue of being able to fight their French or Russian equivalents.

Chapter 9

PATHFINDERS OF EMPIRE

The Royal Navy's long and arduous campaign against the African slave trade must go on record as its most thankless task. With only token co-operation from other nations British men-of war had to linger in the fever-ridden Bight of Benin in the hope of intercepting slave-ships. Most slavers were too fast, while those which were caught often stank so abominably as to disgust the most hardened sailor. As an incentive the men of the Preventive Squadron were paid a bounty for each living slave found, the so-called 'head money'.

By the 1850s expert opinion was generally agreed that the soundest way of checking the slave trade was to patrol close inshore, thus preventing the slavers from picking up cargoes. This meant that sailors were much exposed to yellow fever, and the horrifying mortality rate on the West Coast of Africa Station made the Admiralty reluctant to sanction this method. It was therefore insinuated by critics of the Admiralty that its captains were only conscientious when there was plenty of 'head money' to be won. However, the Admiralty was in favour of anti-slavery patrols off the West African coast; it was only reluctant to lend its support to costly expeditions inland, which abolitionists always recommended as the only sure way to stamp out the trade completely. The other aspect of Admiralty policy which aroused criticism was the age and decrepitude of the ships selected for service with the Preventive Squadron: 'If there was a particularly slow-going old tub … she was sure to be sent to the coast of Africa.'[1]

In time the slave-merchants' influence declined, and by the 1850s, with ceaseless prodding from Palmerston, the Admiralty's efforts were showing results which helped to silence its critics. A report by a Select Committee of the House of Lords in July 1850[2] declared that withdrawal of the Preventive Squadron (which had been suggested in several quarters) would allow the slave trade to expand immediately. Any resurgence of this sort was unwelcome, for it would hamper the developing trade in palm oil, ground nuts and timber. Equally, Palmerston was insistent that this trade had to be fostered to show the local chiefs that it could bring them greater profits than trafficking in human beings. The report recommended the use of smaller vessels, controlled by more detailed instructions to commanders, but otherwise endorsed the Royal Navy's previous measures against slavery.

To mid-Victorian statesmen West Africa was hardly a promising field of commercial endeavour. There were three destitute colonies which played only a minor part in West African trade. Apart from slaves, the staple export of the region was palm oil, which was exported chiefly through the Niger Delta. Although the palm oil trade expanded steadily in the 1840s and 1850s it could never hope to provide enough revenue to finance development. At this time there were no settlements in the Niger Delta, and it was argued that British trade in West Africa could dispense with the impoverished colonies in Gambia, Sierra Leone and the Gold Coast. But trade was not all that interested the British in West Africa in the mid-fifties, and humanitarians were powerful enough to ensure that these colonies would never be abandoned while the slave trade still flourished.

Palm oil profits attracted the worst type of European trader to West Africa, frequently the very people who had formerly dealt in slaves. Their squabbles created new disorder on the coast, and captains of warships in the Preventive Squadron had to intervene frequently to settle disputes over prices and terms of sale. Finally in 1849 a British consul was appointed to supervise the trade of the Niger Delta in order to provide the Navy with better guidance in its dealings with local rulers and white traders. The success of the new consulate at Fernando Po

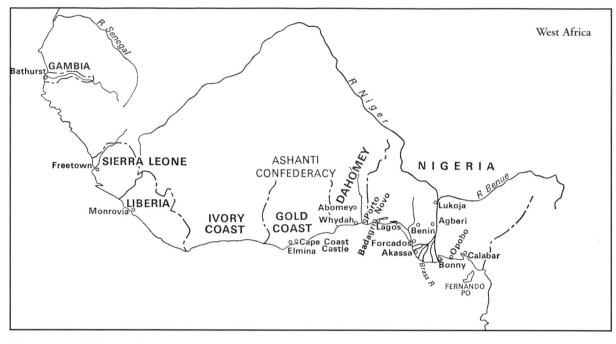

West Africa

led to the establishment of another at Lagos in 1852, as this town was a growing centre of trade with the interior.

The appointment of these and other consuls led to the Navy becoming more closely associated with British policy and forced the Admiralty to make certain dispositions to conform to Foreign Office requirements. In 1857, after a number of overtures to the powerful kingdom of Dahomey had failed, the Foreign Office claimed that if the Admiralty had provided shallow-draught steamers, Whydah (Dahomey's chief port) might have been 'brought to reason'.[3] As a result the West Coast of Africa squadron was reinforced in 1859 by a paddle-wheel steamer, H.M.S. *Brune*, the gunboat *Rainbow*, and two veterans of the Sea of Azov, the gunvessels *Lynx* and *Viper*.[4] *Brune* was an unfortunate choice, for she was a clumsy vessel. Her great length made her hard to steer, and she mounted only one gun on each broadside. When used in an expedition against Porto Novo (the capital of Dahomey) in 1861 she fired only three shells and five shot in three-quarters of an hour![5]

The bombardment of Lagos in 1851 had been a heavy blow to the slave trade, for Lagos controlled two important centres upriver, Porto Novo and Badagry. The slave trade had received a great fillip when the shortage of slaves in Cuba and Brazil forced their price up to £200 a head;[6] as they could be bought on the Gold Coast for as little as £10 a head the enormous profits made any risk seem worthwhile. To try and strangle this new outbreak Palmerston agreed to the occupation of Lagos, since this could be achieved by naval means alone, whereas action against Whydah would have required troops as well. The treaty enforced with King Akitoye allowed British, French and German traders to establish themselves in Lagos, and thus displace the slave-traders. Unfortunately

these European traders employed a number of freedmen, whose privileged status aroused enmity very easily in a society which had only recently been persuaded by force to abandon slavery. To curb this unrest it was thought necessary to moor *Brune* in the lagoon opposite the town.[7] Nevertheless the situation remained threatening, and the consuls at Lagos frequently pressed for the annexation of the town. In April 1860 Consul Brand described the town as the 'natural entrepôt of an immense country abounding in unlimited resources',[8] or the 'natural basis of operations for extending the blessings of industry, commerce and Christian civilisation to this portion of Central Africa'.[9]

The annexation of Lagos was preceded by a demonstration against Porto Novo in April 1861, as a result of the chief's reluctance to expel a number of Brazilian slave-dealers, and to allow them to be replaced by 'respectable' traders. The consul embarked in *Brune*, and was accompanied by several ships' boats provided by the Commodore at Lagos, and a hired steamer. The action was marred by *Brune*'s laboured performance and the fact that her crew of locally-recruited Kroomen[10] ran below at the first shot,[11] but was reasonably successful. Several barracoons (compounds for holding slaves awaiting shipment) were destroyed, and thanks to the compulsory use of quinine there were no deaths from fever.

The lesson was not lost on King Dosumo, and the formal annexation of Lagos followed three months later without any resistance. King Dosumo was left in nominal control, and Sir John Glover was appointed to lay the foundations for the great era of Lord Lugard's administration. In return for the loss of their independence the inhabitants of Lagos gained stable government and freedom from the social chaos engendered by the slave trade.

It might be thought that Palmerston's policy of throttling the slave trade and replacing it with trade in palm oil was nothing more than self-interest masquerading as philanthropy, but this was not entirely true. Unlike many of his contemporaries Palmerston never believed that principles of *laisser faire* would enable legitimate trade to 'root out the overshadowing weed' of slave-trading. Opening up the Niger to trade threatened to undermine the position of the established oil-traders on the coast, who claimed that oil from the interior could be bought for half the price it fetched at the coast. To a certain extent their fears were justified, for two modern advances made it possible to bring large quantities of oil downriver, thus bypassing African middlemen and the white supercargoes. The two advances were quinine and the steam-engine; the one enabled white men to live in the pestilent climate, while the other enabled small vessels to navigate safely against the strong currents of the West African rivers. However, the coastal traders were unduly pessimistic. The price of palm oil upriver was increased considerably by the cost of transporting it to the coast, and as the supply of oil available in the interior was quite inadequate it was years before the position of the coastal traders was seriously threatened.

The great disappointment of European intervention in West Africa was that it never produced the great benefits planned by Palmerston and those who thought like him. First, the trade with the interior proved too meagre after all the sanguine prophecies, and then a decline in world prices for palm oil threatened to destroy the trade of the whole region. West African trade stagnated after the mid-sixties as palm oil prices fell from £40 per ton to £33 per ton in ten years,[12] and in turn produced tribal unrest. Powerful tribes in the interior looked with contempt on the once independent coastal tribes. The installation of British puppets as local rulers in a society already gravely weakened by generations of warfare and slave-trading contributed to the general instability in West Africa, and made it difficult to establish any deep-rooted prosperity.

The appointment of the first British consuls during the palm oil boom in the 1840s and 1850s initiated a new phase in the Navy's involvement with British commercial interests, for although the Admiralty disliked such interference, which took warships into unhealthy rivers and prevented them from catching slavers,

Sir Richard Burton. *(US Library of Congress)*

Palmerston's anti-slavery policy called for the active promotion of trade. The Foreign Office therefore supported requests from the consuls for naval escorts. As the town of Lagos is situated on an island separated from a spit of land forming the seaward bank of a series of shallow lagoons the only vessels which could assist the consuls to any extent were shallow-draught steamers. As we know, gunboats and gunvessels were the only types of shallow-draught steamers available in any numbers in the early 1860s, and they soon played as important a part in the lagoons between Lagos, Badagry and Porto Novo as they had in China in 1857.

In October 1861 the consul at Fernando Po, Richard Burton, complained to Lord Russell that he was 'crippled without a gunboat' permanently available, since the crisis invariably came to a head before a warship could arrive.[13] This plea was accompanied by a request for magisterial powers, which were needed to stop 'the arbitrary and illegal proceedings of British supercargoes',[14] and an admission that on one occasion, when a British warship had not been available, a Spanish vessel had been used to carry out a bombardment.[15] Burton would have been furious if he had known that the Foreign Office doubted his discretion and would not trust him with a gunboat, as he was 'utterly reckless'.[16] However, in normal cases Whitehall supported requests for naval assistance when trade was threatened, with the proviso that 'traders who knowingly place themselves in positions where life and property cannot be protected without danger … should be informed that they must not rely upon receiving armed protection'.[17]

The calls for gunboats went on despite the reluctance of the Admiralty and the Colonial Office to intervene in African affairs. In September 1865 Sir John Glover, the consul at Lagos, called for more action against Porto Novo, the last great outlet for slaves brought out of Yorubaland. When a naval officer refused to co-operate (on the grounds that it would cause unrest among the tribes), he wrote to the Foreign Office demanding 'the most decided interference by H.M.G. at Porto Novo',[18] where, he asserted, human sacrifice was rife. Glover's proposals were: (1) depose the king, or (2) establish a British Residency (which would necessitate the presence of a gunboat), or (3) annex Porto Novo.[19] He also proposed to fine the king to meet the costs of a protective steamer. Then came a suggestion from another consul, McLeod, to send the paddle-vessel *Investigator* up the Niger to deal with unrest. This was turned down firmly by Lord Stanley[20] as this ship had recently completed four trips up the Niger without being attacked. Another dispatch from McLeod convinced the Foreign Office that the consul was out of his mind. This was a proposal to build ships for his own use, on the grounds that the traders of Lokoja (at the confluence of the Niger and the Benue) were prepared to pay three per cent of the cost.[21] He hoped that the Treasury would foot the bill for what amounted to a private navy of his own.

Some of the more farsighted Victorians had doubts about the ultimate outcome of British policy in West Africa. One of them was Sir Frederick Rogers, Permanent Under-Secretary at the Colonial Office.[22] In a minute drafted in 1862 he made these observations:

> Wherever we go in Africa, our views are as enlightened and lofty, compared with those of the barbaric people among whom we find ourselves, as those of a superior race of beings; and if we choose to employ steamers and a few disciplined troops, our influence is paramount. The apparent good is so great that it is very fascinating. But still one cannot help occasionally asking oneself, where is it to end? It is also uncomfortable to reflect on the disparity between our power and our knowledge. The first is so tremendous that we can at will, exalt or destroy, but who is to ensure a corresponding discrimination?[23]

For the moment, however, official British policy in West Africa was more restrained than aggressive. In essence this represented the victory of government departments in Whitehall, anxious to limit British involvement in African politics, over the men on the spot, the missionaries and consuls who demanded annexation in order to bring larger areas under their influence. As another Under-Secretary at the Colonial Office put it, 'These petty and often not wise chief civil authorities in different parts of the coast cannot be made the arbiters of naval movements – not attempted by the governors of more important colonies.'[24] The arguments in favour of annexation made much of the money that could be saved on defence, since it was assumed that the colonies would soon be self-supporting. Knowing better, the Foreign Office ignored all exhortations to move in, until the 'Scramble for Africa' created the possibility that another European Power might do so. Until this change in Britain's world position made expansion necessary the undercapitalised trade of West Africa was not considered worth the upkeep; while the British were able to step in whenever they pleased[25] they chose not to do so.

Until the second generation of gunboats came into service in the early 1870s the gunvessel was the most common type of shallow-draught warship sent to West Africa, where it proved ideal for the shallow reach-es of the Niger and other rivers. The new composite gunvessel *Lynx* reached a point four hundred miles upstream on a 'flag-showing' cruise in 1869, but when she returned to Lagos two months later over seventy of her complement were down with fever, leaving only four ratings fit for duty. To offset the 'sickly season' associated with service in West Africa the Admiralty restricted the time spent by warships on the station to eighteen months if possible. Ships were usually detached to serve the remaining eighteen months or more of the commission on the healthier Mediterranean or North American stations. Bad fever cases went to Ascension and then to Simon's Bay, where the remains of the cable-way for transporting stretcher-cases to the hospital can still be seen.

The firms operating in the Niger Delta seemed to be contributing to West African trade by competing among themselves, and thus bolstering the price of oil shipped from the interior, but as we have seen, by 1864 the world prices for oil were dropping. In these changed circumstances the quasi-monopoly maintained by the Delta traders ran into trouble. To gain more trade some oil merchants offered extravagant credit, which in turn led to disputes when promises could not be met. It was not long before the antics of the Delta traders and their African middlemen were disrupting trade even further. Trouble among the coastal tribes threatened to destroy the trade of firms operating upriver, and violence and gunplay became a normal hazard to vessels using the river. In such a climate violence spreads easily, and soon the unrest among the tribes rebounded on the traders. Early in 1865 the gunvessels *Dart* and *Lee* had to land men at Akatu to prevent warehouses from being burnt and looted, while the paddler *Investigator* was kept busy throughout the year in the Lagos lagoons, as she was one of the few vessels on the station capable of operating in such shallow waters.

Until 1867 the Gold Coast remained at peace with the much-feared Ashanti Confederacy, apart from a close shave in 1863, when the Ashanti invaded the territories of tribes under British protection. This disturbance cost the British Government over £700,000 and the loss of many valuable lives from fever (British forces were not involved in any fighting but much effort was put into organising resistance by the protected tribes). Thereafter relations between the British and this powerful nation deteriorated. After the young King of Ashanti, the Asantehene Kofi Karikari, succeeded to the throne in 1867 he initiated a less prudent course than his predecessor had followed. Alarmed by the pending transfer of Elmina from Dutch to British control in 1871, and by British claims to a protectorate over part of the lower valley of the Volta, the Ashanti pressed claims of their own. After much haggling and vacillation the government in Cape Coast Castle made a vain attempt to persuade the Asantehene to accept goodwill payments (as formerly paid by the Dutch) on the understanding that the Ashanti had no claim to Elmina. It was too late, and before the end of January 1873 60,000 Ashanti warriors were swarming over the coastal tribes' territories, and the Second Ashanti War had begun.

The only British reinforcements available had to be supplied by the Navy, for there were no white troops to defend the coast settlements, and the Fanti allies proved utterly useless. Elmina and Cape Coast Castle were closely invested, and had to rely on sailors and marines to reinforce the West India Regiment and Hausa troops. Fortunately five warships arrived in good time, including two new gunboats, *Decoy* and *Merlin*, but even after every available man had been sent ashore there were only a thousand men to defend all the settlements. For months the Ashanti faced the British forces in Elmina and Cape Coast Castle while the Government pondered on the problem, all the while refusing to allow the troops to take the offensive. When Sir Garnet Wolseley's request for British regulars was finally granted he was sent out in August 1873 to finish off this most unsatisfactory colonial war. With typical dash the 'Wolseley Gang' tidied up the Ashanti War in six months, after burning Kumasi and checking the power of the Ashanti for a few more years.

The Treaty of Fomena concluded between Sir Garnet and the Ashanti is an interesting document in that it made no attempt to dethrone Kofi Karikari, the normal fate of heathen monarchs who opposed the march of liberal imperialism. Instead, an indemnity of 50,000 ounces of gold was demanded, with a *promise* (authors' italics) to reduce human sacrifice. The rest of the treaty consisted of clauses defining the Ashanti territory and influence, and a pious wish that the coastal tribes would be left in peace. The question of Ashanti slave-trading was tactfully ignored, although domestic slavery was abolished in the Gold Coast in the same year, and the importing of slaves made punishable.

Unrest in West Africa was not confined to the Gold Coast. The consulate at Lokoja was closed down in 1869 after only three years' existence,[26] although this was probably due as much to McLeod's impetuous policies as any physical danger from the surrounding tribesmen. In June 1876 a gunboat was requested to protect the West Africa Company's post at Agberi, which was reported to be under fire from natives armed with Snider and Chassepot rifles.[27] The Foreign Office nevertheless continued to be hopeful, and maintained that trade was expanding at a healthy rate,[28] leading Lord Granville to suggest that the annual expeditions upriver by gunvessels should be stopped. This drew a warning from William Wylde, formerly head of the Foreign Office Slave Trade Department, who remained an advocate of force. 'One Gun Boat will be sufficient. This was the plan adopted during the ten years I was head of the S.T. Dept., and I never knew it to fail.'[29]

Sir William Hewett, V.C.
(© *National Maritime Museum, London*)

Granville was against this policy, and had warned that the Government was 'altogether averse from resorting to force unless compelled to do so … it appears hardly justifiable to resort to the armed intervention of Great Britain in a quarrel among natives which may have been originally fomented by British subjects'.[30] The Admiralty's objections were prompted by motives less noble but nonetheless practical. All these expeditions in support of nebulous trade were expensive to maintain, tried morale severely and interrupted the normal routine of the station. Discipline was that much harder to maintain in a small overcrowded warship lingering in an unhealthy river. Reports indicate that the local palm-wine was consumed in near-fatal doses by sailors on shore leave, yet to deny leave to men in such a climate would have been inhuman.

Punitive expeditions were not confined to the Niger, for various river tribes in the Congo occasionally attacked trading schooners on their way upstream. On hearing that the schooner *Geraldine* had been looted after running aground in the autumn of 1875 it was decided to send strong forces from Lagos under none other than Sir William Hewett, V.C., flying his broad pendant in the corvette *Active*. With the corvette *Encounter* and the paddle-sloop *Spiteful* Hewett took all the gunboats on the station, *Merlin*, *Foam* and *Ariel*, and a store-ship. The expedition followed the pattern of scores like it; ships' boats and gunboats shelled empty villages as they made their way upriver, ignoring desultory sniping from the banks until they finally reached the village of the chief

A naval landing party in action against Congo river pirates.
(Radio Times Hulton Picture Library)

thought to be responsible for looting the *Geraldine*. When a demand for the surrender of the culprit was ignored, probably because the inhabitants were all in hiding, the village was set on fire. As usual more men were killed by fever than by bullets, and the expedition withdrew to Lagos as quickly as it could.

The new *Ariel* class composite gunboats were sent to West Africa frequently, and most of them took part in the small skirmishes which took place on the rivers from time to time. They played a big part in a crisis over Dahomey in 1876, when Swanzy & Company's agent was ill-treated at Whydah. Sir William Hewett immediately demanded a fine of £6,000, and instituted a blockade of the coast until this was paid. The Dahomeyans retaliated by seizing French hostages, which ruled out any drastic action by Hewett, and the blockade settled down to a trial of patience. However, with two corvettes,

H.M.S. *Foam*, a composite gunboat of the 1870s; painted white for service in the tropics. *(Imperial War Museum)*

a sloop, two gunvessels and four gunboats[31] against him the King of Dahomey eventually submitted and paid the fine. Hewett's action did not win him unqualified praise from the Admiralty, who objected that 'it is a gunboat policy to back such a trade quarrel'.[32] Some officials regarded the fine as excessive, and thought the Commodore had been too impetuous; Lord Derby's chief fear was that such high-handed action might lead to another West African war.[33]

The history of the Navy's contribution to British expansion in West Africa is one of reluctance alternating with rashness. The Navy was always doing too little or too much, in the eyes of the Foreign Office at least. When the Lagos administration and local traders urged that the Volta should be forcibly opened to trade, the Admiralty objected, but was overruled. Grudging permission was given for the paddler *Pioneer*[34] to accompany the Lagos government steamer *Eyo* (our old friend *Investigator*, recently transferred from the Navy) on the expedition. When the two vessels returned all the Admiralty's gloomy predictions were justified: only five out of thirty-two Europeans were not invalided, and three of these had a mild case of fever.[35] If, on the other hand, an impetuous commander like Hewett came on the scene, naval actions could embarrass the Foreign Office and Colonial Office, for with the slowness of communications between Lagos and London the damage was done before any countermanding orders could be sent.

The Admiralty's critics maintained that the extermination of the Atlantic slave trade left the West African Squadron with nothing to do. Why then, with European trade struggling to establish itself, could the Navy not be compelled to lend its support more frequently? The answer to this was that too frequent naval intervention encouraged the use of force in the most trifling matters. In 1878 there was a complaint that some of the local African government agents (Sierra Leonian freedmen) were in the habit of writing direct to the Secretary of State for assistance. If they received an acknowledgement they were seen strutting about the town with the envelope stuck in their pocket, telling their admirers: 'A letter from Secretary of State, sah – I go bring man-of-war.'[36]

Despite these objections the gunboats continued their activities through the 1870s and 1880s, since British policy was at times virtually impotent without their support. One of the many flag-officers who served part of their careers on the West Africa Station was Sir Walter Cowan.[37] He was appointed to H.M.S. *Redbreast* in 1893 when she was serving in the East Indies, and remained in her after she transferred to West Africa the following year. Many years later he recalled a typical raid at Forcados:

> The procedure was that the ship concerned got as far up
> the creek as the water would permit and then embarked
> the men in boats, which were towed as near as possible to

the town they were to attack. During the boat-trip they invariably had to run the gauntlet past batteries of numerous old cannon stuffed with every sort of missile, such as bits of metal, and bags of nails, and generally a number of bell-mouthed swivel blunderbusses as well. This armament would be mounted in thick bush only a few yards from the water's edge with a track cut through the bush from the mouth of each gun to the water.[38]

These actions were frequent and bloody, for the dense bush always aided the defenders, and the boats' crews were fully exposed to sniping. Fortunately African marksmanship was bad, and British losses from wounds in action were relatively slight. Long after the gunboats were withdrawn from other foreign stations this sporadic warfare continued, and only died out when colonial rule was firmly established between the two world wars.

East Africa
Gunboating was also a feature of naval activity on the east coast of Africa, but with more emphasis on diplomacy and less on trade. Although Great Britain exercised quasi-sovereignty over the east coast by virtue of her sea power, the British trader was hardly known in East Africa in the early 1860s. Informal imperialism worked rather better than it did on the west coast, for the British had a useful ally in the Sultan of Zanzibar, through whom she was able to control an important part of the route to India. Since practically all the principal ports were under British, Portuguese or Zanzibari control (with the exception of the Red Sea ports, which were Turkish) there was more scope for diplomatic action and correspondingly less scope for annexation and involvement in tribal politics.

Seyyid Said, Imam of Muscat and Sultan of Zanzibar until 1856, profited greatly by a judicious partnership with Great Britain, for she helped him regain lost territories and protected him from outside interference. The British refrained from meddling in areas under the Sultan's nominal influence, and in return looked to him to promote their interests. This was done, and done well, without the expense of colonial government and large military forces. Moreover, the Sultan was an enlightened ruler by the standards of the day, and under his benign rule Zanzibar promised to become another Singapore; but until the 1880s Zanzibar's value to Great Britain remained strategic rather than commercial.

Only one sore point marred this happy relationship: Said and his subjects drew much of their revenue from slave-trading, and although Palmerston could appreciate this and be prepared to tolerate it for a while, philanthropists in England could not.[39] Towards the end of his reign Said was forced to carry out the provisions of an anti-slavery treaty pressed on him in 1845,[40] but when he died in 1856 his heirs revolted against this measure. In 1858 an attempt to displace the feeble Sultan Majid

by his brothers Thwain and Barghash had to be suppressed by men from the sloop *Assaye* and the gunvessel *Lynx*, since the new Consul, Colonel Rigby, was determined to stamp out the slave trade. Rigby was also able to turn his attention to the evils of the French *engagé* trade, which was nothing less than slave-trading thinly disguised as the recruitment of indentured labourers. As late as 1871 it was estimated that 2,000 negroes were being shipped to the French settlements in Nossi-Bé (off the north-west coast of Madagascar), Réunion and Mayotta (in the Comoro Islands), on the pretext that they had volunteered to work for five years.[41] However, in the 1860s Rigby's herculean efforts to suppress the slave trade single-handed were rewarded by the allocation of five ships[42] to patrol the east coast from the Mozambique Channel to Cape Guardafui.[43] Despite the age and bad sailing qualities of these warships they were under the energetic leadership of Captain R. B. Oldfield, R.N., and soon reduced the traffic to some extent.

The British foothold in Zanzibar conferred influence over a very wide area, from Mozambique to the Persian Gulf and even further afield. From Simon's Bay, Mauritius and Aden British warships could cover a threat to India from the French in Madagascar, Nossi-Bé, Mayotta and Réunion. Naval forces operating in the area came under the control of the Commodore at Bombay after 1863.[44] Except in unusual circumstances it was laid down that local defence was the responsibility of the Indian Government, and no hostile operations were to be undertaken without the authority of the Viceroy, the C.-in-C. or the Board of Admiralty. The Red Sea, the Persian Gulf and the Straits of Malacca were specifically mentioned as likely trouble-spots, and the instructions were framed accordingly. Small vessels had to visit Aden from time to time in view of a new French steamer service down the Red Sea, which might allow French prestige to flourish unchallenged if no British warship were to show the flag. Visits to the Persian Gulf were needed to check the slave trade and occasional acts of piracy, although these visits were confined to the cool season in view of the unhealthy climate. Provision was also made for joint operations in the Gulf with vessels under the Senior Officer in the Mozambique Channel.[45]

The death of Sultan Majid in 1870 posed a new threat to British interests in East Africa, for his successor was Barghash, the same brother who had disputed his succession in 1858. Barghash had the support of the French, and when he quarrelled with the British Consul it looked as if the carefully fostered British connection might be destroyed. But the position was saved by the new consul, Dr John Kirk, who revived British prestige within a few months.[46] At first Kirk was unable to persuade the new Sultan to intensify his efforts to end the slave trade, which was now flourishing as never before. Although British ships cruised ceaselessly off Zanzibar and Pemba the trade actually seemed to thrive on suppression. But

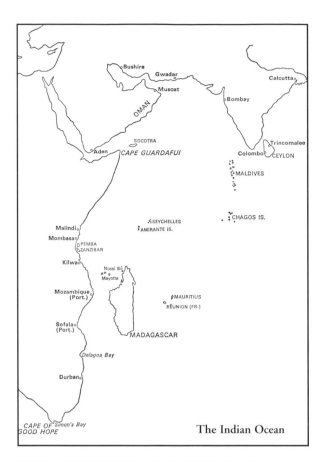

The Indian Ocean

after a Select Committee had recommended the enforcement of a new treaty with the Sultan the position improved. True, the Sultan refused at first to honour the new treaty, but he was forced to by a naval blockade of the coast. The results were dramatic, for the slave trade declined rapidly over the next ten years, and degenerated into occasional smuggling.

In 1873 the forces available for general service in the Indian Ocean included the sloop *Daphne* and the gunvessels *Magpie*, *Nimble*, *Philomel*, *Rifleman* and *Vulture*, with the surveying ship *Nassau* operating off East Africa. Many of their actions were straightforward punitive expeditions. For example, when *Rifleman*'s captain heard that a telegraph station at Gwadar, in Baluchistan, had been attacked, he set sail for the Gulf of Oman (see Map 7), and arrived in time to beat off the marauding Bedouins. In March the following year an expedition was dispatched from Bombay to deal with a troublesome chief at Masnah. Accompanying *Philomel* and *Nimble* was an interesting relic, the Bombay Marine gunboat *Hugh Rose*, a teak-built copy of the old *Algerine* class of 1857; as *Rifleman* was refitting at Bombay she supplied a party of ratings to work *Hugh Rose*'s guns.

A more serious incident at Mombasa began with the capture of an old Portuguese fort by a rival of the Sultan of Zanzibar. This rebellion was a reply to the Sultan's suppression of the slave trade; as we have seen, this policy was unwillingly put into effect under British orders,

The gunvessel *Nimble*. (NPC)

and many of the Sultan's subjects were prepared to defy the ban. A Christian ideal superimposed in this way on a Muslim society succeeded with the backing of gunboats, but at the price of undermining the structure of that society in the process.

The Sultan decided to retake Mombasa early in 1875, but when he learned that the rebel chief Abdullah had destroyed the town he turned to the British Consul for help. Stationed at Zanzibar was the store-ship *London* under Captain George Sullivan, who immediately placed a scratch force of a hundred sailors and marines at the consul's disposal. As *Nassau* was still in the area the naval brigade was embarked in her for passage to Mombasa, where she was joined by *Rifleman*. The two vessels landed the naval brigade and provided covering fire, but it took five hours of shelling before Abdullah conceded victory to the Sultan.

About this time steam launches and picket boats were supplied to sloops and larger vessels, although they were considered too heavy for gunboats and gunvessels. Steam-powered boats were a great advance in the suppression of slave-running as they did away with the exhausting effort of rowing heavy boats under a tropical sun, and the large increase in the number of captures in the 1870s was attributed to this single innovation.[47] Still,

the smaller ships had a good record, and the gunvessels *Lynx* and *Vulture* scored an imposing list of successes in the Gulf between 1877 and 1880, many of them in the face of armed resistance. The Arabs often fought it out with boats' crews, who were no better armed than themselves. Not until 1883 could the Royal Navy finally claim to have throttled the East African slave trade, at which date the anti-slavery patrols were withdrawn.[48] The sloop *Penguin* was able to capture fifteen dhows in eight months as late as 1888. When Zanzibar became a British Protectorate in 1897 the legal status of slavery was abolished, although this privilege was not extended to the Sultan's mainland dominions until 1907.[49]

The Royal Navy's efforts to destroy the slave trade left it in a unique position to further British interests in Africa, for vast areas of the African coastline remained under exclusive British control. Thus, when events forced Britain to consider a policy of colonial expansion she had a considerable advantage over her European competitors. However vague and uncoordinated British colonial policy may have been in the 1860s and 1870s the extensive naval activity during that period laid firm foundations for the subsequent British Empire in East Africa which took shape during the celebrated 'Scramble'.

Chapter 10

SUEZ

The third area in Africa where gunboats found themselves involved – although to a much lesser degree – was Egypt. Britain's interest in Egypt dated from the late eighteenth century, when its importance as a link in communications with the new Indian Empire became vital. In 1869 Egypt's value was still further enhanced by the completion of the Suez Canal, which ran straight through Egyptian territory. From the British viewpoint it was essential that the Canal should never be allowed to fall into unfriendly hands, so in 1875 Disraeli underlined his Government's concern by purchasing a substantial shareholding in the Canal. The shares were offered for sale by the Egyptian ruler, the Khedive Ismail, whose wild extravagances had almost bankrupted his country.

Egypt's position was made even more crucial by the fact that the French also had a stake in the Canal. The British had long since determined not to allow the French to gain a foothold in Egypt, as long ago as 1798, when Nelson annihilated the French invasion fleet at Aboukir Bay. Despite this setback and the subsequent destruction of her army the French had managed to preserve considerable influence in Cairo. By the 1860s they had built the Suez Canal as an outlet to their own Far Eastern empire, and the collapse of 1870 did little to reduce their colonial ambitions. In this atmosphere it is not surprising that French and British interests in Egypt were rarely compatible.

When the Khedive Ismail did at last go bankrupt in 1876 the delicate balance between British and French influence in Egypt was upset. The formidable problem of recovering the money owing to foreign bondholders was answered by rigid Anglo-French control of Egypt's revenues. Lord Salisbury was against acting as bailiff on behalf of the bondholders, but felt it was necessary to prevent the French from gaining ground in Cairo.[1] Accordingly an international Commission of the Public Debt, the *Caisse de la Dette Publique*, was formed to recover the missing millions, and the Egyptians were effectively placed under Anglo-French rule.

The Khedive Ismail.
(US Library of Congress)

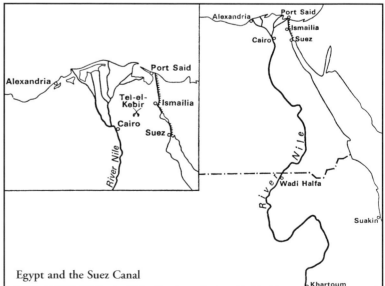

Egypt and the Suez Canal

At once the *Caisse de la Dette* had Egypt by the throat, and was drawing twenty-five per cent of her revenues to pay off the Debt. This was sound Bourse policy, but it took little account of Egyptian sensitivity. The privileged classes resented attempts at fiscal reform, while the burden of the extra taxes lay heaviest on the wretched *fellahin* and brought them more hardship than ever. The result was a nationalist movement to throw off foreign domination, supported for different reasons by pashas and peasants. 'Egypt for the Egyptians' became the cry, until finally in 1879 Ismail dismissed his European ministers and tried to end foreign control over his affairs. But the British and French retaliated by ordering the Sultan of Turkey to dismiss Ismail, who was technically his vassal. The foreign stranglehold was promptly reapplied, but more subtly, and for the moment all seemed well.

The nationalist movement gained new strength from the Army, whose officers had supported Ismail's attempt to expel the foreigners. When the movement felt strong enough to act its first move was a cautious one. This time the nationalists confronted the young Khedive Tewfik with a demand for the dismissal of his Minister for War, which was done. On 9 September 1881 officers surrounded the Khedive's palace and demanded the dismissal of the entire government and the recall of the old Chamber of Notables. Tewfik yielded, and thereafter *de facto* power passed into the hands of Arabi Pasha and his fellow-colonels. By the end of the year Egypt was near to anarchy, and statesmen in London and Paris were considering ways to check Arabi and restore the Khedive's influence.

The British reaction to the crisis in Egypt was affected profoundly by a change of government in the previous year, when the Liberals returned to power under Gladstone. The Liberal Party was divided, since the Whigs supported the Conservatives' calls for intervention while the Radicals denounced them as jingoes. When the French suggested a joint expedition to put down the Egyptian nationalist revolt Gladstone was faced with a conflict of ideals. On the one hand he professed sympathy for all nationalist causes, but on the other hand he could hardly abandon the Canal. In the hope that the nationalists would be sobered by the threat of intervention he agreed to the issue of a Joint Note on 8 January 1882. This was nothing more than a bluff, the Liberals kept reassuring themselves, which would bring Arabi to heel and avert the need for action.

The result was exactly the opposite, for Arabi and the Army took this as proof that the two Powers were determined to intervene, and began to fortify Alexandria as a visible deterrent to an invading force. After much hesitation a strong force of British and French battleships was ordered to concentrate at Alexandria in May 1882. Although only intended as a show of force it was enough to make the Khedive dismiss Arabi and his supporters from the government. But Egypt was gripped by such

nationalist fervour now that the Arabists were back in office five days later.[2]

As rumours of massacres of Europeans reached London Gladstone's Cabinet became more alarmed. Finally, on the pretext that repairs to the ancient forts of Alexandria were acts of aggression, Admiral Sir Frederick Beauchamp Seymour was instructed to deliver an ultimatum to Arabi. This was meant to be a demand to disarm the forts, but Seymour exceeded his instructions by demanding the surrender of the forts.[3] The French had by this time decided not to join the British, so Seymour was left to carry out his threat alone. With the bulk of the Mediterranean Fleet available there were eight battleships, three gunvessels, and two gunboats, giving a preponderance of ninety-seven modern guns in the ships to only forty-four in the forts.[4]

Towards evening on 10 July the bombarding ships took up their positions opposite the forts. The gunvessels and gunboats were told to keep clear of the big ships until 'a favourable opportunity offers itself of moving into the attack on Mex'[5] (this disposition was to have unexpected results the next day). The array of ships under Seymour's command was a good cross-section of the Fleet in 1882, a mixture of sail and steam, of wood and iron. The eight battleships mounted six different calibres of main armament, all rifled muzzle-loaders. The gunvessels included the name-ship of the *Beacon* class, a wooden contemporary of the *Plover* class and a newer composite vessel, H.M.S. *Condor*; the gunboats were two veterans of West Africa, *Decoy* and *Cygnet*. With their teak sides these five small vessels were vulnerable to anything larger than a rifle bullet, but the Admiral kept them in reserve as repeater-ships for signals and for any special task beyond the capabilities of the bigger ships.

The Egyptian gunners had a magnificent view of the

British sailors inspecting the guns of Fort Mex after the bombardment of Alexandria, 1882. (*Radio Times Hulton Picture Library*)

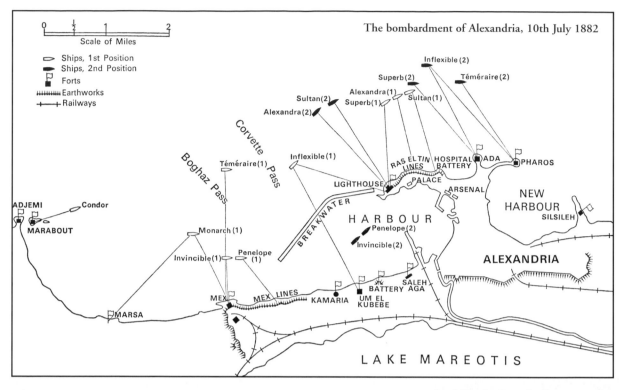

The bombardment of Alexandria, 10th July 1882

Scale of Miles

Ships, 1st Position
Ships, 2nd Position
Forts
Earthworks
Railways

Inflexible (2)

Superb (2)

Téméraire (2)

Alexandra (1)

Sultan (2)

Superb (1)

Sultan (1)

Alexandra (2)

Corvette Pass

Boghaz Pass

Téméraire (1)

Inflexible (1)

RAS EL TIN
LINES

HOSPITAL
BATTERY

ADA

PHAROS

LIGHTHOUSE

PALACE

ARSENAL

NEW
HARBOUR

ADJEMI

Condor

MARABOUT

BREAKWATER

HARBOUR

SILSILEH

Monarch (1)

Penelope (2)

Invincible (2)

ALEXANDRIA

Invincible (1)

Penelope
(1)

MEX

MEX LINES

KAMARIA

UM EL
KUBEBE

BATTERY

SALEH
AGA

MARSA

LAKE MAREOTIS

Lord Charles Beresford's command at Alexandria, the composite gunvessel *Condor*. In action her spars and top-masts would be sent down, and with rigging rove down she would appear more bare. *(Imperial War Museum)*

British squadron next morning. There in the morning sun was a line of black-hulled warships with gleaming white upperworks and buff funnels, in a long straggling line opposite the six miles of forts. The nearest battleships were only a thousand yards away, but the new battleship *Inflexible* lay over two miles out, where her enormous 16-inch, 80-ton guns were equally effective. Firing began at 7 a.m., and after three hours some of the forts were badly knocked about. The light breeze helped the Egyptians, for it failed to clear the vast clouds of powder-smoke and prevented the British gun-layers from seeing their targets. As some of the forts appeared to be silenced the battleships shifted berths to attack fresh targets, allowing the gunvessel *Bittern* to send her dinghy in to disable some of the guns.

The little *Condor* had no intention of playing a subsidiary role, for Commander Lord Charles Beresford could hardly miss such a chance to distinguish himself. One may doubt if 'Charlie B.' would have become a famous flag-officer had he not been so lucky at Alexandria, but this was to be the start of a dazzling career. Seeing that Fort Marabout was firing at the battleships without hindrance Beresford took what he considered a favourable opportunity and steered his little gunvessel in so close that the fort's guns could not be depressed enough to reach him. For an hour-and-a-half *Condor* pestered Fort Marabout with 7-inch shells, while the Egyptian shells roared overhead and deluged her with water. By warping his ship to and fro Beresford avoided being hit, although his rigging was cut by shell-splinters. At about ten o'clock the Admiral signalled to the other gunboats and gunvessels to join Beresford. There could be no doubt that his star was in the ascendant when Seymour later made the signal: 'Well done *Condor*'.

Despite the nonchalant ease with which the ships battered the forts to pieces the bombardment was a tactical error, and had serious repercussions. Rioting broke out all over Egypt, and Arabi warned de Lesseps that he would destroy his beloved Canal in the defence of Egypt.[6] As in 1956 this threat was enough to push Great Britain to the point where she would land an expeditionary force,[7] but if troops were to be used the key point was not Alexandria but Ismailia. The bombardment therefore did nothing to aid the invasion and merely confirmed Arabi's control by arousing patriotic feelings.

After the French decision not to join in the bombardment it was realised that they were not likely to agree to a joint invasion. A reluctant Gladstone was left to justify the necessity of British intervention on the grounds that it might restore law and order. It is a tremendous tribute to the Prime Minister's powers of persuasion that he could carry the Liberals with him in putting down a revolt by a people 'rightly struggling to be free'.[8] On 16 August 1882 Sir Garnet Wolseley's expeditionary force landed in Egypt.

After the bombardment the warships had landed men to police Alexandria until the arrival of troops from

Lord Charles Beresford, later in his career, as Vice-Admiral. *(US Library of Congress)*

Cyprus and Malta. Naval forces in the Red Sea were used effectively to gain control of Suez before Arabi's men could destroy the port. With troops ashore the naval brigade was broken up to allow the men to return to their ships, which were needed to seize the Canal. Wolseley had already decided on a bold outflanking move to outwit Arabi, and asked the Navy to hold Ismailia as a new base for operations against Cairo. Port Said fell to a surprise attack on 20 August, but at Ismailia the Egyptian Army counter-attacked and had to be driven off by naval gunfire. The previous night a force of a hundred men under the commander of the gunvessel *Ready* had swooped on the Suez Canal Company's possessions, including all its dredgers and its private telegraph system. Two gunvessels and two smaller steamers were stationed in the Canal to guard against an attempt to sabotage it, but with the defeat of Arabi at Tel-el-Kebir the Navy's work in Egypt was practically over by September 1882.

Gladstone had assured the Radicals of his party that he would intervene in Egypt, restore law and order, and then withdraw as quickly as possible. The French certainly believed for a while that this would happen, and may have hoped that the British would bear the cost of finding a solution to the Egyptian problem which would benefit both countries. But once in Egypt the British could not resist the temptation to secure their influence before they left. In their attempts to give the *fellahin* good government and his rulers financial stability the well-intentioned British did away with the system of dual control by themselves and France. Then their competent administrators found that Egypt was simply not fit to be abandoned quickly, although Gladstone still clung to this forlorn hope. Not until a whole chain of disasters in the Sudan demonstrated the complete absence of stability in Egypt did he realise how enmeshed he had become in Egyptian affairs.

The Sudan was Egypt's rich dependency, a savage wilderness which supplied ivory, ostrich feathers and gum arabic from the lush equatorial provinces and taxes from the wretched inhabitants. Egypt had misgoverned the Sudan ever since Said Pasha had conquered its black inhabitants. Gordon, when appointed to suppress the slave trade in the Sudan, remarked that the Egyptian rule was 'little better than brigandage'. When a Mahdi rose and preached a holy war against the infidel and the Turk the oppressed Negroes and Arabs found that their valour was enough to overcome incompetent Egyptian armies. It is a measure of the desperate state of the Cairo Government that the army sent southwards in 1883 to quell the Mahdi's revolt was largely made up of the men who had been routed at Tel-el-Kebir, and now had to be manacled to prevent them from deserting. To this incredible host of unfortunates weeping in their chains was added an undisciplined force of Circassians and Bashi-Bazouks, all under the command of Colonel Hicks, a retired Indian Army officer.

When the news came that Hicks Pasha's army had been wiped out in Kordofan the British at last realised that if they did not act quickly their possession of the lower Nile Valley would be jeopardised. Defeated though the Egyptians might be, their Government could not bring itself to abandon the Sudan. Public opinion would not allow such a humiliation, yet the Khedive's ministers were hardly in a position to prevent it. If the British refused to allow Egypt to fight for the Sudan they were likely to find themselves more unpopular than ever. More remote but nonetheless foreseeable was the danger of a Mahdist invasion of Upper Egypt causing unrest among the predominantly Muslim population.

Immediate orders were sent to Rear-Admiral Sir William Hewett[9] to protect the Red Sea coast. As most

The 'flat-iron' gunboat *Medina*, sent to Suez in 1882. *(Conway Maritime Press)*

of Garnet Wolseley's forces had been sent back to England it was absolutely vital for the Egyptians to hold Khartoum until the garrisons could be withdrawn. It was this task which took General Gordon to Khartoum, for it was hoped that his great popularity as a liberator of slaves would pacify the country for a while and make the withdrawal easier.

When Sir William Hewett heard of the destruction of Hicks's army he sent the gunvessel *Ranger* to Suakin, where she was just in time to help beat off an attack by the Arabs. For a while *Ranger* was the backbone of the defence, but reinforcements were being rushed from the Mediterranean Fleet. This tiny port, almost encircled by coral reefs, was essential to any campaign against the Mahdi for it was far closer to Khartoum than Wady Halfa (on the Egyptian border). While Gordon was making his way up the Nile Valentine Baker Pasha[10] was sent to Suakin with 2,500 Egyptian gendarmerie, and Hewett was concentrating his ships. Unfortunately, Baker's force was routed by a small number of Hadendoa tribesmen at El Teb, and Hewett found himself responsible for the defence of Suakin with only 300 Royal Marines and the men from his ships.

With the whole of the eastern Sudan now held by pro-Mahdi tribes any attempt at extricating the two surviving Egyptian garrisons required British troops, which had to be sent from Egypt. These seasoned troops, fighting in hollow square, inflicted fearful slaughter on the Hadendoa, but the effort was too late; one of the garrisons was cut to pieces and the other surrendered in despair. Graham's[11] troops were recalled to Egypt, leaving local defence to Hewett and his sailors. Although Hewett was most successful in organising the defences by landing Gatlings and searchlights, one of his measures caused a storm of protest in England. He put a price on the head of Osman Digna, a former slave-trader who had gone over to the Mahdi and was to prove a troublesome opponent. In the bloodthirsty atmosphere of the Sudan such a move was probably no better and no worse than any other tactics, but the uproar in England caused the Admiralty to make Hewett withdraw the proclamation.

In London Gladstone faced bitter opposition to his Sudan policy from both imperialists and Radicals. The former criticised his unwillingness to reconquer the Sudan, while the latter accused him of surrendering the Sudanese to barbarism. To add to his troubles Gordon took it into his head to remain in Khartoum when he found that it was no longer possible to withdraw all the Egyptian garrisons through hostile country. The Government would have been happy to know that Gordon had helped the European officers to get out, but he refused to abandon the garrisons. Encouraged by his example the Governor of Kordofan held out and Gordon prepared Khartoum for a long siege. By March 1884 it was clear to the British in Egypt, if not clear to the British in London, that Gordon and his garrisons could only be extricated by a military expedition. But the Cabinet saw only the diplomatic and political necessity of jettisoning the Egyptian problem. The Party was divided, and every day spent in Egypt by the army of occupation increased French hostility.

Gladstone resisted pressure to rescue Gordon until August, when he gave in and authorised the Gordon Relief Expedition; on Garnet Wolseley's advice it was decided not to use the route from Suakin to the Nile. Instead the longer route from Wady Halfa and Upper Egypt was chosen. The result of all the months of heartbreaking delays, the last desperate pitched battles and the final sprint to Khartoum was the bitter knowledge that the Relief Column had arrived two days late. The wrath of the public was immediately directed at Gladstone, and encouraged his opponents in both the Liberal Party and the Opposition. Wolseley denounced him as the 'M.O.G.', or Murderer of Gordon, and for a while it looked as if the Government might fall. But the Liberals clung to office until the heavensent Penjdeh Incident gave them an excuse to rush troops from Egypt to the North-West Frontier of India.[12] The avenging of Gordon was gratefully postponed and all British troops were withdrawn to the Egyptian frontier.

Although the Army's responsibilities in the Sudan were drastically reduced after the fall of Khartoum the Royal Navy still had to safeguard the Red Sea coast against the Mahdists.[13] In March 1885, when the Government was still hoping to crush the Mahdi, a strong force was sent once more to Suakin. This time its purpose was to pacify the country long enough to allow the construction of a railway from Suakin to the Nile to ease the problems of supporting an army in a waterless waste. The Red Sea Division of the Mediterranean Fleet, comprising the corvette *Carysfort* the sloops *Dolphin* and *Sphinx*, and gunvessels *Condor*[14] and *Coquette* were ordered to land men and machine-guns for a naval brigade. This force marched out of Suakin on 22 March as part of a division under Major-General Sir John McNeill, V.C., escorting a large number of camels. Only six miles from Suakin the force halted to build a depot.

Working parties were scattered around the convoy cutting thorn scrub for the protective zeribas when the frantic sound of a bugle made them rush for their rifles. But the alarm was given too late to prevent the Hadendoa (Kipling's 'fuzzy-wuzzies') from rushing the camp. Within minutes a horde of brawny barefooted warriors swept through the sailors as they tried to bring their Gardner guns into action. Then they broke into a hur-

riedly formed square of the Berkshires, who were only saved by fighting back to back with rifle-butts and bayonets. Others rushed among the mass of camels, stabbing and hamstringing the wretched beasts until they stampeded through the Royal Marines. In the incredibly short space of twenty minutes 'McNeill's Zeriba' was a bloody shambles of dead camels and men, but the Hadendoa had melted back into the scrub.

Two days later another force moving in square formation was attacked near Tamai and lost a hundred camels, and it became clear to General Graham that loss of transport would cripple his efforts. The Army had bought or requisitioned all the camels possible, and lost a large number of them within a month. When the Gladstone Government decided to take troops from Egypt for the crisis over Afghanistan the fate of the campaign was sealed. By May 1885 the troopships were threading their way out through the coral reefs, leaving the Suakin foreshore piled with unused equipment for the railway and a hundred new crosses in the English cemetery.

Suakin was fought over by Osman Digna and the British for another ten years, during which scores of petty actions were fought between the Arabs and 'friendly' tribes acting on the bribes of the energetic Governor of Suakin, Major Kitchener – the man who would ultimately avenge Gordon at Omdurman. In March 1888 the sloop *Dolphin* was again on hand when Egyptian troops and 'friendlies' attempted to drive the Arabs out of a fort near the town. Unfortunately the sloop dropped a 6-inch shell among the 'friendlies', which did not earn the Governor's approval! The bickering between Osman Digna and the garrison continued intermittently until strong reinforcements were sent to Suakin in 1896 as a prelude to Kitchener's reconquest of the Sudan.

The occupation of Egypt by British forces and the subsequent evacuation of the Sudan were to have incalculable repercussions beyond Egypt. There was a colossal expenditure of lives by both sides, which was only ended after thirteen years by the slaughter at Omdurman. For all the humiliation of British interference Egypt eventually prospered under the direction of Lord Cromer and the devoted paternalism of British civil servants. The rehabilitation of the Egyptian Army was so successful that the reconquest of the Sudan in 1896-98 relied heavily on native troops throughout the campaigns. But the most far-reaching effects were felt on British policy, which was to undergo drastic changes as a result of the events of 1882, changes which in their turn sealed the fate of the Gunboat Navy.

Chapter 11

THE BEGINNING OF THE END

Victorians marvelled at Great Britain's naval and commercial power, and spoke of their Empire on which the sun never set. But to questioning minds it was clear that the British Empire would some day have to yield first place in the world. When at last the combination of factors producing *Pax Britannica* broke down the chief weapons of imperialism lost their edge. The slow dissolution of the old system left no place for the gunboat, for with it went the climate in which the gunboat had managed to thrive.

The first warning came in the 1870s, when British agriculture met severe competition from the vast wheatlands of America and Canada. The slump in farming was followed by a brief but damaging recession in industry, which showed itself in reduced public expenditure, and particularly in reduced Army and Navy Estimates. Worst of all for Victorian complacency, Great Britain found that she had to rely more and more on the goodwill of European Powers. Isolation, once the *sine qua non* of Victorian statesmanship, seemed far from splendid by the 1880s, and was gradually replaced by diplomatic commitments to most of the major European Powers.

This new and unwelcome dependence on Europe stemmed from the British occupation of Egypt in 1882,[1] which led to the collapse of the longstanding 'Liberal Alliance' between Great Britain and France. The French were convinced that the British had used Arabi Pasha's revolt as an excuse to gain paramount control over the Suez Canal, which was quite true; the short route to the East was vital to the British Empire, both in terms of defence and commerce. Not for the last time the British were ready to go to any lengths to retain control of the Canal.

Without French co-operation the British found it increasingly difficult to carry out their policies in Cairo, for they had to win the support of the Austrian, Italian

and German members of the International Debt Commission. In practice this meant relying on the goodwill of the Imperial German Chancellor, Bismarck (the creator of the Triple Alliance with Austria-Hungary and Italy in May 1882). Britain had refused to join the Triple Alliance, but she was forced to conclude secret agreements with Italy and Austria-Hungary in 1887, and at the same time appeased the Germans with colonial concessions in Africa, and the Pacific. Breathing-space had been bought, but commitments on this scale were unprecedented in time of peace, as the Prime Minister, Lord Salisbury, realised only too well.

Egypt brought more tribulations, by causing a reversal of British policy in Africa and the substitution of annexations in place of the old methods of indirect rule. Again it was the Suez Canal forcing the pace, for it was deemed necessary to prevent another European Power from gaining control of the headwaters of the Nile, and thus dominating the exit to the Canal. It was no new argument to suggest that annexation gave more certain control over a territory than any number of gunboats cruising off the coast; this argument had hitherto been rejected by the Foreign Office and the Cabinet, but now world events gave it new force. Moreover, the case for annexation was strengthened by the knowledge that gunboat operations in areas such as West Africa and the Pacific had destroyed primitive societies; the resulting anarchy created a 'power vacuum' which could only be filled by European intervention. The old style of imperialism seemed incapable of serving the Empire's needs in these new circumstances, and consequently gunboats, the tools of that old imperialism, fell into disfavour.

Great Britain's position in the Mediterranean also suffered from her involvement in Egypt. Ever since Waterloo she had regarded Turkey as her first line of defence against Russian encroachment in the eastern

Mediterranean, and the safety of Constantinople had been preserved by British intervention on a number of occasions. The Mediterranean Fleet was maintained at a strength calculated to be capable of beating the Russians, on the assumption that the French would remain neutral, but after the quarrel over Egypt in 1882 the French began to cast about for new allies to offset Salisbury's compromises with Bismarck and the Triple Alliance. Slowly they drifted into an understanding with Russia, and by 1887 the two Powers were sufficiently friendly to embark on joint action in international diplomacy. The two new friends blocked an Anglo-Turkish convention which would have given Great Britain a permanent right to intervene in Egypt after her proposed withdrawal in 1890.

To the Admiralty and the Cabinet it was clear that a Franco-Russian alliance would make the Straits of Gibraltar almost impossible to defend, for if the Mediterranean Fleet were to concentrate in the Levant to pounce on the emerging Black Sea Fleet then France's Toulon Fleet could brush aside the light forces at Gibraltar and escape into the Atlantic. This nightmare haunted naval strategists, for the obvious consequence was that the Toulon Fleet would combine with the Brest Fleet and sweep through the English Channel. The French saw it as their chance to reverse the decision of Trafalgar, and the prelude to a major attack on the British Isles, and both British and French navies conducted their annual manoeuvres on the assumption that this would be the pattern of a future war.

With the Straits of Gibraltar no longer tenable it seemed to Salisbury only political realism to jettison the commitment to support Turkey, as British warships would never be spared to cover the Dardanelles so long as the Toulon Fleet was in a position to reach the Atlantic. Equally, Turkey could hardly protect the Suez Canal better than the British garrisons in Egypt could. Salisbury became convinced that Constantinople had been displaced by Cairo as the centre of gravity of British interests in the Mediterranean. This in itself affords an indication of the declining prestige of the Ottoman Empire, for Egypt was still nominally under Turkish suzerainty.

While Egypt was helping to reshape British foreign policy there was also growing concern for the safety of the colonies and trade-routes.[2] The defenceless state of British coaling-stations and naval establishments abroad had already been noted by Sir William Jervois (shortly before he left for Malaya),[3] but his report was shelved until the Russian War Scare in 1878. Then an exaggerated fear for British ports and naval bases infected both public and official opinion, although the chief bogey, the dreaded Russian Far Eastern Fleet, turned out to be a paper tiger. Nevertheless it was clear that the Empire was frighteningly unprepared for serious attack, and first British reactions showed how little thought had been given to the matter. When it was suggested that the coal-mines of Labuan were vulnerable, the order was given to close them down! Five guns set up to defend the vital base at Simon's Bay were not fired until December 1879,

Simon's Bay at the end of the 1890s – one of the gunboat's last strongholds. Beyond the two *Thrush* class gunboats are the cruisers *Magicienne* and *Doris*, with three 'flat-iron' gunboats, *Griper*, *Gadfly* and *Tickler*, in the foreground. *(Simon's Town Historical Society, South Africa)*

when two of them were promptly disabled. One of Sir Garnet Wolseley's staff remarked to the Governor that the recoil apparatus had long since been condemned in the British Army, and would never be put into a battery in Europe.[4]

An official investigation of Imperial defence was entrusted to a Colonial Defence Committee, but in September 1879 this committee was superseded by a Royal Commission with the broadest possible terms of reference, 'to enquire into the defence of British possessions and commerce abroad'. The chairman was the former Colonial Secretary, Lord Carnarvon.

The Carnarvon Commission made little impression at the time. The Radicals regarded it as an 'insane scheme', in Bright's words, and urged Gladstone to wind it up as soon as he took office in 1880. Invariably bored by the subject of defence, Gladstone merely expressed his wish that the Commission would run its course and thereafter be forgotten. But in retrospect it emerges as the first significant challenge to the concept of 'Fortress England', and a fresh enunciation of Nelson's principle that the nation's first line of defence is the Navy. Men like Jervois and the Colomb brothers had put this principle forward for many years, but without success, and the Commission's reports vindicated them.

The findings of the Carnarvon Commission were so serious that many parts of its reports were suppressed; only extracts of the three reports were published in the proceedings of the 1887 Colonial Conference, but these made bad enough reading. There were no shore defences at Hong Kong and Singapore, and most of the ports of India, Australasia, Canada and the West Indies were open to naval attack. Assuming that the Royal Navy's task in wartime would be to command the seas and deny the enemy the use of his bases (and if this were not the Navy's function, what other could there be?), an entirely new type of Navy was needed. The Royal Navy as it was constituted in 1887 was not equipped or designed to defend the Imperial trade-routes against enemy commerce-raiders. This task called for a number of fast, powerful cruisers operating from a chain of bases and coaling-stations around the world. By implication the existing fleet of police vessels, slow and weak, would have no place in the new Navy.

To the dismay of the politicians a new problem arose to aggravate Britain's diplomatic position. Colonial defence could be shelved, provided the Royal Navy kept its pre-eminent position, but a sudden spate of expansion in European navies was matched by an alarming stagnation in the Royal Navy. The worst example of British backwardness was over that old bone of contention, the breech-loading gun. As we have already seen, the rifled muzzle-loader replaced the Armstrong breech-loader for convincing reasons in the 1860s, but after this unfortunate setback no further effort seems to have been made to develop a reliable breech-loader, regardless of German

and French success in this field. Such was the lack of imagination in the Navy that nobody thought that the revolutionary developments in foreign artillery could be worth imitating. Masts and yards were retained in battleships to provide an alternative to steam-power. Sail-power would enable an ironclad to reach port if she broke down at sea, and would save coal on long voyages, ran the argument. Tacticians ignored the weakness of these arguments: in wartime no sailing battleship with defective engines could escape from an enemy using steam-power, and if endurance were required then coaling-stations would be a more reliable alternative to wind-power.

The other factor highlighting Britain's naval weakness was the Whitehead torpedo. This crude weapon had originally been bought by the Royal Navy as far back as 1870, and by 1879 the first torpedo-boat, H.M.S. *Lightning*, was in service. The Royal Navy's progress with the new weapon was watched by its European rivals, and soon orders for torpedo-boats were placed by every navy. Like the gunboat before her, the little torpedo-boat with her puny 14-inch torpedoes represented defence on the cheap, for could not one tiny 200-ton boat sink a 10,000-ton battleship?

The nation which took this argument most seriously was France. Weary of years of fruitless rivalry with the Royal Navy, the French Navy turned to the torpedo-boat as the equaliser which could send British battleships to the bottom of the sea at a fraction of the cost of a fleet of battleships. Even if torpedo-boats could only operate successfully in the sheltered waters of the Channel and the Mediterranean it did not matter, for large cruisers would sweep British commerce from the seas after disposing of any weak British cruisers which might have enough speed to overtake them. This revolutionary doctrine was widely discussed in naval circles, and its disciples became known as the *Jeune Ecole*, to distinguish them from the older officers brought up in the tradition of fighting the British in line of battle. Many of the rosier dreams of the *Jeune Ecole* foreshadowed developments of the First and Second World Wars, particularly merciless onslaughts on merchant shipping and the use of capital ships in a purely passive strategic role, the 'fleet in being'.

British cruiser design lagged behind, for the watchword was still economy, and naval architects were adept at producing the largest number of cruisers at the lowest cost. There were only two drawbacks: small cruisers were not only weakly armed, but not even capable of fighting their guns in rough weather. In contrast the French built a series of large armoured cruisers with great endurance, clearly designed for running down merchantmen on the high seas. Furthermore, by continuing to build battleships they adhered to the 'fleet in being' concept, and thus forced the British to follow suit by laying down sufficient battleships to maintain their margin of superiority. America was still consuming her energies in expanding her frontiers and settling the West, which left little time or money for giant battleships, but both Italian and Russian battleship designs were causing a degree of consternation in British circles unknown since the Crimean War.

In the autumn of 1884, moreover, Bismarck made a disturbing proposal to the French for an 'equilibrium of the seas', nothing less than a Continental naval league directed against Great Britain. 'I do not want war with England,' said the Iron Chancellor, 'but I want her to understand that if the navies of the other nations unite, they will counterbalance her on the ocean and will compel her to consider the interests of others.'[5]

The Royal Navy was facing challenges from all directions, and influential people were not confident that it was ready to meet them. In September 1884 these influential men put their case before a startled British public in a series of sensational articles in the *Pall Mall Gazette*. Although published anonymously it was soon known that the articles were written by the celebrated journalist W. T. Stead at the instigation of H. W. Arnold Forster, an ardent Big Navy man. The technical comments had been vetted by Captain John Fisher, R.N., once a weedy midshipman at the Peiho River but now in command of the Navy's gunnery school, H.M.S. *Excellent*. This pressure group was much more than a trio of agitators for bigger and better battleships, for their friends were influential beyond the two Services. Fisher in particular cultivated his contacts with the press, and lost no opportunity of hobnobbing with the Prince of Wales.

The agitation which followed Stead's 'Truth about the

Navy' articles resulted in increased expenditure on the Navy, despite Gladstone's misgivings. New ships were not enough, however, to revitalise the establishment of the Navy after its long slumber, and many reforms had to be initiated before the image of H.M.S. *Pinafore* could be eradicated. In the spring of 1885, during one of the many 'Russian War Scares', ships took months to mobilise, and several had not even completed their fitting-out when orders came to demobilise at the end of the crisis.[6] At the Golden Jubilee Review of the Fleet in 1887 Admiral Hewett (the old warrior was now almost at the end of his distinguished career) remarked acidly to a distinguished visitor: 'Most of what you see here is mere ullage.'[7]

Under Lord Salisbury's new Government of 1886 the Board of Admiralty was assured of financial support for its reforms, a state of affairs not enjoyed since the days of Lord Barham. As a concession to public agitation for naval reform the popular Lord Charles Beresford was made Fourth Sea Lord. Despite his connections Beresford was regarded in the Navy as something of a brash upstart, an opinion which must have been shared by Sir Arthur Hood, the First Sea Lord. Only a few months after joining the Board Beresford drew up a confidential memorandum on the Navy's unpreparedness, and pressed for the formation of a War Staff. The Board examined the memorandum, rejected all the charges as exaggerated, and concluded that Beresford was sticking his nose into things which did not concern him.[8] Undaunted, Beresford arranged for Salisbury to see the

H.M.S. *Peacock*, one of the six *Pigmy* class composite gunboats. (*Craig Leaske*)

H.M.S. *Thrush*, photographed in July 1904. *(NPC)*

memorandum, with the result that the Naval Intelligence Department was formed. Then came the final stroke. In September 1886 the memorandum was stolen, and by a strange coincidence found its way to the *Pall Mall Gazette*.

The uproar over this 'leak' (nothing was ever proved, although an Admiralty messenger was prosecuted for the theft) resulted in a reawakened public interest in naval affairs, and the early editions of the new *Brassey's Naval Annual* were crammed with facts and figures showing the relative strengths of the major powers. The accelerating Scramble for Africa also showed, if more proof were needed, that the world had grown highly competitive.

At the Jubilee Colonial Conference in 1887 Lord Salisbury summed up the situation admirably:

> The circumstances in which we live, and the tendencies of human nature as we know it, in all times of history teach that, where there is a liability to attack, and defencelessness, attack will come. The English colonies comprise some of the richest and most desirable portions of the earth's surface. The desire for foreign and colonial possessions is increasing among the nations of Europe. The power of concentrating naval and military force is increasing under the influence of scientific progress. Put all these things together and you will see that the Colonies have a real and genuine interest in the shield which their imperial connection throws over them, and that they have a ground for joining with us in making the defence of the Empire effective.[9]

The Prime Minister's final exhortation meant little, for in her new mood of imperialism the mother country no longer turned her back on colonial defence. London was no longer disposed to leave defence to the colonies, but rather to make the vital decisions on strategy and allow the colonies to help in any small way they could.

One last scare was enough to tip the scales in favour of massive modernisation of the Navy. Early in 1889 the House of Commons and House of Lords received the Report on the Manoeuvres of 1888. This document charged that the Fleet was 'altogether inadequate to take the offensive in a war with only one Great Power', and formulated the principle of the Two-Power Standard, whereby the Fleet should be maintained at a strength equal to any two enemies.[10] Despite efforts to minimise its gravity the Report was taken seriously by both Liberals and Conservatives, and few objections were heard when Lord George Hamilton introduced the great Naval Defence Act on 7 March 1889, providing for seventy new warships at a cost of £21,500,000.

The significance of the Naval Defence Act was tremendous, for it marked a drastic alteration in the composition of the Royal Navy. The 1886-87 Navy Estimates had only provided for small cruisers, sloops and the last composite gunboats, in order to give the Royal Dockyards time to bring their equipment up to date. As the keels of the first Naval Defence Act ships were laid the last composite warships were nearing completion. The following were still on the Navy List:[11]

	EFFECTIVE	NON-EFFECTIVE OR OBSOLETE
Sloops	4 *Swallow* class	7 *Osprey* class
	5 *Osprey* class	1 *Fantome* class
	6 *Mariner* class	
	2 *Dolphin* class	
Gunvessels	2 *Condor* class	1 *Kestrel* class
	2 *Linnet* class	1 *Condor* class
	1 *Arab* class	2 *Algerine* class
Gunboats	3 *Bramble* class	2 *Ariel* class
(1st class)	6 *Pigmy* class	4 *Forester* class
	3 *Albacore* class	
	1 *Banterer* class	
Gunboats	6 *Banterer* class	
(2nd class)	2 *Ariel* class	
	1 *Forester* class	

Note: There were also two steel gunvessels on the effective list, and forty iron 3rd class gunboats suitable only for coastal defence.

Due to join the Fleet were two steel sloops, *Beagle* and *Basilisk*, and another nine 1st class gunboats. Earlier in 1889 the Admiralty had reclassed all gunboats and gunvessels by their armament; those with breech-loading guns became 1st class, while the 2nd class comprised all those which retained their venerable muzzle-loaders. All the iron gunboats had muzzle-loading rifles, and were

The steel sloop H.M.S. *Beagle*. (NPC)

reduced to 3rd class status, but within two or three years the surviving gunvessels were absorbed into the gunboat classes.

As the composite gunboat reached its final stage of development in 1889 it would not be out of place to compare her with H.M.S. *Britomart*, a wooden predecessor of the 1860s. The new gunboat is H.M.S. *Thrush*, commanded for a while by the future King George V. After a busy career on foreign stations up to 1906 she joined the Coastguard and was ultimately wrecked off the Irish coast in World War I while serving as a salvage ship.

	BRITOMART (1862)	*THRUSH* (1890)
Launched	7 May 1860 at North Shields	22 June 1889 at Greenock
Building time	2½ yrs (approx.)	1¾ yrs (approx.)
Length between perpendiculars	120 ft	165 ft
Beam	22 ft	31 ft
Draught	9 ft 3 in.	11 ft 6 in.
Displacement	330 tons	805 tons
Guns	2 68-pdrs (smooth-bore M.L.)	6 4-in. quick-firers (B.L.)
Weight of broadside	176 lb. per min.	450 lb. per min.
Speed	10 knots	13 knots
Complement	40 officers and ratings	76 officers and ratings

In thirty years the gunboat had not grown in size when compared with other warship-types. Apart from her 4-inch quick-firers and a better turn of speed *Thrush* showed no marked advance on *Britomart*; there was little to choose in external appearance, for both featured the standard sail-plan known as 'gunboat rig'. *Thrush* offered better accommodation on account of her roominess, although like all composite and wooden ships she was a veritable 'bug-trap', and was always infested with cockroaches after a commission in the tropics.

Even at this late stage the gunboat had its supporters. Sir George Elliot, who had helped to design the freakish trio of armoured gunboats in the 1860s, was still preaching their virtues twenty years later. Referring to the nation's 'impoverished first line of defence',[12] he claimed that a flotilla of French gunboats[13] and torpedo-gunboats could sweep aside the Channel Fleet and support an invasion. To defeat this possibility Elliot proposed to build two new classes of gunboats, Class I of 1,800 tons, and Class II half that size. In layout they would have been enlarged editions of the little 'flat-irons' built ten years before, with a single heavy gun firing forward. Other details would be as follows:

	ARMOUR	SPEED	GUN	COST
Class I	150 tons	17 knots	1 13.5-in. 67-ton B.L.[14]	£85,000
Class II	120 tons	12 knots	1 12-in. 45-ton B.L.	£40,000

Elliott's critics pointed out that the new 3rd class cruis-

The composite
gunboat *Bramble*,
name ship of a class
of four, which were
rated as 1st Class
gunboats.
(Craig Leaske)

ers of the *Cossack (Archer)* class (1,770 tons, six 6-in.
guns) would be a better investment than the Class I gunboats, which might keep off a small squadron, but not a
determined attack. Although Elliot defended his concept
of 'the largest possible gun in the smallest hull' the battle
experience of two world wars shows that the advantage
of a single big gun against a manoeuvrable target mounting more guns of inferior calibre is usually only theoret-
ical. In December 1939 one 8-inch-gun cruiser and two
small 6-inch-gun cruisers outfought the 11-inch-gun
'pocket battleship' *Graf Spee* by making use of the fact
that the slower German ship could not range effectively
on three moving targets with her six guns in two triple
mountings. The bigger the gun, the harder it is to hit the
target quickly at long range, unless a large number of
guns are fired together in a salvo.[15] With the passing of
the Naval Defence Act, however, the days of all gunboats
were numbered. The emphasis from now on was solidly
in favour of big ships. The only small vessels ordered
were eighteen tiny 'torpedo-catchers', ancestors of the
destroyer; the rest of the programme comprised ten large
battleships and forty-two cruisers. By a belated effort the
Royal Navy had recognised and mastered the technological revolution which had begun thirty years before.
Boldly, if regretfully, Great Britain was taking up the
challenge from Europe, and by turning her back on her
Gunboat Navy she was unwittingly committing herself
to the great naval arms race which was to spend itself in
futility at Jutland.

Lord Salisbury. An early photograph, before he had become Prime Minister. *(US Library of Congress)*

Melita, one of six *Mariner* class composite sloops, was the only one to be constructed abroad. Built at Malta, she took more than twice as long as most of her sisters to complete, and cost considerably more. However, she had a long and varied career, serving with the Mediterranean Fleet until 1902, then fourteen years as a boom defence vessel at Devonport, and finally as a salvage ship until sold in 1920. *(Conway Maritime Press)*

Chapter 12

THE SCRAMBLE FOR AFRICA

The diplomatic pressure on the British Government resulting from its intervention in Egypt brought about a number of changes in Imperial policy. To win German support for his plans in Cairo Lord Salisbury had to agree to various colonial concessions in Africa and the Pacific. The British were also vulnerable to French pressure in West Africa, where France had extensive colonial possessions. In the past the French presence in West Africa had caused little friction, for the long-standing 'Liberal Alliance' had smoothed away many difficulties. Now, however, the French were anxious to offset their severe diplomatic reverse in Egypt. It was natural too for the British to recompense themselves for their concessions to Germany, and the vast areas of Africa were well suited for colonial expansion. These factors all combined to produce the tit-for-tat policy of acquisition which became known as the 'Scramble for Africa', and British gunboats played an important role at almost every stage.

The first moves took place in West Africa, where the 'gentlemen's agreement' between British and French came to a foreseeable end after 1882. The Minister of Marine and Colonies rescinded the previous instructions to French traders to refrain from colonising the hinterland, and ordered them to push up the Niger, where they soon obtained exclusive trading rights from various chiefs. These gestures were not lost on British traders on the Niger, who immediately petitioned the Colonial Office for some form of support. By this time the traders were better organised than they had been in the 1870s, having amalgamated to form an influential group, the National African Trading Company.[1] This group warned the Government about the French activity and suggested that the French should be asked to withdraw from the Lower Niger and the Benue in return for a free hand in the region between Senegal and the Upper Niger. But the French refused to co-operate with the British in any informal arrangements, pointing out that such agreements had not availed them in Egypt.

Despite their continuing aversion to annexation of African colonies the British were acutely aware of the potential trade which they might lose. This fear was reinforced when it was learned that Stanley and Savorgnan de Brazza were opening up the Congo River. The French intention had only been to protect Gabon, but when they realised that the British were uneasy about Brazza's treaty-making they promptly gave him official backing. The British reply to this was to acknowledge Portugal's claims to the Congo basin, although these claims had been studiously ignored by the Foreign Office for forty years! The idea behind this decision was that Portugal would hold the territory on behalf of Great Britain, and thus relieve her of the expense and political difficulties involved in holding it herself. There was even talk of buying out King Leopold's concession in the Congo and turning it into an English company.[2]

To defeat this move the French turned to the Germans, who gladly accepted the chance to drive a wedge between the two former allies. The British were hampered by the fact that they needed Bismarck's assistance in Cairo; without German support on the Debt Commission it was almost impossible to govern Egypt. When it was learned that Bismarck was against the British in their plans for the Congo, their resolution evaporated; all attempts to block the French by means of an Anglo-Portuguese treaty were dropped, and German demands were met. By 1884 it seemed that the British were on the retreat throughout West Africa.

Concessions to the Germans followed in East Africa, where once the Sultan of Zanzibar had enjoyed paramountcy under British protection. Despite the Sultan's misgivings the British allowed the Germans to carve themselves a large holding on the mainland opposite Zanzibar. Further south, the Portuguese showed new initiative in opening the Zambesi River as a route to Central Africa, a move which forced London into negotiations over the control of the hinterland. Lord Salisbury had ignored appeals from missionaries to declare a British protectorate over the area around Lake Nyasa, but he was insistent that the Portuguese should keep out of Matabeleland and Mashonaland. The missionaries and the African Lakes Company which supported them were fighting a constant battle with Arab slave-traders on Lake Nyasa, but London remained unwilling to give any help. There was even talk of the Portuguese closing the Zambesi to British steamers, a state of affairs which would never have arisen ten years before.

Salisbury was not averse, however, to using gunboats to convey a gentle warning to the Portuguese that interference with the African Lakes Company steamers would not be tolerated indefinitely. In 1889 the little survey ship *Stork* (a converted gunboat) was sent to survey the mouth of the Zambesi. When the Portuguese warships in the river threatened to open fire *Stork*'s commander sounded 'Action Stations'. With her two 6-pounders manned, and the boatswain brandishing an enormous axe on the forecastle, she steamed on, while the Portuguese commodore contented himself with firing a round of blank charges![3]

The following year a more determined effort was made to keep the river open. The British Government had tired of negotiating with the Portuguese, and ordered the building of two stern-wheel gunboats, *Mosquito* and *Herald*, to patrol the Zambesi. In view of the probable reaction of the Portuguese authorities a covering force was collected at Zanzibar. When the two stern-wheelers were finally ready two composite gunboats, *Pigeon* and *Redbreast*, were ordered to cross the bar first. The principal difficulty was that the Portuguese had never made available any charts of the river mouth, and *Redbreast*'s navigator was forced to rely on the sketchy survey done by *Stork* the year before. At times the two gunboats were wedged in the channel, and finally *Pigeon* was withdrawn in order to avoid the risk of losing two ships. However, *Redbreast* ultimately forced her way through and became the first British warship to sail on the Zambesi. This exploit had little more than prestige value, as seagoing gunboats drew far too much water to go any higher up the river, but the point had been made, and Portugal acknowledged the African Lakes Company's rights.

Disputes between the French and British over the boundaries of their colonies in West Africa produced a great deal of unrest among the tribes affected. Early in 1891 an Anglo-French boundary commission was attacked near the Gambia River, and although the party was rescued by the paddle-gunboat *Alecto*[4] the tribes in the area remained unsettled. The Senior Officer at

Bathurst ordered the sloop *Swallow* and the gunboat *Widgeon* to join *Alecto* and land some men. Peace was restored for the moment, but when rumours of fresh disturbances reached the Governor in Bathurst at the end of the year further action had to be taken. Three gunboats, *Sparrow*, *Widgeon* and *Thrush*, were ordered to round up the rebellious chief believed to have caused the original attack.

The expedition mustered in the Gambia River on New Year's Day 1892, but the chief proved particularly elusive. Although the Naval Brigade burnt all his strongholds before withdrawing, the chief returned to the area within two weeks, and the Naval Brigade had to be called in again. By the end of January it was clear that reinforcements were needed, and eventually close on 500 men were hunting fruitlessly through villages and bush. The expedition was finally recalled in February 1892, when it was learned that the fugitive had crossed the border and gone over to the French. No attempt appears to have been made to arrange for his extradition.

Two years later another outbreak of unrest in the Gambia River provoked naval intervention on a small scale, but this was followed by an insurrection in the Brass River district, where a warehouse at Akassa was burned down. The punitive expedition organised was bigger than usual, and comprised two cruisers and the gunboats *Thrush* and *Widgeon*. This time the show of force met with rather more success than usual, although there were several casualties.

The encroachments made by the Germans in East Africa strained relations between Great Britain and the Sultan of Zanzibar, and created fresh problems in a part of the world that had once been almost exclusively under British control. The Zanzibaris, after sullenly concurring in the suppression of the slave trade, were further humiliated when the Germans encroached on their mainland territories. Step by step the extensive possessions of the Sultan were being whittled away, and since Great Britain was acquiescent her puppet ruler had to submit as well.

The death of the reigning Sultan on 25 August 1896 precipitated yet another succession crisis, a rebellion by one of the royal princes, Seyyid Khalid ben Barghash. The pretender broke into the palace with his followers and presented the British Agent with a demand for recognition as the new Sultan. This demand carried some considerable weight, for most of the Zanzibari Army had deserted to him, and arms had been distributed to the mob. Seyyid Khalid repeated his demand to the European consuls, who all replied that they would recognise him as Sultan if the British did so.

The first British reaction was to fortify the English Club, and then as an afterthought, to defend the Agency. In harbour at the time were the cruiser *Philomel* and the gunboat *Thrush*, which landed every man they could spare. Later that morning another gunboat arrived from Aden, and it began to look as if the situation might be retrieved. *Thrush* was warped across the harbour so that her guns could bear on the palace as a prelude to negotiations. No further action was taken that day, but as the sun set the Sultan's 'gunboat' *Glasgow* (now in rebel hands) fired a salute. Next morning the deadlock continued, although two more cruisers arrived within a few hours of one another, *St George* and *Racoon*. By nightfall the five warships were moored in line with every available gun trained on the palace.

With the arrival of the flagship *St George* the pace of events had already quickened on shore, for Rear-Admiral Sir Harry Rawson was a man of action. With his black beard and stocky figure he looked every inch a sailor, and was a veteran of African coastal warfare. At seven o'clock on the morning of 27 March 1897 he gave Seyyid Khalid a last warning that he had two hours to strike his colours. While foreign vessels got clear of the harbour and the British ships went to action stations a number of armed dhows mustered near the *Glasgow*. Clearly Seyyid Khalid felt confident enough to fight and on the face of it his preponderance in artillery gave him the advantage.

The palace clock struck nine o'clock, and a 4-inch gun on *Thrush*'s forecastle belched smoke. Within seconds the sound of gunfire rolled around the harbour as *Racoon* and *Sparrow* joined in. The *Glasgow* fired a few shots, but this only drew the fire of the three cruisers, and she was quickly silenced. The bombardment lasted exactly thirty-seven minutes, the time it took Seyyid Khalid to strike his flag. *Glasgow* was a burning wreck, and the warships' shellfire had destroyed the palace and sunk several dhows. In another two hours Rawson's ships were firing a 21-gun salute in honour of the new Sultan, and another incident had ended. As usual the British losses were trifling, a seaman wounded compared to the hundreds killed and wounded by the bombardment.

Rawson was also in command of two of the last important naval operations on the coast of West Africa. The first was the provision of a naval contingent for the final Ashanti War of 1895-96, which ended in the capture of King Prempeh and the elimination of the Ashanti threat to the Gold Coast. The second operation was on a far bigger scale, calling for six cruisers and three gunboats. The Benin Expedition was conceived to put an end to the threat to the Niger Coast Protectorate from the powerful kingdom of Benin. The campaign was a masterpiece of planning and brevity, especially when one considers that it was mounted by the Royal Navy with only Hausa troops in support.

Rawson received his orders on 15 January 1897, and concentrated his squadron off the Benin and Brass Rivers on 3 February. In addition to the four cruisers from the Cape of Good Hope[5] and the gunboats *Alecto*, *Widgeon* and *Magpie* he had the welcome reinforcement of the cruisers *Forte* and *Theseus* from the Mediterranean. The key to success was speed, since delay would cause fearful wastage of men from fever, so Rawson kept his landing force embarked until the Hausas and porters had been collected on shore. Rawson took 1,200 men ashore on 9 February and began his march on Benin. To mislead the enemy a small force was sent to cover the main road and make a feint attack on Benin, while the main column fought its way through the bush, relying on its speed of advance to take the enemy by surprise.

In spite of constant sniping and a shortage of water the column reached Benin on 18 February after a running fight. The stench was appalling, for the king had ordered a fresh batch of sacrifices to propitiate the gods and to delay Rawson. Huge pits were found full of decapitated and mutilated bodies, and the smell of corruption hung over the city. The place was patently unhealthy, and Rawson prepared to leave as quickly as possible, leaving the Hausas to garrison it. As soon as the palaver between the Beni chiefs and the political officer from Lagos was concluded the British forces were withdrawn, but although they were re-embarked by 27 February the losses from fever were very high. After only eighteen days on shore the expedition's surgeons recorded 2,290 cases of fever, nearly all among the 1,200 men who marched to Benin.[6]

Return to the Sudan

When it was realised in London that a hostile European power at the head of the Nile could control the Suez Canal the destiny of the Sudan suddenly became identified with British interests. For eleven years the Khalifa had ruled this vast land from his gloomy capital at Omdurman with only occasional interference from the Anglo-Egyptian garrisons on his frontiers. It had been known for some time that the French were prepared to make the Khalifa promises of arms, and that French rifles had reached Abyssinia.[7] In Gladstone's time the problem of European powers establishing relations with the Khalifa had never arisen, for no European nation established in Central Africa was capable of pursuing such a course. But in 1895 the Italians had begun an advance into the uplands of Abyssinia. In March 1896 the Abyssinians routed the Italians at Adowa; not only was the Italian dream of colonial glory shattered but the balance of power was rudely upset. Lord Salisbury realised that the possibility of an alliance between the Emperor of Abyssinia and the Khalifa would be a menace to Egypt and the Canal, and immediately ordered the first move in the reconquest of the Sudan.

The power of the Khalifa had been steadily declining since the death of the Mahdi in 1886, but the Dervish strength was still formidable. In contrast the British position was immeasurably stronger than it had been in the days of Hicks Pasha and the Gordon Relief Expedition. Years of work by Cromer and his subordinates had put Egypt on an even keel, and by 1895 the country was looking forward to a budget surplus for the first time. The Egyptian Army had been carefully trained and nursed through a number of small battles with the Dervishes until it achieved full confidence in itself. Apart from the cost, Egypt was fully prepared for an attempt to recover her lost dominion. However, a Treasury loan of £800,000 tided the Egyptian Exchequer over for the moment, and provided for a railway and a flotilla of river-gunboats.

The railway was the key to the problem of fighting in the arid wastes of the Sudan, for it was the only means of supplying an army operating a thousand miles and more from its main base. The gunboats would ensure the safety of the railway while it was under construction, as well as providing vital reconnaissance. Officers and men were seconded from the Mediterranean Fleet, and the flotilla was placed under the command of the Sirdar of the Egyptian Army, Herbert Kitchener. Although Kitchener's campaign was severely limited, for reasons which will be seen, his gunboats reached as far south as Meroë before they were recalled, and distinguished themselves in an action at Hafir on 19 September 1896. In spite of a warning that a French expedition was on the way to the Upper Nile from West Africa Kitchener's forces were halted in 1897, when they were only 200 miles from Khartoum.

The delay was deliberate, for Salisbury wished to see if certain diplomatic overtures to the Emperor of Abyssinia would bear fruit before he sanctioned the final overthrow of the Dervish Empire. Unfortunately French diplomacy had forestalled the British, and Sir Rennell Rodd was unable to convince Menelik that his government could make a better offer. After toying with the idea of an advance from Uganda[8] Salisbury realised that speed was of paramount importance, and ordered Kitchener to make the final advance in 1898. This time British troops were used for the final destruction of the Dervish Army, just in case the ghastly fiascos of 1882-84 were repeated. The naval contingent was doubled, and some of the future flag-officers of the 1914-18 War were sent out to man the gunboats, including Beatty, Cowan and Hood.

The gunboats were manhandled through the Cataracts[9] and accompanied the final drive on Omdurman, where their bombardment demoralised the Dervishes. One of them was able to exert a decisive influence at one stage of the battle. The Camel Corps had suffered heavy losses, and had been detached by General Broadwood to return to the main zeriba. Unfortunately the course lay over rocky ground, and when a large force of Dervishes moved up to cut them off their position became most dangerous. Moving at over seven miles an hour the Arabs were soon within four hundred yards of the Camel Corps, and it seemed that the situation could only be retrieved by a suicidal charge from the reserve cavalry. 'The Camel Corps were already close to the river. But thousands of Dervishes were running swiftly towards them at right angles to their line of retreat, and it was certain that if the camelry attempted to cross this new front of the enemy they would be annihilated.'[10]

Fortunately two of the gunboats busy shelling the city and the Mahdi's tomb had been ordered to cover the retreat of the Camel Corps, and the first boat arrived just in time. '... The gunboat arrived on the scene and began suddenly to blaze and flame from Maxim guns, quick-firing guns and rifles. The range was short; the effect tremendous. The terrible machine, floating gracefully on the waters – a beautiful white devil – wreathed itself in smoke. The river slopes of the Kerreri Hills, crowded with the advancing thousands, sprang up into clouds of dust and splinters of rock. The charging Dervishes sank down in tangled heaps. The masses in the rear paused, irresolute. It was too hot even for them.'[11]

Apart from holding the Army's left flank at Omdurman and providing invaluable fire-support, the gunboats' most important work was done immediately after the battle. On 7 September 1898 a small Dervish steamer arrived with the news that the French had reached the Upper Nile. It was the Marchand expedition, which had set out from French West Africa at the end of 1896 to stake a French claim to the Nile Valley, and Kitchener was just in time to defeat an audacious *coup*. The next day five steamers, including the powerful new gunboat *Sultan*, two Sudanese battalions and some artillery, set off on the long journey southward to Equatoria.

Ten days later Kitchener's flotilla reached the little mud fort at Fashoda, where they found Major Marchand with eight French officers and some hundred Senegalese soldiers. Ignoring the Tricolour hanging limply from a crude flagstaff Kitchener's party hoisted the Union Jack and the Egyptian flag, to signify that the country now belonged jointly to Great Britain and its former rulers. Poor Marchand could do little to oppose this humiliation, for his force had hardly any ammunition left after its incredibly heroic journey across Africa, and would have been annihilated by Dervish forces if Kitchener's army had not won at Omdurman.

The subsequent 'Fashoda Incident' brought Britain and France close to war, for the French tried to insist that Marchand had conquered the Sudan in France's name. But the total victory of Omdurman and the strength of the Anglo-Egyptian Army made the French pretensions too hopeless to be continued. Had the territory not previously belonged to Egypt, and had the conquest not been undertaken on Egypt's behalf, with Egyptian money, the French claim to have 'discovered' the Upper Nile might have been valid. But when the awesome might of the Royal Navy was mobilised, and war seemed certain, the French retreated from the brink.[12] France swallowed her pride and accepted concessions elsewhere. With the British in control of the entire Nile Valley, the Scramble was over. But Britain's so-called splendid isolation was over too, and in the decade that followed a revolution in British policy was to take place; this revolution would in turn cause drastic changes in the country's naval organisation.

Chapter 13

THE FISHER AXE

The Naval Defence Act struck the first blow at the Gunboat Navy, and the gunboat's standing declined still further in the 1890s. Thus the *coup de grâce* from Fisher was inevitable. However, the process of deterioration must not be exaggerated. Although the Act had provided for rapid replacement of obsolete warships, in fact only thirty old ships were deleted from the Navy List between 1889 and 1894; eight of these were wooden sloops and ten were gunvessels.[1] The building of large numbers of cruisers meant the end of the Gunboat Era but the race took some time to die out.

The gunboat's decline was the logical result of the rising challenge to Britain's status as a world power. The Naval Defence Act was the first official recognition that such a challenge existed, and the next fifteen years saw successive British governments making fresh appraisals of the country's diplomatic position and the naval resources behind it.

The first revision of policy stemmed from the situation in the eastern Mediterranean. As we have seen, Franco-Russian co-operation made the Admiralty doubtful of its ability to protect Turkey from a Russian attack. In the summer of 1893 this nebulous fear was crystallised by the news that a Russian squadron was due to pay a courtesy visit to Toulon. The predictable upshot was yet another naval scare, with the usual calls for vast increases in the naval estimates. As in the past these demands were fought tooth and nail by the Liberals and Radicals of the old school, whose archetype, Gladstone, was in his fourth term as Prime Minister. Even Gladstone could not prevail against this wave of agitation, and his resignation on 1 March 1894 symbolised the defeat of the pacific, frugal philosophy of the Gunboat Era, which he had carried to such extremes. In the new building programmes for the years 1894-98 no fewer than seven battleships were provided for, two 1st class cruisers, nine 2nd class cruisers, eight 3rd class cruisers, two sloops, seven torpedo-gunboats and eighty-two destroyers.[2] These last were the Admiralty's defiant answer to the swarms of French torpedo-boats built to conform to the *Jeune Ecole*'s concept of hit-and-run warfare; so successful was the new 'torpedo-boat destroyer' that it not only drove the torpedo-boat from the scene within ten years, but took over its function as well.

These reinforcements were not due to join the Fleet until 1899 at the earliest, and long before that a Turkish crisis forced a radical change in Britain's Middle Eastern policy. Late in 1894 the Sultan Abdul Hamid began a systematic extermination of the Armenian population of the Ottoman Empire, at which British opinion clamoured for some form of intervention. But the Admiralty was by now convinced that the risks inherent in forcing the Dardanelles were unacceptable in the face of Turkish opposition (and in view of the damage wrought by a makeshift defence in 1915 we must assume that the Admiralty's fears were justified). Moreover the French revealed in June 1895 that an alliance existed between themselves and the Russians; the probability of Franco-Russian collusion against Great Britain was now almost a certainty.

Given these harsh conditions the new Conservative Government under Lord Salisbury (which had returned to power in the summer of 1895) decided to make a virtue of necessity by abandoning the long-standing British connection with Constantinople. It had long been obvious (see Ch. 11) that Cairo was now the pivot of Great Britain's strategy in the Levant, but overt recognition of this fact meant jettisoning the century-old British protection of the Turks, leaving them open to the influence of other powers. Salisbury found this prospect less disagreeable than most, having been pessimistic about the Sultan's survival for some twenty years. On his return to office he had even gone so far as discussing a possible partition of the Ottoman Empire with the German Ambassador. The deciding factor was the firm British hold on Egypt and the Suez Canal, for with these aces in his hand Salisbury could see no point in propping up the Turks any more.

The Director of Naval Intelligence supported the new move wholeheartedly. In a memorandum dated October

1895 (following a second bout of Armenian massacres) he argued that 'there would be only one way in which England could not only sustain herself in the Mediterranean at all, but continue to hold India, and that is by holding Egypt against all comers and making Alexandria a naval base'. Shortly afterwards Salisbury told Austria and Italy that he did not wish to renew the Mediterranean Agreements guaranteeing the *status quo* in Turkey. The consolidation of the British position in Egypt – already begun by Rosebery's seizure of Uganda in 1894 – was completed by the reconquest of the Sudan by Kitchener in 1898. The headwaters of the Nile were now firmly in British hands, and the withdrawal of support from Constantinople was irreversible.

Securing Egypt solved only one problem, however, and there were many more on the horizon. In December 1895 the United States presented a major challenge to British influence in the Western Hemisphere by claiming the right to arbitrate in a border dispute between British Guiana and Venezuela; the following month Kaiser Wilhelm II's famous 'Kruger Telegram' showed that Germany was itching to take a hand in the worsening relations between London and the Boer Republics. In each case the crisis was soon over, for neither the Germans nor the Americans had the naval strength to back up their pretensions. But both the Cabinet and the Admiralty knew how badly

stretched Britain's resources would be if she should face simultaneous threats from various quarters, since the margin of superiority over the Franco-Russian Alliance was not enough to allow ships to be detached from the Mediterranean to reinforce the vessels in the Caribbean during the Venezuelan affair.

The first British reaction was merely an increase in the Navy Estimates, and in March 1896 Salisbury's First Lord, Goschen, announced an expanded building programme calculated to appease all but the most insatiable navalists. It was clear that the country was entering a period altogether unlike the palmy days of *Pax Britannica*, and that a police-force Navy would no longer do if the Fleet were to be kept on a war footing to meet the challenges from abroad. The long Victorian peace now seemed nothing more than an interlude, not the dawn of the liberal millennium. Naval strategists and theorists found themselves looking back to the forgotten principles of the eighteenth century and the wars against Napoleon as their guide to an uncertain future. It was then, as the American naval historian Alfred Mahan pointed out, Britain had developed the superb weapon of sea power which had saved her from military defeat and invasion, and had in turn given her an enormous maritime empire. In his widely-read books, *The Influence of Sea Power upon History* and *The Influence of Sea Power upon the French Revolution and Empire*, Mahan showed

Rinaldo, one of six *Condor* class steel sloops built around the turn of the century. *(Craig Leaske)*

that the benefits of sea power were no accident of history, but the logical outcome of a series of cardinal principles. It was now time for the Royal Navy to relearn these principles to enable the Empire to survive against the most powerful land armies on earth.

At such a time it is hardly surprising that the gunboat was under fire. In 1896 the influential new yearbook *Brassey's Naval Annual* remarked that 'the number of ships absolutely valueless for war purposes which we maintain in commission on foreign stations is very large', and suggested that 2nd and 3rd class cruisers should replace these craft as they wore out. This argument was taken a step further by a well-known journalist, G. W. Steevens, in a book called *Naval Policy*, which appeared in the same year. Steevens tried to translate the endless annual returns of warships and statistics into language which the layman could understand. In one vivid example he showed that the obsolete ships on the Australian and Pacific Stations absorbed 1,600 seasoned sailors. Since these craft were 'too weak to fight, and too slow to run away', they would be forced to skulk in harbour at a time when men might be desperately needed to man cruisers and battleships in Home waters. An alternative suggested by Steevens was to maintain cruisers in reserve at important foreign bases like Hong Kong and Esquimalt. A Naval Defence Act cruiser of the *Apollo* class (3,400 tons) could have been commissioned by laying up three sloops, although a larger type might require the crews of five sloops or gunboats.

In spite of such critics the Admiralty was not yet entirely converted to the new way of thinking. In 1896 there were still twenty-two sloops and twenty-five gunboats on the Navy List, but only four gunvessels. The disposition of those in commission was as follows:[3]

Cape of Good Hope	6
North America	6
East Indies	3
China	8 (not including river-craft)
Australia	3
Pacific	3
	29

Between 1893 and 1904 the Admiralty built sixteen vessels rated as sloops, but actually little more than steel editions of the gunboats built before the Naval Defence Act. Like the gunboats they were fully rigged and armed with six 4-inch guns. They were beautiful little ships, with yacht-like lines and slim graceful funnels, but they were obviously not meant to fight. Cheapness was their real virtue, for they lacked all the refinements of bigger ships, such as steam-capstans and electric lighting. They were steered by an enormous double wheel aft, which took two men to hold it in normal weather. Fresh meat was provided by sheep and cattle penned on the upper deck, usually two or three cows and eight to ten sheep. It was as if the designers had deliberately worked in as many reminders of the Navy of 1875 as they could, and as a final touch of unrepentant decadence the new ships even had figureheads!

In direct contrast the last proper gunboats to be ordered were quite modern in appearance. The only traditional point about them was their names: *Dwarf,*

The steel sloop *Cadmus,* launched in 1903, was the last ship to be built for the Royal Navy at Sheerness. She may well also have been the last to have had a figurehead. *(Craig Leaske)*

The *Bramble* class gunboat *Britomart*,
photographed in 1910. *(Craig Leaske)*

Bramble, *Britomart* and *Thistle* had all been borne by
gunboats and gunvessels before. Designed for service in
West Africa and China, they were built of steel, and had
two light masts. Like the steel sloops their equipment
was simple; all ground tackle was worked by hand, and
although a searchlight (and later, wireless) was provided,
all lighting was by candle-lamp.

The logic of events, however, was spelling out the
doom of all these craft, as British statesmen found that
the most astronomical expenditure on the Navy could
still not buy security from the international challenge.
The first German Navy Law of 1897 brought this fact
home, with its bald announcement that the Kaiser also
wanted a formidable fleet of battleships. For a time many
navalists argued that this threat could be met by boosting
the Naval Estimates, as had been done in 1889, 1894
and 1896. Since Britain was successfully outbuilding the
French and Russians, surely she could take on the
Germans as well? But on reflection this proved a vain
hope, for the cost of maintaining British isolation was
becoming prohibitive; if further competition were to
come from the United States and Japan (which both pos-
sessed growing fleets) the expense would be intolerable.
What was needed was not what commentators like
Steevens suggested – a preventive war against the new
rivals – but a drastic pruning of British world-wide commitments in order to enable the Navy to meet the most
fundamental threats to the country's security. In other
words, Britain was now forced to admit that she could no
longer control the seas without a second thought. As

Lord Rosebery emphatically put it: 'We cannot afford to
be the Knight Errant of the world, careering about to
redress grievances and help the weak.' Gunboat diplomacy had become a dangerous luxury.

Who, then, represented the greatest danger to British
interests? To most people the answer was simple: France
and Russia were Britain's traditional enemies. The
instinctive reaction was to associate with the rising power
of Germany, and thus redress the European naval balance. So thought Joseph Chamberlain, perhaps the most
important figure in the Conservative Cabinet after
Salisbury himself. In the spring of 1898 Chamberlain
offered the Germans an alliance entirely on his own
responsibility, and in spite of Salisbury's disapproval
negotiations dragged on for three years. But the Germans
were not interested in the idea for various reasons, and by
the end of 1901 even Chamberlain admitted defeat.

The outbreak of the Boer War made it imperative to
consolidate the Empire's defences, since Britain found
herself more isolated than at any time since the American
War of Independence in the 1770s. During this disastrous war the long-heralded redisposition of naval
strength began. The first area to be affected by this was
the Caribbean, where American pressure was mounting.
For decades the Americans had endeavoured to maintain
their interests in the region, and now they were determined to be masters of the new canal to be cut across the
Isthmus of Panama, just as the British held Suez. By the
Clayton-Bulwer Treaty of 1850 Great Britain and the
United States had agreed to respect one another's inter-

ests in the area, but Washington, with its prestige enhanced by the triumph over Spain, now asked for British recognition of American paramountcy. In November 1901 this demand was recognised, and Great Britain forfeited her position as the leading naval Power in the West Indies. The alternative was an arms race with the United States, which was unthinkable unless Britain was prepared to cut her commitments in Home waters and elsewhere.

The second important realignment was in the Far East, where British differences with the Russians had been unsettled for years. But the Russian occupation of Manchuria in 1900, taking into account the Franco-Russian Alliance, made Britain's position precarious. The First Lord, Selborne, pointed out in September 1901 that Great Britain would be outnumbered by the French and Russians in the Far East to the tune of nine battle-ships to four. Since both Germany and the United States had rejected British overtures for a Far Eastern partnership Britain was forced to turn to Japan, the greatest Asian naval Power. The Japanese themselves had made approaches to London in 1898, with a suggestion for a naval combination against the Russians which would 'sweep the sea', and this was still in their minds when the British renewed the discussions in 1901. British motives were less belligerent: a wish to create an equilibrium in naval strength in the Far East, so as to avoid the need to reinforce the squadrons there with units from Home waters. As in the Caribbean, British policy was dictated by the basic requirement for defence of the British Isles. The Japanese, on the other hand, did not see things this way, and looked on the Anglo-Japanese Alliance (signed in January 1902) as the green light for their intended war with Russia, since Great Britain agreed to remain neutral in any such war.

The British concern for Home defence which influenced both these settlements was caused by the rapid build-up in the strength of the German battle-fleet. In 1900 von Tirpitz had steered a second Navy Law through the Reichstag; its provision for a North Sea Squadron pointed to only one possible adversary. By the following year the British Director of Naval Intelligence was convinced that Germany was Britain's most likely enemy, and Selborne drafted a memorandum to the Cabinet in which he declared that 'the great new German navy is being carefully built up from the point of view of a war with us'. Since Germany had rejected Chamberlain's approaches, it now seemed that the only course was to seek a European alliance with France or Russia, Britain's chief antagonists of only four years before!

An attempt to come to terms with St Petersburg had, in fact, been made since 1901. When the Marquess of Lansdowne, the Foreign Secretary, placed the outline of the Japanese alliance before the Cabinet he also set out proposals for an understanding with Russia over Persia

Sir John Fisher, as Vice Admiral, in 1902.
(Conway Maritime Press)

and Manchuria. Early in 1903 the new Prime Minister, Balfour, was prepared to let the Russians have Constantinople if they had wanted it. Nevertheless relations between Britain and Russia remained difficult for various reasons, not least the Anglo-Japanese Alliance, so the British diplomatic effort was concentrated on France. A rapprochement with the French had actually begun immediately after the Fashoda crisis in 1898, when the French formally renounced all claims to the Nile Valley. This welcome new trend was hastened by an agreement over Siam in 1902, and then in the spring of 1903 came King Edward's famous visit to Paris.

The outbreak of the long-expected Russo-Japanese War in February 1904 gave a sharp impetus to the negotiations between France and Great Britain. The treaty with Japan bound the British to aid the Japanese in a war with France *and* Russia, although the British had agreed to remain neutral in a war between Japan and Russia alone. Thus an understanding with France was the only way of avoiding the nightmare of a conflict with France and Russia, the fear which had dominated British strategy since 1887. The Entente Cordiale was signed in April 1904, and Great Britain took yet another step away from isolation.

The Entente Cordiale was ostensibly concerned with the settlement of colonial squabbles. The French finally recognised the British seizure of Egypt, while Britain for her part acknowledged France's claims to Morocco, with the proviso that the coastline opposite Gibraltar should be undefended, and should go to Spain. But its underlying significance was strategic, though it was far from a naval or military alliance as originally conceived in 1904. Its implications affected the Royal Navy profoundly, and as the two countries drew closer together, so naval and military cooperation grew. Just as the treaties with Washington and Tokyo allowed the Admiralty greater freedom in the allocation of British naval resources, the Entente paved the way for a still more fundamental redistribution of the Fleet. At a single stroke the pressure on the Mediterranean, the Atlantic and the Channel disappeared, allowing the Royal Navy to be marshalled in the North Sea to face the growing menace from Germany. The moment was also ripe for a massive shake-up to improve the Fleet's efficiency.

The man chosen to initiate this revolution in naval policy was Admiral Sir John Fisher, the same 'Jacky' Fisher who had helped W. T. Stead to rouse the nation with his 'Truth about the Navy' series in 1884. Fisher was convinced that the Royal Navy must be transformed as fast as possible to be ready for its 'Armageddon' with Germany. Apart from a whole series of overdue administrative reforms four points distinguished his grand design. First, new ships were needed to take advantage of the current revolution in gunnery; in other words, the all-big-gun battleship, the *Dreadnought*, was to provide the first line of defence against a German attack. With the *Dreadnought* went the fast battle-cruiser to protect British merchant shipping against marauders. The second point in the Fisher plan was a full-scale redistribution of the Fleet which would concentrate the best fighting ships in Home waters; this was a fascinating echo of the Childers policy of 1869-71, but rendered possible this time by the dictates of a radically different international situation. 'The principles upon which the present peace distribution of His Majesty's ships and the arrangement of their stations are based', declared a scathing Admiralty statement, 'date from a period when the electric telegraph did not exist and when wind was the motive power.'[4] All this was to change, as it was decreed that 'the peace distribution of the fleet should also be its best strategical distribution for war' – a far cry from the philosophy of *Pax Britannica*.

The third point was the creation of an efficient reserve of ships which would be ready to reinforce those in commission. These vessels would be manned by 'nucleus crews' to keep them in fighting trim, and to provide trained cadres to bring the ships to full efficiency in time of war. Finally came the corollary to this scheme, which sounded the death-knell of the gunboat, for Fisher ordered all obsolete warships to be withdrawn from for-

eign stations to provide the manpower for the nucleus crews. This was, in effect, the plan outlined by Steevens in 1896. These ships, argued Fisher, were now a positive hindrance to the Navy if a war broke out. 'What will happen to our *Odins*, *Redbreasts*, *Fantomes*, *Dwarfs* &c.?' With characteristic glee he provided the answer: 'An enemy cruiser would lap them up like an armadillo let loose on an ant-hill.' He concluded that the broadcast use of gunboats was 'a marked strategic weakness … the gunboat is merely a symbol of the power of the nation, not a concrete embodiment of it'. The Navy's first duty was not to show the flag, but to be 'instantly ready to strike', and this could only be brought about by 'concentrating our strength into ships of undoubted fighting value, ruthlessly discarding those that have become obsolete'. The only areas where Fisher saw any possible scope for gunboat operations were China and West Africa, 'where the civilisation of the inhabitants of the shores is such as … to preclude them obtaining and mounting guns of sufficient size to put the vessels to any considerable inconvenience'.[5]

So Fisher pronounced sentence of death upon the gunboat. The surviving vessels were all pigeonholed under the unflattering labels of 'sheep', 'goats' and 'llamas' as follows:[6]

THE 'SHEEP' – SHIPS FOR SALE AND SOLD

Battleship	*Simoom* (ex-*Monarch*)		
Cruisers	*Warspite*	*Mersey*	*Fearless*
	Australia	*Raleigh*	*Mohawk*
	Galatea	*Boadicea*	*Porpoise*
	Orlando	*Iris*	*Tartar*
	Northampton	*Active*	*Racoon*
	Hector	*Archer*	*Barracouta*
	Arethusa	*Cossack*	*Barrosa*
	Severn	*Marathon*	*Magicienne*
	Melpomene	*Blonde*	*Pearl*
	Blanche	*Ringarooma*	*Mildura*
	Phoebe	*Katoomba*	*Wallaroo*
	Pallas	*Tauranga*	
Torpedo-gunboats	*Sandfly*	*Karrakatta*	*Salamander*
	Jaseur	*Grasshopper*	*Renard*
	Gleaner		
Sloop	*Beagle*		
Gunboats	*Bouncer*	*Redwing*	*Pickle*
	Sparrow	*Starling*	*Snake*
	Pincher	*Tweed*	*Pigmy*
	Fancy	*Pike*	*Lizard*
	Partridge	*Skylark*[7]	

OBSOLETE VESSELS

Gunboats	*Widgeon*	*Dapper*[8]
Gunvessel	*Curlew*	

THE 'LLAMAS' – SHIPS AVAILABLE FOR SUBSIDIARY PURPOSES OF WAR

Cruisers	*Mercury*	*Amphion*	*Brisk*
	Calliope		
Torpedo-gunboats	*Rattlesnake*	*Onyx*	
Sloops	*Alert*	*Algerine*	*Cadmus*
	Clio	*Fantome*	*Mutine*
	Melita	*Torch*	*Merlin*
	Phoenix	*Racer*	*Rinaldo*
	Rosario	*Vestal*	*Odin*
Gunboats	*Bramble*	*Britomart*	*Magpie*
	Peacock	*Pheasant*	*Pigeon*
	Rattler	*Redpole*	*Ringdove*
	Thistle	*Thrush*	*Cockchafer*
	Albacore	*Stork*	
Gunvessels	*Landrail*	*Flamingo*	

THE 'GOATS' – SHIPS STRUCK OFF THE EFFECTIVE LIST[9]

Battleships	*Sans Pareil*	*Collingwood*	*Conqueror*
	Hero		
Cruisers	*Immortalité*	*Narcissus*	*Undaunted*
	Aurora	*Tribune*	*Andromache*
	Pique	*Naiad*	*Apollo*
	Melampus	*Intrepid*	*Spartan*
	Rainbow	*Retribution*	*Pomone*
	Pactolus	*Medusa*	*Medea*
	Philomel	*Pylades*	
Torpedo-gunboats	*Alarm*	*Sheldrake*	*Antelope*

True, not all the ships Fisher had wished to liquidate found their way on to these black lists, and even the lists were misleading. Certain venerable warriors went to the scrapheap, but many vessels on the Sale List actually survived for many years. There seemed little rhyme or reason about the selection of ships for the lists; sister-ships could be found on the Effective List, the Sale List and the Subsidiary List. The majority appeared to have been picked at random, but the result was the same. By 1914, ten years later, there were scarcely a dozen seagoing sloops and gunboats left in service.

A contemporary depiction of some of the ships that Fisher proposed to discard or reduce to 'subsidiary purposes', including a number of gunboats. The artist, Norman Wilkinson, went on to become one of Britain's greatest maritime painters. *(US Library of Congress)*

Chapter 14

THE LAST OF THE GUNBOATS

W hile the echoes of Fisher's naval reforms were still reverberating around the Admiralty the forces of opposition were gathering. Aptly enough, the leader of the anti-Fisher party was Lord Charles Beresford,[1] who had earned his laurels in the palmy days of gunboating.

Both Fisher and Beresford had qualities of their own, but their great dispute was marred by petty, vindictive actions. Sordid quarrels between the First Sea Lord and the Commander-in-Chief became common knowledge, not only in the Navy, but in the press. Beresford and his supporters criticised every detail of the redistribution of the Fleet, while the Fisherites vehemently defended it. Each side flooded the newspapers with pamphlets, articles and letters, and by 1908 the rift had become so great that the unity of the service was greatly impaired.[2] Fortunately in addition to those naval officers in the 'Fishpond' and those out of it, there was a third body who refused to take sides; by remaining aloof they helped to re-create the atmosphere of Nelson's 'band of brothers' before 1914.

Far from being satisfied with purging the Navy of its older ships, Fisher continued to rail at the whole concept of the Navy's police duties:

…Gunboats, and all vessels of like class, have been gradually losing value except for definite purposes under special conditions. As far as this country is concerned, the very places consecrated as the spheres of gunboat activity are those remote from the covering aid of large ships…
…since the redistribution of the Fleet the Empire has had to do without the ubiquitous gunboat, and, if the truth be told, scarcely seems to have missed it. There are one or two valuable cases in point. For a long time the Foreign Office, or rather the Ambassador at Constantinople, pressed for the restoration of the second stationnaire.[3]

The Admiralty sternly refused. The only noticeable result of this dangerous policy so far has been that the French have followed our example, and withdrawn their second vessel.

An even more remarkable example occurred in Uruguay. A poaching Canadian sealer had been captured by the Uruguayan authorities, and language was used as if the disruption of the Empire would follow a refusal on the part of the Admiralty to liberate her crew by force. For a time the Admiralty was practically in revolt against H.M. Government, and then – everything blew over. The dispute was settled by diplomatic action and the local courts of law.

The question of the small vessel for police duties will long be with us. Vice-Consuls and Resident Commissioners will, no doubt, continue to act on the great principle: When in doubt wire for a gunboat. The Foreign and Colonial Offices, to whom the dispatch of a gunboat means no more than persuading a gentleman in Whitehall to send a telegram saying she is to go, will probably never realise why the gentleman should be so perverse as to refuse. But the matter is really now a 'Chose jugée'; the Admiralty battle has been fought and won, and it only remains for the Admiralty to adhere to its principles and decline to give way simply for the sake of a quiet life.[4]

To this the opposition countered with the argument that while Fisher's policy certainly covered the heart of the Empire (the British Isles), it left the arteries (that is, the supply routes) wide open. In other words, although the Navy was to have its battle-fleet to defend Home waters against enemy attack, it was to be denied the equally vital supporting craft indispensable in a national emergency. The result would be a service as top-heavy – and as vulnerable – as an Army consisting solely of artillery. When war broke out the force of these claims was at once revealed. Ruthless scrapping of small ships of all kinds left the Royal Navy without the precious escorts and minesweepers needed to fight the U-boats and indiscriminate mine-laying which nearly brought Great Britain to her knees in 1917. For Fisher believed in only two types of warship, the battle-cruiser or fast battleship and the large destroyer – all else was 'junk', to use a typical Fisher pejorative. Fisher's prejudice against cruisers left the Navy with a woeful shortage of ships to meet such German commerce-raiders as the *Emden* and the *Königsberg*, and on the eve of war the only fleet minesweepers were the remaining torpedo-gunboats (some of them listed as 'goats' back in 1904).

At the time of the reforms, of course, the critics were fighting on poor ground. Given the need to work within fairly tight budgets, both in terms of manpower and money, the Fisher programme was the only way in which a modern battle-fleet could have been built quickly. The war, however, vindicated the critics' insistence on a balanced Navy and showed how short-sighted Fisher had been in dismissing all small ships out of hand. It is one of the minor ironies of naval history that soon after Fisher returned to the Admiralty in 1914 he was forced to order a new generation of steel sloops, this time for use as minesweepers, convoy escorts and maids-of-all-work. Like the Crimean gunboats after the Peace of Paris, these *Flower* class sloops were later the only vessels available for police work on distant stations. After 1920 the new convoy sloops were sent out to China, the Persian Gulf and other traditional gunboat stations, where they also fulfilled a function which their designers had never envisaged.

So it was against a background of considerable strife that the survivors of the gunboats carried on with their work. Fisher's reorganisation took a long time to take effect, and many ships were left on foreign stations until new arrangements could be made for patrolling their areas. It is surprising to find how many spheres of gunboat operations still survived on the eve of the great reforms; in several cases the small craft continued their duties for some years.

The China gunboats, for instance, continued their familiar routine of calling at the Treaty Ports, and occasionally entered the rivers, but were slowly being replaced by specially built river-gunboats drawing less water. In the 1870s and 1880s it had been customary to leave a gunvessel frozen in the ice at Tientsin to protect the Legation there each winter in case of rioting. The idea was that the Legation staff could hold out for a while in the gunvessel, since troops would have difficulty in reaching Tientsin quickly during the winter months, but this idea was abandoned when China became more settled. So far as is known it was done each year, but was never put to the test.

The British position in the Far East had changed considerably since the days of Sir James Hope. When Chinese resentment against foreign interference came to a head in 1900 the principal Western interests threatened were American and British. Yet the Boxer Rebellion was made an excuse for an international expedition to Peking, with Japanese, Russian, Austrian, French, Italian and German troops. Great Britain could no longer act alone without arousing the suspicions of her European neighbours, who insisted in joining in the last great occasion of gunboating. A force of cruisers and gunboats shelled the Taku forts, and easily silenced their obsolete guns, although the Russian gunboat *Gilyak* and the British sloop *Algerine* sustained some slight damage.

The next stage of the campaign was more hazardous, for when word came that the Legations in Peking were about to surrender (a false alarm, as it turned out) all the available sailors and marines were formed into a naval brigade and rushed by rail to Tientsin. Here they found that the Boxers had torn up the railway line, leaving the Relief Column stranded in the middle of hostile country. But troops were being rushed from India and South Africa, and it was not long before the Relief Column was relieved. The last part of the story was sheer farce; while the various detachments advanced independently of one another, each one trying to be the first to reach the embattled Legations, the British contingent was hoodwinked into leaving two hours late, took the wrong road, but arrived first. After all the dangers of the advance from the coast to Peking, the midshipman who scaled the wall of the Legations found the ladies taking tea on the lawn!

In the Pacific sloops and gunboats had inherited a special task. In addition to policing the islands, for which their sail-power made them ideal, H.M. ships tried to control the practice of 'blackbirding'. This had grown up in the 1870s as a means of procuring cheap labour for the sugar plantations of Queensland and Fiji, and was similar to the French *engagé* traffic in East Africa. But a long campaign by missionaries and their sympathisers in New Zealand led to its suppression by naval action. As this work was carried out mainly by sloops and larger vessels it falls outside the scope of this book, and, incidentally, explains why the early gunboats and gunvessels played no vital role in the Pacific. The lack of shallow harbours and populated river estuaries meant that the peculiar qualities of the gunboat were not required, whereas the bigger warships, sloops, frigates and corvettes were more use because of their greater endurance. Paradoxically, the later composite gunboats were most useful in the Pacific, since their size and seakeeping qualities were so much improved. Even at the turn of the century gunboats were patrolling the vast wastes of the south-western Pacific in much the same manner as their predecessors had done thirty years before.

Service on the Pacific Station was arduous, even as late as 1903, and it was not unusual to go for months with-

The composite sloop *Daphne* was a victim of the 'Fisher Axe' in 1904, but her sister *Nymphe*, attached to H.M.S. *Wildfire* at Sheerness, served throughout the First World War. *(NPC)*

out sighting another ship. H.M.S. *Dart*, for example, left Sydney in April 1901 and returned from a surveying voyage in December. While at sea between 1901 and 1904 she sighted only one other British warship, the gunboat *Sparrow*. The two ships met for a few days at Tulagi, in the Solomon Islands, but before *Sparrow* arrived *Dart's* captain learned that a missionary had been murdered on the island of Malatea, and immediately reported the matter to the Commissioner at Tulagi. As H.M.S. *Sparrow* turned up the same day she was sent to the scene of the murder with a detachment of native police. The police disembarked some distance from the village to round up the inhabitants, while *Sparrow* appeared at daylight and shelled the village with her 4-inch guns. At the time this was considered a sufficiently severe punishment, rather than fines or sentences of imprisonment.

Even in 1903 the food consisted of salt beef which had been in brine since 1863 in the victualling yard at Sydney. Australian ship's biscuit had the reputation of being unusually hard, and had to be soaked or boiled for an hour or two before eating; it was often necessary to skim the weevils off the water. All the ships were alive with cockroaches; hence the familiar reference to gunboats as 'bug-traps'. The diet was varied by salt pork and dried peas, with fish on the menu when available. One of the items missed most was fresh bread, for often enough there was no flour. Without refrigerators there could be no milk or butter either. Still, the men were said to be very happy in small ships. Survey work was especially interesting since the men were frequently away from the ship for days. In shallow waters surveying had to be done in boats, and the men would be at it from dawn to dusk. As a form of compensation survey ships were issued with small extras such as coffee, tinned mutton and pickles. The standard ration was tea, bread, sugar and fresh meat in harbour; at sea it was always salt pork or beef, with

corned beef once a week to break the monotony, and vegetables while they lasted.[5]

The vessels on the North America and West Indies Station were usually serving out the balance of their commissions after a spell in West Africa. Their duties were by this time confined to fishery protection and visits to various ports to 'show the flag'. Similarly a handful of steel sloops continued the Persian Gulf patrols right up to 1914. Although the slave trade had been stamped out a good deal of gun-running was going on among the independent states in the Gulf and in southern Arabia. In addition merchant ships were occasionally looted, and the only way to check these random outbreaks of lawlessness was to maintain frequent patrols.

The gunboat days left their mark, and many tried to emulate their tradition. In 1911 the Kaiser attempted to turn the Agadir Crisis to his advantage by sending the gunboat *Panther* to the trouble-spot. This proved disastrous, and showed that a nation cannot afford to make idle threats of war when her opponents are ready to take up the challenge. The only positive result of the *Panther's* visit to Morocco was to transform the hitherto nebulous Entente Cordiale into firm solidarity between France and Great Britain and a promise of an alliance against Germany.

As far as the Royal Navy was concerned, it can be seen in retrospect that when the gunboat passed from the scene it took with it certain advantages. One noticeable casualty was the independence of junior officers.

The independent commands offered to lieutenants and commanders in the heyday of the gunboat and the sloop gave great scope for initiative. It is no coincidence that many distinguished flag-officers served in gunboats in their younger days,[6] just as destroyer-flotillas were to be the nursery of another generation of gifted sailors. With the introduction of wireless, however, junior commanders could no longer disappear for months in the south Pacific, and they could no longer plead the excuse that a situation demanded quick action without reference to the Senior Naval Officer. Not only was the Senior Naval Officer in constant touch, but the Admiralty was always ready to issue numerous orders to change naval dispositions.

On the other hand, the gunboating days bequeathed a curse which only showed itself in World War I. Throughout the nineteenth century British warship commanders were required to form landing-parties from their ships' companies. The naval brigade was a feature of almost every land campaign during the reign of Queen Victoria, and came to be lauded as an example of naval ingenuity, instead of being recognised as the makeshift which it was. The naval brigade was an inefficient substitute for combined operations between the Army and the Navy; it not only relieved the Army of the necessity to develop a doctrine of amphibious warfare, but also impaired the operational efficiency of the Fleet by wasting large numbers of men ashore.

Bearing in mind the large number of expeditions undertaken in tropical Africa it is not unfair to say that the continuing calls for naval brigades seriously affected the health of the men by exposing them needlessly to fever. The fact that a landing-party from the Fleet at Simon's Bay nearly defeated the local garrison during manoeuvres was read as proof of the Navy's versatility, whereas it was more likely to prove the incompetence of the garrison. In the Boer War the Army's weakness in artillery had to be remedied by stripping cruisers of their 6-inch, 4.7-inch and 12-pounder guns, while a colossal blunder was committed by allowing the Naval Brigades to be used as assault troops at Graspan, when regular troops were available.

The lesson was not learned by 1914, despite the anti-gunboat mentality of Fisher. That brilliant man had an appalling blindness to tactical problems, and gave his new Navy no guidance in planning for amphibious war-

H.M.S. *Dwarf,* photographed in 1910. *(Craig Leaske)*

fare. His loudly proclaimed plan for landing 100,000 men on the Pomeranian coast was typical – none of the practical problems of penetrating the Baltic had been examined. The landings at Gallipoli in 1915 had advanced little further in technique from the days of the Second China War. In fact, the first landings at Sedd-el-Bahr were made by bluejackets and marines from the Fleet's picket boats. This gunboat outlook hindered the whole British attitude to amphibious warfare at the time, and must be partly blamed for the inept manner in which most operations were executed during World War I. Not until the Zeebrugge Raid in 1918 could the Royal Navy be said to have recaptured its ancient flair for surprise attacks from the sea.

After all the criticism of gunboats at the turn of the century it is curious to find that ten sloops and five gunboats were still in service in 1914. Another three sloops were on surveying duties, but were quickly rearmed for war service. For most of them war duties were merely an extension of their peacetime role, but they proved invaluable in some of the overseas campaigns.

While a huge fleet of dreadnought battleships was gathering for the Royal Navy's test mobilisation in July 1914 the little steel gunboat *Dwarf* was completing a refit at Gibraltar. This tiny vessel had seen fifteen years of service on foreign stations, and belonged to that category of vessels stigmatised by Fisher as useless for the purposes of war. Yet when her captain received a wireless message at Las Palmas warning him to stand by for further orders *Dwarf* began a ritual which was being repeated all over the world by British warships of all sizes. She took on extra coal and jettisoned as much woodwork as could be spared. When the signal to 'commence hostilities against Germany' came at last the gunboat was in as warlike a state as she could be.

The British strategic plan called for a blockade of all German colonies, so early in August 1914 the ships off West Africa were ordered to destroy the German wireless station and base at Duala, in the Cameroons. Although the armoured cruiser *Cumberland* was present it was clear that a gunboat would be the most suitable type of ship for the winding creeks and mangrove swamps around Duala. *Dwarf* found herself the major unit in a strange flotilla which comprised the Nigerian Government yacht *Ivy* and a motley collection of launches. However the scarcity of troops prevented any serious attempts at combined operations, and after a preliminary bombardment a landing had to be cancelled in the face of German troops.

Dwarf's next venture was more successful, for on the night of 6 September she crept up the river and sent a landing-party ashore armed only with revolvers. When they returned they had captured four lighters without firing a shot, an exploit reminiscent of the cutting-out expeditions of old. It was learned afterwards that the affair had taken place under the noses of 200 German soldiers.

The approaches to Duala had been mined, and several German steamers had been sunk in the navigable channel. While the British flotilla was reconnoitring this channel *Dwarf* was engaged by the armed yacht *Herzogin Elisabeth*, but drove her opponent off with a few accurate rounds of 4-inch fire. Next morning as the launches began sweeping for mines they came under heavy fire from a battery of field-guns on shore. This time when *Dwarf* intervened to cover the retreat of her flotilla she was hit under the bridge. Although her quartermaster was hit while the ship was in a narrow channel she escaped without further damage. But the incident convinced the Germans that of all the British ships lying downriver *Dwarf* was the most dangerous. Within a week or two they devised a crude weapon which could destroy her; a German officer wrote in his diary, 'tonight a launch with a mine built in under her keel is to be let loose on her'.[7]

The 'mine' was in fact a gas-cylinder filled with dynamite and capped with a home-made firing device; three launches were fitted to carry two of these improvised torpedoes below the waterline, and three volunteers were picked to ram the *Dwarf*.[8] But the attacks all proved abortive, for *Dwarf*'s searchlight always picked out the launches before they could get within range, and the final attempt was ruined when the leading launch was abandoned by her steersman; with her lethal load she careered around in circles and frightened off the other launch. Only when the abandoned launch was examined did the gunboat's captain realise how close his escape had been.

The most important German unit left was the armed steamer *Nachtigal*,[9] and *Dwarf* was ordered to find her and bring her to action. She was hiding up one of the many shallow creeks south-west of Duala, so *Dwarf* searched the Bimbia River on the night of 16 September 1914. With the ship completely darkened and all guns manned the tension among the men on *Dwarf*'s bridge could be felt. Suddenly the look-out spotted a grey steamer heading downriver at full speed – it was the *Nachtigal*, and she struck the gunboat amidships with a tremendous crash. Fortunately the few seconds had been enough warning; the searchlight was switched on and the helm was put hard over, so that the steamer was raked by 4-inch and 12-pounder shellfire as she ground down the port side. At twenty feet or less the shells riddled the *Nachtigal*'s hull; she drifted away blazing like a torch, and blew up a few minutes later. Afterwards *Dwarf* picked up four Germans and ten negroes, the survivors of a band of very brave men.

When Duala fell two weeks later *Dwarf* was present, sporting a large patch in her side. The Senior Naval Officer paid a handsome tribute to the little gunboat after the surrender, and it is sad to reflect that subsequent events did not match the brilliant opening to the campaign. Despite the lack of troops ambitious landing operations were eventually undertaken in 1915 and came to nothing. Skilful fighting by the numerically inferior German forces and the effects of dysentery made for slow progress, and by the middle of 1915 the Anglo-French offensive petered out.

The Mesopotamian Campaign was another attempt to use sea power to attack the enemy's distant possessions, and like Gallipoli and the minor colonial operations proved a bigger drain on the Empire's resources than was first imagined. Apart from the obvious need to safeguard Persian oil supplies it was hoped that an offensive in the Middle East would weaken Turkish influence,

The old 'flat-iron' gunboat *Bustard*, re-armed, serving off the Belgian coast during the First World War. *(Craig Leaske)*

The sloops *Shearwater* (above) and
Vestal (below) both served throughout
the First World War. *(Craig Leaske)*

but the lure of easy victories was a delusion. After the
capture of Kurnah at the end of 1914 the Expeditionary
Force was unable to advance, and had great difficulty in
holding its ground.[10]

The troops were sorely harassed by sniping from the
Arabs who inhabited the swamps of the Euphrates, and
it was to check this nuisance that the sloops *Espiègle*,
Odin and *Lawrence* (Indian Marine) were stationed in
the river. The three vessels achieved little of importance
but their shallow draught did enable them to keep the

tribesmen in check. On 6 January 1915 *Espiègle* and two converted commercial river-steamers raided the village of Kubaish after the Chief Political Officer had learned that the local shcikh was a Turkish sympathiser. The raid was a complete success, for the sloop reached the village without grounding, while the accompanying launches pursued the Arabs into a nearby lake; in true gunboat fashion the recalcitrant sheikh was deposed at Kurnah as a lesson to his followers.

A more serious threat was a southward offensive by Turkish troops; by January 1915 advanced outposts were only eight miles from Kurnah, and the whole British enterprise was in jeopardy. After a series of reconnaissances *Espiègle* and two smaller vessels supported a sortie by British forces above Abu Aran which met with limited success. But the Turks were moving on Basra and the oil pipeline in a two-pronged attack which the British were too weak to counter. For the moment the naval forces had to concentrate on interfering with the Turks' communications by raids on the enemy's waterborne supply routes. The Admiralty, worried about the danger to the Anglo-Iranian Oil Company's oilfields (in which it had a large shareholding), sent the sloop *Clio* from Egypt to reinforce her sisters, while an Indian brigade was at last spared from guarding the Suez Canal.

The reinforcements were just in time, for in April 1915 the long-awaited Turkish offensive began with a bombardment of Kurnah. The first attack was repulsed with heavy loss, and this was followed by a successful counter-attack which cost the Turks some 6,000 casualties. When this success was followed up, the river flotilla had to be called upon again to dislodge the Turks from their strong position above Kurnah.

The operation was singularly difficult. Not only were the enemy outposts within 2,000-3,000 yards on either side, but the surrounding countryside was so marshy that the attacking troops had to be embarked in native boats. *Espiègle* and *Odin* were sent upriver to turn the Turkish flank, while *Clio* and *Lawrence* remained to reinforce the artillery with their gunfire. The initial attack was successful, and was followed by a series of victories which forced the Turks to abandon all their precious gains. By the beginning of June the enemy was in full flight, pursued by the three sloops and their supporting launches. In four days' operations the troops and supporting warships captured the important town of Amara, three steamers and 1,700 men.[11] At one stage General Townshend embarked in *Espiègle* and far outstripped his command, as the sloops scraped their way through tortuous channels and rounded up boatloads of Turkish soldiery.

Although the Army was continuing its campaign in Mesopotamia the sloops played little part after June 1915; as the troops penetrated further upriver the water became so shallow that specially designed gunboats had to be sent out from England. However, German propaganda was successful in stirring up unrest in the Persian Gulf, and the sloops found useful employment in 'showing the flag' at various Gulf ports. The old *Alert*, which had been sold out of the Navy some years before the War, was pressed into service to act as a guardship at Basra, where she had been stationed, and reverted to her civilian duties after the Armistice.

The Easter Rising of 1916 produced its own gunboat action in Dublin, when H.M.S. *Helga* was brought up the Liffey to shell the Volunteers holding out in the General Post Office. Although described in all accounts as a 'special gunboat of light draught' *Helga* was in fact only an armed yacht serving in the Auxiliary Patrol at Kingstown (Dun Laoghaire). Her 12-pounder shells failed to evict the Volunteers, but her exploit won her a surprising notoriety; it is therefore amusing to find that she was finally transferred to the newly independent Irish government in 1922 as the fishery patrol vessel *Muirchu*.

Early in 1919 the Admiralty reinstituted the Persian Gulf patrols to try and bring the area under control again. There were no modern vessels available, so the three old sloops were commissioned once more after a refit to remedy some of the defects accumulated in four years' war service. *Espiègle* was stationed in the Red Sea, with the Senior Naval Officer, Persian Gulf, in the old cruiser *Topaze*, and *Odin* and *Clio* under his orders. In 1920 came their last action of any consequence, when they helped to round up the 'Mad Mullah of Somaliland', who had been eluding British forces since 1901. The ultimate eclipse of the Gunboat Era was symbolised by the presence of the aircraft-carrier *Ark Royal* alongside the twenty-year-old sloops.

Fantome, *Merlin* and *Mutine* went back to surveying duties for a while, but *Shearwater*, which had been the Canadian Navy's first submarine depot-ship in 1914, failed to survive the rapid run-down of Canada's naval forces in 1921-22. *Mutine* lingered on until 1932 as a training hulk for the Newport Division of the Royal Naval Volunteer Reserve. She was thus the last of the old sloops to remain in nominal commission.

The four steel gunboats of the *Bramble* class all survived the War, but *Bramble* and *Britomart* were 'axed' in 1920. Native shipbreakers bought them for scrapping at Bombay, but their sister-ships were more fortunate. *Dwarf* and *Thistle* were found indispensable for patrolling the West African rivers, where they served for another seven years. The long gunboat lineage which began in 1854 ended on 13 July 1926, when a firm of shipbreakers bought two rusty old ships. Today the only reminder of the Gunboat Navy is a sooty, battered hulk in Blackwall Reach, launched as H.M.S. *Foxhound* in 1877, a forlorn memorial to a vanished era.

Chapter 15

CONCLUSION

Having looked at the evolution of the gunboat from 1854 to 1914 we come to the question: what was the ultimate achievement of those sixty years? Did gunboat diplomacy influence the subsequent course of history, and are its doctrines relevant to the Nuclear Age?

One could say that after two world wars and the end of the cosiness of *Pax Britannica* the gunboat might as well not have existed. Furthermore, the arrogance which allowed the British to intervene at will in the affairs of other nations is no longer acceptable. With the upsurge of nationalism in Africa and Asia since 1945 the British find it almost impossible to justify gunboat tactics. As Suez showed, such ventures are hostages to fortune if they lack international support, even if Great Britain still had sufficient naval and military might to carry them out efficiently. Even the Super-Powers, the United States and Russia, would hesitate to take repeated offensive action against sovereign states.

There is clearly no place in the world today for a purely peacetime force of ships such as the sloops and gunboats which existed before the Naval Defence Act. Yet this type of force may be currently evolving in a new shape. The 1966 *Defence Review*[1] uses phrases which might almost have featured in a Victorian appreciation of strategy.

> Much of Africa, the Middle East and Asia, is going through a period of revolutionary change, which may sometimes spill across national frontiers... When such instability leads to open war, it may imperil not only economic interests in the area, but even world peace... On more than one occasion in the recent past, we have seen how local conflict in a far away country has threatened to embroil the major powers in a direct confrontation, directly endangering world peace... Recent experience in Africa and elsewhere has shown that our ability to give rapid help to friendly governments, with even small

British forces, can prevent large-scale catastrophes. *In some parts of the world, the visible presence of British forces by itself is a deterrent to local conflict.*[2]

Here in essence is the traditional 'police-force' role of the Royal Navy, for which is allocated the incredibly slender force of four aircraft-carriers,[3] two commando ships (helicopter-carriers) and their escorts. To supplement the ability of the commando ships to land Royal Marines in areas of local conflict, the Royal Navy is commissioning two assault ships capable of landing tanks and troops, while the Army operates three 'logistic' ships with a similar basic function. A considerable amount of money is spent on this portion of the Navy's combat forces, which reflects the current policy of the United States Navy in keeping a large number of ships on 'assault' duties. These naval forces, British and American, are the principal agents of gunboat diplomacy in the 1960s.

In terms of our original definition of gunboat diplomacy, the Western Alliance has continued to use its naval forces to further its political aims. Since 1945 there have been many examples of the use of British and American ships to carry out some specific task of importance to national policy. Two of the best examples are the 'Confrontation' in Malaysia and the Cuban Quarantine. In both cases the diplomatic problems could not have been solved by direct military intervention, although a state had been reached where normal diplomatic pressure was no longer effective. It is this situation of stalemate which lies under shadow of the nuclear deterrent, when the doctrine of limited options comes into play and makes a gunboat policy feasible.

In the Cold War the United States has come close to enjoying the monopoly of power which was once the privilege of Great Britain in the nineteenth century. She is above all the greatest maritime nation in the world, and when the conditions are favourable she has repeatedly fallen back on the basic tactics of gunboat diplomacy. The circumstances have changed but the principles remain very similar. Yesterday a cruiser might have landed men to prevent the Chinese from looting a tea-merchant's warehouse; today the U.S. Marines land in Santo Domingo to 'restore equilibrium in Latin America'.

The invention of the atomic bomb exerted a hypnotic influence on strategy after 1945, and only now can we see the advantages of the relatively subtle tactics of modern gunboat diplomacy. Like the old-style gunboats, today's destroyers are visible deterrents to ill-organised local military action, and can therefore still be used to reinforce policy. This is not advocacy of large-scale intervention by American or British warships in the affairs of neutral countries; it would be no more possible for the United States to stamp out Communist influence wherever it appears than it was for Great Britain to outbuild the French, Russian, German and American navies in the 1890s. However, as long as it remains expedient for a powerful nation to intervene in the affairs of a weaker nation *intervention will occur*, and we are concerned only with the methods of intervention. Gunboat diplomacy has always had an implied quality of 'controlled response', as opposed to the uncontrolled response of, say, nuclear bombardment.

A crisis overseas might have caused the Admiralty to send a gunboat to investigate. Let us suppose that the outbreak of violence was more serious than it had seemed; the Senior Naval Officer would dispatch another vessel, possibly under an officer senior to the lieutenant in command of the gunboat in order to give himself more control over the direction of affairs. Assuming the crisis grew worse the 'response' by the Senior Naval Officer was always capable of being increased gradually, with the ultimate threat of intervention by stronger British forces if the situation got out of control. Through its chain of command the Admiralty kept in touch with local commanders, and thus indirectly had a hand on the shoulder of the most impetuous lieutenant. Beyond the Admiralty was the Cabinet to advise where the national interest lay, so that in most cases precipitate action was avoided. '[The gunboats'] arrival gave early warning of the purposes of the statesmen who directed them, while the pressure they exerted could be varied from hour to hour.'[4]

In many ways the main fleets of the Royal Navy represented the ultimate deterrent. The mighty battle squadrons were always in the background, ready for use if the humbler instruments failed in their tasks. Like the Bomb, mobilisation of the Royal Navy was used at the last possible moment as a threat. Twice, at the time of the Kruger Telegram (the Jameson Raid) and the Fashoda Incident, when there was open talk of war, mobilisation of the British Fleet was enough to bring both sides to their senses. One of the most important lessons of the Cuban crisis is that a headlong clash of American and Russian armed strength, universally heralded as the automatic prelude to a nuclear holocaust, was avoided by an old-fashioned naval blockade. The institution of a 'quarantine squadron' off Cuba enabled the American High Command to watch the Russian ships without harming them, to check the rate at which Russian ordnance was entering Cuba. No other service could have monitored the Russians tactfully, but at the same time demonstrate to them that they could be destroyed at will. The result of the naval quarantine was that President Kennedy controlled the situation without resorting to any of the wilder counter-measures proposed, such as invading Cuba or sinking the Russian merchantmen at sight. In this instance the main fleet was not the ultimate deterrent, but rather a more acceptable alternative.

The Suez Canal crisis of 1956 might have been another case-history of gunboat diplomacy in the 1950s, but is now held up as proof of the limitations of this type of operation in modern conditions. Not only was the political direction of the military expedition so inept as to make failure certain, but the rundown in British military strength since 1945 had been so fast that the forces were, on paper at least, barely adequate for the task. One cannot avoid comparing the execution of the military plan unfavourably with the Egyptian campaign of 1882, when the Canal, the prize for which everything was risked, was captured in twenty-four hours; in 1956 the Anglo-French forces were only in possession of half the length of the Canal after forty-eight hours.[5] Furthermore the British military effort in 1882 was hindered by the bombardment of Alexandria, a blunder which gave plenty of warning to the defenders. In the debacle of 1956 one can detect little sign of the nineteenth-century 'will to act'. If pressure of world opinion weighed so heavily on the minds of the politicians who ordered the operation, the four days' delay before troops were landed becomes indefensible, since it gave world opinion time to harden against the enterprise.[6]

Numerical strength is essential if any type of gunboat diplomacy is to work, which explains why the latter-day American brand works more spasmodically than the original. In the nineteenth century the sheer size of the Gunboat Navy made it possible to keep warships constantly on the move, visiting distant ports and lonely anchorages, and always giving visible proof of the British Empire's influence. Today the occasional visit of an American aircraft-carrier on a goodwill cruise has even greater effect, for the propaganda value is fully exploited by publicity which could scarcely have been available to the Victorians. All Western navies take care to foster this aspect by organising entertainments for local dignitaries, as well as the more significant displays of fighting efficiency. The Royal Navy's apt description of these diversions gives the clue to their real character: 'Exercise Shopwindow'.

One problem affecting the practice of gunboat diplomacy today is the dwindling number of bases. Eighty years ago the Royal Navy used a chain of bases stretching from Plymouth to Sydney, and turned them to good account in both world wars. So much admired was this complex of harbours, anchorages and dockyards that the Anglo-U.S. Agreement of 1940 stipulated a 99-year lease of specified British bases to the United States in return for the loan of fifty ancient destroyers. Then came the catastrophic series of defeats at the hands of the Japanese in 1941-42, when British, American and Dutch sea power in the Far East was virtually wiped out in six months. Apart from irreparable harm to the prestige of the white races few of the old bases remained under full British control for very long after the war. The rising tide of nationalism has threatened those bases which remain on foreign soil, although the adverse effect of this on naval operations has been partially offset by the introduction of refuelling at sea and the consequent greater mobility of fleets. The future of such bases as Guantánamo Bay and Singapore will continue to worry defence planners unless quite unforeseeable political changes take place in the countries offering base facilities to foreign powers.

Closely connected with the problem of bases is consideration of the effect of periodic warship visits to foreign ports. There can be little doubt that the occasional calls on Mediterranean ports by the U.S. Sixth Fleet are far more popular than they would be if the countries concerned had large American garrisons. Anything which can be construed as an army of occupation excites chauvinistic passions, whereas naval forces are seen on rare occasions. In Malta ill-feeling was caused by the Admiralty decision to close the Dockyard, since this threatened large-scale unemployment; local agitation was only appeased by the concession to allow the Dockyard to pass into commercial hands, and an assurance that American warships would call for refits.

The current trend of the Royal Navy shows it to be developing along the lines pioneered by the United States Navy, i.e. making its chief contribution to intervention in 'limited wars', the so-called conventional warfare in which nuclear weapons are either unsuitable or politically impossible to use.[7] The most important single warship type in this type of warfare is inevitably the aircraft-carrier, since she is designed to provide air cover for landings of troops as well as carrying out strikes against any surface warship attempting to interfere with the landing. This is how modern gunboat diplomacy differs from the old style, for in the last decade the Western Powers and the Communists have made large amounts of military material available to their satellites. All too frequently this equipment has been misused, and often helps to promote a switch of allegiance. In the past this was relatively unimportant, since the equipment was old-fashioned and already phased out of service, but in 1955 the Russians broke new ground by supplying modern arms to President Nasser. Since then British and American naval forces have frequently faced possible opposition from countries possessing the latest Soviet aircraft and missiles. The forces supporting 'limited war' operations or 'brush-fire'[8] wars must therefore be provided with the most up-to-date defence, by carrier-borne fighters or guided weapons.

The British *Defence Review* of February 1966 will attempt to put the clock back, since it recommends the retention of the assault-forces but discards the powerful protection afforded by the carrier. There is an echo of Gladstone's 'recall of the legions' in the 1860s in the defence planners' pleas that 'to maintain all our current military tasks and capabilities outside Europe would impose an unacceptable strain on our overstretched forces'.[9] To reduce the commitments outside Europe the decision has been made to abandon Aden and, Indonesian intentions permitting, Singapore. To offset Aden's vital role in safeguarding the flow of oil from the Persian Gulf it is hoped that bombers will be able to operate from a 'chain' of Indian Ocean island airfields (in fact likely to be three). The traditional Persian Gulf patrols are to be increased, although the military effectiveness of this measure without support from Aden is open to question.

These forecasts for the 1970s would seem to spell the end of any effective British contribution to the type of gunboat diplomacy which has been developing since 1945, for the main requirement, adequate retaliatory power held in reserve, will shortly disappear. The theory underlying this reversal of policy seems to be that future 'limited wars' will be undertaken with the blessing of the United States, and will therefore qualify for protection from American sea power. Since it is hard to visualise a situation in which the U.S. Navy would allow one of its precious attack carriers to be earmarked for support of a British landing, the Royal Navy's operations will be increasingly restricted to minor police work. In fact without its strike aircraft (and it has not yet been shown that a 1,500 m.p.h. bomber can carry out the precise bombing required for naval support) it would prove necessary to allow British amphibious forces to operate only against those opponents unable to retaliate.

Despite the gloomy future predicted for the Royal Navy the principles of gunboat diplomacy remain valid for the future. Gunboating will last as long as any Power continues to adopt a maritime strategy in peacetime, for it offers a sane alternative to the deadlock caused by nuclear parity. Far from being the bludgeon of imperialism, it has developed into the precise instrument of Western policy. Whatever the size of the 'gunboat', whether aircraft-carrier or frigate, the principles will apply as long as the warship exists. Here, as elsewhere, the Victorian experience holds many lessons for us today.

AFTERWORD

Dr Eric Grove
Director of the Centre for International Security and War Studies
University of Salford

Four years after the appearance of *Send a Gunboat* another major work on the subject appeared, *Gunboat Diplomacy* by James Cable, the distinguished diplomat. He had used a period of reflection at the Institute for Strategic Studies to produce a work that was intended to prove that gunboat diplomacy, 'the use or threat of limited naval force, otherwise than as an act of war, in order to secure advantage or avert loss',[1] was still very much alive and well. The book was a resounding 'yes' to the question asked at the beginning of John Major and Antony Preston's conclusion – gunboat diplomacy had indeed influenced the course of history after the First World War, and its doctrines were very relevant to the nuclear age.

By the third edition of his book, which appeared in 1994 and covered the period from 1919 to 1991, Sir James (as he later became) listed around 250 examples of gunboat diplomacy, in which Britain had often been the 'assailant'. Britain had found it far from difficult to justify 'gunboat tactics' after 1945; indeed she had indulged in the activity some 35 times between 1946 to 1991, from sending a cruiser and a sloop to Basra in the context of anti-British rioting at Abadan to the diversion of the frigate *Ambuscade* to Grenada to reassure the local Prime Minister who feared civil unrest.

Cable defined four kinds of gunboat diplomacy: definitive, when a *fait accompli* is achieved; purposeful, when armed coercion is carried out to achieve a change of policy; catalytic, when forces are deployed to intervene if necessary and as required (the modern British doctrinal concept of 'poise'); and expressive, beautifully defined as when warships 'are employed to emphasise attitudes, to lend verisimilitude to otherwise unconvincing statements, or to provide an outlet for emotion.'[2] Cable convincingly argued that the Beira patrol which had begun as a purposeful activity blockading Rhodesia had become merely expressive in its later stages.

As the authors of *Send a Gunboat* had made clear, gunboat diplomacy in the mid to late twentieth century was the task of naval forces in general rather than specialised 'gunboats'. Apart from the specialised China gunboats built for riverine duties in the pre-war days of extraterritoriality the Royal Navy found it difficult even in the inter-war period to obtain ships with only a peacetime role. This had negative effects on sloop numbers, even though the utility of these vessels in a mercantile escort role was recognised.[3] The heavily armed definitive 'sloop' design – the *Black Swan* class – proved itself after the war as an effective 'gunboat' just as it had done as a convoy escort in higher-level operations. Post-war 'frigates' – the common term adopted for escorts in the late 1940s – had 'gunboat' duties as their major peacetime role, especially as the role of naval forces in general war became increasingly and officially 'doubtful' in the late 1950s. Some ships were indeed built for primarily for presence and gunboat duties, notably the 'Tribal' class 'second rate' general purpose frigates of the 1960s which were considered by their designers to be latter-day colonial sloops. The need for guns for more limited duties was reflected in the design of the contemporary 'County' class guided missile destroyers which sacrificed anti-air warfare sensor and control capabilities to retain them. 'Confrontation' with Indonesia during the same decade demonstrated the continued need for light automatic weapons that had been abandoned with the advent of missiles. These were put back into frigates.

The withdrawal from east of Suez that was brought forward to 1967 just as *Send a Gunboat* was published coupled with the advent of surface-to-surface missiles saw the temporary demise of 4.5-in guns in frigates. These were, however, restored after the Falklands War, which followed the temporary success of Argentina's 'definitive' gunboat diplomacy in seizing the islands and the 'purposeful' movements of the task force before the outbreak of hostilities at the beginning of May 1982.[4] This decision, together with improvements in light guns also resulting from Falklands experience, effectively gave the entire surface fleet a gunboat capability. This has stood the Royal Navy in good stead in the post-Cold War world.

Where Preston and Major's understandable pessimism

happily proved less than well founded was in the rebirth of the Royal Navy's carrier capability in the form of the *Invincible* class 'through-deck cruisers'. These and embarked Sea Harriers and other aircraft proved invaluable in a wide range of 'gunboat diplomacy' situations in the 1990s both in the Adriatic and the Gulf. In the former theatre Serbia was the target of a purposeful sanctions operation enforced by multinational surface forces while carriers patrolled off shore in a catalytic role. The presence of a British carrier under national command prepared to come to the aid of British troops in trouble ashore in their ill-defined 'enhanced peacekeeping' role was a vital factor in the deployment of those forces as the Prime Minister made clear on a visit to *Ark Royal* as she 'poised to protect' in 1994. In the Gulf the ability of carriers to operate without host-nation support was a key factor in their use in the attempted coercion of Iraq.

Both these scenarios greatly supported the programme that began in the 1990s to replace the carriers and culminated in the announcement in the 1998 Strategic Defence Review that two large carriers with joint RAF-Navy air groups would be built. These are intended for a self-consciously interventionist expeditionary strategy for a world in which the UK had to go to the crisis rather than wait for it to come to it. At the end of 2005 it was confirmed that the carriers would be 65,000-ton monsters, the largest warships ever built in Britain. How far these will allow autonomous British or European action rather than the current emphasis on making a contribution to US-led coalition (that is, if anything even greater now than in 1967) remains to be seen.

The primary purpose of the new carriers is power projection ashore and this has become the major role of the entire fleet (surface and subsurface) as the blue-water warfare of the Cold War has been replaced by the 'littoral warfare' of the current age. The future surface combatant plans of the Royal Navy, like those of other navies, reflect this. The Type 45 air-defence destroyers (the first of which, *Daring*, launched in February 2006 and for which, initially, land attack capabilities beyond a 4.5-in gun could not be afforded) will be followed, on current plans, first by land attack/anti-submarine derivatives. These will be followed by a new class of versatile surface combatant capable of being swung between various roles, probably as a result of modularity. 'Gunboat' bombardment duties will be an important role for these vessels using missiles and a new 6-in gun that takes only the same space of the present 4.5-in weapon and which can use new ammunition to range far inland. Soon 6-in GPS-guided rocket-assisted gun-launched 'long range land attack projectiles' (LOLAPs) being developed in the USA will be able to hit targets with great precision

eighty or more miles away. The 'gun boat' (in the narrowest sense) will have more potential than ever.

The increasing cost of naval forces means that difficult choices have to be made as to the balance of the fleet. The current interventionary policy has emphasised carriers and the amphibious fleet. The latter has received enormous enhancement recently with the second generation of amphibious assault ships (LPDs) and the replacement of the old Landing Ships Logistic (LSLs) by much more capable dock landing ships (LSDs). Unfortunately this has meant significant cuts in numbers of surface warships. This has meant that certain 'presence' duties have had to be curtailed. At the beginning of 2006 the retiring First Sea Lord made it clear that this could not go on and indeed it had gone rather too far already; 25 frigates and destroyers were being called upon to do the tasks of 30.

It is possible that the new versatile combatants may be built in larger numbers because of their planned assumption of part of the mine countermeasures role. It is interesting however that studies have been going on into a 'global corvette' to allow larger numbers of assets to meet 'gunboat' commitments. This low end of a 'high-low mix' has usually been anathema to the Royal Navy in recent decades (although an enhanced 'OPV3' offshore patrol vessel was considered in the aftermath of the Falklands War). It seems, however, that funding pressures may be causing a rethink. The gunboat may therefore be undergoing a renaissance in the RN as it is in the USN, as Professor Lambert explained in the introduction.

Certainly the outlook for gunboat diplomacy in general looks even brighter now than it did in 1967. This will be done, at least for the time being, more in the context of a 'Pax Americana' rather than a 'Pax Britannica', but this does not mean that significant national British action is not possible in certain circumstances. The year 2000 saw the UK take very significant unilateral action, Operation 'Palliser', which involved a British maritime deployment off and in Sierra Leone to help stabilise the chaotic local situation. The force consisted of the aircraft carrier *Illustrious* with a joint Sea Harrier/Harrier air group; the Amphibious Ready Group based around 42 Commando, the helicopter-carrying amphibious transport (LPH) *Ocean* and two LSLs; the frigates *Chatham* and *Argyll* and two fleet auxiliaries. The frigates came inshore to bombard with their 4.5-in guns and *Chatham* moved upriver to support forces inland. The operation was a big success. As Antony Preston and John Major concluded their own account almost four decades ago, 'Here, as elsewhere, the Victorian experiment holds many lessons for us today.' In the context of 'Palliser' this might be asserted in 2006 with more conviction than even the two original authors might have imagined in 1967.

Foreword

[1] J. Cable, *Gunboat Diplomacy: Political Applications of Limited Naval Force.* (London, 1971). See also M. Hood, *Gunboat Diplomacy 1895-1905: Great Power Pressure on Venezuela* (London, 1975). Neither text made reference to *Send a Gunboat*.

[2] D. R. Headrick, *The Tools of Empire: Technology and European imperialism in the nineteenth century* (New York, 1981).

[3] Professor Schurman's important thesis was published as *Imperial Defence 1868-1887* (London, 2000), with a fine introduction by Professor John Beeler.

[4] The standard account of this process is: P. J. Cain & A. G. Hopkins, *British Imperialism: Innovation and Expansion 1688-1914* (London, 1993); see esp. pp. 125-177. P. J. Cain, 'Economics and Empire: The Metropolitan Context', in A. Porter, ed., *The Oxford History of the British Empire: vol. III The Nineteenth* Century (Oxford, 1999), esp. pp. 42-50. For links between government and finance, and the City's bellicose attitude to securing investments see pp. 206-8. A. H. Imlah, *Economic Aspects of the Pax Britannica* (Harvard, 1958), pp. 186-8. M. Lynn, 'British Policy, Trade, and Informal Empire in the Mid-Nineteenth Century' in Porter ed. pp. 101-121. J. Y. Wong, *Deadly Dreams: Opium and the Arrow War (1856-1860) in China* (Cambridge, 1998), pp. 470-78 argues that British imperialism was complex, and included key economic elements. N. Ferguson, *The World's Banker: The History of the House of Rothschild* (London, 1998), pp. 817-26. D. Kynaston, *The City of London: Vol I. A World of its Own 1815-1890.* (London, 1994), pp. 335-40.

[5] Specification for *Fairy*: 142' x 20' x 9' 6"; draught 5'; 173 tons; 120 hp engines. 22.11.1844: ADM 83/33 2612. Admiralty Order 31.5.1845 to use the *Fairy* design for two new gunboats: ADM 83/35 4269.

[6] M. Burrows, *Memoir of Admiral Sir H. D. Chads* (Portsea, 1869), p. 27-8

[7] Ibid. pp. 27-34, 36

[8] Chads to Northumberland 1.7.1852: ADM 13/185 ff. 88-92. For details of the experiments see: Chads to Sir Thomas Briggs, 7.10.1852: WO 33/6B A1493.

[9] Chads to Admiral Sir A. Fanshawe (Portsmouth), 23.12.1852: WO 44/502.

[10] Chads to C-in-C Portsmouth, 23.12.1852: WO 502. Graham to Aberdeen 26.1.1853: Add. Mss 43, 191 f1 6.

[11] F. H. Winter, *The Golden Age of Rocketry* (Washington, 1990), pp. 31-42.

[12] Chads to Graham (Confidential), 1.10.1853: ADM 13/185 ff. 93-6.

[13] A. D. Lambert, *The Crimean War: British Grand Strategy against Russia 1853-1856* (Manchester, 1990).

[14] A. D. Lambert, 'Looking for Gunboats. British Naval operations in the Gulf of Bothnia, 1854–55', *Journal of Maritime Research*, June 2004.

[15] R. Winfield & D. Lyon, *The Steam Navy List: All the Ships of the Royal Navy 1815-1889* (London, 2004), pp. 218-9, 246.

[16] A. D. Lambert, 'Under the Heel of Britannia: The Bombardment of Sweaborg, August 1855', in Hore, P. ed., *Seapower Ashore* (London, 2001).

[17] D. K. Brown, *Before the Ironclad: Development of Ship Design, Propulsion and Armament in the Royal Navy , 1815-1860* (London, 1990), p. 148.

[18] D. Evans, *Building the Steam Navy: Dockyards, Technology and the Creation of the Victorian Battlefleet 1830-1906* (London, 2004), pp. 141-7.

[19] *The Times* Editorial, April 24th 1856: in A. D. Lambert & S. Badsey, eds, *The War Correspondents: The Crimean War* (Gloucester, 1994), pp. 304-5.

[20] A. D. Lambert, *The Crimean War: British Grand Strategy against Russia 1853-1856* (Manchester, 1990).

[21] H. Douglas, *A Tract on the Naval, Littoral and Internal Defence of England* (London, 1859), p. 191

[22] H. Douglas, *Observations on Modern Systems of Fortifications* (London, 1859), p. 191.

[23] Brown, p. 149

[24] Admiralty to War Office 2.12.1861: ADM 13/47/158 & 162. Admiralty to Controller 2.12.1861: ADM 13/47/160.

[25] P. Kennedy, *The Rise and Fall of British Naval Mastery* (London, 1976), p. 180. Kennedy cites *Send a Gunboat*, but not to sustain this argument.

[26] A. Preston & J. Major, *Send a Gunboat* (London, 1967), pp. 96-7, 215-6.

[27] D. K. Brown, *Warrior to Dreadnought: Warship Development 1860-1905* (London, 1997), p. 122.

[28] T. Ropp, *The Creation of a Modern Navy* (Annapolis, 1989), pp. 14-16. S. Sandler, *The Emergence of the Modern Capital Ship.* pp. 60- 70, 157-173, 198, 242-3. Admiral Sir P. Colomb, *Memoirs of Sir Astley Cooper Key* (London, 1898), p. 348.

[29] Philip Colomb's *Naval Warfare* of 1891 was taken far more seriously in Russia than in Britain because, uniquely, it focused on the offensive use of sea power and examined the experience of the nineteenth century. See R. W. Herrick, *Soviet Naval Theory and Practice* (Annapolis, 1988), pp. 192-200.

[30] A. D. Lambert, 'Part of a long line of circumvallation to confine the future expansion of Russia: Great Britain and the Baltic 1809-1890', in G. Rystad, K-R Bohme & W. M. Carlgren, *In Quest of Trade and Security: The Baltic in Power Politics 1500 - 1990* (Volume 1, Stockholm, 1994), pp. 310-322.

[31] T. Ropp, *The Development of a Modern Navy, 1871-1904.* ed. S. Roberts, (Annapolis, 1989), p. 261. A. J. Marder, *The Anatomy of British Seapower* (London, 1940), pp. 550-567.

[32] I. N. Lambi, *The German Navy and Power Politics 1862-1914* (London, 1984), pp. 158, 215.

[33] G. Martel, *Imperial Diplomacy: Rosebery and the Failure of Foreign Policy* (Kingston, 1986), pp. 150-3, 238-9, 257-61.

[34] J. S. Corbett, *Some Principles of Maritime Strategy* (London, 1911), p. 14.

[35] See http://www.lmlcsteam.com/media.html for the Lockheed Martin Littoral Combat Ship project; http://peoships.crane.navy.mil/lcs for the United States Navy's LCS website.

Chapter 1

[1] See G. S. Graham, *The Politics of Naval Supremacy*, pp. 112-16 (hereafter cited as Graham).

[2] Cf. London's position as the most important European airline terminal for trans-Atlantic flights; similarly the Port of London, crowded and old-fashioned as it is, continues to attract a large share of North Sea shipping.

3   See Graham, pp. 102-3.

4   Graham, p. 110.

5   C. J. Bartlett, *Great Britain and Sea Power 1815-1853*, pp. 254-5.

6   Admiral C. C. Penrose Fitzgerald, *Memories of the Sea*, p. 35.

7   Graham, p. 112.

8   Palmerston, 25 June 1850; *Hansard*, third series, vol. 112.

9   Parliamentary Papers for 1883, 47 (C. 3814); the writer was Captain Maxwell of H.M.S. *Emerald*, who had been ordered to take reprisals for the killing of several of the crew of H.M.S. *Sandfly*.

Chapter 2

1   To Lord Paget, captain of H.M.S. *Princess Royal*; quoted in *Russian War 1854, Baltic and Black Sea; Official Correspondence*, p. 5 (hereafter cited as *Russian War 1854*).

2   *The Times* leader, 3 April 1855; quoted in *Russian War 1855, Baltic; Official Correspondence*, p. 7 (hereafter cited as *Russian War 1855 (Baltic)*).

3   Letter from Napier to First Lord, 18 July 1854; *Russian War 1854*, p. 127.

4   *Russian War 1854*, pp. 17-18. Leader of 13 September 1854.

5   This heeling over was common to vessels much larger than gunboats and persisted until the 1880s, when the lighter Vavasseur 'pedestal' mounting was introduced.

6   *Russian War 1854*, p. 346

7   *Ibid.*, p. 351

8   *Ibid.*, p. 361.

9   *Russian War 1855, Black Sea; Official Correspondence*, p. 73. This is hereafter cited as *Russian War 1855 (Black Sea)*.

10 *Russian War 1855 (Black Sea)*, pp. 296-7.

11 *Ibid.*, pp. 319-23.

12 *Ibid.*

13 *Russian War 1855 (Black Sea)*, pp. 419-21.

14 According to the biographer of Gordon, Sir William Butler, in *Charles George Gordon* (London, 1920), p. 32.

15 In this action one of *Magicienne*'s lieutenants and an A.B. won the Victoria Cross for their bravery in dealing with the accidental explosion of a rocket-fuse.

16 *Russian War 1855 (Baltic)*, p. 12.

17 *Ibid.*, pp. 382-98.

18 See G. A. Osbon's articles 'The Crimean Gunboats – Parts I and II'.

19 See Parliamentary Papers for 1860, 1861, 1867 and 1876 – particularly 1860, 8 (545).

20 One of the shadier transactions of the period; H.M.S. *Victor* was ostensibly sold in November 1863 to Gordon Coleman & Co. for mercantile use after being in Reserve at Sheerness. Once at sea her 'merchant' crew hoisted the Confederate ensign (see Part II). Despite this audacious attempt at evading British neutrality, C.S.S. *Rappahannock* was interned by the French at Cherbourg.

Chapter 3

1   D. C. Gordon, *The Dominion Partnership in Imperial Defense 1870-1914*, p. 54.

2   *Ibid.*, p. 56.

3   *Ibid.*

4   Laird to the Secretary of the Admiralty, July 1859, Parliamentary Papers, 1860, 42 (497); they would have been manned by the Coast Volunteers.

5   Gordon, *The Dominion Partnership*, p. 52.

Chapter 4

1   Sir Michael Seymour, K.C.B., C.-in-C. East Indies and China Station.

2   *The Second China War*, p. 171.

3   H.M.S. *Starling* was the only gunboat to earn Battle Honours for Sveaborg and China.

4   Later Vice-Admiral Sir William Kennedy, K.C.B.

5   *The Second China War*, pp. 204-8.

6   *Algerine, Lee, Leven, Slaney*.

7   *Banterer, Firm*.

8   *Clown, Drake, Janus, Kestrel, Watchful, Woodcock*.

9   For a detailed analysis of the R.N.'s approach to Chinese piracy, see G. Fox, *British Admirals and Chinese Pirates* (hereafter cited as Fox).

10 An Act to repeal an Act of George IV for encouraging the capture or destruction of piratical ships and vessels.

11 The average of annual awards for the periods 1851-57 is actually lower, since the Admiralty was deliberately keeping bounties as low as possible.

12 Fox, p. 157.

13 Adm. Sir William Kennedy, *Hurrah for the Life of a Sailor! Fifty Years in the Royal Navy*.

14 Kennedy, *Hurrah for the Life of a Sailor*, p. 103. Gunboats' captures were treated as being effected by their parent ship (see Chapter 2).

15 For a full description of this phase see Edgar Holt, *The Opium Wars in China*.

16 *The Second China War*, p. 318.

17 Written at Tientsin, 6 July 1858, *The Second China War*, p. 346.

18 America, Holland and France had concluded their treaties some months earlier while Elgin had been absorbed in his Chinese negotiations.

19 *Plover, Janus, Banterer, Forester, Haughty, Kestrel, Lee, Opossum, Starling, Nimrod, Cormorant*.

20 Adm. Sir Reginald Bacon, *The Life of Lord Fisher of Kilverstone*, p. 13.

21 Adm. Lord Fisher, *Records*, p. 14.

22 There is some doubt that Tattnall said these words, but the Royal Navy was quite satisfied that he did, and held him in great esteem. Tattnall fought for the Confederacy in the Civil War, and like many rebel officers found himself in penury after the South's collapse. When news of his plight reached England, a number of naval officers started a fund for his benefit.

23 Butler, *Charles George Gordon*, p. 45; Beatty, *His Country was the World* (London, 1954), p. 25.

Chapter 5

1   Quoted by Fox, pp. 4-5.

2   By an Order in Council of 30 August 1862.

3   See Fox, p. 148, and Sir W. Laird Clowes, *The Royal Navy, A History* (here after cited as Laird Clowes), vol. 7, p. 181. Many officers and men were on loan from the Indian Navy.

4   Fox, p. 62.

5   Admiralty to Rear-Admiral Hope, 26 March 1859, quoted in Fox, p. 63.

6   Laird Clowes, vol. 7, p. 161.

7   *Ibid.*

8   *Ibid.*, p. 163 (quoting a letter from Russell to Bruce).

9   H.M.S. *Hardy* and *Kestrel* and French *Étoile* and *Confucius*.

10 Assumed command 29 October 1862.

11 Quoted in Fox, p. 63.

12 Oscar Parkes, *British Battleships*, p. 36.

13 It could be significant that this arrangement was considered for R.-Adm. Hope, but was not carried out. See Fox, p. 64 n.

14 This system has been adopted extensively since 1920 by most navies.

15 Fox, p. 9.

16 *Kestrel, Hardy, Flamer, Bustard, Haughty, Grasshopper, Opossum, Leven, Janus, Bouncer, Cockchafer,* and *Algerine*.

17 *Snake* and *Osprey*.

18 Fox, pp. 203-4.

19 H. B. Morse and H. F. MacNair, *Far Eastern International Relations*, p. 197.

Chapter 6

1 Sir Henry F. Woods, *Spunyarn from the Strands of a Sailor's Life Afloat and Ashore*, pp. 28-30.

2 See R. Van Alstyne, *The Rising American Empire*, in which the author claims that some form of American take-over in Cuba would have been inevitable but for the outbreak of the Civil War.

3 Extract from the Governor's address to the Legislative Session of 1865.

4 Adm. 128/48, *Jamaica Rebellion Papers*.

5 *Ibid.*

6 It would appear from this that Brand was temporarily in command of *Nettle* instead of *Onyx*.

7 In his testimony to the Royal Commission Brand denied most of the charges, but admitted that he had handled Gordon roughly before his execution. In *Memories of the Sea* Admiral Penrose Fitzgerald mentions (pp. 13-14) a 'bumptious midshipman' who bullied his juniors, and 'later gained an unenviable notoriety through the exhibition of an abnormal zeal for hanging niggers at the time of the Jamaica disturbances'. He also gives the impression that, in his ship at least, the consensus of opinion was that they were glad not to be involved in such dirty work, which suggests that men of Brand's calibre were the exception rather than the rule.

8 *The Times*, 4 June 1868.

9 See Bernard Semmel, *The Governor Eyre Controversy*.

10 Adm. 128/48, *Jamaica Rebellion Papers*, p. 374.

11 Adm. 128/48 – letter dated 6 July 1866.

12 Adm. 1/5969 (memo. Y.81/1866).

13 Rear-Admiral Sir Thomas Maitland (1803-78).

14 Letter from Maitland in *Bacchante* at Esquimalt, 27 August 1861 (see Adm.Y.333/236).

15 Sir James Hope, the former C.-in-C. China Station.

16 The gunvessel *Star* was ordered to reinforce Hope, but was not sent up to the St Lawrence (Adm. 1/6042).

17 *Ibid.*

18 *Ibid.*

19 R.-Adm. John Kingcome (?-1871), C.-in-C.

20 Adm. 1/5826; from *Sutlej* at Esquimalt 11 August 1863, enclosing copy of instructions issued at Valparaiso on 13 June.

21 Adm. Sir G. Elliot, 'Coast Defence by Gunboats'.

Chapter 7

1 See Appendix B. *Algerine, Slaney* and *Leven* (under repair) were listed in Admiralty returns as gunvessels.

2 See Parliamentary Papers, 1860, 8 (545).

3 See Part II, pp. 147-158, and Appendix B, p. 190.

4 It was considered essential that the machinery be below the waterline, where it could not be easily disabled; this meant comparatively compact, high-performance (by 1856 standards!) machinery. Later it was realised that this requirement was absurd in unarmoured warships, and it was quietly dropped.

5 See Part II, p. 147 and Ch. 2.

6 Parkes, *British Battleships*, p. 19.

7 *Ibid.*, p. 34.

8 Screw-propellers in gunvessels of the period ranged from 9 to 13 feet in diameter.

9 To call it a mistake is perhaps less than fair to the designers of these vessels. To have fitted hoisting screws would have necessitated filling the after part of the hull with hoisting gear. As this would have taken up a lot of space and would drastically reduce astern fire from the after gun, twin screws were adopted as the lesser evil.

10 For a full description of this and succeeding classes of warships see *The Mariner's Mirror* articles by Adm. Ballard, October 1939 to January 1941.

11 The sloops *Gannet* and *Dolphin*, and the gunboats *Stork* and *Foxhound*, all over eighty years old (See Part II).

12 In a sloop or corvette the fore and main masts were in three sections, lower mast, topmast, and topgallant mast. In a gunvessel the masts were merely in two parts, i.e. lower mast and pole topmast. Thus the gunvessel, with yards on both fore and main masts, looked superficially similar to the sloop but had a lighter rig (see Part II, pp. 175-6).

13 The corvette and the frigate were both ancestors of the cruiser, and both types were later reclassified as cruisers at the time of the Naval Defence Act.

14 Extract from the Navy List as corrected to December 1873.

15 *United Service Journal*, 1873, p. 10; see also Part II, pp. 162-7.

16 See Part II.

Chapter 8

1 Harry St George Ord, a former Royal Engineer, transferred to the Colonial Office in 1855; Lt-Governor of Dominica 1857, Governor of Bermuda 1861-66 (Lt-Col. and C.B.) and Governor of Straits Settlements 1867-73.

2 In 1869 the C.O. had no idea where Johore was, although it was this state which had ceded Singapore to the Crown in 1819.

3 C. D. Cowan, *Nineteenth-Century Malaya* (hereafter cited as Cowan), p. 55.

4 *Ibid.*, p. 55.

5 *Ibid.*, pp. 35-41.

6 Dispatch of 8 April 1868, quoted by Cowan, p. 60.

7 This nominal suzerainty had been recognised since 1826, but friction occurred when the Siamese influence threatened to become effective. Not until Weld's governorship in the 1880s was there an attempt to argue that the states were independent.

8 Secretary of State to Governor of Straits Settlements, 22 April 1868; CO. 809/1 (quoted by Cowan, p. 64).

9 Anticipating little trouble, *Rinaldo's* captain left his ship downriver and sent his boats to join *Pluto*.

10 C. Northcote Parkinson, *British Intervention in Malaya 1867-1877*.

11 V.-Adm. Sir Henry Kellett, K.C.B., C.-in-C. China Station.

12 What was normally classed as piracy by the Admiralty could better be described as internal interference with the flow of trade. Piracy in the true sense hardly ever involved European vessels in this part of the world (although some cases did occur in Borneo); local seafarers suffered far more.

13 N. Tarling, *Piracy and Politics in the Malay World*, pp. 169-70.

14 *Ibid.*, p. 178.

15 *Ibid.*, p. 180.

16 *Ibid.*

17 *Ibid.*, p. 181.

18 In effect a deck over the bows of the ship from bulwark to bulwark providing a shelter.

19 A light fore-and-aft deck, not part of the structure of the vessel, used to stow boats and spare spars.

20 Parkinson, *British Intervention*, p. 61, in which he quotes from a petition drawn up by the Malacca merchants.

21 H.M.S. *Nassau* was originally a wooden screw gunvessel launched in 1866 and completed for surveying work. Like all R.N. survey ships of the time she had a light gun-armament (in her case four Armstrong 20-pounders) for emergencies.

22 Parkinson, *British Intervention*, p. 79.

23 A minute from Kimberley dated 10 July 1871, see Cowan, p. 174. His decision to reverse the old policy was prompted by fear of foreign intervention, either from Germany or France.

24 The ironclad *Iron Duke*, the composite gunvessels *Midge* and *Frolic* and the dispatch vessel *Salamis*.

25 Parkinson, *British Intervention*, p. 143.

26 Letter from Clarke quoted by Parkinson, *British Intervention*, p. 146.

27 The only chief acceptable to the British was too unpopular with the Malays to be considered.

28 After the Second Burmese War Great Britain annexed Pegu and allowed a friendly ruler to look after her interests; after his death in 1878 the Resident's position became precarious, and he had to be withdrawn temporarily to Rangoon.

29 Quoted in Laird Clowes, vol. 7, p. 376; the French denied that this alliance existed, but H.M.G. had already discovered proof.

30 To the Indian Government the most alarming aspect of the alliance was a promise by the French to supply arms to Burma as soon as their Tonkin war was over.

Chapter 9

1 Palmerston to Russell in 1862, quoted by C. Lloyd, *The Navy and the Slave Trade*, p. 155.

2 C. W. Newbury, *British Policy Towards West Africa*, pp. 175-6.

3 F.O. 2/20.

4 F.O. 84/1088 and Navy List for December 1859.

5 F.O. 84/1147.

6 Lloyd, *The Navy and the Slave Trade*, p. 27.

7 *Ibid.*, p. 160.

8 *Ibid.*

9 F.O. 84/1115.

10 From the middle of the nineteenth century Kroomen were recruited for service in ships on the West Africa coast as boatmen, since they were accustomed to the heat.

11 F.O. 84/1147.

12 J. Gallagher, R. Robinson with A. Denny, *Africa and the Victorians* (hereafter cited as *Africa and the Victorians*), p. 38, n. 4.

13 F.O. 84/1147.

14 *Ibid.*

15 *Ibid.*

16 *Ibid.* Despite Burton's reputation as a scholar and traveller, he was little but a burden to the Foreign Office.

17 F.O. 2/45 (1864).

18 F.O. 84/1250.

19 *Ibid.*

20 F.O. 84/1278 (May 1867).

21 F.O. 84/1292 (April 1868).

22 Later Lord Blatchford; he filled this post from 1859 to 1871.

23 C.O. 147/1 (22 February 1862).

24 T. F. Elliot, talking of the consul at Lagos, in January 1864 (C.O. 147/1).

25 See *Africa and the Victorians*, p. 41.

26 See *Africa and the Victorians*, p. 40, and F.O. 84/1292.

27 F.O. 84/1343.

28 *Africa and the Victorians*, p. 40.

29 Newbury, *British Policy Towards W. Africa*, p. 33.

30 F.O. 84/1343 (September 1871), talking of Harry Johnston's deposing of Ja-Ja.

31 H.M. ships *Sirius, Tourmaline, Spiteful, Avon, Seagull, Ariel, Mallard, Cygnet* and *Contest*.

32 F.O. 84/1464.

33 *Ibid.*

34 A paddle-wheel gunboat which served for most of her career in West Africa; she was launched in 1874 and carried six 20-pounders.

35 C.O. 147/19 (1870).

36 F.O. 84/1508 (August 1878).

37 Admiral Sir Walter Cowan, K.C.B., D.S.O. and Bar, M.V.O. (1871–1956).

38 Captain Lionel Dawson, *The Sound of the Guns* (London, 1949), p. 28.

39 See *Africa and the Victorians*, p. 44.

40 The so-called Hamerton Treaty, which banned the export of all slaves from Africa to Arabia, but permitted the importation of slaves to Zanzibar and Pemba. As there were hardly any R.N. ships available to enforce this, reliance was placed on the Sultan's 'navy', which could not put to sea! Lloyd, *The Navy and the Slave Trade*, pp. 234-5.

41 See *ibid.*, pp. 226-7.

42 *Lyra, Gorgon, Penguin, Sidon* and *Wasp*, out of a total of eight ships on the station; see *ibid.*, p. 242.

43 *Ibid.*

44 Adm. 1/5832 – Instructions to the Commodore in India (24 February 1863); the Cape and East Indies stations were united in 1865, but separated again in 1867.

45 After 1889 East Africa and Zanzibar became part of the Cape of Good Hope Station.

46 Lloyd, *The Navy and the Slave Trade*, p. 261.

47 See Laird Clowes, vol. 7, p. 264.

48 Lloyd, *The Navy and the Slave Trade*, p. 271.

49 *Ibid.*, p. 272.

Chapter 10

1 See *Africa and the Victorians*, p. 84.

2 See *Africa and the Victorians*, pp. 100-4.

3 *Ibid.*, p. 112.

4 See Laird Clowes, vol. 7, p. 325; there was also a considerable number of obsolete smooth-bores in the forts, which could inflict damage at short ranges.

5 *Ibid.*, p. 327 (Seymour's orders).

6 See *Africa and the Victorians*, p. 113.

7 However in both cases troops were already mobilising before any outright threats had been made to harm the Canal; as early as 15 July 1882 officers had been standing by for Egypt.

8 The phrase later used by Gladstone to describe the Sudanese rebellion against Egyptian rule.

9 Now C.-in-C. in the East Indies.

10 Valentine Baker was the former Colonel of the 10th Hussars, cashiered after being found guilty of assaulting a girl in a railway carriage; he then enlisted in the Turkish Army and served with great bravery against the Russians.

11 Sir Gerald Graham, V.C., who commanded two expeditions to Suakin.

12 The incident was caused by the alleged presence of Russian officers

in an obscure Afghan village, and was very quickly forgotten – once it had served its turn.

13 Within a short while gun-running by French steamers became an additional source of annoyance.

14 She was now commanded by Cmdr William Domville, as Beresford had accompanied the Gordon Relief Expedition.

Chapter 11

1 See Ch. 10.

2 D. M. Schurman, *Imperial Defence 1868-1887*.

3 Sir William Jervois was at this time Inspector-General of Fortifications; his memorandum was dated January 1875.

4 Schurman, *Imperial Defence*, p. 122.

5 See W. L. Langer, *European Alliances and Alignments*, p. 302.

6 A. J. Marder, *The Anatomy of British Sea Power*, p. 133.

7 *Ibid.*, p. 136.

8 Parkes, *British Battleships*, p. 350.

9 *Cambridge History of the British Empire*, vol. 3, p. 338.

10 Parkes, *British Battleships*, p. 253.

11 Extract from Navy Lists and Parliamentary Papers; for fuller details see Part II, pp. 181-6, and Appendix B, p. 190.

12 See Adm. Sir G. Elliot, 'Coast Defence by Gunboats'.

13 The French had recently built some armoured gunboats armed with 9.4-in. and 10.6-in. guns.

14 In his article Elliot proposed a 63-ton gun, but a gun of this weight did not feature in British ordnance lists.

15 This, of course, remained true of all naval gunnery until the introduction of radar-assisted fire control in the 1940s.

Chapter 12

1 This group was formed in 1879 by George Goldie Taubman, later Sir George Taubman Goldie (1846-1925).

2 *Africa and the Victorians*, p. 171.

3 See Adm. Sir William James, *A Great Seaman*, p. 37.

4 This little paddler was permanently stationed in West Africa for river service from 1883 to 1899.

5 *St George* (flagship), *Philomel*, *Phoebe* and *Barrosa*.

6 Laird Clowes, vol. 7, p. 443.

7 W. S. Churchill, *The River War*, vol. 2, p. 302.

8 In fact the Expedition's Sudanese troops mutinied within two days of landing at Mombasa; Churchill, *The River War*, vol. 2, pp. 302-3.

9 In addition to three paddle-gunboats and four older vessels, the Nile Flotilla was reinforced in 1898 by three large screw-gunboats, assembled above the Cataracts.

10 Churchill, *The River War*, vol. 2, p. 125.

11 *Ibid.*

12 The French were still deeply divided over the Dreyfus Affair; Sir John Fisher is credited with a proposal to kidnap the wretched Dreyfus from Devil's Island and land him on French soil immediately war was declared, in order to embarrass the French Government at a critical moment.

Chapter 13

1 Parkes, *British Battleships*, p. 351.

2 *Ibid.*, p. 381.

3 *Brassey's Naval Annual* – 1896 (London).

4 Cd 2335.

5 Kemp (ed.), *Fisher Papers*, vol. 1, p. 36, and *ibid.*, vol. 2, pp. 14-15; Marder, *The Anatomy of British Sea Power*, pp. 489 and 494.

6 Cd 2791.

7 The old Crimean gunboat which had been in harbour service. *Skylark* was the last Crimean gunboat to retain her identity as a gunboat, as she was retained as a gunnery tender until July 1906; see Part II, p. 149.

8 Another old Crimean gunboat, still in service as a tender to *Britannia* in 1904.

9 This list comprised ships which were not to be disarmed, but were to be kept in Material Reserve without any expenditure on their upkeep. However, this decision was partly rescinded, and several vessels became minelayers and minesweepers by 1914.

Chapter 14

1 Beresford was C.-in-C., Mediterranean, 1905-7 and C.-in-C., Channel, 1907-9.

2 See Marder, *From the Dreadnought to Scapa Flow*, vol. 1, pp. 88-104.

3 At the request of the Foreign Office, two warships had previously been based on Constantinople.

4 *Fisher Papers*, vol. 1, pp. 117-20; these extracts are from the 'Cawdor memorandum', in which Fisher set out his views to Lord Cawdor, the First Lord (Feb.–Dec. 1905).

5 From information supplied by D.C. Holbrow, who served in *Dart* at the turn of the century.

6 However, by 1901 the status of the sloop had declined to such an extent that Commander Pakenham thought his career was finished when he was posted to *Daphne* in the Pacific; he nevertheless survived to command a battle-cruiser squadron in World War I.

7 See E. Keble Chatterton, *Gallant Gentlemen*, p. 135.

8 Cf. the device imagined by C. S. Forester in *The African Queen*.

9 Named after the explorer Dr Gustav Nachtigal, whose discoveries helped to open up Equatorial Africa.

10 Sir J. Corbett, *Naval Operations*, vol. 3, p. 9.

11 Corbett, *Naval Operations*, vol. 3, pp. 22-3.

Chapter 15

1 Cd 2901 (H.M.S.O.).

2 *Defence Review*, p. 7. Our italics.

3 A fifth carrier is paid off (in reserve) with little likelihood of seeing service again.

4 Capt. S. W. Roskill, *The Strategy of Sea Power*, p. 251.

5 See 'The Suez Operation' by Lt-Cdr J. Stewart in *U.S. Naval Institute Proceedings*, April 1964.

6 The slow assault convoys took some four or five days to reach the eastern Mediterranean, yet the nationalisation of the Canal took place three months before. In addition, when the crisis blew up only *one* British carrier was operational.

7 This generalisation does not ignore the strategic importance of Polaris submarines or of nuclear bombers flown from large carriers.

8 An American term, based on the brush-fire's ability to spread easily.

9 *Defence Review*, p. 7.

Afterword

1 Cable, *Gunboat Diplomacy: Political Applications of Limited Naval Force* (3rd edition, London, 1994), p. 14.

2 Ibid. p. 62.

3 See G. Franklin, *Britain's Anti-Submarine Capability 1919-39* (London, 2003) for an excellent discussion of this problem.

4 For the reality of the diplomatic dimension of British deployments in April 1982 see Sir Lawrence Freedman, *The Official History of the Falklands Campaign* (London, 2005).

Rosario, a *Condor* class steel sloop and one of the last units of the gunboat navy, rides at her buoy, probably in the Nore. *(Conway Maritime Press)*

PART 2

THE GENEALOGY OF THE GUNBOAT NAVY

Notes

The following tables contain the names of all gunboats and gunvessels built between the Crimean War and 1914. For purposes of comparison the later sloops from the *Fantome* class have been included; earlier sloops had been a considerably larger warship type, nearer to frigates than gunvessels. River gunboats (i.e. craft built solely for river service) are not included.

For the earlier vessels, the tonnage is always 'builder's old measurement', a figure arrived at by an old formula. By 1873 warship tonnages were calculated on the basis of displacement, or in other words, the actual weight of the ship calculated by estimating the amount of water displaced. 'Navy List Displacement' was the normal figure calculated when the ship was built, or at the time of her latest reconstruction; not until the twentieth century did the varying Standard and Full Load Displacement tonnages come into vogue.

Abbreviations

The following are used throughout:

b.o.m.	Builder's Old Measurement.
ind.	Indicated (horsepower); reflects the approximate h.p. developed.
nom.	Nominal (horsepower); an arbitrary figure calculated by formula, considerably below the real or indicated h.p.
M.L.R.	Muzzle-loading rifle (used of heavy guns)
B.L.	Breech-loading.
M.L.	Muzzle-loading.
S.B.	Smooth-bore.
Q.F.	Quick-firer (a later development of the B.L. gun).
in.	Inch (usually calibre of gun).
pdr	Pounder (usually shell weight but used to describe a gun).
S.B. Co.	Shipbuilding company.
h.p.	Horsepower.

Dimensions

Figures represent length x beam x draught. Length is always given 'between perpendiculars', i.e. between a perpendicular from the forward end of the keel and another perpendicular through the rudder-post. This gives an idea of the relative size of the vessel since it ignores the inessential space taken up by the overhang of bows and stern, which frequently had only a decorative function. Beam refers to the outside measurement of the hull at its maximum width, but draught varies. Designed draught is an estimate made before launching, whereas mean draught is the actual figure discovered in service, and is the mean between draught forward and draught at the stern. Maximum draught refers to the ship when fully loaded and manned.

Half block models of the hulls of various representatives of the gunboat navy, on display at the Admiralty Experiment Works, Haslar. From top: *Plucky, Clown, Albacore, Algerine, Angler, Britomart.* Originally these models were used in the laying out of the run of the planking or plating of the hulls. *(Private collection)*

The 'flat-iron' gunboat *Drudge*, which served as a tender to the gunnery school H.M.S. *Excellent.* *(Private collection)*

Builders

The builders mentioned in the following tables were located as shown. In many cases they were later known by other names. In the early days installation of the engines was so specialised a task that it was usually entrusted to the leading firms, Penn and Maudslay, although other firms were granted contracts. Not until much later did the practice arise of the builder constructing and installing the machinery if the facilities were available.

BUILDER	LOCATION
Armstrong Mitchell	Newcastle.
Barrow Shipbuilding Co.	Barrow-in-Furness (later Vickers).
Wm Briggs	Sunderland.
Chatham	Royal Dockyard, Chatham.
Courtenay	Newhaven.
Deptford	Royal Dockyard, Deptford.
Devonport	Royal Dockyard, Devonport (Plymouth).
Dixon & Co. (better known as Sir Wm Raylton Dixon & Co.)	Middlesbrough.
Wm Doxford	Sunderland.
Dudgeon	Limehouse.
Earle	Hull.
Elder	Glasgow.
Elswick (Sir Wm Armstrong, formerly Armstrong Mitchell)	Newcastle.
Fletcher	Limehouse.
Green	Blackwall.
Harland & Wolff	Belfast.
Hill	Bristol.
Wm Laird (later Cammell, Laird)	Birkenhead.
C. Lamport	Workington.
Laurie	Glasgow.
London Engineering Co.	
London & Glasgow Co.	Govan (Glasgow).
Lungley	Deptford.
Malta	Royal Dockyard, Malta.

BUILDER	LOCATION
Mare	Blackwall.
Milford Haven	
W. C. Miller	Liverpool.
Napier	Govan.
Patterson	Bristol.
Pembroke	Royal Dockyard, Pembroke.
Perm	Stockton-on-Tees.
Pitcher	Northfleet.
Portsmouth	Royal Dockyard, Portsmouth (the early Crimean gunboats were built at Haslar).
Potter	Liverpool.
Reid	Glasgow.
Rennie	Greenwich.
Samuda	Poplar.
Scott	Greenock.
Scott Russell	Millwall.
Sheerness	Royal Dockyard, Sheerness.
T. & W. Smith	North Shields and Newcastle.
Thames Ironworks	Blackwall.
Thames Shipbuilding Co.	
Thompson	Rotherhithe.
J. & G. Thompson (later John Brown & Co.)	Clydebank.
Westbrook	Blackwall.
J. S. White	Cowes.
Wigram	Blackwall and Northam.
Woolwich	Royal Dockyard, Woolwich.
Young Son & Magnay	Limehouse.

The sloop *Buzzard*, built at the Royal Dockyard at Sheerness between 1886 and 1888. *(NPC)*

Summary of launchings 1854-1903

	1854		1855		1856		1857		1858
g.v.s	6 Arrows	g.v.s	3 Intrepids	g.v.s	3 Intrepids	ʒ.v.s/g.b.s	6 Algerines		–
			2 Vigilants		12 Vigilants				
g.b.s	6 Gleaners	g.b.s	20 Dappers	g.b.s	79 Albacores				
			19 Albacores		18 Cheerfuls				
			2 Cheerfuls		12 Clowns				

	1865		1866		1867		1868		1869
g.b.s	2 Britomarts	g.v.s	2 Cormorants	g.v.s	1 Cormorant	g.v.s	5 Plovers	g.v.s	2 Plovers
	2 Vixens	g.b.s	2 Britomarts		1 Philomel		11 Beacons		
			1 Vixen		4 Plovers				
					7 Beacons				
				g.b.s	2 Britomarts				
					1 Staunch				

	1875		1876		1877		1878		1879
g.b.s	2 Foresters	Sloops	3 Ospreys	Sloops	2 Ospreys	Sloops	2 Ospreys	Sloops	3 Ospreys
		g.v.s	3 Condors	g.v.	1 Condor			g.v.	1 Linnet
		g.b.s	4 Medinas	g.b.s	6 Foresters			g.b.s	4 Gadflys
					8 Medinas				

	1885		1886		1887		1888		1889
Sloops	1 Mariner	g.v.	1 Curlew	Sloop	1 Nymphe	Sloops	1 Mariner	Sloops	2 Beagles
	1 Nymphe	g.b.s	4 Brambles				2 Nymphes	g.b.s	9 Redbreasts
g.v.	1 Curlew					g.b.s	6 Pigmys		

	1899		1900		1901		1902		1903
g.b.s	2 Brambles	Sloops	4 Condors	Sloops	3 Cadmuses		–	Sloops	2 Cadmuses
			1 Cadmus						

An *Arrow* class gunvessel. *(NPC, Antony Preston Collection)*

	1859		1860		1861		1862		1863-64
g.v.s	2 *Philomels*	g.v.s	14 *Philomels*	g.v.s	2 *Philomels*	g.v.	1 *Philomel*		–
			5 *Cormorants*		1 *Cormorant*				
		g.b.s	9 *Britomarts*	g.b	1 *Britomart*				

	1870		1871		1872		1873		1874
g.b.s	1 *Staunch*	g-v.	1 *Plover*	g.v.s	4 *Frolics*	Sloops	5 *Fantomes*	Sloop	1 *Fantome*
	2 *Ants*	g.b.s	5 *Ariels*	g.b.s	2 *Ariels*	g.b.s	2 *Ariels*	g.v.s	2 *Arabs*
			9 *Ants*		5 *Ants*		3 *Ants*	g.b.s	3 *Foresters*
									1 *Ant*

	1880		1881		1882		1883		1884
Sloops	3 *Ospreys*	g.b.s	2 *Banterers*	Sloop	1 *Dolphin*	Sloops	1 *Mariner*	Sloops	3 *Mariners*
g.v.s	3 *Algerines*		2 *Bouncers*	g.b.s	3 *Banterers*		1 *Dolphin*		
	1 *Linnet*					g.b.s	3 *Albacores*		
g.b.s	6 *Banterers*								

	1890-93		1894		1895		1896-97		1898
	–	Sloops	2 *Alertes*	Sloops	2 *Phoenixes*		–	Sloops	2 *Condors*
								g.b.s	2 *Brambles*

Arrow Class gunvessels (wooden)

NAME	BUILT	LAUNCHED	FATE
Arrow	Mare	June 1854	Sold May 1862 (see *Lynx* and *Viper*).
Wrangler	Green	June 1854	Towed to Charlton for scrapping May 1866.
Beagle	Mare	July 1854	Sold by Admiralty Order 16 July 1863.
Viper	Green	July 1854	Sold (with *Arrow* and *Lynx*) to Messrs Marshall 19 May 1862.
Lynx	Mare	July 1854	Sold May 1862.
Snake	Mare	Sept. 1854	Sold to Marshall 1865.

Tonnage: 477 b.o.m.
Dimensions: 160 ft x 25 ft 4 in. x 11 ft 6 in. (mean), 12 ft 3 in. (max.)
Guns: 2 68-pdrs M.L.
Machinery: Single-screw reciprocating, 160 h.p. (nom.), 670 h.p. (ind.) = 11 knots
Complement: 65 officers and ratings

Notes: Although these six ships were not the first to be classed as gunvessels, they were the first *class* to be known by this name. Rated originally as screw vessels, then dispatch vessels, and unofficially as sloops or gunboats; entered service as dispatch vessels and rerated in 1856 as gunvessels.

Roomier than gunboats owing to greater length and depth of hold but drew more water. From the *Arrow* class onwards gunvessels remained independent commands, whereas the first gunboats were always tenders to bigger ships. In recognition of this difference gunvessels were commanded by commanders after the Crimean War, whereas they had previously been lieutenants' commands.

Built at an average cost of £9,500 between April and December 1854. Their 68-pdrs were Lancaster guns, a new type of rifled gun which was finally withdrawn owing to its lack of reliability.

Gleaner Class gunboats (wooden)

NAME	BUILT	LAUNCHED	FATE
Badger	Pitcher	Sept. 1854	Broken up at Portsmouth June 1864.
Gleaner	Deptford	Oct. 1854	Sold at Montevideo April 1868.
Pelter	Pitcher	Aug. 1854	Sold for breaking up Jan. 1864.
Ruby	Deptford	Oct. 1854	Broken up Oct. 1868.
Snapper	Pitcher	Oct. 1854	Hulked 1865 and sold 1906.
Pincher	Pitcher	Sept. 1854	Broken up 1864.

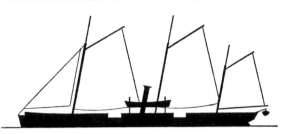

The original sail-plan of H.M.S. *Gleaner* before modification.

Tonnage:	216 b.o.m. (designed)
Dimensions:	100 ft x 22 ft x 6 ft 6 in. (designed draught)
Guns:	1 68-pdr S.B./M.L., 1 32-pdr S.B./M.L., 2 24-pdr howitzers
Machinery:	Single-screw, 60 h.p. (nom.) reciprocating engine = 8 knots (maximum)
Complement:	36 officers and ratings

Notes: The original Crimea gunboats, ordered in June 1854 to the design of Mr W. H. Walker, and completed for service early in 1855. Three masts, with only dipping lugsails as first designed, but this rig was greatly increased before they went to the Baltic. All engined by Penn with trunk engines. It was hoped that they could carry two 68-pdr shell-guns but their margin of stability was too low, and a 32-pdr was substituted for No. 2 gun.

Dapper Class gunboats (wooden)

NAME	BUILT	LAUNCHED	FATE
Biter	Pitcher	May 1855	Hulked 1865.
Boxer	Pitcher	April 1855	Discarded 1865 and broken up 1866.
Clinker	Pitcher	April 1855	Sold to Castle 6 June 1871.
Cracker	Pitcher	April 1855	Broken up 12 April 1864.
Dapper	Green	March 1855	Hulked 1885; became *YC.37* in 1909; sold 10 May 1922.
Fancy	Green	March 1855	Hulked 1876; sold 11 July 1905.
Grinder	White	March 1855	Broken up at Haslar 15 July 1864.
Hind	Thompson	May 1855	Broken up 1872.
Jackdaw	Thompson	May 1855	Hulked 1868 and sold Nov. 1888.
Jasper	White	April 1855	Wrecked in Sea of Azov 24 July 1855.
Lark	Deptford	March 1855	Sold at Devonport 18 July 1878.
Magpie	Deptford	March 1855	Wrecked in Galway Bay 3 April 1864.
Redwing	Pitcher	March 1855	Sold 2 Dec. 1878 and broken up.
Skylark	Pitcher	May 1855	Became gunnery tender; sold 10 July 1906.
Snap	Pitcher	Feb. 1855	Sold at Hong Kong 1868; became Japanese warship *Kaku-ten-kan;* renamed *Snap* (mercantile) in 1872.
Starling	Pitcher	Feb. 1855	Sold at Hong Kong 1 Dec. 1871.
Stork	Pitcher	April 1855	Hulked 1874 and sold for breaking up April 1884.
Swinger	Pitcher	May 1855	Broken up 1864.
Thistle	Pitcher	Feb. 1855	Broken up 1863.
Weazel	Pitcher	March 1855	Sold at Hong Kong 18 Nov. 1869.

Tonnage:	232 tons b.o.m. (displacement 284 tons)
Dimensions:	106 ft x 22 ft x 6 ft 9 in.
Guns:	1 68-pdr S.B./M.L., 2 24-pdr howitzers
Machinery:	Single-screw 60 h.p. (nom.) reciprocating engine = 8 knots (maximum)
Complement:	36 officers and ratings

Notes: Successors to the *Gleaners*, ordered in October 1854 before the first class had entered service. Slightly larger dimensions, but otherwise differed little. *Dapper* outlasted her sisters by a good margin after serving as a tender to *Britannia* at Dartmouth. Hulked in 1885 and finally converted into a cooking vessel, she lasted until 1922. Her sister-ship *Skylark* ended her days as a gunnery tender to H.M.S. *Excellent*, and was the last of her

Redwing, serving as tender to H.M.S. *Cambridge*, the gunnery training ship, at Plymouth. *(Plymouth Naval Base Museum)*

class to remain on the Navy list as a gunboat, being stricken in 1906. Like the earlier class they were unable to mount their designed armament, and shipped a 32-pdr in place of the second 68-pdr.

Intrepid Class gunvessels (wooden)

NAME	BUILT	LAUNCHED	FATE
Intrepid	Wigram	Nov. 1855	Sold to Marshall Oct. 1864.
Victor	Mare	Nov. 1855	Sold to Gordon Coleman & Co. Nov. 1863, as S.S. *Scylla*; resold the same month as C.S.S. *Rappahannock*.
Flying Fish	Pembroke	Dec. 1855	Broken up at Charlton Aug. 1866.
Pioneer	Pembroke	Jan. 1856	Sold to Marshall Oct. 1864.
Roebuck	Scott Russell	March 1856	Sold to Castle 1864.
Nimrod	Scott Russell	April 1856	Sold to White at Cowes 2 June 1865.

Tonnage: 868 b.o.m. (displacement 1,042 tons)
Dimensions: 200 ft x 30 ft 4 in. x 10 ft 6 in. (normal draught), 12 ft 6 in. (deep load draught)
Guns: 1 110-pdr, 1 60-pdr, 4 20-pdrs (all B.L.)
Machinery: 2-cylinder reciprocating engine, single shaft; 350 h.p. (nom.), 930-1,193 h.p. (ind.) = 11 knots
Complement: 100 officers and ratings

Notes: Rated as 1st Class Gunvessels on account of their size. All built between May 1855 and October 1857 (*Intrepid* and *Nimrod* lagging thirteen and six months respectively behind the rest of the class). Twin funnels and three masts, presenting a graceful profile. Cost £17,000 each, but do not appear to have been successful ships; the official reason for *Victor*'s sale after seven years' life was 'numerous mechanical defects'. *Flying Fish* was selected for hull tests after completion; with a false bow fitted, adding eighteen feet to her length, she reached 12.43 knots on trials.

Vigilant Class gunvessels (wooden)

NAME	BUILT	LAUNCHED	FATE
Vigilant	Mare	March 1856	Sold at Bombay 25 Feb. 1869.
Alacrity	Mare	March 1856	Sold to Castle 7 Oct. 1864.
Assurance	Green	March 1856	Sold to Marshall 8 March 1870.
Cormorant	Fletcher	Feb. 1856	Sunk in action against Peiho forts, China, 28 June 1859.
Foxhound	Mare	Aug. 1856	Broken up by Castle Oct. 1866.
Lapwing	White	Jan. 1856	Sold 1864; broken up by Marshall 1865.
Mohawk	Young	Jan. 1856	Sold 20 Sept. 1862 to Emperor of China as *Pekin*; resold to Egyptian Govt 30 Dec. 1865.
Osprey	Fletcher	March 1856	Wrecked off South Africa June 1867.
Renard	Mare	April 1856	Arrived at Charlton for scrapping by Castle March 1866.
Sparrowhawk	Young	Feb. 1856	Sold at Esquimalt 1872.
Surprise	Wigram	March 1856	Broken up by Marshall Nov. 1866.
Ringdove	White	Feb. 1856	Sold 2 June 1865; broken up by White of Cowes 1866.
Coquette	Green	Oct. 1855	Sold 1868.
Wanderer	Green	Nov. 1855	Arrived at Charlton for scrapping by Castle Aug. 1866.

Tonnage: 670 b.o.m.
Dimensions: 181 ft x 28 ft 6 in. x 8 ft (designed draught)
Guns: 1 110-pdr, 1 68-pdr, 2 20-pdrs
Machinery: Single-screw reciprocating, 200 h.p. (nom.), 640-770 h.p. (ind.) =11 knots
Complement: 80 officers and ratings

Notes: Rated as 2nd Class Gunvessels, and reflected the need for smaller vessels than the *Intrepids*. Cost £14,000, and were all laid down between May and August 1855; most were completed by June 1856, but three were much delayed by the cessation of hostilities.

Albacore Class gunboats (wooden)

NAME	BUILT	LAUNCHED	FATE
Albacore	White	April 1856	Converted to tank vessel at Bermuda in 1874 and broken up there in June 1885.
Amelia*	White	May 1856	Broken up at Pembroke 29 Sept. 1865.
Banterer	Pitcher	Sept. 1855	Sold at Hong Kong 30 Dec. 1872.
Beacon†	Laird	Feb.1856	Discarded 1864.
Beaver†	Wigram	Nov. 1855	Broken up 1864.
Blazer*	Laird	Feb. 1856	Became *YC.29* at Portsmouth and later transferred to Gibraltar; sold at Gib. 4 May 1877.
Bouncer	Mare	Feb. 1856	Sold at Hong Kong 1 Feb. 1871.
Brave†	Laird	Feb. 1856	Broken up at Portsmouth 25 March 1869.
Brazen†	Laird	Feb.1856	Broken up Aug. 1864.
Bullfinch*	Laird	Feb.1856	Broken up Aug. 1864.
Bullfrog*	Pitcher	Oct. 1855	Broken up 8 June 1878.
Bustard	Pitcher	Oct. 1855	Sold 18 Nov. 1869 at Hong Kong to Cheeong Loong.
Camel†	Green	May 1856	Breaking up completed 30 June 1864.
Carnation	Pitcher	Oct. 1855	Broken up at Sheerness 1863.
Caroline†	Green	May 1856	Broken up 1862.
Charger†	Pitcher	Nov. 1855	Became *YC.6* at Halifax 1866; sold July 1887 and became S.S. *Rescue* (lasted until 1921).
Charon*	Pitcher	Feb. 1856	Broken up by Marshall Oct. 1865.
Cherokee†	Green	April 1856	Broken up at Portsmouth 25 March 1869.
Cochin†	Green	April 1856	Broken up 1863.
Cockchafer	Pitcher	Nov. 1855	Sold at Shanghai to Telge Northing Co. 1872.
Confounder†	Green	May 1856	Discarded under Admiralty order and breaking up completed 4 Oct. 1864.
Crocus†	Green	June 1856	Discarded under Admiralty order and breaking up completed July 1864.
Delight	Wigram	March 1856	Sold Nov. 1867 at Halifax; became *M.A.Starr;* broken up 1894.
Dove	Pitcher	Nov. 1855	Sold at Shanghai to P. & O. Steam Navigation Co. 14 April 1873.

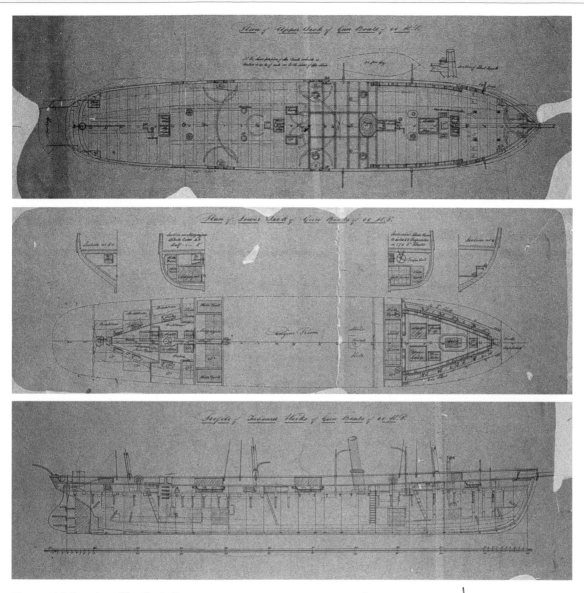

Plans and inboard profile of a 60 h.p. gunboat. *(NPC, Antony Preston Collection)*
The annotated drawing of H.M.S. *Beacon*
shows the basic rig and some of the vessel's
principal features. *(Private collection)*

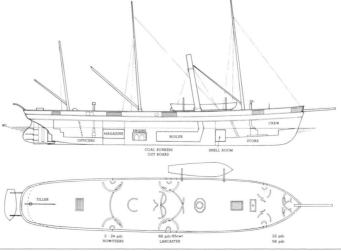

NAME	BUILT	LAUNCHED	FATE
*Earnest**	Patterson	March 1856	Deleted from Navy List and sold 17 Jan. 1885.
*Erne** (ex-*Spray* or *Surge*)	Smith	Feb. 1856	Deleted 1874 and broken up at Chatham.
*Escort**	Patterson	May 1856	Broken up at Pembroke Oct. 1865.
*Fervent**	Green	Jan. 1856	Broken up at Devonport Feb. 1879.
Firm	Fletcher	March 1856	Sold at Shanghai to Telge Northing Co.
Flamer	Fletcher	April 1856	Hulked at Hong Kong 1867 and sold 1874 as a stranded wreck.
*Fly**	Fletcher	April 1856	Broken up 1862.
*Foam**	Wigram	May 1856	Broken up June 1867.
Forester	Green	Jan. 1856	Hulked at Hong Kong as *YC.7* and lost in a typhoon 1871.
Forward	Pitcher	Dec. 1855	Sold at Esquimalt 28 Sept. 1869.
*Goldfinch**	Wigram	Feb. 1856	Broken up at Pembroke June 1869.
*Goshawk**	Wigram	Feb. 1856	Broken up at Devonport March 1869.
Grappler	Wigram	March 1856	Sold June 1868 at Esquimalt as a tug; burnt 3 May 1883 and broken up 1884.
Grasshopper	Pitcher	Dec. 1855	Sold at Newchang May 1871.
*Griper**	Green	Dec. 1855	Broken up at Devonport March 1869.
Growler	Wigram	May 1856	Broken up at Malta Aug. 1864.
Hardy	Hill	March 1856	Sold at Hong Kong 9 Feb. 1869.
*Hasty**	Pitcher	Jan. 1856	Broken up by Castle 1866.
Haughty	Pitcher	Feb. 1856	Sold at Hong Kong 1867.
Havock	Hill	March 1856	Sold at Yokohama 31 March 1871.
*Herring**	Pitcher	Jan. 1856	Broken up at Sheerness Aug. 1865.
*Highlander**	Hill	April 1856	Converted to a dredger (*YC.51*) at Chatham 1868; sold May 1884.
*Hyaena**	Mare	April 1856	Sold 8 March 1870 for conversion to salvage ship; broken up 1894.
Insolent	Pitcher	Jan. 1856	Sold at Chefu March 1869.
*Julia**	Fletcher	Nov. 1855	Broken up at Devonport Dec. 1865 to Feb. 1866.
*Leveret**	Pitcher	March 1856	Broken up at Portsmouth Oct. 1867.
Lively * (ex-*Surge* or *Spray*)	Smith	Feb. 1856	Wrecked 23 Dec. 1863 off Dutch coast; salvaged and became S.S. *Helgolanderin* (German).
*Louisa**	Fletcher	Dec. 1855	Sold 27 Aug. 1867.
Mackerel†	Pitcher	March 1856	Broken up July 1862.
*Magnet**	Briggs	Jan. 1856	Broken up at Chatham 1874.
Manly†	Briggs	Jan. 1856	Broken up at Chatham 1863.
Mastiff† (ex-*Hound*)	Briggs	Feb. 1856	Broken up at Chatham 1863.
*Mayflower**	Pitcher	Jan. 1856	Broken up at Sheerness Sept. 1867.
*Mistletoe**	Briggs	Feb. 1856	Broken up at Sheerness Sept. 1864.
*Nightingale**	Mare	Dec. 1855	Sold to W. Lethbridge, 16 July 1867.
Opossum	Wigram (Northam)	Feb. 1856	Hospital hulk in 1876; mooring vessel 1891; renamed *Siren;* sold 1896 at Hong Kong as *Opossum* (ex-*Siren*).
Parthian†	Wigram	May 1856	Breaking up completed 14 Sept. 1864.
Partridge†	Wigram (Northam)	March 1856	Sold to Habgood 8 Sept. 1864.
Peacock†	Pitcher	April 1856	Broken up at Portsmouth March 1869.
*Pheasant**	Pitcher	May 1856	Broken up at Sheerness Aug. 1877.
Pickle†	Pitcher	May 1856	Breaking up completed 12 April 1864.
Plover	Pitcher	Sept. 1855	Sunk in action against Peiho forts, 25 June 1859.
Porpoise	Pitcher	June 1856	Breaking up completed 22 Feb. 1864.
Primrose†	Pitcher	May 1856	Breaking up completed 25 May 1864.
Procris	Pitcher	May 1856	Hulked 1869 and sold 31 May 1893.
Prompt†	Pitcher	May 1856	Breaking up completed 6 May 1864.

NAME	BUILT	LAUNCHED	FATE
Quail	Wigram	June 1856	Broken up at Malta Sept. 1861.
*Rainbow**	Laird	March 1856	Hulked as R.N.R. Volunteers' drill ship in 1873; sold Nov. 1888 to Castle.
*Raven**	Laird	March 1856	Breaking up completed 24 Sept. 1864.
Redbreast†	Laird	March 1856	Breaking up completed 24 Sept. 1864.
Ripple†	Wigram	June 1856	Broken up by Marshall April 1866.
Rocket†	Laird	April 1856	Broken up Oct. 1864.
Rose†	Laird	April 1856	Broken up at Devonport Aug. 1868.
*Sandfly**	Pitcher	Sept. 1855	Sold to W. Lethbridge 1867.
Savage†	Mare	May 1856	Became mooring lighter at Malta (*YC.3*) 1863; broken up at Malta Sept. 1888.
*Seagull**	Pitcher	Aug. 1855	Sold to Marshall 7 Oct. 1864.
*Sepoy**	Smith	Feb. 1856	Broken up April 1868.
*Shamrock**	Pitcher	March 1856	Sold to Marshall April 1867.
Sheldrake	Pitcher	Sept. 1855	Sold at Montevideo 30 June 1865.
Skipjack	Pitcher	Aug. 1855	Hulked 1874 and broken up Jan. 1879.
*Spanker**	Green	March 1856	Broken up at Chatham 1874.
Spey†	Pitcher	April 1856	Broken up 1864.
Spider	Smith	Feb. 1856	Sold to Castle 12 May 1870.
Staunch	Pitcher	Jan. 1856	Sold Dec. 1866 at Hong Kong and broken up.
*Surly**	Smith	March 1856	Sold to T. J. Begbie 1869.
Swan†	Smith	April 1856	Hulked 1869 and discarded 1906.
*Thrasher**	Green	March 1856	Sold 1883.
Tickler†	Pitcher	Sept. 1855	Broken up 1863.
Tilbury†	Pitcher	March 1856	Broken up 1865 (completed 2 Aug. by Marshall).
*Traveller**	Green	March 1856	Broken up 1864.
*Violet**	Mare	Jan. 1856	Sold 7 Oct. 1864.
Wave†	Wigram	June 1856	Renamed *Clinker* 30 Dec. 1882 when converted to coal depot; sold 1890 (never completed as g.b.).
*Whiting**	Wigram	Jan. 1856	Broken up Dec. 1881.
Wolf†	Mare	July 1856	Broken up 1864 (completed 8 July).

Tonnage: 232 tons average as built
Dimensions: 106 ft x 22 ft x 6 ft 6 in.
Guns: 1 68-pdr S.B., 1 32-pdr S.B., 2 24-pdr howitzers
Machinery: One set 2-cylinder reciprocating, 60 h.p. (nom.), 203-233 h.p. (ind.) = 7 ½ knots (service speed)
Complement: 36-40 officers and ratings

Notes: Identical copies of the *Dappers*, ordered as a result of the success of the first twenty vessels, and the need for a larger number. Ninety-eight vessels were ordered in all, as follows: twenty-three in May and June 1855, another twenty-three in July, and no fewer than fifty-two in October and November. Although none would be completed before the end of the Crimean War all had been launched by June 1856. Half were engined by Maudslay and half by Penn, and the size of the order has led naval historians to believe that some form of sub-contracting was necessary, and that components were supplied by other firms for assembly by either Penn or Maudslay.

When refitted for foreign service this class were given a heavier rig, enabling them to set a topsail and topgallant on the foremast as well as a flying jib. It was this combination of fore-and-aft and square rig which became the characteristic 'gunboat rig'. Ventilating cowls

Raven at Kingstown.
(NPC, Antony Preston Collection)

and additional water-tanks were fitted on the upper deck, and internal arrangements were altered to improve living conditions.

The haste with which these vessels were built necessitated the use of unseasoned timber, and thirty-two (marked †) fell to pieces although they saw no service whatsoever. Many were laid up incomplete, and never stirred from their berths until towed away for breaking up. Those marked * served as tenders for part of their lives, but many of these also fell to pieces after a short time. Engines from these two groups were used later in the *Beacon* class, as they were practically unused.

Cheerful Class gunboats (wooden)

NAME	BUILT	LAUNCHED	FATE
Angler	Devonport	March 1856	Broken up at Haslar Jan. 1869.
Ant	Devonport	March 1856	Broken up at Haslar Feb. 1869.
Blossom (ex-*Careful*)	Laird	April 1856	Broken up at Haslar Oct. 1864.
Cheerful	Deptford	Oct. 1855	Broken up at Haslar Jan. 1869.
Chub	Sheerness	Oct. 1855	Broken up at Haslar Jan. 1869.
Daisy	Westbrook	March 1856	Broken up at Haslar Jan. 1869.
Decoy	Pembroke	Feb. 1856	Broken up at Haslar Feb. 1869.
Dwarf	Westbrook	April 1856	Broken up at Haslar by Hood 1863.
Fidget	Joyce	April 1856	Broken up at Haslar 1863.
Flirt	Joyce	June 1856	Breaking up completed at Haslar 30 April 1864.
Gadfly	Laird	April 1856	Broken up Nov. 1864.
Garland	Laird	May 1856	Broken up June 1864.
Gnat	Laird	May 1856	Breaking up completed 10 Aug. 1864.
Midge	Young	May 1856	Broken up Oct. 1864.
Nettle	Pembroke	Feb. 1856	Broken up at Bermuda Oct. 1867.
Onyx	Young	April 1856	Sold at Jamaica after conversion to a steam lump 8 July 1873.
Pert	Young	April 1856	Discarded 1864: breaking up completed 12 March.
Pet	Pembroke	Feb. 1856	Converted to a coal depot in 1865, and finally sold to Castle 12 April 1904.
Rambler (ex-*Ramble*)	Pembroke	Feb. 1856	Broken up at Haslar Jan. 1869.
Tiny	Young	May 1856	Discarded 1863; breaking up completed 28 Jan. 1864.

Tonnage: 212 b.o.m.
Dimensions: 100 ft x 21 ft 10 in. x 4 ft 6 in. (designed)
Guns: 2 32-pdrs S.B.
Machinery: One set of single-cylinder reciprocating, 20 h.p. (nom.) = 8 knots (designed)
Complement: 30-6 officers and ratings

Notes: The least successful of the Crimean gunboat designs, this class resulted from experience with the *Dappers* and *Gleaners* in the Baltic in 1855. As there were many instances of gunboats grounding in water less than six feet deep the Admiralty ordered a class which would float in four feet. But to accomplish this the builders probably carried weight-saving to extremes; whatever the cause only two of these 20 h.p. gunboats saw service. Eighteen were put straight into reserve and later broken up or used as hulks.

All ordered between July and November 1855. Two masts, and could only set 1,919 square feet of canvas (as against at least 2,426 sq. ft on the original *Gleaner* design). All engined by Penn.

H.M.S. *Ant* of the *Cheerful* class. *(Private collection)*

Clown Class gunboats (wooden)

NAME	BUILT	LAUNCHED	FATE
Clown	Miller	May 1856	Converted to coal lighter *YC.6* at Hong Kong in 1867 and lost 1871.
Drake	Pembroke	March 1856	Sold at Hong Kong 9 Feb. 1869.
Fenella	Pitcher	May 1856	Converted to a dredger March 1867 and broken up 14 Nov. 1878.
Garnet	Pitcher	May 1856	Discarded 1864; breaking up completed 25 May 1864.
Handy	Pitcher	May 1856	Sold at Lagos May 1868.
Hunter	Pitcher	June 1856	Sold 1884 (never completed for sea).
Janus	Pembroke	March 1856	Sold at Hong Kong 1871.
Kestrel	Miller	May 1856	Sold to Glover & Co. at Yokohama 16 March 1866 and resold to Japanese Govt.
Ready	Briggs	May 1856	Breaking up completed 25 Jan. 1864.
Thrush	Briggs	May 1856	Breaking up completed 14 March 1864.
Watchful	Smith	June 1856	Sold at Hong Kong 1 Feb. 1871.
Woodcock	Smith	June 1856	Sold at Hong Kong 1 Feb. 1871.

Tonnage: 233 b.o.m.
Dimensions: 110 ft x 22 ft x 4 ft
Guns: 1 68-pdr S.B., 1 32-pdr S.B.
Machinery: One set of single-cylinder reciprocating, 40 h.p. (nom.), 145 (ind.) = 8 knots
Complement: 30 officers and ratings

Notes: Improved *Cheerfuls*, with greater length, heavier armament and more powerful machinery. Like the *Dappers* many were adapted for foreign service, and received square rig on the foremast. Even before these modifications it is clear that the *Clowns* were to carry more sail than the 20 h.p. gunboats; their sail-area was

The sail-plan of the 40 h.p. *Clown* class gunboats as modified for China service.

increased from 2,466 sq. ft to 4,889 sq. ft. Like the other wooden gunboats built at this time some deteriorated rapidly from being built of unseasoned wood.

Algerine Class gunboats (wooden)

NAME	BUILT	LAUNCHED	FATE
Algerine	Pitcher	Feb. 1857	Sold at Hong Kong 2 April 1873, but continued in mercantile service until 1894.
Jaseur	Green	March 1857	Wrecked on Baxo Nuevo, West Indies, 26 Feb. 1859.
Jasper (ii)[1]	Green	March 1857	Became Chinese *Amoy* 1862, but returned and sold to Egypt.
Lee	Pitcher	Feb. 1857	Sunk by gunfire at Peiho 25 June 1859.
Leven	Pitcher	March 1857	Sold at Shanghai 21 July 1873.
Slaney	Pitcher	March 1857	Wrecked near Hong Kong 9 May 1870.

Displacement: 370 tons (301 tons b.o.m.)
Dimensions: 125 ft x 23 ft x 7 ft 9 in.
Guns: 1 10-in. S.B./M.L., 2 24-pdr howitzers or 1 68-pdr S.B. and 2 howitzers (in 1863 all had 1 110-pdr and 1 40-pdr B.L.)
Machinery: Single-screw 2-cylinder reciprocating, 80 h.p. (nom.), 294 h.p. (ind.) = 9 knots
Complement: 50 officers and ratings

Notes: All ordered in September 1856. The most powerful gunboats yet built, although for some years they were officially referred to as gunvessels. The great increase in size reflects the transition from the purely coastal function of gunboats to the deep-water cruising required of later vessels of this type. Had greatly improved accommodation by virtue of their size, and since they were the first gunboats to have a hoisting screw they proved very handy under sail. So well thought of that two copies, *Clyde* and *Hugh Rose*, were built of teak at Bombay for the Indian Marine. But in spite of their qualities they were the unluckiest of all the classes; two were lost within two years of first hoisting the pendant, and a third was sold three years later.

Four made the journey to China around the Cape of Good Hope in 1857-58 almost without assistance.

The last man to be hanged at the yardarm was a marine executed on 13 July 1860 in H.M.S. *Leven*.

[1] (ii) or (iii) indicates that this is the second or third ship of the same name.

Britomart Class gunboats (wooden)

NAME	BUILT	LAUNCHED	FATE
Bramble	Portsmouth	—	Cancelled on stocks 1863.
Britomart	Smith	May 1860	Sold Castle 1892; resold and became mooring hulk at Dagenham; broken up 1946.
Bruizer	Portsmouth	April 1867	Broken up at Devonport May 1886.
Cherub	Portsmouth	March 1865	Sold for breaking up 1890.
Cockatrice	Smith	May 1860	Became a luggage lighter at Malta (*YC.10*) 1882; sold 1885.
Cromer	Portsmouth	Aug. 1867	Sold 24 May 1886.
Crown	Portsmouth	—	Cancelled on stocks 1863.
Doterel	Miller	July 1860	Sold to Marshall for breaking up 6 June 1871.
Heron	Miller	July 1860	Broken up at Jamaica June 1879.
Linnet	Briggs	June 1860	Broken up at Chatham July 1872.
Minstrel	Portsmouth	Feb. 1865	Hulked (coal depot) at Bermuda 1874 and discarded 1907.
Netley	Portsmouth	July 1866	Sold at Portsmouth 1885.
Orwell	Portsmouth	Dec. 1866	Discarded 1890.
Pigeon	Briggs	June 1860	Broken up at Devonport Sept. 1876.
Protector	Portsmouth	—	Cancelled on stocks 1863.
Speedy	Lamport	July 1860	Discarded 1889.
Trinculo	Banks	Sept. 1860	Wrecked near Gibraltar 5 Sept. 1870 after collision with S.S. *Moratin*.
Tyrian	Courtenay	Sept. 1861	Sold at Jamaica 1891.
Wizard	Smith	Aug. 1860	Broken up at Malta Sept. 1878.
Danube	Portsmouth	—	Not laid down; order cancelled 1863.

Tonnage: 268 b.o.m. (displacement 330 tons)
Dimensions: 120 ft x 22 ft x 8 ft
Guns: 2 68-pdrs (later 2 64-pdrs M.L.R.)
Machinery: 2-cylinder reciprocating 60 h.p. (nom.), 260 h.p. (ind.) = 9 knots
Complement: 36-40 officers and ratings

Notes: Ten were ordered from private builders in 1859 as 'Improved *Dappers*', and proved most successful in service. Hoisting screws remedied the defective handling of earlier types, and the leisurely pace of construction ensured that they were sturdily built. Ten more were ordered from Portsmouth Dockyard in 1861, but only six were completed, five or six years later. The remaining four were cancelled by an Admiralty order dated 12 December 1863 (*Danube* had never been laid down, but the other three had been lying on the stocks for two years).

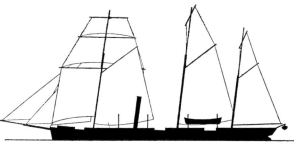

The *Britomart* class as completed; this sail-plan became known as 'gunboat-rig'.

Philomel Class gunvessels (wooden)

NAME	BUILT	LAUNCHED	FATE
Philomel	White	March 1860	Sold to White, Cowes, 2 June 1865.
Dart	Mare	March 1860	Renamed *Kangaroo* 1882; sold 1884.
Espoir	Pembroke	Jan. 1860	Converted to dredger at Bermuda (*YC.19*) 1869.
Griffon	Pitcher	Feb. 1860	Collided with *Pandora* off Little Popo, W. Africa, Oct. 1866, and stranded.
Jaseur (ii)	Deptford	May 1862	Sold to Irish Lighthouse Commissioners Dec. 1874.
Landrail	Deptford	March 1860	Sold Sept. 1869 and renamed *Walrus*.
Lee (ii)	Wigram	Jan. 1860	Broken up at Sheerness March 1875.
Mullet	Lungley	Feb. 1860	Sold at Hong Kong 25 April 1872.
Newport	Pembroke	July 1867	Completed April 1868 as survey vessel (see Notes). Sold May 1881 to Allen Young for polar exploration and crushed in the ice as S.S. *Pandora* 11 June 1881.
Nimble	Pembroke	Sept. 1860	Hulked 1878; sold to W. R. Jones 10 July 1906.

NAME	BUILT	LAUNCHED	FATE
Pandora	Pembroke	Feb. 1861	Sold 13 Jan. 1875; later lost and replaced by *Newport* (date unknown).
Penguin	Miller	Feb.1860	Sold 26 Feb. 1870 and broken up by Lethbridge & Drew.
Plover (ii)	Green	Jan. 1860	Sold 12 Sept. 1865 to Messrs Bowring and renamed *Hawk;* crushed in ice 1876.
Ranger	Deptford	Nov. 1859	Sold to Moss Isaacs 3 Nov. 1869.
Snipe	Scott Russell	May 1860	Sold 1869.
Sparrow	Scott Russell	July 1860	Broken up by Marshall 1868.
Speedwell	Deptford	Feb. 1861	Broken up at Chatham 2 Aug. 1867.
Steady	Miller	Feb. 1860	Sold to W. & T. Jolliffe 12 May 1870.
Torch	Green	Dec. 1859	Broken up at Malta Sept. 1881.
Cygnet	Wigram	June 1860	Broken up at Portsmouth Aug. 1868.

Nimble as in 1875. *(Conway Maritime Press, drawing by John Roberts)*

Tonnage:	428 b.o.m. (570 tons displacement)	
Dimensions:	145 ft x 25 ft 4 in. x 11-12 ft	
Guns:	1 68-pdr S.B., 2 24-pdr howitzers, 2 20-pdrs B.L. (68-pdr replaced by 110-pdr B.L.)	
Machinery:	One set single-screw reciprocating, 80 h.p. (nom.) = 9 knots; 276-382 h.p. (ind.) = 8-11 knots	
Complement:	60 officers and ratings	

Notes: Enlarged editions of the *Algerine* class, with greater length and draught to improve seaworthiness, and heavier rig (square rig on foremast and main). As a class had chequered careers; eight were disposed of for scrapping after five to nine years' service, yet others of the class survived until the 1880s. *Newport* was laid down in 1860, suspended in February 1863, and finally completed as a survey ship in November 1866. Six more were cancelled in 1863, *Discovery, Humber, Alban, Portia, Rye* and *Undine.*

Laid down between November 1857 and January 1861; completed June 1860 to September 1863 (except *Newport* – see above).

Cormorant Class gunvessels (wooden)

NAME	BUILT	LAUNCHED	FATE
Cormorant (ii)	Wigram	Feb. 1860	Sold at Hong Kong for breaking up by Admiralty order of 7 June 1870.
Eclipse	Scott Russell	Sept. 1860	Broken up at Sheerness July 1867.
Lily	Scott Russell	Feb. 1861	Broken up at Sheerness Oct. 1867.
Myrmidon	Chatham	June 1867	Completed as survey vessel Oct. 1867; sold at Hong Kong 1889.
Nassau	Pembroke	Feb. 1866	Completed as survey vessel July 1866; broken up at Sheerness April 1880.
Racehorse	Wigram	March 1860	Wrecked near Chefu 4 Nov. 1864.
Serpent	Mare	June 1860	Sold to Castle April 1875.
Star	Mare	Dec. 1860	Broken up at Devonport 1877.
Sylvia	Woolwich	March 1866	Completed as survey vessel Oct. 1866; sold 1890.

Tonnage:	695 b.o.m. (877 tons displacement)	
Dimensions:	185 ft x 28 ft 2 in. x 8 ft (designed), 11-12 ft draught (as completed)	
Guns:	2 68-pdrs S.B., 2 32-pdrs S.B. as designed, but 1 68-pdr was replaced by a 110-pdr B.L., and 2 20-pdrs replaced the 32-pdrs; later the class was rearmed with 1 7-in. 6½-ton M.L.R. and 2 64-pdrs	
Machinery:	Single-screw reciprocating, 200 h.p. (nom.), 690-774 h.p. (ind.) =10 knots	
Complement:	90 officers and ratings	

Notes: A return to the dimensions of the old *Intrepid* class in an attempt to provide fire-power equal to two gunboats. However, the relatively deep draught must have outweighed the advantage of gunpower in coastal operations. This class was very active on foreign stations, but like so many vessels of this period, they seem to have passed out of service unusually quickly. Two were broken up or sold after five and six years' service respectively, and with the exception of the survey vessels

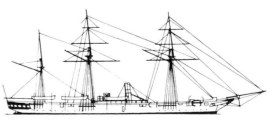

Nassau as in 1875.
(Conway Maritime Press, drawing by John Roberts)

the survivors lasted only eight to ten years. *Albatross*, *Guernsey*, *Pegasus* and *Tartarus* were cancelled, while the three survey vessels were laid down in 1862 but suspended until 1865.

Serpent, of the *Cormorant* class of wooden gunvessels. *(NPC)*

Vixen Class armoured gunboats

NAME	BUILT	LAUNCHED	FATE
Vixen	Lungley	Nov. 1865	Sold at Bermuda 1896.
Viper (ii)	Dudgeon	Dec. 1865	Reduced to harbour service 1890 (became tank vessel 1901); sold at Bermuda 1908.
Waterwitch	Thames Iron Works	June 1866	Sold to Castle 26 April 1890.

Tonnage: *Vixen* and *Viper* 754/737 b.o.m. (displacement 1,230 tons); *Waterwitch* 777 b.o.m. (displacement 1,205 tons, later 1,280 tons)

Dimensions: *Vixen* 160 ft x 32 ft 5 in. x 10-12 ft; *Viper* 160 ft x 32 ft x 10-12 ft; *Waterwitch* 162 ft x 32 ft x 11 ft 6 in.

Guns: 2 7-in. M.L.R., 2 20-pdrs B.L.

Machinery: (*Vixen* and *Viper*) twin-screw horizontal reciprocating, 612/740 h.p. (ind.) = 9.24 knots

Complement: 80 officers and ratings

Armour: 4½ in. of iron on 10-in. backing

Viper as completed in 1867. *(Conway Maritime Press, drawing by John Roberts)*

Notes: Designed by Rear-Admiral George Elliot and the Controller's Department, and were largely experimental. *Vixen* was the first composite-hulled gunboat, whereas *Viper*'s hull was built of iron. These two were the first warships with twin screws. *Waterwitch* was double-ended, and when it was decided to install the Ruthven turbine in her she was given a rudder under the bow. Their 4½-in. armour belt was the same thickness as the protection of the famous ironclad *Warrior*.

Waterwitch tested the revolutionary Ruthven turbine, which needed no screws. Although Ruthven's invention

had much to recommend it, a less suitable guinea-pig could not have been found. *Waterwitch* was a failure in every respect, as she was unmanoeuvrable and lacked seaworthiness; the results of her trials were enough to condemn Ruthven's invention for all time. All three ships spent the rest of their lives in harbour service, but their failure did not deter other navies from toying with the idea of armoured gunboats. Both the French and the Russians produced similar vessels, but they likewise disappointed their designers.

A large-calibre Armstrong 7-inch breech-loading gun; the example shown is a 110-pounder, introduced in 1860.

Plover Class gunvessels (wooden)

NAME	BUILT	LAUNCHED	FATE
Plover (iii)	Deptford	Feb. 1867	Sold 1886.
Ringdove (ii)	Portsmouth	Sept. 1867	Sold 17 May 1882.
Philomel (ii)*	Deptford	Oct. 1867	Sold at Bombay 1887.
Lapwing (ii)	Devonport	Nov. 1867	Sold to Castle 15 April 1885.
Magpie (ii)*	Portsmouth	Feb. 1868	Sold Sept. 1885.
Bullfinch (ii)	Sheerness	Feb. 1868	Sold June 1885.
Seagull (ii)*	Devonport	March 1868	Sold Nov. 1887.
Curlew	Deptford	Aug. 1868	Sold 7 Nov. 1882.
*Swallow**	Portsmouth	Nov.1868	Sold to Mr Tobin 18 Oct. 1882.
Bittern	Pembroke	Sept.1869	Sold 1887.
*Vulture**	Sheerness	Nov. 1869	Sold to Castle Sept. 1885.
*Woodlark**	Chatham	March 1871	Sold at Bombay 9 March 1887.

Seagull. Commissioned in 1871, she served on the Cape of Good Hope and West Coast of Africa and North America and West Indies Stations, as well as in the Mediterranean. *(Conway Maritime Press)*

Tonnage: 663 b.o.m. (755 tons displacement)
Dimensions: 170 ft x 29 ft x 9 ft 6 in.-10 ft 6 in.
Guns: 1 7-in. 6½-ton M.L.R., 2 40-pdrs B.L. (Armstrong); later some had 1 7-in. 4½-ton M.L.R. and 2 64-pdrs M.L.R.
Machinery: Twin-screw simple-pressure reciprocating, 800-970 h.p. (ind.) = 10 knots (average)
Complement: 90 officers and ratings

Notes: The last wooden gunvessels built for the Royal Navy. Built between 1865 and 1871 and served on most foreign stations. Part of the large replacement programme undertaken in the late 1860s as a result of the early deterioration of previous gunboats and gunvessels. Designers forced to adopt twin screws owing to the shallow-draught hull, an innovation which met with little support. However, they were highly successful in service, apart from a tendency to lateral drift in a beam sea; not being fitted with hoisting screws they steered sluggishly under sail.[1] Their unusually high coal capacity was offset by excessive consumption.

In common with all gunvessels of the period they were barque-rigged without royals. They were the smallest vessels to have telescopic funnels, and had a pronounced rake to their masts. Six (marked *) were altered after their first commissions by the addition of topgallant forecastles and poops to improve habitability in the tropics (see Ch. 8); this alteration increased displacement to 805 tons. Later all except *Bittern*, *Lapwing* and *Ringdove* were rearmed with the lighter 7-in. 4½-ton gun, and two 64-pdr rifled muzzle-loaders in place of the Armstrong guns.

[1] As explained earlier the adoption of non-hoisting screws in this class and the contemporary *Beacons* was owing to lack of space, and the need to allow a good arc of fire for the stern-chaser.

Beacon Class gunvessels (composite)

NAME	BUILT	LAUNCHED	FATE
Beacon (ii)*	Chatham	Aug. 1867	Sold Dec. 1888.
Avon	Portsmouth	Oct. 1867	Sold 1890.
Boxer (ii)*	Deptford	Jan. 1868	Sold 1886.
Cracker (ii)	Portsmouth	Nov. 1867	Broken up at Portsmouth 1889.
Dwarf (ii)*	Woolwich	Nov. 1867	Broken up at Devonport April 1886.
*Elk**	Portsmouth	Jan. 1868	Reduced to harbour service 1890; sold 1905 as a dredger.
Flirt (ii)*	Devonport	Dec. 1867	Sold 1888.
Fly (ii)	Devonport	Dec. 1867	Sold Nov. 1887.
Gnat (ii)	Pembroke	Nov. 1867	Wrecked off Balabac Island, China Sea, 15 Nov. 1868.
Growler (ii)	Laurie	Dec. 1868	Sold Nov. 1887 and renamed *Branksea*.
Hart	Thompson	Aug. 1868	Sold Dec. 1888.
Hornet	Penn	March 1868	Discarded 1889.
Lynx (ii)	Harland & Wolff	April 1868	Sold Dec. 1888.
Midge (ii)*	Elder	May 1868	Reduced to harbour service 1891; sold 15 March 1907.
Pert (ii)	Reid	June 1868	Sold Dec. 1888.

Dwarf of the *Beacon* class, seen leaving Portsmouth. Note the differences in her rig and colour scheme compared with the photograph on pages 70-71. *(Conway Maritime Press)*

NAME	BUILT	LAUNCHED	FATE
Rocket (ii)	London Eng. Co.	April 1868	Sold Dec. 1888.
*Teazer**	Laird	April 1868	Broken up at Chatham Dec. 1887.
Thistle (ii)	Deptford	Jan. 1868	Sold to Read, Portsmouth, Nov. 1888.

Displacement: 576 tons designed (465 tons b.o.m.); 603 tons actual
Dimensions: 155 ft x 25 ft x 7 ft 6 in. (designed), 8-9 ft 6 in. (actual)
Guns: Designed to mount 2 68-pdrs S.B., but completed with 1 7-in. 6½-ton M.L.R., 1 64-pdr M.L.R., 2 20-pdrs B.L.
Machinery: 2 sets horizontal direct-acting reciprocating, 120 h.p. (nom.), 465-696 h.p. (ind.) = 9-10¼ knots
Complement: 80 officers and ratings

Notes: Designed for service in China, and combined shallow draught with a heavy armament. When their armament came under review the Armstrong gun crisis was in full swing, so it was decided to give them two 68-pdrs each. However, the crisis was resolved by the arrival of the 'Woolwich' rifled muzzle-loader, and the new ships received a 7-in. and a 64-pdr instead. To obtain maximum hull strength these ships were composite built, the first class of gunvessels to feature this extremely durable form of construction. Highly successful on all foreign stations, and saw much action during their two decades of service.

Unique in that they were engined with two sets of 60 h.p. machinery removed from rotten Crimean gunboats. The original manufacturers were responsible for the re-installation, i.e. Maudslay engines were installed for the second time by Maudslays while Penns did the same for their sets of machinery. Steam was provided by three

cylindrical boilers working at 80 lb. (Penn) and 60 lb. (Maudslay).

After their first commissions those ships marked * were altered by the addition of poops. When newer ordnance was developed it was hoped to rearm the whole class, but as it turned out *Flirt*, *Hornet*, *Lynx* and *Rocket* received two 7-in. 4½-ton guns in place of their 6 ½-ton gun and 64-pdrs; *Avon* and *Elk* only exchanged the heavy 7-in. gun with its massive wooden carriage for the new 4½-ton pattern on an iron carriage. Thus most of the ships remained saddled with the curse of three different patterns of gun, which in turn meant three sets of spares, and three magazines and shell rooms.

Although their excessively shallow draught made them sail 'like tea-trays' and their steering was erratic they were steady gun-platforms and highly seaworthy. Built under 1867-68 Estimates.

Ariel Class gunboats (composite)

NAME	BUILT	LAUNCHED	FATE
Ariel	Chatham	Feb. 1873	Sold Aug. 1889.
Coquette (ii)	Pembroke	April 1871	Sold Aug. 1889.
Decoy (ii)	Pembroke	Oct. 1871	Sold Oct. 1885.
Foam (ii)	Pembroke	Aug. 1871	Broken up June 1887.
Goshawk (ii)	Pembroke	Jan. 1872	Hulked 1902; sold 1906(?).
Merlin	Pembroke	Nov. 1871	Sold 27 Feb. 1891.
Mosquito	Pembroke	Dec. 1871	Sold Dec. 1888 and broken up by Cohen.
Swinger (ii)	Pembroke	Feb. 1872	Hulked 1895; sold to Rogers & Co., Plymouth, June 1924.
Zephyr	Chatham	Feb. 1873	Sold to G. Cohen Aug. 1889.

Displacement: 430 tons (*Ariel* and *Zephyr* 438 tons)
Dimensions: 125 ft x 22 ft 6 in. x 8 ft 6 in.-10 ft 6 in. (*Ariel* and *Zephyr* 23 ft beam)
Guns: 2 64-pdrs M.L.R., 2 20-pdrs B.L.
Machinery: Single-screw horizontal compound reciprocating, 60 h.p. (nom.), 400-540 h.p. (ind.) = 9½-10½ knots
Complement: 60 officers and ratings

Notes: The first composite-built gunboats, the *Ariel* class represented a big advance in offensive power. Embodying all the improvements of the old *Algerines* and *Britomarts*, they also had watertight bulkheads and improved ventilation. Although contemporaries of the *Beacon* and *Plover* classes they were designed with a view to ocean work, and therefore mark a slight weakening of the 'coastal' theory of naval warfare. They were among the first vessels fitted with compound engines, in accordance with the Admiralty practice of trying new engines in small hulls.

Frolic Class gunvessels (wooden)

NAME	BUILT	LAUNCHED	FATE
Frolic	Chatham	Feb. 1872	Converted to R.N. Volunteers' drill ship 1888; became Coastguard 'Watch Vessel' *W.V.30* 1893 (renumbered *W.V.41* in 1897); sold 7 April 1908.
Kestrel (ii)	Chatham	Feb. 1872	Sold 1888.
Ready (ii)	Chatham	Sept. 1872	Reduced to harbour service 1892; re-named *Drudge* 1916; sold at Bermuda 25 Feb. 1920.
Rifleman	Chatham	Nov. 1872	Sold 26 April 1890.

Displacement: 610 tons
Dimensions: 155 ft x 25 ft x 7 ft 9 in.-9 ft 6 in.
Guns: 1 7-in. 6½-ton M.L.R., 1 64-pdr M.L.R., 2 20-pdrs B.L.
Machinery: 2 sets compound trunk engines, twin-screw, 100 h.p. (nom.), 830-90 h.p. (ind.) = 10½-11 knots
Complement: 80 officers and ratings

Notes: Repeat editions of the *Beacons* laid down in 1871, on the same dimensions. As no ex-gunboat engines were available by this time the contract was given to Penn, who took the opportunity to try compound pressures (one of the earliest instances). The experiment fully justified itself, and the engines were so economical that bunkerage was reduced by fifteen tons to allow more weight to be devoted to increasing the horsepower and speed.

Two were partially rearmed on the lines of the *Beacons*, *Rifleman* receiving two 4½-ton 7-in. guns in place of her two largest guns, while *Frolic* exchanged the 6½-ton 7-in. for the newer 4½-ton mark.

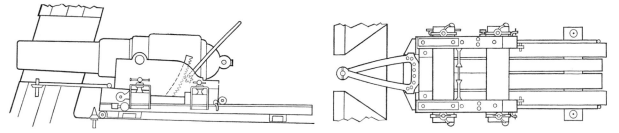

Side view of a large rifled muzzle-loader on its broadside pivot, ready for firing; the plan view shows only the carriage. The basic simplicity of the mounting can be seen clearly.

Coastal gunboats (iron type)

During the late 1860s and early 1870s, when the 'coastal' theory of naval warfare held sway and the Army indulged its 'fortress mania', there was great pressure on Parliament to authorise the construction of small gunboats for coastal defence. This resulted in a series of small iron craft known as the 'flat-irons' from their tubby hulls. As they were under 100 feet long and steamed at less than nine knots there was no question of employing them on the high seas, and they could have been omitted from this survey. They were failures in their designed role, but outlasted many composite ships as tenders and gunnery trials ships. Late in their careers some served on foreign stations, but mainly in a subsidiary role.

Three classes were built, twenty *Ant* type (following the construction of two prototypes, *Staunch* and *Plucky*),

four *Gadfly* type and two *Bouncer* type. All mounted a single 10-in. gun originally, and had a sea speed in the region of 7½ knots. They were built intermittently between 1867 and 1881, and were rerated as 3rd Class gunboats after the Naval Defence Act. The gunnery tender *Bustard* had been rearmed before World War I, and joined Rear-Admiral Hood's bombardment force off the Belgian coast late in 1914, and thus became the first and last 'flat-iron' to fire her guns in anger.

The two gunboats *Handy* and *Drudge* were somewhat larger, and were built in the early 1880s by Armstrong for testing gun-mountings. Both were bought by the Admiralty and used for the same purpose. As the tender *Excellent*, *Handy* served off the Belgian coast in 1914-15 in Rear-Admiral Hood's makeshift bombarding force.

Haslar Gunboat Yard, 1878. Ten covered sheds and a large open storage area were constructed in 1855 on the site of Haslar Farm, surrounded by a wall, complete with watchtowers at the corners. The yard was served by a single slipway, the gunboats then being moved around using a 'traverser', a wheeled platform designed by IK Brunel and driven by steam, which became known as 'The Elephant'. In 1952 this was broken up and replaced by an electrically-operated transporter; by this time the Yard had long been carrying out maintenance and refitting of a whole variety of small naval craft. The Gunboat Yard was scheduled as an Ancient Monument in 1976, and ceased to be used for refitting vessels two years later. Today the sheds survive, albeit much altered, within Haslar Marine Technology Park (formerly the Admiralty Experiment Works). The site of the slipway and transporter can also be seen. *(Above: private collection, right: Fort Blockhouse)*

Above: The 'flat-iron' gunboat *Handy* while serving as tender to H.M.S. *Excellent*. In the background are *Royal George* and *Actaeon* (ex-*Vernon*). *(Private collection)*

Right: *Handy* as she is today (2006), in a creek at the back of Portsmouth Harbour. *(Geoffrey Dennison)*

Prototype iron coastal gunboats

NAME	BUILT	LAUNCHED	FATE
Plucky	Portsmouth	July 1870	Renamed *Banterer* c.1916; sold 1928.
Staunch (ii)	Armstrong	Dec. 1867	Sold 1904-5.

Displacement: *Staunch* 200 tons, *Plucky* 212 tons
Dimensions: *Staunch* 75 ft x 25 ft x 6 ft 6 in. (light). *Plucky* 80 ft x 25 ft 1½ in. x 6 ft 1½ in. (light)
Guns: 1 9-in. 12-ton M.L.R.
Machinery: 2 sets of 2-cylinder engines, twin-screw, 25 h.p. (nom.), 134 h.p. (ind.) = 7½ knots; *Plucky*'s machinery developed 224 h.p. (ind.).
Complement: 31 officers and ratings

Ant Class

NAME	BUILT	LAUNCHED	FATE
Ant (ii)	Laird	Aug. 1874	Sold to Granton Shipbreaking Co. 2 June 1926.
Arrow (ii)	Rennie	April 1871	Sold to W. H. Webber 1 March 1922.
Badger (ii)	Chatham	March 1872	Sold to Loveridge, W. Hartlepool, 6 Oct. 1908.
Blazer (ii)	Portsmouth	Dec. 1870	Sold to Loveridge 19 Aug. 1919.
Bloodhound	Armstrong	April 1871	Sold to F. Bevis Ltd 28 June 1921.
Bonetta	Rennie	May 1871	Sold 12 Jan. 1909 after conversion to salvage vessel *Dispenser*.
Bulldog	Campbell Johnston	Sept. 1872	Sold to R. Gillham for £900 16 July 1906.
Bustard (ii)	Napier	Jan. 1871	Sold to Ward, Milford Haven, March 1923.
Comet	Portsmouth	Dec. 1870	Sold in Holland to J. Pas for £900 12 May 1908.
Cuckoo	Laird	Aug. 1873	Renamed *Vivid* 19 Feb. 1912; *Vivid II* Jan. 1920; became *YC.37* in 1923 and sold to Hocking, Plymouth, 1959.
Fidget (ii)	Chatham	March 1872	Sold 1905 (possibly became Yard Craft *C.21*).
Hyaena (ii)	Laird	Aug. 1873	Sold to Merveille, Dunkirk, for £850 3 April 1906.
Kite	Napier	Feb. 1871	Sold to Hughes Bolckow partly dismantled (for conversion to a dredger) 18 May 1920.
Mastiff (ii)	Armstrong	April 1871	Renamed *Snapper* 1914; sold to Thames Shipbreakers Ltd 28 Nov. 1931.
Pickle (ii)	Campbell Johnston	Nov. 1872	Sold 1906 (may have become a dockyard lighter).
Pike	Campbell Johnston	Oct. 1872	Became boom defence vessel at Southampton from 1908; sold to G. Sharpe 27 March 1920.
Scourge	Chatham	March 1871	Converted to tank vessel *C.yg* 1903.
Snake (ii)	Chatham	March 1871	Became cable lighter *YC.15* 23 Sept.1907.
Snap (ii)	Campbell Johnston	Dec. 1871	Sold to Deaker, Hull, for £900 at Chatham 11 May 1909.
Weazel (ii)	Laird	Sept. 1873	Became oil lighter *C.118* 1904.

Arrow as completed, 1872. *(Conway Maritime Press, drawing by John Roberts)*

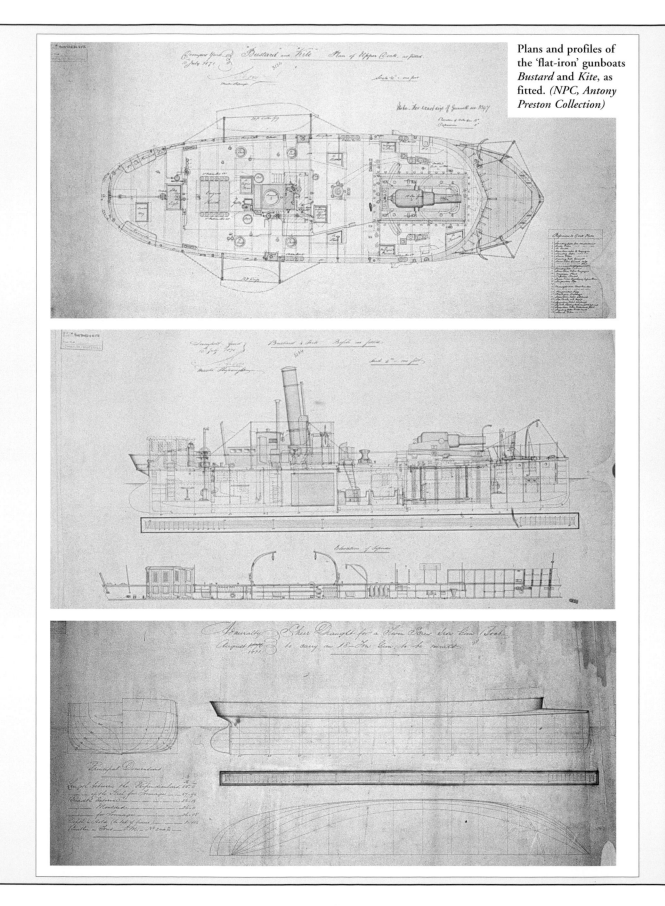

Plans and profiles of the 'flat-iron' gunboats *Bustard* and *Kite,* as fitted. *(NPC, Antony Preston Collection)*

Displacement: 254 tons
Dimensions: 85 ft x 26 ft 1½ in. x 6 ft-6 ft 6 in.
Guns: Originally 1 10-in. 18-ton M.L.R., but various pieces were mounted in vessels which served as tenders
Machinery: 2 sets of 2-cylinder reciprocating engines, 28 h.p. (nom.), 260 h.p. (ind.) = 8½ knots
Complement: 30 officers and ratings

'Flat-iron' gunboats *Pike* (left) and *Gadfly*. *(Private collection)*

Gadfly Class

NAME	BUILT	LAUNCHED	FATE
Gadfly (ii)	Pembroke	May 1879	Became coal lighter at Simon's Bay 18 May 1900; later renamed *YC.230;* sold 1918.
Griper (ii)	Pembroke	Sept. 1879	Became steam lighter *YC.373* c. 1905; renamed *Flora* 19 June 1923; became *Afrikander* in 1933.[1]
Pincher (ii)	Pembroke	May 1879	Sold 11 July 1905.
Tickler (ii)	Pembroke	Sept. 1879	Converted to steam lighter at Simon's Bay 1902; renamed *Afrikander* 26 Feb. 1919; became *Afrikander II* 1933 and broken up 1937.

Notes: Repeat editions of the *Ant* type, with identical particulars. Originally ordered at the same time as the *Ant* class, but the orders were suspended by an Admiralty order dated 23 July 1872, and all four were not laid down until 29 April 1878.

[1] A former flat-iron gunboat is said to have been broken up at Simon's Town in 1951, and if correct it would probably have been *Griper*.

Kite in 1911, serving as a gunnery tender. *(NPC)*

Bouncer Class

NAME	BUILT	LAUNCHED	FATE
Bouncer (ii)	Pembroke	March 1881	Ordered to be converted to a tank vessel Oct. 1904, but sold at Sheerness for £740 4 April 1905.
Insolent (ii)	Pembroke	1881	Foundered in Portsmouth Harbour 1 July 1922; wreck sold to J. H. Pounds 18 June 1925.

Displacement: 265 tons
Dimensions: 87 ft 4 in. x 26 ft 1½ in. x 6 ft-6 ft 6 in.
Guns: 1 10-in. M.L.R.
Machinery: Similar to *Ant* class, 268 h.p. (ind.) = 8½ knots
Complement: 30 officers and ratings

Notes: Similar to *Ant* and *Gadfly* classes, but built with slightly greater length; steel was used in place of iron for the first time.

Insolent pictured off Southsea, fitted with the Battenberg Signalling Device. This was an invention of Captains Prince Louis of Battenberg and Percy Scott of the Ordnance Committee, and consisted of a collapsible canvas sphere fitted with ribs, rather in the manner of an umbrella, and made to open and close by way of collars attached to rods passing through the interior of the mast. It had the advantage of being operated by personnel stationed safely below decks. Trials aboard *Insolent* in the autumn of 1894 were deemed successful, signals being read at a distance of 18 miles. *(Conway Maritime Press)*

Medina Class gunboats (iron)

NAME	BUILT	LAUNCHED	FATE
Dee	Palmer	April 1877	Used for torpedo instruction at Malta 1892-1902; sold for £620 10 July 1902.
Don	Palmer	April 1877	Reduced to harbour service at Malta (used as concrete barge 1906-8); converted to lighter 1911, and sold in 1914.
Esk	Palmer	April 1877	Sold at Hong Kong April 1903.
Medina	Palmer	Aug. 1876	Sold with *Medway* at Bermuda for £570 1904.
Sabrina	Palmer	April 1877	Renamed *Sabine* 1916; *Vivid* late 1919; sold to B. Fryer July 1922.
Slaney (ii)	Palmer	April 1877	Sold to Ward, Grays, 30 Aug. 1919.
Spey (ii)	Palmer	Oct. 1876	Deleted about 1915; sold 1923.
Tay	Palmer	Oct. 1876	Sold to Stanlee S.B. Co. 22 Oct. 1920.
Tees	Palmer	Oct. 1876	Sold to Harris Bros of Bristol for £1,750 9 July 1907.
Trent	Palmer	Aug. 1877	Renamed *Pembroke* Sept. 1905; *Gannet* June 1917. sold to Dover Shipbreaking Co. 21 Feb. 1923.
Tweed	Palmer	Aug. 1877	Sold at Hong Kong for £987 1 Nov. 1905.

Medina as completed, 1877.
(Conway Maritime Press, drawing by John Roberts)

Displacement: 386 tons (designed); later given as 363 tons
Dimensions: 110 ft x 34 ft x 5 ft 7 in. - 5 ft 9 in.
Guns: 3 64-pdrs M.L.R.
Machinery: 2 sets of 2-cylinder reciprocating engines, 310 h.p. (ind.) = 9½ knots (designed)
Complement: 51 officers and ratings

Notes: Totally unlike any other British gunboat, before or since. While the *Ant* type were clearly intended for local service, the addition of masts and yards to the *Medina*'s design shows that the Admiralty expected her to serve further afield. With one of her guns firing forward on a fixed bearing she showed the influence of the *Ant*'s design, but *Medina* was given a bow rudder to improve her handling.

The *Medina* class were suited for river work, and so several found their way out to China. *Dee* and *Medina* were sent out to Egypt in 1882 for possible use in the Suez Canal, but achieved nothing. To give greater stability they were designed with a marked 'tumble-home', i.e. their sides sloped inwards above the waterline, giving the hull a bulged appearance. This in conjunction with a vestigial poop and forecastle and three-masted rig made them the most grotesque craft ever seen.

Dee, pictured sometime after 1887. *(Private collection)*

Medina. (Private collection)

Fantome Class sloops (composite)

NAME	BUILT	LAUNCHED	FATE
Albatross	Chatham	Aug. 1873	Broken up at Chatham Feb. 1889.
Flying Fish (ii)	Chatham	Nov. 1873	Sold Dec. 1888 (converted to survey ship 1878).
Fantome	Pembroke	March 1873	Sold 1889.
Egeria	Pembroke	Nov. 1873	Converted to survey ship in 1886; sold at Esquimalt to Vancouver Branch of Navy League Oct. 1911.
Sappho	Wigram	Nov. 1873	Sold to Castle Dec. 1887.
Daring	Wigram	Feb. 1874	Sold to Cohen Aug. 1889.

Displacement: 894 tons designed (949 tons actual), 727 tons b.o.m.
Dimensions: 160 ft x 31 ft 4 in. x 12 ft 6 in. – 14 ft
Guns: 2 7-in. M.L.R., 2 64-pdrs M.L.R.
Machinery: Single-screw compound reciprocating, 120 h.p. (nom.), 836-1,011 h.p. (ind.) = 10½-11½ knots
Complement: 125 officers and ratings

Notes: Although the sloop had once been a warship type of considerable importance, its status declined after the introduction of steam power. For a while during the period of transition the sloop held its own as the equivalent of the modern cruiser. By the 1870s, however, the sloop was clearly reduced to junior rank, intended only for detached cruising and police duties. In short she was now the senior member of the Gunboat Navy: although equal to the gunvessel by virtue of the rank of her captain, the sloop's more weatherly qualities and heavy armament were better suited to deep-water cruising. Sloops, being fewer in number than gunboats and gunvessels, were used to reinforce the lesser vessels, but in general their size was against them in coastal or estuarial waters.

The *Fantome* class were the largest warships in the Navy to retain the pivot system for all guns; larger sloops had a mixture of traversing and broadside guns. They were like gunvessels in having a partial main deck, although this feature was by no means common to all sloops. In 1875 a sloop was defined as a vessel of cruising type with fewer than 200 officers and ratings but more than 100. [1]

---

[1] Adm. G. A. Ballard, *Mariner's Mirror*, vol. 25 (1939). 220

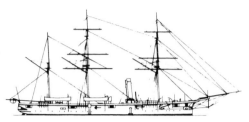

Daring as in 1876. *(Conway Maritime Press, drawing by John Roberts)*

Albatross. (Conway Maritime Press)

Arab Class gunvessels (composite)

NAME	BUILT	LAUNCHED	FATE
Arab	Napier	Oct. 1874	Sold in 1889.
Lily (ii)	Napier	Oct. 1874	Wrecked off Point Armour, 16 Sept. 1889; wreck sold Labrador, 1890-91.

Displacement: 620 tons
Dimensions: 150 ft x 28 ft 6 in. x 10 ft 6 in. – 12 ft 10 in.
Guns: 1 7-in. M.L.R., 2 64-pdrs M.L.R.
Machinery: Single-screw 2-cylinder compound reciprocating, 570 h.p. (ind.) = 10½ knots
Complement: 90 officers and ratings

Notes: Composite gunvessels intended as successors to the *Frolic* class, but with deeper draught. By simplifying the main armament the drawbacks of the *Beacon* and *Frolic* classes were avoided. *Arab* partially rearmed about 1879, when her after 64-pdr was replaced by three 20-pdr Armstrong guns.

Osprey Class sloops (composite)

1ST GROUP

NAME	BUILT	LAUNCHED	FATE
Penguin (ii)	Napier	March 1876	Completed conversion to survey ship Jan. 1890; reduced to harbour service 1909 and transferred to R.A.N. 18 March 1913; sold at Sydney 1924, and finally lost as a crane hulk 13 Dec. 1960.
Cormorant (iii)	Chatham	Sept. 1877	Reduced to harbour service at Gibraltar Nov. 1889; renamed *Rooke* July 1946; broken up at Malaga 1949.
Gannet	Sheerness	Aug. 1878	Renamed *President* May 1903; became *President II* 1909; lent to Mr C. B. Fry Oct. 1913 and renamed T.S. *Mercury* (still afloat).

NAME	BUILT	LAUNCHED	FATE
Kingfisher	Sheerness	Dec. 1879	Renamed *Lark* 10 Nov. 1892 when reduced to harbour service; renamed *Cruiser* 18 May 1893; sold 1919.
Osprey (ii)	Sheerness	Aug. 1876	Sold 29 April 1890.
Pelican	Devonport	April 1877	Sold to Hudson Bay Co. 22 Jan. 1901; hulk scuttled off Sydney (Nova Scotia) 1953.
Wild Swan	Napier	Jan. 1876	Renamed *Clyde* 1 May 1904 when reduced to harbour service; renamed *Columbine* 1912; sold 4 May 1920 to Forth Shipbreaking Co.

2ND GROUP

NAME	BUILT	LAUNCHED	FATE
Doterel (ii)	Chatham	March 1880	Sunk by internal explosion off Puntas Arenas (Straits of Magellan) 26 April 1881.
Dragon	Devonport	May 1878	Sold 24 Sept. 1892.
Espiègle	Devonport	Aug. 1880	Reduced to harbour service 1889; renamed *Argo* 1900; sold to W. Thorpe 25 Aug. 1921.
Miranda	Devonport	Sept. 1879	Sold 24 Sept. 1892.
Mutine	Devonport	July 1880	Reduced to harbour service 1899; renamed *Azov* 1900; sold to C. A. Beard 25 Aug. 1921.
Pegasus	Devonport	June 1878	Sold 1892.
Phoenix	Devonport	Sept. 1879	Wrecked on Prince Edward Island 12 Sept. 1882.

Displacement: 1,130 tons
Dimensions: 170 ft x 36 ft x 13-15 ft
Guns: 2 7-in. M.L.R., 4 64-pdrs
Machinery: Single-screw compound reciprocating, 900 h.p. (ind.) as designed, but developed 950-1,100 h.p. in service = 11½-12½ knots
Complement: 140 officers and ratings

Notes: Enlarged editions of the *Fantome* class designed for handiness and speed. Unfortunately the designers tried to achieve this with very full lines and mediocre machinery. Nevertheless they proved extremely handy in service. Group 1 were laid down 1874-76 and completed 1877-80, and had graceful knee-bows; Group 2 were laid down 1877-79 and completed 1879-81, and could be distinguished by their vertical stems.

Like all composite-built vessels these sloops were very durable as their teak skins (oak was no longer in use by this time) were impervious to rust and corrosion; furthermore their iron ribs and frames prevented the continual leakage of water which was characteristic of wooden hulls. Out of fourteen ships, seven survived for forty years or more, and two were afloat for over seventy years.

The class were all poor steamers, and in view of the contemporary advances in marine engineering this must

Dragon as in 1880. (Conway Maritime Press, drawing by John Roberts)

be taken as a bad reflection on the Admiralty's policy. *Wild Swan* and *Penguin* failed to reach their contract speed on trials, and were re-engined by Devonport Dockyard after their first commission.

To take advantage of the heavier broadsides possible with breech-loading ordnance the Admiralty rearmed as many vessels as possible after 1884. In some of the

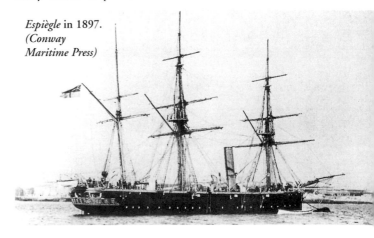

Espiègle in 1897. (Conway Maritime Press)

Gannet at Malta in 1891. (Chatham Historic Dockyard)

Penguin alongside as a stationary depot ship in Sydney, NSW, 12 April 1908. *(Royal Australian Navy)*

Dragon being broken up, location possibly Portsmouth. *(NPC)*

Osprey class the traversing 7-in. 4½-ton guns were replaced by broadside-firing 6-in. breech-loaders, while the four 64-pdrs were replaced by six 5-in. guns. Although the weight of a single broadside was reduced, the higher rate of fire doubled the weight of shells fired per minute. As in so many other classes the process of rearmament took much longer than expected, and never extended to the whole class. Many ships were not worth refitting as they were near the end of their useful lives, and soldiered on with their antiquated muzzle-loaders.

Like other composite sloops they were barque-rigged, a practice which continued until the very last class was built (the *Nymphe* class).

H.M.S. *Foxhound*, one of the *Forester* class and the only gunboat still afloat at the time the original edition of this book was published. This photograph was taken during her service in the Coastguard. *(Imperial War Museum)*

Forester Class gunboats (composite)

NAME	BUILT	LAUNCHED	FATE
Forester (ii)	Earle	Feb. 1877	Coal depot 1894; sold 1904 but believed to be in existence 1914.
Foxhound (ii)	Barrow	Jan. 1877	Removed from effective list 1895; sold after service as coal haul-about Aug. 1920 (see Notes).
Firefly	Thompson	June 1877	Hulked, and renamed *Egmont* 3 April 1914; reverted to *Firefly* 1 March 1923; sold May 1931.
Forward (ii)	Barrow	Jan. 1877	Sold 1903.
Firm (ii)	Earle	Feb. 1877	Sold to Cox, Falmouth, 14 May 1907.
Firebrand	Thompson	April 1877	Sold 1905 and became S.S. *Hoi Tin*; deleted from mercantile register 1911-1912 after transfer to Chinese registry.
Contest	Doxford	Aug. 1874	Broken up at Devonport 1889.
Cygnet (ii)	Doxford	May 1874	Broken up 1889.
Express	Doxford	July 1874	Sold Aug. 1889.
Mallard	Earle	Aug. 1875	Sold 1889.
Moorhen	Napier	Sept. 1875	Sold Nov. 1888.
Sheldrake (ii)	Napier	July 1875	Renamed *Drake* 13 Jan. 1888 when converted to drill ship for Artillery Volunteers; renamed *W.V.2g* in 1894; sold at Chatham 3 April 1906.

Displacement: 455 tons
Dimensions: 125 ft x 23 ft 6 in. x 8 ft 6 in.-10 ft 6 in.
Guns: 2 64-pdrs M.L.R., 2 20-pdrs B.L.
Machinery: Single-screw reciprocating (compound in all except *Moorhen* and *Sheldrake*), 387-515 h.p. (ind.) = 10 knots
Complement: 60 officers and ratings

Cygnet. (Conway Maritime Press, drawing by John Roberts)

Notes: Similar to *Ariels* in every respect. Most served on foreign stations and were only retired after the Naval Defence Act. Like the earlier class some received 5-in. breech-loaders in place of their 64-pdrs, and 4-in. in place of the 20-pdr Armstrongs, which resulted in their reclassification as 1st Class gunboats after 1889. Many spent their last years in the Coastguard or on Fishery Protection duties, and *Firefly* was called in to help keep order during the Hull dock strike of 1893. Average cost was £20,000 each.

The only member of this class to survive is *Foxhound*, which found a resting place on the Thames, where she can still be seen. After two commissions on the China Station lasting from 1877 to 1884 she paid off, and served the

H.M.S. *Foxhound* in service. (NPC)

remainder of her active career in the Coastguard. She was offered for sale from 1894 to 1896, but as the Admiralty received no offers for her she was converted to a coal haul-about for use in Portsmouth Dockyard. Finally, as *YC.20* she was sold in 1920 to a firm of London coal-merchants who have used her since then as a depot and floating workshop. Although scarcely recognisable as a gunboat she is a fascinating vessel, for many details of her construction can still be seen.

A corner of the forecastle, showing the hammock hooks in the deckhead beams, and the original scuttles. *(© National Maritime Museum, London)*

Arabel, ex-H.M.S. *Foxhound*, as she was in October 1975. *(GA Osbon)*

A close up showing the composite construction. *(© National Maritime Museum, London)*

The upper deck forward. While the cable arrangements and the bitt in the foreground are probably original, the hatchway and other fittings are more recent. (© *National Maritime Museum, London*)

The upper deck, showing the hatches and derrick post from her coal haul-about days. The retention of the bulwarks fore and aft allowed filled bags of coal to be stacked ready for hoisting. (© *National Maritime Museum, London*)

Condor Class gunvessels (composite)

NAME	BUILT	LAUNCHED	FATE
Condor	Devonport	Dec. 1876	Sold Aug. 1889 and broken up by Cohen.
Falcon	Laird	Jan. 1877	Reduced to harbour service 1890; sold to E. W. Payne 25 June 1920.
Griffon (ii)	Laird	Dec. 1876	Sold to Board of Trade 28 Sept. 1891 as hulk and renamed *Richmond*.
Flamingo	Devonport	Dec. 1876	Reduced to harbour service in 1892; lent 1909 to Plymouth Port Sanitary Authority to whom she was sold 25 May 1923; broken up 1930.

Displacement: 774 tons designed, 780 tons actual
Dimensions: 157 ft x 29 ft 6 in. x 13 ft
Guns: 1 7-in. 4½-ton M.L.R., 2 64-pdrs M.L.R.
Machinery: Single-screw compound reciprocating, 750 h.p. (ind.) as designed, 721-95 h.p. actual = 11½ knots
Complement: 100 officers and ratings

Griffon at Malta. *(NPC)*

Notes: Like the *Ariel* class and later gunboats these composite gunvessels reflected the swing away from the 'coastal' theory in the 1870s, in that they had deeper draught and were more suited to ocean work than earlier gunvessels. The armament was intended to be equal to that of the rearmed *Plovers*. Unfortunately they reverted to single-screw machinery as twin-screw propulsion was still not recognised as being more efficient; however, to a certain extent this was offset by the introduction of compound pressures.

Griffon and *Flamingo* were rearmed in 1884-87 with two 5-in. Vavasseur B.L. in place of their single 7-in. guns, but retained the antiquated 64-pdrs. In place of the more usual hoisting propellers *Falcon* and *Griffon* had feathering screws.

This class resembled sloops in their rig, since they had a barque-rig in place of the traditional gunvessel-rig. The distinguishing feature of barque-rig was the mizzen, which had only a pole topmast. In succeeding classes this arrangement was continued, while older gunvessels were often reduced to barquentine-rig; this involved the loss of the yards on the main, and resembled gunboat-rig.

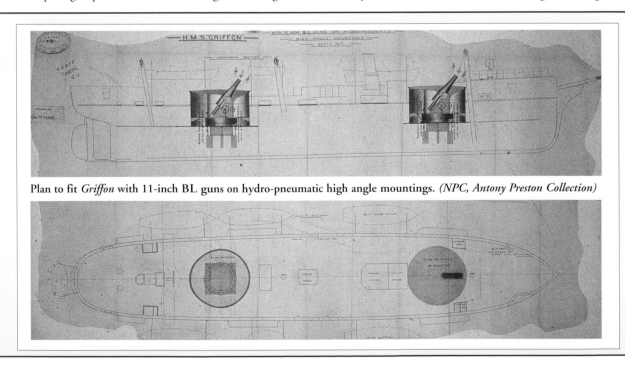

Plan to fit *Griffon* with 11-inch BL guns on hydro-pneumatic high angle mountings. *(NPC, Antony Preston Collection)*

Linnet Class gunvessels (composite)

NAME	BUILT	LAUNCHED	FATE
Linnet (ii)	Thames S.B. Co.	Jan. 1880	Sold 27 April 1904 but retained her name.
Swift	Thames S.B. Co.	Nov. 1879	Sold by Admiralty order dated 4 Feb. 1902 and retained her name for a while; listed in 1908-9 mercantile register as *Hoi Ching*.

Displacement: 756 tons designed, 788 tons actual
Dimensions: 165 ft x 29 ft x 10 ft 3-10 in.
Guns: (designed) 1 7-in. 4½-ton M.L.R., 1 64-pdr M.L.R., 2 20-pdrs B.L.; (actual) 2 7-in. 4½-ton M.L.R., 3 20-pdrs B.L.
Machinery: Single-screw reciprocating, 870 h.p. (ind.) = 11.8 knots
Complement: 92 officers and ratings

Linnet as completed, 1880. *(Conway Maritime Press, drawing by John Roberts)*

Notes: Slightly enlarged *Condors* with a somewhat heavier armament and higher speed. Laid down in 1878 and completed late in 1880.

Algerine Class gunvessels (composite)

NAME	BUILT	LAUNCHED	FATE
Algerine (ii)	Harland & Wolff	Nov. 1880	Sold 10 May 1892.
Rambler (ii)	Elder	Jan. 1880	Completed as a surveying vessel 1884; sold 23 Jan. 1907.
Ranger (ii)	Elder	Feb. 1880	Sold 24 Sept. 1892 as salvage vessel; broken up at Liverpool 1954.

Displacement: 835 tons
Dimensions: 157 ft x 29 ft 6 in. x 13 ft 6 in.
Guns: 1 7-in. M.L.R., 2 64-pdrs M.L.R.; (later) 2 5-in. B.L., 2 64-pdrs M.L.R.
Machinery: Single-screw reciprocating, 810 h.p. (ind.) = 10½ knots
Complement: 100 officers and ratings

Algerine as completed, 1883. *(Conway Maritime Press, drawing by John Roberts)*

Notes: Repetitions of the *Condor* class, but drew slightly more water as they were fitted with poops. These were the last composite gunvessels built, and the last to carry yards on the mainmast. In common with the earlier class those rearmed with 5-in. Vavasseur breech-loaders were reclassed as 1st Class gunvessels after the Naval Defence Act.

Rambler. (Private collection)

Banterer Class gunboats (composite)

NAME	BUILT	LAUNCHED	FATE
Banterer (ii)	Barrow	Nov. 1880	Sold to Harris Bros, Bristol, 14 May 1907.
Cockchafer (ii)	Pembroke	Feb. 1881	Sold 6 Dec. 1905.
Espoir (ii)	Barrow	Nov. 1880	Deleted 1904.
Bullfrog (ii)	Pembroke	Feb. 1881	Renamed *Egmont* March 1923; *St Angelo* 1 July 1933.
Grappler (ii)	Barrow	Oct. 1880	Sold to King Garston 14 May 1907.
Raven (ii)	Samuda	May 1882	Tender to Diving School from 1904 until sold 13 March 1925.
Redwing (ii) (ex-*Espoir*)	Pembroke	May 1880	Sold at Chatham 4 April 1905.
Starling (ii)	Samuda	April 1882	Sold at Chatham 4 April 1905; became *Stella Marts;* lost March 1925.
Stork (ii)	Samuda	May 1882	Completed as surveying vessel; became Navy League training ship at Hammersmith 28 March 1913; sold to Shaws of Kent 1950 (see Notes).
Wrangler (ii)	Barrow	Oct. 1880	Sold to J. H. Lee 2 Dec. 1919.
Wasp	Barrow	Oct. 1880	Wrecked off Tory Island (Donegal) 22 Sept. 1884; wreck sold Nov. 1910.

Displacement: 465 tons
Dimensions: 125 ft x 23 ft 6 in. x 10 ft (mean)
Guns: 2 64-pdrs M.L.R., 2 20-pdrs B.L.
Machinery: Single-screw reciprocating, 440 h.p. = 9½ knots
Complement: 60 officers and ratings

Notes: Improved *Ariels* built 1879-82, but could be distinguished from them by their vertical stems. *Redwing* was completed for service as a Coastguard cruiser (after being renamed in June 1879), and differed from her sisters by having a knee-bow, which made her look like the older *Ariels* and *Foresters*. Some were rearmed with 5-in. and 4-in. breech-loaders and became 1st Class Gunboats after 1889. The rest were soon placed on the non-effective list or transferred to the Coastguard. *Stork* can still be seen at Lower Rainham, where her hull forms part of a jetty.

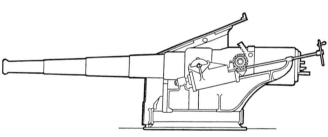

A 6-inch breech-loader of the 1880s, typical of the Vavasseur mountings which replaced broadside pivot guns in the Fleet.

Cockchafer at Plymouth. *(Conway Maritime Press)*

Albacore Class gunboats (composite)

NAME	BUILT	LAUNCHED	FATE
Albacore (ii)	Laird	Jan. 1883	Sold 18 May 1906.
Mistletoe (ii)	Laird	Feb. 1883	Sold to Shipbreaking Co. 14 May 1907.
Watchful (ii)	Laird	Feb. 1883	Sold to Harris, Bristol, 14 May 1907.

Displacement: 560 tons
Dimensions: 135 ft x 26 ft x 7 ft-10 ft 3 in.
Guns: 2 5-in. B.L., 2 4-in. B.L.
Machinery: Single-screw reciprocating, 650 h.p. (ind.) = 10.7 knots
Complement: 60 officers and ratings

Notes: Built 1881-83 and were the first gunboats to reflect the Royal Navy's swing back to breech-loading guns. They were also the last composite gunboats to mount their guns on centre-line pivot mountings, the system which had been common to all classes since 1854.

Albacore at the Diamond Jubilee Review, 26 June 1897. Prominent amongst the vessels in the background is the armoured cruiser H.M.S. *Warspite*. *(Private collection)*

Watchful. (Conway Maritime Press)

Albacore. (Craig Leaske)

Mariner Class sloops (composite)

NAME	BUILT	LAUNCHED	FATE
Acorn	Milford Haven	Sept. 1884	Sold to Harris, Bristol, 15 Dec. 1899 and broken up at Milford Haven 1904.
Icarus	Devonport	July 1885	Sold 1903.
Mariner	Devonport	June 1884	Reduced to harbour service 1903; became salvage ship 1917; sold to Hughes Bolckow 19 Feb. 1929.
Melita	Malta	March 1888	Harbour service 1905; renamed *Ringdove* (salvage ship) 1917; sold to Falmouth Docks Board 9 July 1920.
Reindeer	Devonport	Nov. 1883	Harbour service 1903; salvage ship 1917; sold to Halifax Shipyard Ltd 12 July 1924.
Racer	Devonport	Aug. 1884	Training ship 1896; salvage ship 1917; sold to Hughes Bolckow 6 Nov. 1928.

Displacement: 970 tons
Dimensions: 167 ft x 32 ft x 14 ft
Guns: 8 5-in. B.L., 8 machine-guns
Machinery: Single-screw, 920 h.p. (ind.) = 11½ knots (with forced draught, 1,380 h.p. = 12.2 knots)
Complement: 126 officers and ratings

Melita as completed, 1889. *(Conway Maritime Press, drawing by John Roberts)*

Melita at Malta, where she was built. *(Conway Maritime Press)*

Notes: Rated originally as gunvessels but rerated as sloops 26 November 1884. Similar in size to *Fantome* class, but adopted a breech-loading armament. The four vessels converted to salvage vessels served for a considerable time after disappearance from the Navy List (e.g. *Reindeer* was still working in Canadian waters in 1930). Laid down 1882-83 and completed 1884-85 (excepting *Icarus*, *Acorn* and *Melita* which took three, four and six years to build respectively). *Melita* was ordered from Malta to provide employment and experience for the dockyard staff, and as a result cost over £10,000 more than the average of £50,000 for the rest of the class. The experiment was not repeated.

Racer. (Craig Leaske)

Dolphin Class sloops (composite)

NAME	BUILT	LAUNCHED	FATE
Dolphin	Dixon & Co.	Dec. 1882	Boilers and engines removed 1899 for service as boys' training ship at Portland; accommodation hulk at Gosport 1907; Flagship, R.-Adm. commanding submarines 1912; sold 13 March 1925 (see Notes).
Wanderer (ii)	Dixon & Co.	Feb. 1883	Reduced to harbour service 1894 and converted to sail training ship (engines and boilers removed); sold Feb. 1907.

Displacement: 925 tons
Dimensions: 157 ft x 32 ft x 12 ft 4 in.-14 ft 2 in.
Guns: 2 6-in. B.L., 2 5-in. B.L.
Machinery: Single-screw triple-expansion, 750 h.p. = 11¼ knots.
Complement: 115 officers and ratings

Dolphin as in 1884. *(Conway Maritime Press, drawing by John Roberts)*

Notes: Both these vessels had active careers, *Dolphin* in particular distinguishing herself in the defence of Suakin on three ocasions. Both vessels were selected for conversion to sail training ships, but when *Wanderer* was sold in 1907 *Dolphin* survived. At Gosport she housed submarine crews, and ultimately gave her name to the submarine base. Her subsequent career is not without interest, as she is still afloat. She was bought by a Glasgow shipowner for conversion to a youth centre at Leith, but foundered on 19 April 1925 while under tow in the Firth of Forth. The towing party beached her in Fisherrow Bay, where she lay for eight months; she was finally patched up and docked at Leith. Since then she has been owned by the Dolphin Training Ship Society, and is currently leased to Leith Nautical College as accommodation and classrooms for boys under training. She retains her name and much of her original appearance, so far as her hull is concerned.

Wanderer in 1901, after conversion to sail training ship. *(Craig Leaske)*

Dolphin moored at Fort Blockhouse, Gosport, as accommodation for submarine crews, in around 1908. She later became depot ship for the 2nd Submarine Flotilla, while the base which took her name survived until 1999. *(Royal Navy Submarine Museum)*

Dolphin as training ship at Leith Nautical College. Popular with students, she was still afloat when the original edition of this book was published; however the decline in Britain's merchant fleet hit the college hard, and she was towed away for scrapping at Bo'ness in July 1977. *(Heriot-Watt University)*

Curlew Class gunvessels (steel)

NAME	BUILT	LAUNCHED	FATE
Curlew (ii)	Devonport	Oct. 1885	Sold 10 July 1906.
Landrail (ii)	Devonport	Jan. 1886	Sank in tow in Lyme Bay after use as a target 4 Oct. 1906.

Displacement: 790 tons (later increased to 950 tons)
Dimensions: 195 ft x 28 ft x 10 ft 6 in.
Guns: 1 6-in. B.L., 3 5-in. B.L., 7 machine-guns
Machinery: Twin-screw reciprocating, 850 h.p. (ind.) = 14½ knots
Torpedoes: 1 bow tube, 2 launching carriages
Complement: 46 officers and ratings

Notes: Strictly speaking these vessels have little claim to be included in a list of gunvessels. In many ways they were miniature cruisers rather than the final developments of the gunvessel, and were presumably only classed as such because they were inferior to the latest sloops in gunpower. Differed from all preceding gunvessels in being built of steel, being armed with torpedoes, and lacking masts and yards. In place of the traditional gunvessel rig they had only two light masts. Although representing quite a radical departure when first conceived they were made obsolete by the Naval Defence Act construction.

Landrail's varied career included service in the Mediterranean and off West Africa; fishery protection duties (during which she ran aground); and collision with, and sinking of, the barque *Siren* off Portland. (*Conway Maritime Press*)

Bramble Class gunboats (composite)

NAME	BUILT	LAUNCHED	FATE
Bramble (ii)	Harland & Wolff	Dec. 1886	Renamed *Cockatrice* June 1896, and sold 3 April 1906.
Lizard	Harland & Wolff	Nov. 1886	Sold at Sydney for breaking up 1905.
Rattler	Elswick	Aug. 1886	Reduced to harbour service 1910; renamed *Dryad* 1919; sold 1924.
Wasp (ii)	Elswick	Sept. 1886	Lost without trace after leaving Singapore, but believed to have foundered in Sept. 1887.

Displacement: 715 tons (670 tons designed), 810 tons full load
Dimensions: 165 ft x 29 ft x 11 ft
Guns: 6 4-in. Q.F.
Machinery: Single-screw triple-expansion, 1,000 h.p. (ind.) = 13 knots (designed)
Complement: 76 officers and ratings

Notes: With the laying down of these four vessels in 1885 the composite gunboat entered on its last stage of development. In every respect they were better than preceding classes, and they served as models for another fourteen years. Retained the traditional three-masted rig, but the layout of armament was revised. Since a greater number of the new light 4-inch guns could be carried the old centre-line arrangement gave way to broadside mountings, one on either side of the forecastle, a pair amidships and another pair aft. Rated as 1st Class gunboats.

Rattler (centre) reduced to harbour service at Portsmouth, in the years immediately prior to the First World War. She is lying alongside the battleship *Renown* (1895), by now a harbour training ship for stokers. To port is the torpedo school *Vernon*, consisting of the hulks of the wooden ships of the line *Donegal* (1858) and *Marlborough* (1855) and the ironclad *Warrior* (1860). A few years prior to this photograph *Rattler* had been lent to Clyde RNVR when she became the first ship to be fully RNVR officered and manned. Her varied harbour service at Portsmouth included, like *Renown,* as a training ship for stokers; then a repair ship for trawlers; and finally as a navigation school ship attached to H.M.S. *Dryad. (Conway Maritime Press)*

Nymphe Class sloops (composite)

NAME	BUILT	LAUNCHED	FATE
Nymphe	Portsmouth	1 May 1888	Reduced to harbour service 31 Dec. 1906 and renamed *Wildfire*; became *Gannet* 1916; *Pembroke* 1917; sold 10 Feb. 1920.
Daphne	Sheerness	May 1888	Sold to McCausland & Sons Feb. 1904.
Swallow (ii)	Sheerness	Oct. 1885	Sold to McCausland & Sons 1904.
Buzzard	Sheerness	May 1887	Reduced to harbour service 1909 and renamed *President*; loaned to Marine Society 1918-21 and sold Sept. 1921.

Daphne as completed, in 1889. *(Conway Maritime Press, drawing by John Roberts)*

Displacement: 1,140 tons
Dimensions: 195 ft x 28 ft x 11 ft 6 in.-12 ft 7 in.
Guns: 8 5-in. B.L., 8 machine-guns; some rearmed with 6 or 8 4.7-in. Q.F.
Machinery: Twin-screw triple-expansion, 1,400 h.p. (ind.) = 11-13 knots
Complement: 135 officers and ratings

Swallow as completed, in 1886. *(Conway Maritime Press, drawing by John Roberts)*

Buzzard at Sheerness. *(NPC)*

Notes: The last composite sloops built, and the only ones to adopt twin-screw propulsion. Their rig was similar to the *Condors* and *Algerines*. *Daphne* and *Swallow* were victims of the Fisher Axe in 1904, but *Nymphe* and *Buzzard* survived World War I in subsidiary roles. *Nymphe* became the gunnery tender *Wildfire* at Sheerness and was pressed into service with Rear-Admiral Hood's squadron off the Belgian coast; with a motley collection of old iron gunboats and tenders she bombarded the German right flank in the early months of 1915 and earned a Battle Honour.

Pigmy Class gunboats (composite)

NAME	BUILT	LAUNCHED	FATE
Pheasant (ii)	Devonport	April 1888	Sold to Cox of Falmouth 15 May 1906.
Partridge (ii)	Devonport	May 1888	Sold at Simon's Town to Ward Preston (prepared for sale March 1912).
Peacock (ii)	Pembroke	June 1888	Sold to Ellis of Chepstow 15 May 1906.
Pigmy	Sheerness	July 1888	Sold to Cox of Falmouth 15 May 1905.
Plover (iv)	Pembroke	Oct. 1888	Reduced to harbour service in 1904; sold at Gibraltar 27 April 1927.
Pigeon (ii)	Pembroke	Sept. 1888	Sold to Greek, London, 15 May 1906 as salvage ship (in mercantile register until 1908-9).

Displacement: 755 tons
Dimensions: 165 ft x 30 ft x 11 ft 3 in.
Guns: 6 4-in. Q.F.
Machinery: Single-screw triple-expansion, 1,200 h.p. = 13.2 knots
Complement: 76 officers and ratings

Notes: Built between 1887 and 1889 at an average cost of £37,000 each. All built in Royal Dockyards.

*Plover.
(Craig Leaske)*

*Pigmy.
(Conway
Maritime
Press)*

H.M.S. *Pigmy*, name ship
of her class of composite
gunboats. *(Craig Leaske)*

Beagle Class sloops (steel)

NAME	BUILT	LAUNCHED	FATE
Beagle (ii)	Portsmouth	Feb. 1889	Sold 11 July 1905.
Basilisk	Sheerness	April 1889	Sold as *Maggie Grace* 1905.

Displacement: 1,170 tons
Dimensions: 195 ft x 30 ft x 10 ft 8 in.-13 ft 4 in.
Guns: 8 5-in. B.L., 8 machine-guns
Machinery: Twin-screw triple-expansion,
               1,400-2,000 h.p. (ind.) = 13-14 knots (designed)
Complement: 135 officers and ratings

Basilisk in 1900. *(Conway Maritime
Press, drawing by John Roberts)*

Notes: Steel versions of the *Nymphe* class, the last of the line of development initiated by the *Fantome* class. At this stage of its development the sloop foreshadowed the light cruiser, having a heavy gun armament and a fair turn of speed by the standards of the day. Unfortunately the new cruiser construction of the Naval Defence Act made it ludicrous to build scouting vessels with speeds under 18-20 knots, and so the sloop suffered a further decline in importance.

Redbreast Class gunboats (composite)

NAME	BUILT	LAUNCHED	FATE
Magpie (iii)	Pembroke	March 1889	Reduced to harbour service 1902, but re-rated as g.b. 1915; converted to depot ship Oct. 1915; sold to Duguid & Stewart 1921.
Lapwing (iii)	Devonport	April 1889	Sold at Bombay 10 Nov. 1910.
Redbreast (ii)	Pembroke	April 1889	Sold 1910.
Ringdove (iii)	Devonport	April 1889	Renamed *Melita* on conversion to salvage ship 1917; sold to Ship Salvage Corp. 22 Jan. 1920.
Goldfinch (ii)	Sheerness	May 1889	Converted to survey ship 1902; sold to shipbreaking co. 14 May 1907.
Redpole	Pembroke	June 1889	Sold to Cox, Falmouth, 15 May 1906.
Thrush (ii)	Scott	June 1889	Coastguard 1906; cable ship 1915; salvage ship 1916; wrecked off Northern Ireland 11 April 1917.
Widgeon	Pembroke	Aug. 1889	Sold to Castle 15 May 1906.
Sparrow (ii)	Scott	Sept. 1889	Renamed *Amokura* 25 Oct. 1906 and became N.Z. Govt. training ship; sold as coal hulk 1922 and broken up 1955.

A view of a model of the composite gunboat *Thrush*, one of the last of her kind. *(© National Maritime Museum, London)*

Displacement: 805 tons
Dimensions: 165 ft x 31 ft x 11 ft-13 ft 9 in.
Guns: 6 4-in. Q.F., 2 3-pdrs
Machinery: Single-screw triple-expansion, 1,200 h.p. = 13 knots (max.)
Complement: 76 officers and ratings

Notes: The last composite gunboats to be built, and just escaped the Naval Defence Act. All actively employed until the Fisher Axe, but *Lapwing*, *Redbreast* and *Ringdove* lasted some time longer; *Ringdove* became a mine-laying tender attached to H.M.S. *Vernon*, and as such was still on the Navy List in 1914.

Ringdove at Devonport. Initially she served mainly in Australian waters, then in fishery protection duties off Scotland, before ending up as a salvage ship at Falmouth. *(Conway Maritime Press)*

Lapwing. Apart from refits, she spent her entire career in the East Indies. *(Craig Leaske)*

Alert Class sloops (steel)

NAME	BUILT	LAUNCHED	FATE
Alert	Sheerness	Dec. 1894	Lent to Basra civil authorities 1906; sold Basra 12 Jan. 1926 (see Notes).
Torch (ii)	Sheerness	Dec. 1894	Transferred to N.Z. Govt. 1917 and renamed *Firebrand;* sold July 1920.

Displacement: 960 tons
Dimensions: 180 ft x 32 ft 6 in. x 10-13 ft
Guns: 6 4-in. Q.F., 4 3-pdrs
Machinery: Single-screw vertical triple-expansion,
1,400 h.p. = 13¼ knots (max.)
Complement: Approximately 106 officers and ratings

Torch as completed, in 1895. *(Conway Maritime Press, drawing by John Roberts)*

Notes: When the sloop reappeared in 1893 she was little more than an enlarged steel edition of the composite gunboat. The armament was the same, and was even arranged exactly as before. The designers included every traditional feature imaginable, even a figurehead. Cost £60,000 each, and took just under two years to build.

With their yacht-bows, tall slim funnels and three-masted rig, these sloops were extremely graceful, but proved to be unstable under canvas. As a result they were soon reduced from sloop-rig to barquentine-rig by the removal of yards from their main masts. *Alert*, although no longer a commissioned warship by 1914, formed part of the naval force at Shatt-el-Arab during the Mesopotamian campaign in 1915. She was sold in 1926 to the Basra port authorities as a pilot vessel for use in the Inner Bar Reach, where she remained until broken up in October 1949.

Phoenix Class sloops (steel)

NAME	BUILT	LAUNCHED	FATE
Phoenix (ii)	Devonport	April 1895	Capsized in dock at Hong Kong during typhoon 18 Sept. 1906; sold 7 Jan. 1907.
Algerine (iii)	Devonport	June 1895	Sold to British Columbia Salvage Co. as salvage vessel 11 April 1919, lost Jan. 1924.

Displacement: 1,050 tons
Dimensions: 185 ft x 32 ft 6 in. x 11 ft 3 in.
Guns: 6 4-in. Q.F., 4 3-pdrs
Machinery: Twin-screw vertical triple-expansion, 1,400 h.p. = 13 knots
Complement: 106 officers and ratings
Notes: Twin-screw versions of the *Alert* class, laid down a year later. Differed only in detail and cost nearly £64,000.

Thistle later in her career – note the topmasts and aerials for wireless. *(Craig Leaske)*

Bramble Class gunboats (steel)

NAME	BUILT	LAUNCHED	FATE
Dwarf (iii)	London & Glasgow Co.	Nov. 1898	Sold to Ward, Pembroke, 13 July 1926.
Bramble (iii)	Potter, Liverpool	Nov. 1898	Sold at Bombay 26 Jan. 1920.
Britomart (ii)	Potter, Liverpool	March 1899	Sold at Bombay for use as passenger vessel 10 June 1920.
Thistle (iii)	London & Glasgow Co.	June 1899	Sold with *Dwarf* 1926.

Displacement: 710 tons
Dimensions: 180 ft x 33 ft x 8 ft
Guns: 2 4-in. Q.F., 4 12-pdrs
Machinery: Twin-screw triple-expansion, 1,300 h.p. = 13 knots (max.)
Complement: 85 officers and ratings

Thistle as completed, in 1900. *(Conway Maritime Press, drawing by John Roberts)*

Notes: The last of the breed, these four little vessels saw out the Gunboat Era, did sterling service in World War I, and served in their traditional role after the Armistice. They were specially designed to undertake duties beyond the capabilities of larger ships, and although their equipment was crude, they were well enough equipped for their tasks. They were the only gunboats, apart from the later China river gunboats, to be built of steel, and they were sheathed and coppered to prevent fouling in tropical waters.

In appearance quite unlike their composite and wooden predecessors, having two light masts without yards. There was no attempt to preserve traditional lines, and by the standards of the day they looked very modern. Nevertheless, they were among the last vessels in the Royal Navy to lack wireless, although this was fitted later in their careers.

The sloop *Phoenix* off the naval ordnance depot at Bull Point, Plymouth. In the distance, Brunel's Royal Albert Bridge. *(Craig Leaske)*

Condor Class sloops (steel)

NAME	BUILT	LAUNCHED	FATE
Condor (ii)	Sheerness	Dec. 1898	Foundered off Cape Flattery on her first commission 3 Dec. 1901.
Rosario	Sheerness	Dec. 1898	Converted to depot ship 1911; sold at Hong Kong n Nov. 1921.
Shearwater	Sheerness	Feb. 1900	Converted to depot ship for Canadian submarines *CC.1* and *CC.2* in 1915; sold to Western Shipping Co., Canada, May 1922.
Vestal	Sheerness	Feb. 1900	Sold 21 Oct. 1921 to W. Thomas, Anglesey.
Mutine (ii)	Laird	March 1900	Completed conversion to survey ship in 1907; reduced to harbour service in 1925; R.N.V.R. drill ship until sold 16 Aug. 1932.
Rinaldo	Laird	May 1900	Sold with *Vestal*.

Displacement: 980 tons
Dimensions: 180 ft x 33 ft x 11 ft 6 in. (*Condor* and *Rosario* 33 ft 3 in. beam)
Guns: 6 4-in. Q.F., 4 3-pdrs
Machinery: Twin-screw vertical triple-expansion, 1,400 h.p. = 13¼ knots (nom.)
Complement: 120 officers and ratings

Notes: Laid down in 1898 (first four) and 1899 (*Shearwater* and *Vestal*), and differed little from the *Phoenix* class. *Vestal* and *Mutine* survived to see considerable service in World War I.

Shearwater as completed, 1902. (*Conway Maritime Press*)

Shearwater as in 1905, with reduced rig. (*Conway Maritime Press, drawing by John Roberts*)

Cadmus Class sloops (steel)

NAME	BUILT	LAUNCHED	FATE
Espiègle (ii)	Sheerness	Dec. 1900	Sold at Bombay 17 Sept. 1923.
Fantome (ii)	Sheerness	March 1901	Converted to survey ship 1906; sold at Sydney Jan. 1925.
Merlin (ii)	Sheerness	Nov. 1901	Converted to survey ship 1906; sold at Hong Kong 3 Aug. 1923.
Odin	Sheerness	Nov. 1901	Sold at Bombay 12 Nov. 1920.
Clio	Sheerness	March 1903	Sold at Bombay with *Odin*.
Cadmus	Sheerness	April 1903	Sold at Hong Kong 1 Sept. 1921.

Displacement: 1,070 tons
Dimensions: 185 ft x 33 ft x 11 ft 3 in.
Guns: 6 4-in. Q.F., 4 3-pdrs
Machinery: Twin-screw vertical triple-expansion, 1,400 h.p. = 13 knots
Complement: 120 officers and ratings

Notes: The last true sloops built for the Royal Navy (the term was introduced again in 1915 for convoy escort vessels). Laid down in 1900 (first pair), 1901 (second pair), and 1902 (third pair). Took on average two years to build.

All survived World War I, and some even took up their traditional police duties East of Suez after the Armistice. *Fantome* is said to survive in a 'Ships' Graveyard' in Tasmania.

Fantome in 1913. (*Craig Leaske*)

Appendix A

Ships lost otherwise than in action 1854-89[1]

DATE	NAME	DESCRIPTION	COMMENT
23 May 1854	*Jasper*	Steam gunvessel[2]	Burnt in Channel.
1855	*Jasper*	Steam gunboat	Wrecked in the Sea of Azov. Lt J. S. Hudson admonished.
20 Feb. 1859	*Jaseur*	Steam gunvessel	Wrecked in Caribbean.
23 Dec. 1863	*Lively*	Steam gunboat	Wrecked off coast of Holland. Lost through stress of weather.
3 April 1864	*Magpie*	Steam gunboat	Wrecked in Galway Bay. Lt Bell severely reprimanded and admonished.
4 Nov. 1864	*Racehorse*	Steam gunvessel	Wrecked near Chefu. Cdr Boxer admonished.
Oct. 1866	*Griffon*	Steam gunvessel	Stranded at Little Popo, West Africa, after collision with *Pandora*. Cdr Davidson severely reprimanded.
1867	*Osprey*	Steam gunvessel	Wrecked on coast of South Africa. Cdr. Menzies loses 4 years' seniority and severely reprimanded.
15 Nov. 1868	*Gnat*	Steam gunvessel	Wrecked off Is. of Balabac (China). Cdr Theobald admonished.
9 May 1870	*Slaney*	Steam gunvessel	Wrecked off China. Acquitted.
5 Sept. 1870	*Trinculo*	Steam gunboat	Wrecked off Gibraltar. Acquitted.
21 May 1874	*Niobe*	Sloop	Wrecked on the China Station. Cdr Stephenson admonished.
26 April 1881	*Doterel*	Sloop	Sunk by an explosion in the Straits of Magellan. Cdr Boyle acquitted.
12 Sept. 1882	*Phoenix*	Sloop	Wrecked off Prince Edward Is. Cdr Grenfell severely reprimanded and dismissed from *Phoenix*.
12 Sept. 1884	*Wasp*	Steam gunboat	Wrecked off Tory Is. Only 6 out of 58 saved. Survivors acquitted.
Sept. 1887	*Wasp*	Steam gunboat	Lost on passage to Hong Kong. All 73 lost.
6 Sept. 1889	*Lily*	Steam gunvessel	Went ashore in fog off Labrador, 7 lost. Cdr Russell severely reprimanded and dismissed from *Lily*.

[1] Extract from Parliamentary Papers for 1890/91-51(176).
[2] Although this vessel is described as a gunvessel she will not be found in Part II, as she belongs to the assorted group of steamers built before 1854 and variously rated as gunboats, dispatch vessels, etc.

Officers and ratings of H.M.S. *Wasp*, lost on passage between Singapore and Hong Kong, probably as a result of a typhoon in the South China Sea on 19 September 1887. Seated at the front are (left to right) Surgeon Nunan, MD; *Wasp*'s commanding officer, Commander BJH Adamson; and Mr Attwood, Engineer; while standing to either side of them are Mr Holge, Gunner (left); and Mr Greenwood, Paymaster. *(Conway Maritime Press)*

Appendix B

Gunvessels and gunboats afloat on 1 April 1867[1]

IN COMMISSION

Star, Vigilant, Penguin (all right until 1870)	EAST INDIES
Cormorant, Serpent, Sylvia (Japan), *Osprey* (ordered home), *Slaney, Algerine, Hardy, Havock, Grasshopper, Insolent, Cockchafer, Weazel, Haughty, Bustard, Banterer, Firm, Snap, Forester, Bouncer, Drake, Janus*	CHINA
Nassau	STRAITS OF MAGELLAN SURVEY
Assurance, Espoir, Landrail, Torch, Mullet, Ranger, Dart (all except *Assurance* to serve to 1870), *Snipe* (ordered home with *Ranger*)	WEST AFRICA
Sparrowhawk, Forward	PACIFIC
Steady (ordered home) *Nimble, Cygnet* (ordered home), *Britomart, Heron, Cherub, Minstrel, Delight, Albacore, Nettle*	NORTH AMERICA AND WEST INDIES
Speedy	CHANNEL ISLANDS
Pigeon	CHANNEL FLEET
Cockatrice, Tyrian, Wizard, Trinculo, Skylark	MEDITERRANEAN
Doterel, Linnet, Spider, Gleaner	S.E. COAST OF AMERICA
Stork, Fancy	PORTSMOUTH
Dapper	DARTMOUTH
Redwing (Ireland), *Clinker*	DEVONPORT
Griper, Highlander, Lark, Sandfly, Whiting	QUEENSTOWN
Raven (Coastguard)	KINGSTOWN
Hyaena (Coastguard)	MILFORD HAVEN
Bullfrog	NORTH SHIELDS
Fervent	BRISTOL

Miscellaneous: twelve 60 h.p. gunboats on Coastguard duties

OUT OF COMMISSION

Lily, Eclipse, Coquette, Sparrow – Rotten and not worth repairing.
Plover – New.
Lee, Jaseur, Pandora, Speedwell – Defective, and under repair (*Lee* completing).
Leven (indifferent condition) *Dove, Starling, Grappler, Onyx* – Laid up abroad.
Another 28 gunboats – Laid up, some incomplete and some for breaking-up; 7 used for harbour service.

Gunboats and gunvessels afloat on 1 April 1876[1]

IN COMMISSION

Torch, Dart, Nimble, Cockatrice, Wizard, Heron, Tyrian, Speedy, Cherub, Netley, Orwell, Bittern, Cromer, Bruizer, Fervent, Earnest, Pheasant, Thrasher, Flamingo, Griffon, Condor, Cracker, Fly, Flirt, Dwarf, Beacon, Lapwing, Philomel, Ringdove, Myrmidon, Hornet, Rocket, Sylvia, Lynx, Nassau, Teazer, Woodlark, Midge, Pert, Hart, Coquette, Curlew, Growler, Foam, Decoy, Merlin, Mosquito, Kestrel, Frolic, Ready, Rifleman, Goshawk, Swinger, Ariel, Zephyr, Cygnet, Express, Contest, Mallard, Sheldrake, Moorhen, Thistle, Bullfinch

1ST RESERVE

Britomart, Pigeon, Avon, Plover, Waterwitch, Magpie

4TH RESERVE

Star, Newport, Vulture, Swallow, Boxer, Elk, Seagull

FOR DISPOSAL

Speedwell

IN RESERVE AT BERMUDA

Viper, Vixen

Sloops afloat on 1 April 1876[3]

IN COMMISSION

Vestal, Peterel, Rapid, Nymphe, Daphne, Dryad, Dido, Wild Swan, Osprey, Penguin

1ST RESERVE

Danae, Blanche, Eclipse, Reindeer

4TH RESERVE

Enterprise (armoured), *Gannet, Cameleon, Rinaldo, Rosario, Greyhound, Perseus*

Ships afloat on 1 January 1889[4]

17 SLOOPS ON EFFECTIVE LIST:

Daphne, Nymphe, Buzzard, Swallow, Pelican, Gannet, Kingfisher, Mutine, Espiègle, Mariner, Racer, Reindeer, Acorn, Melita, Icarus, Dolphin, Wanderer

8 GUNVESSELS EFFECTIVE:

Curlew, Landrail, Flamingo, Griffon, Linnet, Swift, Lily, Rifleman

62 GUNBOATS EFFECTIVE:

9 1st Class, 13 2nd Class, 40 3rd Class

8 SLOOPS NON-EFFECTIVE OR OBSOLETE:

Wild Swan, Penguin, Osprey, Cormorant, Dragon, Pegasus, Miranda, Daring

4 2ND CLASS GUNVESSELS NON-EFFECTIVE OR OBSOLETE:

Ranger, Algerine, Falcon, Ready

6 2ND CLASS GUNBOATS CLASSED AS OBSOLETE:

Firm, Forester, Firebrand, Firefly, Zephyr, Merlin

---

[1] From Parliamentary Papers for 1867-44 (349); see also Part II.
[2] From Parliamentary Papers for 1876-45 (297), setting out the state of the Fleet at 1 April 1876; iron gunboats are not included in this extract – most were hauled up at Haslar or in the 1st Reserve, and only two or three were in commission.
[3] *Ibid.*
[4] From Parliamentary Papers for 1889-50 (90).

Appendix C

Applications made for ships of war to be sent to foreign stations, 1857-61[1]

A Return of all Applications, as far as can be obtained, that have been made by the Commercial and other Interests during the last Five Years to the Government of the Day, for Ships of War to be sent to Foreign Stations, or to be employed on Foreign Stations, for the Protection of British Interests and Commerce.

DATE OF APPLICATION	BY WHAT DEPARTMENT OR PERSONS MADE	NATURE OF APPLICATION	REMARKS
1857			
22 Jan.	Foreign Office.	Ship to visit Island of Spalinadair (Island of Greek Archipelago), to prevent plunder of wrecks.	Orders given to the Admiral in Mediterranean to send a ship.
27 Jan.	Gentlemen connected with Honduras, through Colonial Office.	Ship of war to be stationed at Belize, to protect settlements.	Directions given to the Admiral on the West India Station.
10 Feb.	Governor of Mauritius, through Colonial Office.	Ship of war to visit dependencies of Mauritius in consequence of murders and outrages committed by Indian labourers.	H.M.S. *Frolic* sent on this service.
9 March	Governor of New Zealand, through Colonial Office.	Ship to be stationed at Auckland, to provide against an attack by natives.	Orders given for a man-of-war to be sent from China when one could be spared.
23 March	Messrs Hindson & Hayes, merchants, of Liverpool.	Ship of war to be sent to Kooria Mooria Islands, to preserve order among shippers of guano.	Informed that a vessel will be sent by August, when season for loading guano would commence.
3 April	Governor of Mauritius, through Colonial Office.	Asks for service of gunboat to protect colony, and enforce quarantine laws.	Informed that there is no gunboat available.
27 April	Governor of Newfoundland.	Asks for efficient naval protection for fisheries.	H.M.S. *Basilisk* and *Atalanta* ordered to Newfoundland.
6 May	Colonial Office.	Ship of war to be sent to Kooria Mooria Islands, to preserve order among the shippers of guano.	H.M.S. *Cordelia* ordered on this service.
– June	Chargé d'Affaires in Mexico, through Foreign Office.	Asks for naval force to protect British interests in Mexico.	Force sent.
17 July	Governor of New Zealand, through Colonial Office.	Asks for adequate naval protection.	Informed that Australian squadron will be strengthened as soon as more pressing demands permit.
31 July	Colonial Office.	Asks for steamer to be stationed at Galle until military force in Ceylon can be strengthened.	Informed that squadron will be sent to Bay of Bengal and to Ceylon.
4 Aug.	Consul General in Borneo, through Foreign Office.	Asks for ship of war occasionally to visit Brunei.	Orders given to Admiral on China Station to take necessary steps.
22 Sept.	Foreign Office.	Protection of British trade in San Domingo.	Vessels of war ordered there.
24 Sept.	Foreign Office.	To prevent foreigners occupying Point Barima, at the mouth of the Orinoco, to search for gold in Venezuela.	Orders given to Admiral on West India Station, and to H.M.S. *Atalanta*.
3 Oct.	Mr Tait, merchant at Amoy.	A vessel to visit Formosa, to inquire whether Europeans are detained as captives in the interior.	Vessel sent.

DATE OF APPLICATION	BY WHAT DEPARTMENT OR PERSONS MADE	NATURE OF APPLICATION	REMARKS
8 Oct.	Governor of Sierra Leone.	A vessel to visit the town of Monbolo, in the Scarcias River, to demand the release of British subjects detained as prisoners.	H.M.S. *Brune* ordered on this service.
– Oct.	Foreign Office.	Conveyance of Siamese Embassy to Suez.	H.M.S. *Encounter* ordered to perform this service.
23 Nov.	Chargé d'Affaires at Guatemala, through Foreign Office and Governor of Jamaica.	Protection from aggression of Caribs from Spanish Honduras upon Island of Bonnacca.	H.M.S. *Arachne* sent to Bay Islands, to inquire into circumstances, and prevent recurrence.
1858			
6 Jan.	Colonial Office.	That H.M.S. *Cordelia* should again be sent to Kooria Mooria Islands, to protect guano trade.	Orders to that effect sent.
– Jan.	Foreign Office.	Conveyance of Siamese Embassy from England to Bangkok.	H.M.S. *Caradoc* and *Pelorus* employed on this service.
7 Jan.	Foreign Office.	A ship of war to convey sappers and miners from Panama to Vancouver.	H.M.S. *Havannah* so employed.
15 Feb.	Governor of Sydney, New South Wales.	Ship to proceed to Tanna, New Hebrides, to investigate a case of murder.	*Iris* sent on this service.
16 Feb.	Board of Trade.	A ship to assist in erection of a light house at Cay Lobos.	Orders sent accordingly.
19 Feb.	Foreign Office.	Assistance to Dr Livingstone on Zambesi Expedition.	Orders given to Admiral on Cape of Good Hope Station.
19 March	Colonial Office.	That a vessel may be placed at the service of the Governor.	Orders sent for two vessels to be detached from China for this service.
24 March	Governor of Honduras, through Governor of Jamaica.	That a vessel may be sent to protect British Honduras from a threatened attack by Central American Indians.	H.M.S. *Leopard* accordingly sent.
24 March	The General commanding the Forces, Jamaica.	Vessel to convey troops to protect British Honduras.	H.M.S. *Leopard* accordingly sent.
– April	Foreign Office.	Protection of British interests in the River Plate.	A small vessel sent.
– April	Registrar of High Court of Admiralty.	A vessel to watch wrecking at the Bahamas.	A ship sent there.
29 April	Foreign Office.	Protection of British interests at Sarawak.	Attention of Admiral on the China Station called to this case.
1 May	Foreign Office.	A vessel to protect British interests at Alexandria.	H.M.S. *Wanderer* sent.
12 May	Governor of Vancouver.	Presence of a ship of war at British Columbia, on account of the excitement on the discovery of gold.	A vessel ordered on this service.
26 May	Foreign Office, on behalf of the Borneo Company.	Naval protection to British interests at Sarawak.	Informed of the orders sent to the Admiral on the China Station.
18 June	Consul at Mozambique.	Requests naval protection.	H.M.S. *Persian* and *Lyra* ordered on this service.
5 July	Foreign Office.	That a ship may be sent to Vera Cruz for protection of British interests, and that a gunboat may be stationed at Tampico.	H.M.S. *Buzzard* and *Basilisk* ordered to Vera Cruz.
10 July	Foreign Office.	Further protection to fisheries in Newfoundland.	Two gunboats sent there from Halifax.
17 July	Foreign Office.	A ship of war occasionally to visit Bangkok, in Siam.	Orders given to the Admiral on the China Station.
5 Aug.	Messrs Hindson & Hayes, through Colonial Office.	Further protection to guano trade at Kooria Mooria Islands.	Senior Officer on East India Station.

DATE OF APPLICATION	BY WHAT DEPARTMENT OR PERSONS MADE	NATURE OF APPLICATION	REMARKS
11 Aug.	Colonial Office.	As large a force as possible to be sent to assist Governor of British Columbia.	As large a force as can possibly be spared to be sent there.
20 Aug.	Colonial Office.	Urging continuance of a naval force in British Columbia.	H.M.S. *Tribune* to proceed from China with as many marines as possible, to Vancouver's Island.
25 Aug.	Foreign Office.	Presence of a squadron in the Red Sea, on account of an outrage at Jeddah.	Squadron sent.
29 Aug.	Consul at Tangiers.	Protection of a cruizer on account of the disturbances on the Riff Coast.	H.M.S. *Curlew* ordered on this service.
1 Sept.	Colonial Office.	A gunboat to proceed up the Hondo River, to protect Mr Seymour, resident in Honduras.	Commodore in Jamaica to act according to his discretion, taking into account the risk of fever, &c, to the ship employed.
21 Oct.	Foreign Office.	Protection of British interests in Morocco.	A vessel ordered to that coast.
29 Oct.	Governor of New South Wales.	A vessel of war at Keppel Bay, on account of Fitzroy gold diggings.	H.M.S. *Iris* sent.
3 Nov.	Foreign Office.	A vessel of war to be constantly stationed on the Coast of Syria.	Ordered.
13 Nov.	Colonial Office.	Further protection to New Zealand.	Informed that orders have been given for keeping a vessel at New Zealand, and a steamer will, if possible, be made available for that service.
16 Dec.	Borneo Company, through Foreign Office.	Continuing naval protection to Borneo.	Orders sent to the Admiral on the China Station.
1859			
25 Jan.	Consul, Vera Cruz, through Foreign Office.	For presence of British ships of war in consequence of the disturbed state of the Mexican Coast.	Instructions accordingly to Commander-in-Chief on the station.
8 Feb.	Governor of New South Wales, through Colonial Office.	General question of naval and military defences of colony, and of costs of conveyance of troops, mails, &c.	Two additional ships of war sent to the station.
3 March	Foreign Office.	British cruizers necessary for protection of Bahama vessels fishing on the Coast of Cuba, &c.	Instructions accordingly to the Admiral of the station.
5 March	Governor of British Columbia, through Colonial Office.	For one or two light draught gunboats capable of navigating Fraser's River.	Two sent out.
7 March	Foreign Office.	That a ship may be sent to the Orinoco, in event of disturbances in Venezuelan Guiana.	Ordered.
9 March	Foreign Office.	Request for presence of a ship on Coast of Ecuador, in consequence of the Peruvian blockade of coasts.	Ordered.
9 April	Foreign Office.	For naval protection in Chili, on account of its disturbed state, as represented by H.M. Chargé d'Affaires, Mr Thowson.	Force increased.
5 May	Colonial Office.	An armed blockship for the Colony of Victoria, and the establishment of an Admiral's station there.	No blockship available. The squadron lately increased, and become an independent commodore's command.

DATE OF APPLICATION	BY WHAT DEPARTMENT OR PERSONS MADE	NATURE OF APPLICATION	REMARKS
19 May	Foreign Office.	That a ship of war be sent to Valentia, to prevent illegal proceedings of guarda costas.	Ordered.
27 May	War Office.	For more frequent visits of a ship of war at Barbadoes.	Instructions to Sir H. Stewart accordingly.
7 June	Foreign Office.	Request that ports in Redhea may occasionally be visited.	Ordered.
7 June	Consul at Fernando Po.	Requests a ship for protection.	The *Lynx* sent.
22 June	Her Majesty's Consul for Bight of Biafra.	For a man-of-war steamer to be permanently attached to the Consulate.	Informed that British interests sufficiently protected by cruizers on station.
31 My	Governor of Bahamas, through Colonial Office.	A small vessel to suppress collusive wrecking in Bahama waters.	No vessel suitable or available.
15 Sept.	Foreign Office.	A ship of war to visit Sarawak for protection of British subjects.	Orders to senior officer at Singapore accordingly.
26 Sept.	Archbishop of Canterbury through Foreign Office.	A ship of war to call at Borneo for protection of missionaries.	Orders to senior officer at Singapore accordingly.
2 Oct.	Foreign Office.	For reinforcements to Vancouver's Island and to Bermuda.	Informed that *Topaze* and *Clio* are ordered to Pacific, and *Nile* to Halifax.
12 Oct.	Foreign Office.	Request a ship of war may be stationed at Vera Cruz.	Ordered.
18 Oct.	Sir H. Stewart, *Indus*, at Halifax.	Advantages of construction of small schooners for Bahama waters.	Two vessels ordered to be built.
27 Oct.	Governor of Bahamas, through Colonial Office.	Ship of war to suppress abstraction of guano from Bahamas by United States' vessels.	Orders accordingly.
8 Dec.	Governor of Victoria, through Colonial Office.	Four steam frigates and three men-of-war for protection of the port and colony.	Compliance impossible, with due regard to demands from other important Colonies.
30 Dec.	Foreign Office.	Naval force for suppression of disturbances in Mexico.	Orders accordingly.
1860			
9 March	Foreign Office.	For a ship of war periodically to visit the dependencies of Mauritius.	Ordered.
– March	Cotton Supply Association at Manchester.	For a vessel to be sent up the Niger occasionally to protect trade.	Informed that this service can only be undertaken under special circumstances, and for some specific object.
– April	The King, Consul, and principal merchants of Lagos to Commodore Edmonstone.	Pointing out how impolitic and injudicious it would be to remove H.M.S. *Brune* from Lagos.	H.M.S. *Brune* ordered to remain at Lagos for protection of life and property.
4 April	Foreign Office.	Vessel of war to visit Zanzibar in consequence of insurrection there.	Ordered.
7 April	Foreign Office.	Vessel of war to visit Dominican ports to protect British trade.	Ordered.
– April	Foreign Office.	Vessel of war to protect British interests in Sicilian ports.	Ordered.
25 April	Foreign Office.	Squadron to be sent to Japan on account of disturbed state of affairs there.	Orders given to the Admiral on the China Station.
2 May	Foreign Office, on behalf of Borneo Company.	Vessel of war to visit Sarawak to protect British interests in Borneo.	Ordered.

DATE OF APPLICATION	BY WHAT DEPARTMENT OR PERSONS MADE	NATURE OF APPLICATION	REMARKS
20 May	Governor of Leeward Islands, through Colonial Office.	Ship of war to occasionally visit Dominica and other Leeward Islands.	Ordered.
30 May	H.M. Consul General in Syria to Admiral Fanshawe.	Vessel of war to proceed off Beyrout to protect British subjects and interests, in consequence of a civil war in Mount Lebanon between Christians and Druses.	H.M.S. *Queen* and *Mohawk* sent.
30 May	Mrs M'Kinley and another, through Colonial Office.	Vessel of war to be sent to Torres Straits to ascertain whether any of the crew of the ship *Sapphire* of Liverpool, wrecked on the barrier reefs, were in existence.	Senior officer at Sydney to use his discretion as to sending a ship to make inquiries, should he not be aware of H.M.S. *Herald* already having done so.
31 May	Colonial Office.	Protection and assistance to New Zealand in the event of rebellion.	Commodore Loring desired, with reference to former instructions, on receiving requisition from the Governor of New Zealand, not to consider himself precluded from adopting any measures which might appear to afford the most prompt means of assisting the Governor in the effectual assertions of Her Majesty's authority in the event of disturbances.
16 Nov.	Foreign Office.	For a ship to be stationed at Panama to protect British life and property, in consequence of the disturbed state of New Grenada.	Ordered.
1861			
1 Jan.	Governor of Mauritius, through Colonial Office.	For a ship of war to visit the distant dependencies of the Mauritius Government, and for the commanding officer to report upon their condition.	Orders given accordingly.
16 Jan.	Governor of Bahamas, through Commander-in-Chief on North American Station.	Naval co-operation with the local authorities in endeavouring to put an end to collusive wrecking.	Commander-in-Chief to send occasionally vessels of light draught to endeavour to put some check on this evil.
23 Jam.	Foreign Office.	Protection to British Consul at Lagos against a threatened attack of King of Dahomey.	Orders given.
31 Jan.	Messrs Coward & Co., through Foreign Office.	Protection to British subjects and property at the Isthmus of Panama, in consequence of the disturbed state of New Grenada.	Orders given for protection to be afforded.
11 Feb.	Foreign Office.	Two frigates required at Gibraltar to prevent seizure of vessels by Spanish revenue authorities in British waters.	Frigates sent accordingly.
16 Feb.	Foreign Office.	A ship of the line to be stationed at Naples or Palermo.	Directions given to the Admiral in the Mediterranean.
26 Feb.	British merchants, through the Commander-in-Chief in the Mediterranean.	Protection of British property at Messina.	Orders given.
16 March	Trustees of the British Museum.	For a ship to be sent to Mersa Louza, in Cyrene, to assist in researches after antiquities, &c, conducted by Lieutenant Smith, R.E., and Lieutenant Porcher, R.N.	Orders given.
23 March	Colonial Office.	For naval assistance in operations against King Badiboo on the West Coast of Africa.	The necessary instructions given to the Commodore on the West Coast of Africa.

DATE OF APPLICATION	BY WHAT DEPARTMENT OR PERSONS MADE	NATURE OF APPLICATION	REMARKS
2 April	Foreign Office.	For protection to Consul and British subjects in Japan; presence of the Commander-in-Chief himself requested.	Instructions sent to the Admiral.
9 April	British Consulate at Zanzibar, forwarded through Naval Commander-in-Chief.	Presence of H.M.S. *Lyra* requested to be prolonged at Zanzibar, for protection against the outrages of Arab slave traders.	Request complied with.
22 May	Foreign Office.	For a vessel to afford protection against violence from the natives in Brass River.	Orders given.
29 May	Governor of Singapore.	For a ship of war to accompany him to effect a mediation between hostile chiefs on the Malay coast.	H.M.S. *Charybdis* ordered on this service.
6 June	Messrs Hunt & Henley, merchants of London.	For a vessel of war to cruize off the coast of Labrador during the fishing season to preserve order.	Sir A. Milne instructed accordingly.
6 June	Colonial Office.	For a vessel to protect British territory from aggressions of Indians of Yucatan.	The Admiral on the West India Station ordered to give all assistance in his power.
1 July	Foreign Office.	Naval aid to prevent the illegal seizure and carrying away of goods of British merchants by insurgents in New Grenada.	Orders given.
28 Aug.	Governor of Newfoundland, through Commander-in-Chief on North American Station.	For a ship to be on the coast of Newfoundland to preserve peace during apprehended riots.	A ship to be sent.
– Sept.	The British Consul at the Fijis, through the senior naval officer.	For protection against the natives of Viti Leva.	A ship accordingly sent.
13 Oct.	Foreign Office.	For two gunboats to be sent to Zanzibar to prevent slave trade.	Vessels to be sent as often as other claims admit.
22 Oct.	Messrs Tobin, of Liverpool	For protection to British trading vessels in the river Congo.	Ordered.
26 Oct.	Liverpool African Association, through Foreign Office.	A vessel of war to be stationed in the Bonny River to protect British interests.	Orders given to the Commodore on the West Coast of Africa.
6 Dec.	Messrs Gibbs, Bright & Sons, of Liverpool.	For protection to homeward trade from the Australian Colonies, on account of the critical state of the critical state of relations with America.	The Commodore on the Australian Station to afford such assistance as the force at his disposal will allow.

1 Taken from Parliamentary Papers for 1862-34 (380).

Appendix D

HMS *Gannet*: survival and restoration

Lindsay Doulton, Curator of Maritime Engineering and Technology, The Historic Dockyard, Chatham

HMS *Gannet* was built at Sheerness Dockyard on the River Medway in 1878. The ship is a composite screw sloop and is typical of the smaller gunboats built by the Victorian Navy to patrol the shores of the British Empire. As the last surviving small ship of Queen Victoria's Royal Navy, HMS *Gannet* is a nationally important vessel. Her composite construction and transitional design reflects a key period of development in the field of ship design and marine engineering technology that culminated in wood giving way to iron and steel, and sail giving way to steam. Today HMS *Gannet* is preserved at The Historic Dockyard, Chatham, where she forms part of the core collection of the registered museum and is open to the public. She is also listed on the core collection of the National Register of Historic Vessels.

HMS *Gannet* had two very different lives: operational warship and drill ship. Between 1878 and 1895 she served as an operational sloop of the Royal Navy until being converted into a drill ship in 1902. From then until 1911 she served as HMS *President*, the Headquarters ship of the Royal Naval Volunteer Reserve, and from 1914 to 1968 as the dormitory ship for a boys' pre-sea training school, TS *Mercury*, moored on the River Hamble. With the closure of TS *Mercury* in July 1968, *Gannet*'s role as a school accommodation ship ended and responsibility for her reverted to the Royal Navy, from whom she had been on loan for nearly sixty years. In 1971 the Royal Navy transferred the ownership and the responsibility for the restoration and preservation of the *Gannet* to The Maritime Trust.

In 1987 The Historic Dockyard at Chatham chartered *Gannet* from The Maritime Trust and started a restoration programme. The objective of the programme was to return *Gannet* to her 1886 appearance – when she saw action for the only time in her naval career at the defence of the Sudanese port of Suakin. In 1994 ownership of the vessel was passed to the Chatham Historic Dockyard Trust. The restoration, completed by late 2003, has seen the ship's largely original hull fully conserved and re-coppered, as well as the re-fitting of the original decks, cabins, masts and spars. The restoration was made possible by the generous support of the Heritage Lottery Fund, Medway Council and the European Regional Development Fund.

The Ship

HMS *Gannet*, an *Osprey/Doterel* class sloop, was ordered by the Admiralty on 14 February 1876. She was laid down in December 1876 and launched 20 months later

Gannet under sail in the Mediterranean in the late 19th Century. During her last commission the ship undertook hydrographic work around the Mediterranean and the Red Sea. *(Chatham Historic Dockyard)*

on 31 August 1878. In 1875, three years before her launch, sloops had been re-defined as any vessel of cruising type, carrying between 100-200 officers and men; they were generally the largest type of Royal Navy vessel to carry a Commander's pennant. When launched, HMS *Gannet* was classified as both a sloop of war and as a colonial cruiser, with a Commander in command. As such, she was ranked between a corvette (commanding officer, Captain, RN) and a gun vessel (commanding officer, Lieutenant, RN) and therefore could operate as an independent command, although often such ships operated in Squadrons when stationed overseas.

HMS *Gannet* – data as built

Length:	190ft oa (57.91m); 170ft (pp)
Beam:	36ft (58.81m)
Draught:	16ft maximum
Displacement:	1130 tons
Machinery:	Single shaft two cylinder horizontal compound expansion steam engine; three cylindrical boilers
Speed:	15 knots (under sail); 12.5 knots (under steam)
Range (under steam):	2,014 nautical miles @ 11.5 knots (7.3 days); 3,240 nautical miles @ 5 knots (27 days)
Complement:	13 Officers and Warrant Officers; 27 Petty Officers; 64 Seamen; 11 Boys; 24 Marines
Armament :	2 x 7" muzzle loading rifled guns (pivoting); 4 x 64 pdrs (2 pivoting, 2 broadside)
Ship's boats:	1 x 25 ft steam cutter; 1 x 30 ft cutter; 2 x 27ft whalers; 1 x 16 ft jolly boat; 1 x 12 ft dinghy

Building the Ship

HMS *Gannet* cost a total of £57,290 to build, with the

hull costing the greatest amount at £39,581, the propeller and other machinery £12,889, and other works and fitting out £4,820. HMS *Gannet* is built of composite construction with an iron frame supporting timber hull planking, decks and superstructure. This type of construction technique was only in vogue for around thirty years and marks the significant transitional period when wood gave way to iron and steel. Composite construction meant some of the restrictions of building ships in timber could be overcome. Larger ships with increased cargo carrying capacity could now be built, which if copper-bottomed, like HMS *Gannet*, could be protected from fouling and marine borers. Furthermore, repairs to hull planking could be carried out at considerably less well equipped dockyards, which was of particular importance to ships operating in less developed areas of the world.

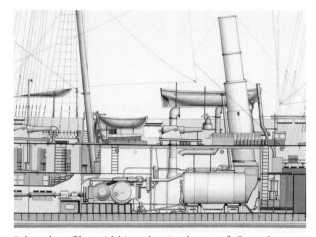

Inboard profile amidships, showing layout of *Gannet*'s machinery. *(Chatham Historic Dockyard)*

Layout of the Ship

The ship was built with three decks; main, lower and hold. The main (upper) deck was largely open, although the forecastle was enclosed to house a 64 pdr gun and heads for Warrant Officers, Petty Officers and Seamen. The main deck was also the ship's gun deck and was where the main armament was mounted. A simple open 'flying bridge' was also fitted at the after end of this deck. The lower deck, separated midships by the engine and boiler rooms, provided accommodation for the crew forward of the machinery spaces and officers aft of them. A significant feature of the layout of the ship as built was a passageway constructed within the port side machinery space coalbunkers that allowed internal access fore and aft at lower deck level. As well as providing the location for the main machinery spaces, the hold deck also was the location for the ship's main stores, magazines and water tanks, all accessed vertically from the deck above. A propeller shaft space ran aft from the engine room along the centreline of the ship above the keel. This necessitated mounting both main and mizzen masts on mast steps at lower deck level rather than on the keel itself, as is the case for the fore mast.

Propulsion

HMS *Gannet* could be propelled by either sail or steam. Her ship's log demonstrates that during her first commission, when stationed in the Pacific between 1879 and 1883, the ship sailed to most destinations. However by her second commission, 1885-1888, in which she saw a more active period engaged in anti-slavery patrols around the Red Sea, she steamed far more often. This presumably reflects the fact that coal had by this point become more readily available around the world. In fact the *Gannet*'s top speed of around fifteen knots was achieved when under sail, whilst under steam her top speed was a lesser twelve and a half knots.

The rig of the ship incorporates traditional masting and sparring, with lower mast, top mast and combined topgallant and royal above on both the fore and main masts. With four yards on each of these masts, the sails were moderately small and therefore required slightly reduced handling. It is unusual for a ship as late as 1878 to have single topsails but again this is a concession to the unusual service of this ship. This old-fashioned sail design comes from the use late into the nineteenth century of the Admiralty Rigging Warrants. All materials were easily obtained and all ropes man-made. In general the ship could be self-sufficient from the rigging point of view, and it is certain that she carried spare spars.

The machinery arrangement onboard *Gannet* incorporated a 2-cylinder compound steam engine which drove a 13ft 1in diameter lifting screw propeller designed by Griffiths. The aperture for lifting the propeller in and out of the water was located within the commander's cabin. When under sail the propeller would be hauled up so as to reduce drag. Steam was provided to the engine by three Humphrey & Tennant cylindrical boilers, each 7ft 10 inches in diameter and 15 feet in length. Finally, a telescopic funnel completed the machinery arrangement which like the propeller could be raised or lowered when at steam or not.

Armament

On completion, *Gannet*'s main armament comprised six rifled muzzle-loading guns, two 7-in and four 64 pdrs. Of these, two of the 64 pdrs were in fixed broadside positions within the forecastle, whilst the remaining weapons were mounted on pivoting carriages normally stowed on the centreline of the ship but capable of being moved to either side of the ship as required.

Operational Refits

During her operational service the ship underwent two minor mid-commission refits, in 1881 and 1888. However in 1884, after her first commission, she returned to Sheerness port for a major year-long refit which cost around £18,000. This refit saw the ship equipped for her second commission in service off the coast of Sudan. The main change saw the replacement of the original flying bridge with a full poop (or quarter) deck. This deck provided space underneath for the commander's cabin as well as offering space for additional armament which included two new 5-in breech-loading guns on Vavasseur mountings and two four-barrelled machine guns. In order to compensate for the extra weight added aft by the fitting of the poop deck the ship's rig was accordingly lightened.

Life on Board

The majority of the accommodation for the crew was provided on the lower deck. When built, all the officers' accommodation was located at the aft end; this included the commander whose cabin was aft of the wardroom. However a major refit between 1884 and 1885 saw the addition of a poop deck fitted onto the main deck at the after end of the ship, with the area enclosed below the poop deck fitted out as the Commander's cabin. These quarters comprised a day room, a couch, and a bed space located on the forward port side with a curtained-off area aft containing the tiller. The propeller-lifting aperture was also located in the centre of the cabin. A spare cabin for the commander's use was still retained on the lower deck.

The remainder of the officers' accommodation was located at the after end on the lower deck with cabins fitted around the outside of the wardroom. Various stores, the petty officers' mess and the wardroom and commander's pantries were also located in this area of the ship. Separated midships by the engine and boiler rooms was the seamen's accommodation. This open mess deck accommodated 101 men with nine mess tables. This relatively small space also included the galley, and provided access to four chain lockers, the fresh water tanks, the sail locker, two provision lockers, the magazine, warrant officers' stores and the gunner's stores, and storage for domestic items such as plates, dishes and basins. Finally this space, the total area amounting to only 56 feet x 32 feet and tapering to just 6 feet wide at the fore end had also to accommodate space for the slinging of the crew's hammocks, leaving each seaman with a mere 14 inches for his hammock and a small-lidded locker for his working gear. Additionally the fore mast ran through this space.

Active Service

During her service in the Victorian navy, HMS *Gannet* served on four commissions. The variety of activities she was engaged in and the different areas of the world in which she served very much reflect both the active and 'diplomatic' role of the navy during this period of British imperial expansion. Essentially the role *Gannet* was designed to perform was a global one, maintaining

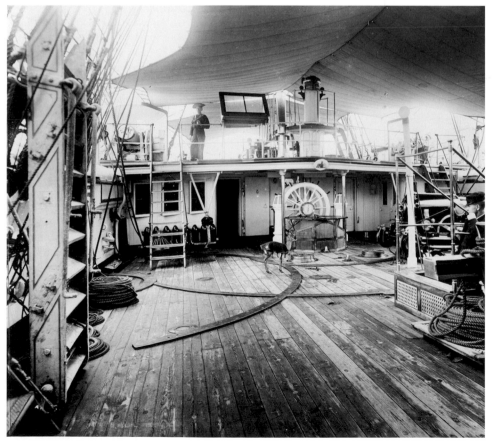

Looking aft on *Gannet*'s poop deck, photographed in 1884. Of note is the white awning overhead that was fitted for service in the Red Sea. On the deck can be seen the ship's mascot, a gazelle named 'Mr Willliams'. (*Chatham Historic Dockyard*)

British influence worldwide. The key duties of such ships were three-fold: protection of trade and empire, the suppression of slavery and piracy and the surveying of the world's seas.

First Commission

Pacific Station; 17 April 1879 – 20 July 1883

Soon after her completion in 1879, HMS *Gannet* was ordered to the Pacific Station to serve her first commission under the flag of Admiral De Horsey. In May 1879, she sailed from Portsmouth, via the Atlantic Ocean, for the Pacific port of Panama, arriving there the following year. *Gannet* shadowed the action during the 'nitrate' war between Chile and the Peru-Bolivia Alliance and she was present off Callao, Peru, when the Peruvians scuttled their own fleet to prevent it from falling into the hands of the enemy. After a long cruise around the Pacific, *Gannet* returned to pay off at Sheerness in July 1883. During her four-year commission on the Pacific Station, *Gannet* sailed over 60,000 miles.

Second Commission

Mediterranean Station;
3 September 1885 – 1 November 1888

Complement:

Officers	10
Petty Officers	24
Seamen	69
Boys, 1st and 2nd class	11
Marines	24
Total:	138

Commander:	Barton R Bradford
Lts:	Alfred R. A. Stock; William G Stewart; Bertram C Wolferstan
Staff Surgeon:	William P Boyle
Paymaster:	Reginald C Hodder
Chief Engineer:	Richard J Trench
Sub Lt:	Arthur P James
Gunner:	John Sime
Carpenter:	Thomas J Roady

Whilst HMS *Gannet*'s first commission had been largely a question of 'showing the flag' of the British Empire her second was of a markedly different nature. In 1885, following a two-year refit, *Gannet* re-commissioned at Sheerness and sailed for the Mediterranean Station, where she was initially used in fleet support duties to General Graham's forces in the Sudan and in slavery patrols. The ship's log show that much time was spent patrolling the Red Sea looking for ships that were involved in the slave trade, with vessels frequently being stopped, searched and any slaves rescued from their captors and taken aboard. Such excursions seemed in the main peaceful; however, the death of one of the ship's

Gannet's crew photographed on the main deck during the late 19th Century. They are wearing tropical rig. Note the ship's mascot again. *(Chatham Historic Dockyard)*

officers, Lieutenant Stewart, during one such search party, whilst reported with the normal succinct formality in the ship's log, caused such a reaction as to be fully reported back in England in *The Times* newspaper.

After some time stationed in the Red Sea HMS *Gannet* was ordered to join the squadron protecting the Sudanese port of Suakin.[1] Suakin was a protectorate of the British Empire and so the task of defending the port to enemy or rebel threats fell to the Royal Navy. The ship was in fact recalled from a mid-commission refit at Malta and ordered to relieve HMS *Dolphin* at Suakin on 11 September 1888, and on 17 September opened fire with her poop deck 5-in guns in support of land forces against an attack by rebel forces. On Tuesday the 19th, the ship's commander, Barton Bradford, moved the *Gannet* closer to the rebels' position so that the deck-mounted Nordenfelt machine guns could be brought within range. During the following 27 days *Gannet*'s main armament fired over 200 shells and her Nordenfelt machine guns fired nearly 1,200 rounds in the defence of Suakin. The entry in the ship's log for Thursday 20 September gives an indication of the action the *Gannet* faced during her time in Suakin. This excerpt also demonstrates that even in times of conflict shipboard life still continued as normal with the 'make and mend' of the sailors' uniforms still taking place, as Royal Naval tradition dictates, on a Thursday:

> Moored a.m.
> 5.15 warped ship round; commenced firing 5-in and 64-pdr, fired 11 shell; fired 2 shell from 5-in BL, tested life buoys, making and mending clothes;
> 5.15 fired 4 shells from 5-in BL[2]

HMS *Starling* relieved *Gannet* on 15 October. Although Osman Digna's rebel forces were not defeated until December 1888, the siege was lifted and with it the immediate threat to Suakin. Without *Gannet*'s assistance the port of Suakin may well have fallen to the rebel besiegers and the British and Egyptian forces could have suffered another major defeat. HMS *Gannet* paid off at Malta on 1 November 1888.

Third Commission
Mediterranean Station;
10 November 1888 – December 1891
HMS *Gannet* recommissioned at Malta on 10 November 1888, nine days after she was paid off from her second commission. She spent the next three years engaged in surveying work in the Mediterranean, before being paid off at the end of her third commission in December 1891.

Fourth Commission
Mediterranean Station; 26 January 1892 -16 March 1895
HMS *Gannet*'s final period of active service began with the start of her fourth and final commission at Malta in January 1892. Engaged in hydrographic work in the Mediterranean and Red Sea, *Gannet* paid off for the last time on 16 March 1895 at Chatham.

Life after Action
Although HMS *Gannet*'s role as an active ship in the Royal Navy was over, the vessel still had a varied future ahead. In December 1895, *Gannet* was transferred to the Harbour Service List and returned to Chatham the following June, where she remained until 1900 when she was placed on the List of Non-Effective Vessels. Between the years of 1900 and 1902 she was leased to the South Eastern & Chatham Railway and operated as an accommodation hulk at the 'cross-channel' railway terminal at Port Victoria on the Isle of Grain. From 1903-1913 she was ordered to relieve HMS *President*, the Royal Naval Reserve drill ship, then berthed in the West India Docks of the Port of London. In order to be fit for this role *Gannet* underwent major alterations before being renamed HMS *President*. In June 1903 she thus became the Headquarters ship of the London Royal Naval Reserve in the West India Docks. However the ship's longest role came from 1913 until 1968 when she was lent to Mr C B Fry (the cricketer) for use as an accommodation ship for the Training Ship *Mercury* based on the river Hamble near Southampton.

Restoration
Since 1987 the ship has been in dry dock at the Historic Dockyard Chatham and in 1994 ownership passed to Chatham Historic Dockyard Trust. Since that time a major restoration programme has taken place, with the ship now restored back to her original appearance of when she served in the Victorian Royal Navy. The long life that the ship has had since active service had resulted

TS *Mercury* moored on the Hamble. *(Chatham Historic Dockyard)*

The ship under canopy early on during restoration. *(Chatham Historic Dockyard)*

in many changes to her physical appearance, with the time served as a drill ship and as the accommodation ship to TS *Mercury* especially resultant in some significant alterations. Therefore, before any restoration work could even be undertaken, an extensive programme of historical research was required in order to establish the original specification of the ship and all its fixtures and fittings. With the latter achieved, a full schedule of works formulated, and the securing of vital funding achieved, restoration work could begin. Although many of the internal compartments await further restoration, work to date has seen the conservation and re-coppering of the ship's largely original hull, as well as the re-fitting of the original decks, cabins, masts and spars. Since her official public opening in 2003 HMS *Gannet* has now seen many visitors to The Historic Dockyard walk across her decks and experience something of what a gunboat in the Victorian Navy would have been like.

Undertaking the Ship's Restoration
Initial investigations by the restoration team showed that below the level of the main deck around ninety percent of the original iron framing and teak planking of the external hull remained intact and therefore only relatively minor repairs were required. However, above this level the extensive corrosion of deck beams and hull frames required large-scale restoration. The former, together with the replacement of the four substantial bulkheads that had been removed during her time as an accommodation ship, plus the insertion of the original coal bunker, all meant that the ship's structural integrity was now insured.

Of the decks, the upper, poop and forecastle deck all required full replacement and recaulking, the latter of which was carried out using traditional oakum. The timbers around the poop deck had particularly suffered from

Members of the restoration team re-caulking *Gannet*'s hull. Oakum is forced between the planks, before sealing with pitch, making the ship watertight. *(Chatham Historic Dockyard)*

Replacement of the foremast, July 2002. *(Chatham Historic Dockyard)*

Bow view of the ship in drydock during restoration. *(Chatham Historic Dockyard)*

decay and so it was necessary to give particular attention to this part of the ship. Replacement of the poop deck also included renewal of the commander's cabin, which was internally refitted. An important alteration to the forecastle deck was to bring its level down from following the line of the hull to its original position of being recessed in line with the gun embrasure.

Another significant aspect of the ship's restoration was her rig. All the masts and spars had to be newly manufactured to original specification from seasoned mast-quality timber, in *Gannet*'s case Douglas fir. In fact suitable timber was sourced in the Forest of Dean from trees that had been blown down during the great storm of 1987. The masts were then seasoned in the water of the dry dock underneath the ship and replaced using a tower crane.

Finally, across the decks non-original inserts such as hatch openings and ladders were removed and replaced to Victorian specification. A number of other fittings such as the original 'Downton' pump were restored to working order and some original and replica pieces of ordnance fitted.

Whilst much of the ship has now been restored, her upkeep and general maintenance, like any other vessel exposed to the elements, is still a full-time job. Jobs required on a day-to-day basis include simple tasks such as keeping the scuppers clear, and scrubbing the decks to ensure they stay watertight. Small areas of the deck caulking are repaired on a yearly basis and the task of painting the hull and masts is ever ongoing. In addition,

Above: The hull has now been fully conserved; this included re-caulking and re-coppering. Similarly, whilst the decks were in relatively good condition all were re-caulked using traditional oakum. Today visitors can watch and even have a go at helping in this process. *(Chatham Historic Dockyard)* Right: Three views on board the restored vessel today. Compare with the photograph on p.199. *(Stephen Dent)*

the standing rigging requires regular dressing with a mixture of tar and linseed oil in order to keep it fully preserved. Finally, the list of more long term objectives that will ensure the continued conservation of HMS *Gannet* includes the renewal of the standing rigging and some of the spars, and a programme of regular dry-docking where the copper-sheathed hull can be inspected and general maintenance tasks carried out.

Notes

[1]   During the mid-nineteenth century Egypt was troubled and territory disputed. In 1820 a 'quasi-empire' began, occupied by the 'Khedives of Egypt'. However, the Mahdi (a Dervish chief) raised the people of Sudan to revolt against Egyptian rule. Egypt was a 'protectorate' of Britain and General Gordon was one of a band of international administrators for the Khedive. In 1877 he was formally appointed as Governor General of the Sudan. His specific task from Cairo was to suppress slave trading. The fortified port of Suakin on Sudan's Red Sea coast came under Egyptian control in February 1885 when British and Indian troops landed there. Following the fall of Khartoum and the death of General Gordon on 26 January 1885, a small Anglo-Egyptian relief column advanced up the Nile as far as Dongola, but were prevented from advancing any further by the Mahdi's rebels. The troops who landed at Suakin hoped to force a railway through the Red Sea hills to Berber on the Nile, before linking up with the Anglo-Egyptian troops advancing on Khartoum from Dongola. This operation failed and the rebels under the command of Osman Digna continued to hold the countryside around the port of Suakin. However, Suakin remained under Egyptian control and was used as a base for the Royal Navy in the Red Sea. Between August 1886-September 1888, Suakin's Commandant was Colonel Herbert Horatio Kitchener. In September 1888, Osman Digna's rebels attacked Suakin.

[2]   PRO, ADM 53/13737

Bibliography

1. Parliamentary Papers

The references are by year, volume and number of paper in brackets. A bracketed number by itself refers to a House of Commons paper; prefaced by 'C.' or 'Cd' it refers to a Command paper.

1860-8 (545) Report of the Select Committee of Evidence on the defective gun and mortar boats built for the Crimean War.

1860-23 (2682) Report of the Committee on the defence of the United Kingdom.

1860-41 (282) Report of the Committee on the Expense of Colonial Military Defence.

1860-42 (365) Copy of a contract between the Admiralty and Messrs Green for building gunvessels, and a report on the state of *Coquette* and *Caroline*.

1860-42 (497) Correspondence between John Laird and the Admiralty regarding the fitting out of Mersey ferry and tug boats as auxiliary gunboats.

1861-13 (423) Report of the Select Committee on Colonial Military Expenditure.

1861-38 (206) Names of all dispatch vessels, gunvessels and mortar boats built since 1852, giving the original cost, expense of repairs, contractors' names, etc.

1862-34 (380) Return of applications for ships of war to be sent to foreign stations for the protection of British commerce, 1857-61.[1]

1863-35 (34) Order in Council authorising the enlistment of officers and men, and the equipment of vessels of war, for the service of the Emperor of China.

1866-30 (3683) and 31 (3683-1) Report of the Royal Commission into the Jamaica Rebellion, with minutes of evidence.

1866-51 (504) Correspondence between the Board of Admiralty and Admiral Hope on the conduct of naval officers during the Jamaica Rebellion.

1867-44 (349) Return of all gunvessels in and out of commission on 1 April 1867, stating how employed, condition, draught, tonnage, horse-power, date of building, etc.

1868/69-38 (89) Instructions granting discretionary powers to naval officers with respect to requisitions addressed to them by diplomatic or consular authorities.

1876-45 (297) Return showing particulars of vessels launched and added to the Navy in each year from 1855, and new building, and showing when such vessels were broken up, sold, whether in commission or reserve.

1887-66 (C. 5091 and C. 5091-1) Extracts from the report of the Carnarvon Commission on the defence of British colonies and trade (included in the proceedings of the 1887 Colonial Conference).

1888-68 (444) Return of actual naval expenditure, ships added and struck off the Navy lists, with other details, from 1859 to 1888, with totals and averages of triennial periods.

1889-5 (186) The Naval Defence Act.

1889-50 (C. 5648a) Return of the number of ships 'which will probably be removed from the list of the Navy as obsolete, or not worth repair' between 1 April 1889 and 1 April 1894.

1889-50 (C. 5648b) Return of the number of ships, 'including those in the proposed new ship-building programme' to be added to the Navy between 1 April 1889 and 1 April 1894.

1890/91-51 (176) Return of the number of H.M. ships lost otherwise than in action, 1841-90.

1905-48 (Cd 2335) The distribution and mobilisation of the Fleet.

1905-48 (74 and 74-I) Return of the vessels struck off the list of effective ships of war.

1905-48 (Cd 2430) Arrangements consequent on the redistribution of the Fleet.

1906-70 (Cd 2791) Statement of Admiralty policy.

2. Unpublished Theses

Rooney, M. J. *Aspects of Imperial Defence*. The relevance of the 1879 Royal Commission on the defence of British possessions and commerce abroad. 1963 (held in the Library of the Royal Commonwealth Society, London).

Schurman, D. M. *Imperial Defence 1868-1887*. A study in the decisive impulses behind the change from 'Colonial' to 'Imperial' defence. 1955 (held in Cambridge University Library).

3. Articles

Ballard, Adm. G. A. 'British Gunvessels of 1875; The Larger Twin-Screw Type', *The Mariner's Mirror*, January 1940.

—'British Gunvessels of 1875; The Smaller Twin-Screw Type', *ibid.*, March 1940.

—'British Gunvessels of 1875; The Larger Single-Screw Type', *ibid.*, October 1940.

—'British Sloops of 1875; The Smaller Composite Type', *ibid.*, October 1939.

—'British Gunboats of 1875', *ibid.*, January 1941.

—'The Fighting Ship from 1860 to 1890', *ibid.*, February 1952.

Elliot, Adm. Sir George. 'Coast Defence by Gunboats', *Journal of the Royal United Service Institution*, 1887-88, vol. 31, pp. 77-93.

Osbon, G. A., 'The Crimean Gunboats; Part I, *The Mariner's Mirror*, May 1965.

—'The Crimean Gunboats; Part II, *ibid.*, August 1965.

4. Books

GENERAL

Gretton, Adm. Sir Peter. *Maritime Strategy*. London, 1965.

Roskill, Capt. S. W., R.N. *The Strategy of Sea Power*. London, 1962.

PAX BRITANNICA

Bartlett, C. J. *Great Britain and Sea Power 1815-1853*. Oxford, 1963.

---

[1] Quoted in full in Appendix C.

Gordon, D. C. *The Dominion Partnership in Imperial Defense 1870-1963.* Johns Hopkins, 1965.

Graham, G. S. *The Politics of Naval Supremacy.* Cambridge, 1965.

Langer, W. L. *European Alliances and Alignments.* New York, 1964 (Vintage edn.).

THE CRIMEAN WAR
Bonner-Smith, D., and Dewar, Capt. A. C, R.N. (ed.). *Russian War 1854, Baltic and Black Sea; Official Correspondence.* London, 1943.

Bonner-Smith, D. (ed.). *Russian War 1855, Baltic; Official Correspondence.* London, 1944.

Dewar, Capt. A. C, R.N. (ed.). *Russian War 1855, Black Sea; Official Correspondence.* London, 1945.

CHINA
Bonner-Smith, D., and Lumby, E. W. R. (ed.). *The Second China War 1856-1860.* London, 1954.

Fox, G. *British Admirals and Chinese Pirates 1832-1869.* London, 1940.

Holt, E. *The Opium Wars in China.* London, 1964.

Morse, H. B., and MacNair, H. F. *Far Eastern International Relations.* Boston, 1931.

Waley, A. *The Opium War Through Chinese Eyes.* London, 1958.

THE CARIBBEAN
Olivier, S. *The Myth of Governor Eyre.* London, 1933.

Semmel, B. *The Governor Eyre Controversy.* London, 1962.

Steinbeck, A. *Filibusters and Buccaneers.* London, 1930.

Van Alstyne, R. W. *The Rising American Empire.* Oxford, 1960.

AFRICA
Churchill, W. S., *The River War.* London, 1900.

Gallagher, J., and Robinson, R., with Denny, A. *Africa and the Victorians.* London, 1961.

Lloyd, C. *The Navy and the Slave Trade.* London, 1949.

Newbury, C. W. *British Policy towards West Africa; Select Documents 1786-1874.* Oxford, 1965.

Oliver, R. *Sir Harry Johnston and the Scramble for Africa.* London, 1957.

MALAYA
Cowan, C. D. *Nineteenth-Century Malaya.* Oxford, 1961.

Parkinson, C. Northcote. *British Intervention in Malaya 1867-1877,* University of Malaya Press, 1960.

Tarling, N. *Piracy and Politics in the Malay World.* Melbourne, 1963.

INDIAN OCEAN AND RED SEA
Marston, T. E. *Britain's Imperial Role in the Red Sea Area 1800-1878.* Connecticut, 1961.

PACIFIC
Legge, J. D. *Britain in Fiji 1858-1880.* London, 1958.

Morell, W. P. *Britain in the Pacific Islands.* Oxford, 1960.

Ross, A. *New Zealand Aspirations in the Pacific in the Nineteenth Century.* Oxford, 1964.

Ward, J. M. *British Policy in the Pacific 1786-1893.* Sydney, 1948.

FIRST WORLD WAR
Chatterton, E. Keble. *Gallant Gentlemen.* London, 1931.

Corbett, Sir Julian. *Official History of the Great War: Naval Operations,* vol. 3. London, 1920.

THE VICTORIAN AND EDWARDIAN NAVY
Briggs, J. H. *Naval Administrations 1827-92.* London, 1892.

Busk, Hans (the younger). *The Navies of the World.* London, 1859.

Clowes, Sir W. Laird. *The Royal Navy, A History.* Vol. 6, *1816-1856.* London, 1901; Vol. 7, *1857-1900.* London, 1903.

Marder, A. J. *The Anatomy of British Sea Power; British Naval Policy 1880-1905.* New York, 1940.

— *From the Dreadnought to Scapa Flow; The Royal Navy in the Fisher Era 1904-1919.* Vol. 1, *The Road to War, 1904-1914;* Vol. 2, *The War Years: To the Eve of Jutland, 1914-1916.* London, 1961 and 1965.

Parkes, O. *British Battleships 1860-1950.* London, 1957.

Schurman, D. M. *The Education of a Navy; the Development of British Naval Strategic Thought 1867-1914.* London, 1965.

Steevens, G. W. *Naval Policy.* London, 1896.

IMPERIAL DEFENCE
Graham, G. S. *Empire of the North Atlantic.* 2nd edn. London, 1958. Tunstall, W. C. B. 'Imperial Defence 1815-1870' in *The Cambridge History of the British Empire,* vol. 2. Cambridge, 1940.

— 'Imperial Defence 1870-1897' and 'Imperial Defence 1897-1914' in *The Cambridge History of the British Empire,* vol. 3. Cambridge, 1959.

MEMOIRS AND BIOGRAPHIES
Bacon, Adm. Sir R. H. *The Life of Lord Fisher of Kilverstone.* 2 vols. London, 1929.

Beresford, Adm. Lord Charles. *Memoirs.* 2 vols. London, 1913.

Colomb, Adm. P. H. *Memoirs of Sir Astley Cooper Key.* London, 1898.

Fisher, Adm. of the Fleet Lord. *Records.* London, 1919.

Fitzgerald, Adm. C. C. Penrose. *Memories of the Sea.* London, 1913.

James, Adm. Sir William. *A Great Seaman.* London, 1955.

Kemp, Lt-CdrP. K. (ed.). *The Papers of Admiral Sir John Fisher.* 2 vols. London, 1960, 1964.

Kennedy, Adm. Sir W. R. *Hurrah for the Life of a Sailor! Fifty Years in the Royal Navy.* London, 1900.

Marder, A. J. (ed.). *Fear God and Dread Nought; the Correspondence of Admiral of the Fleet Lord Fisher of Kilverstone.* 3 vols. London, 1952-59.

Smith, Vice-Adm. Sir H. H. *A Yellow Admiral Remembers.* London, 1930.

—*An Admiral Never Forgets.* London, 1936.

Woods, Sir H. *Spunyarn from the Strands of a Sailor's Life Ashore and Afloat.* 2 vols. London, 1924.

Index of Ships

This Index contains the names of all gunboats, gunvessels and sloops featured in the book. Foreign vessels and other British warships are cross-referenced to the General Index that follows. References to Chapter Notes are by page, chapter and note, e.g. 138:7/1. Numbers in *italics* denote captions; numbers in **bold** denote maps.

General Index